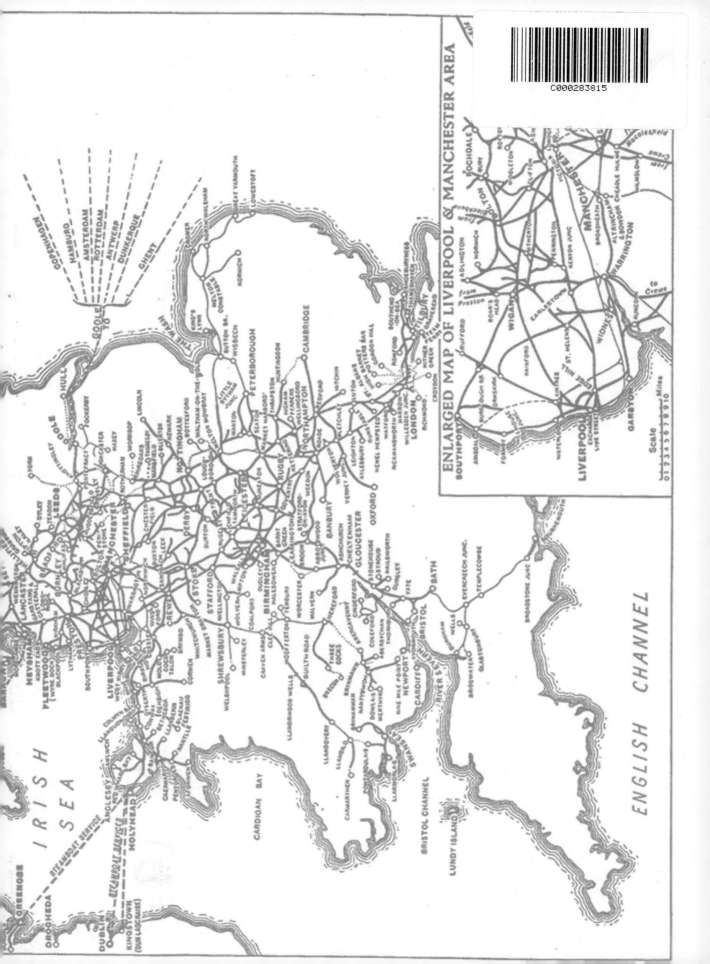

ENLARGED MAP OF LIVERPOOL & MANCHESTER AREA

LMS
HANDBOOK
1923-1947

LMS

HANDBOOK

THE LONDON MIDLAND & SCOTTISH RAILWAY **1923-1947**

DAVID WRAGG

First published in December 2010

A catalogue record for this book is available from the British Library

ISBN 978 1 84425 828 4

Library of Congress catalog card no 2010927383

Published by Haynes Publishing,
Sparkford, Yeovil, Somerset BA22 7JJ, UK
Tel: 01963 442030 Fax: 01963 440001
Int.tel: +44 1963 442030 Int.fax: +44 1963 440001
E-mail: sales@haynes.co.uk
Website: www.haynes.co.uk

Haynes North America Inc.,
861 Lawrence Drive, Newbury Park, California 91320, USA

Designed and typeset by Dominic Stickland

Printed and bound in the USA

Contents

Acknowledgements

I should like to thank Paul Chancellor of Colour-Rail and both Trevor Johnson and John Hancock of the Historical Model Railway Society (HMRS) for their help in providing copies from their vast stock of excellent images, and the staff of the Search Engine at the National Railway Museum in York for their help, and in particular making available so many LMS publications.

David Wragg
Edinburgh
2010

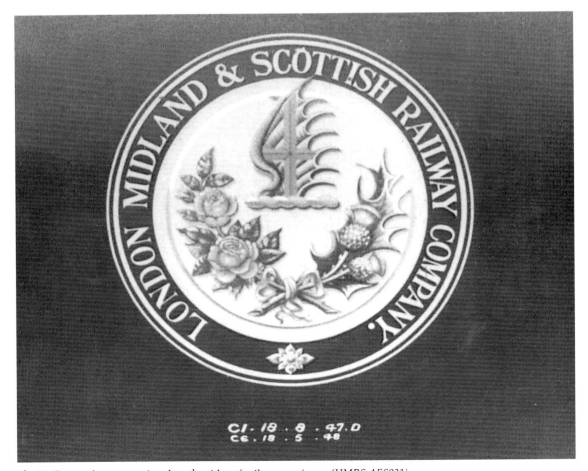

The LMS coat of arms as painted on the sides of railway carriages. *(HMRS AES931)*

Preface

My first memory of railway travel was probably on what had been part of the LMS, the former Northern Counties Committee in Northern Ireland. Father was in the Fleet Air Arm and had been posted to the Royal Naval Air Station at Eglinton, near Londonderry, HMS *Gannet*. I remember getting off the train, which then steamed away through a level crossing. With the exception of three years in Malta, the rest of my childhood and much of my adult life was spent fairly and squarely in Southern Railway territory. Nevertheless, for family reasons visits to Northern Ireland continued and for me *the* train was the 'Ulster Express', leaving Euston for Heysham late in the afternoon. My mother insisted on travelling first class, and on the Southern's Portsmouth line this meant sitting in carriage compartments with doors, so that the view was never as good as on the 'Ulster Express' with its huge picture windows, and a small notice telling passengers the type of wood used to complete the interior.

Of course, these were the days when as a youngster, I looked longingly at the magnificent steam locomotives and tended to disparage the efficient Southern 4-COR electric multiple units. As the train headed northwards to Heysham, with a reversal at Preston, it passed successive suburban steam trains, and in my childish innocence I rather envied those who caught such trains to work.

At Heysham, one walked down the slope at the end of the platform to get to the ship, and here one had a true trackside view looking up at the mighty locomotive.

There was even a final treat on the way home, having crossed from Belfast overnight, and then having breakfast aboard the 'Ulster Express', and being called 'sir' by a dining car attendant. All very heady stuff when just nine years old!

The one drawback was that I never again re-established any link with the NCC. The one time I travelled by train in Northern Ireland in later years was on the former Belfast & County Down Railway to Bangor, in a filthy diesel multiple unit.

Later, while working for P&O, owners of the Belfast Steamship Company, most of my visits to Belfast were by air, but when time permitted, I then had to use the London Midland Region service to Liverpool. I was gently reminded by a master aboard the *Ulster Queen* that 'the quality always travelled by Belfast Steamship from Liverpool, and never from Heysham!' After a disappointing experience one night aboard 'The Liverpool Pullman', I did at least know that the better dinner was to be had aboard the ship!

There was no doubt about it, the LMS was a great railway. That it could provide some of the best locomotives, once Stanier was wooed away from the Great Western, there was no doubt. My model railway at home included *Princess Elizabeth*, although I had a meagre stud of locomotives otherwise. Not least because the nomadic quality of service family life meant that there was never an opportunity to establish something really worthwhile.

As for locomotives in real life, my favourites, I have to admit, nevertheless, were Stanier's famous 'Black Five' 4-6-0s, and they remain so. This is perhaps not good news to those who are appalled at how many have been preserved, rather than a more representative collection of steam locomotives. Yet, this is inevitable, given not just the numbers built but the way in which they pervaded the system and, of course, because the restoration and preservation movement was run from the bottom up, with small and unconnected groups and individuals doing their own thing. There was no controlling hand in preservation, and after all, that is how our home railways developed, locally and regionally, but never nationally.

Quite right too!

Note: 'up' and 'down'

Anyone with an interest in Britain's railways will know that 'up' has traditionally meant the line leading to London or the train heading for the Capital, while 'down' means exactly the opposite. In considering the railways that cross the border into Scotland, however, the situation is more complicated. North of the border, 'up' means Edinburgh-bound and 'down' means the train heading from Edinburgh or the line leading away from the Capital.

In short, a train from London to Aberdeen via Edinburgh heads down to the Scottish border, then up to Edinburgh and then down to Aberdeen.

The exceptions to this included the Midland Railway, which retained its headquarters in Derby even after St Pancras opened, and rightly regarded trains as running from Derby as 'down' and those heading towards it as 'up'.

Introduction

Britain's largest railway – reaching all four corners of the Kingdom

'"This is your way Sir" in England, Scotland, Ireland, Wales' boasted the poster advertising the only railway company to operate throughout the Kingdom, it was the LMS. Never the LMSR but always the LMS, in contrast to the LNER and this was followed, even when the 'Big Four' took a joint advertisement, and also, when spelt out completely, it was 'London Midland and Scottish Railway', never 'London, Midland and Scottish Railway'. This was not the only distinguishing feature of the new company that came into being on 1 January 1923. Uniquely, the London Midland & Scottish Railway was, during its brief history, the only railway to cover all parts of the United Kingdom, and beyond, for although British Railways operated ferries to Ireland it never actually operated trains there, as Northern Ireland Railways, which took over the three Irish 'standard' gauge (5ft 3in) railway companies, was 'owned' by the government of Northern Ireland.

The LMS route network extended to Thurso in the north of Scotland and reached the South Coast of England through its involvement with the Somerset & Dorset Railway; it stretched into Essex with an isolated line from Fenchurch Street to Southend and Shoeburyness; ran along the coast of North Wales to Anglesey, with other lines reaching down into South Wales. It included the Northern Counties Committee, using the Midland Railway name for the former Belfast & Northern Counties Railway (BNCR), a railway with crack expresses, boat trains and commuter lines, and which through its joint ownership of the County Donegal Railway, an Irish narrow gauge line, with the Great Northern Railway of Ireland (GNR (I)), extended across the border into the Irish Republic. Then there was the Dundalk, Newry & Greenore Railway using the Irish gauge of 5ft 3in, and even a short length of track by the Dublin North Wall steamer berths.

No other railway demonstrated the importance of this mode of transport to the economy as did the LMS, which many maintain was the largest business in the British Empire. Created from no fewer than 33 mainland companies (the Belfast & Northern Counties was owned by the Midland Railway), its early history was marred by in-fighting between the managements of the two strongest constituent companies, the London & North Western Railway (LNWR) and the Midland Railway (MR). During the Second World War, it lost its chairman in an air raid, an event that may eventually have affected the deal between the Ministry of War Transport and the 'Big Four' railway companies.

The LMS was famed for its crack expresses, and the work of its longest reigning chief engineer, Sir William Stanier, influenced the first locomotive and carriage designs for the nationalised British Railways. Yet, many of its branch lines and stopping trains reflected unfavourably on the company, and, due in no small part to its financial situation and the emphasis on crack expresses, its attempts at electrification were half-hearted compared with the work done by the Southern Railway. Not for nothing was the Somerset & Dorset, operated jointly with the Southern Railway, known as 'Slow and Dirty'. Like the Southern, however, it had several London termini, including not only Euston and St Pancras, but also Broad Street and Fenchurch Street, terminus for what had been the London, Tilbury & Southend Railway.

LONDON AND NORTH WESTERN AND CALEDONIAN RAILWAYS.

WEST COAST ROUTE TO and FROM

SCOTLAND.

Shortest Route to and from GLASGOW.

CORRIDOR, LUNCHEON, DINING, AND SLEEPING CARS.

COMMENCING JULY 10th, 1922. Week Days.   **Sun. ngt & Mon. mrn.**

STATIONS.		h			g		a	a		b	b			b	d	b	a				
		mrn	mrn	mrn		aft	aft	aft		aft	aft	aft	mrn	aft	aft	aft	aft	aft	aft	aft	aft
London (Euston) ......dep		5 0	6 45	10 0		....	1 30	....		7 30	....	9 20	....	11 0	11 0	1140	11 45	7 40	9 30	11 0	1140
Birmingham (New St.).	,,	3 50	7 15	9 10	11 0	12 15	2 50	....		8 20	....	10 50	....				12 25	6 50	10 15	....	
Liverpool { Lime Street	,,			h							1040	....	12 45	12 45	1245	....		9 V 0	12 45	....	
{ Exchange..	,,	9 47	9 47	12 40		....	3 20	....	5 8	....		....	1250	1 50	....		1 40	....	1 50	....	
Manchester { Exchange	,,							....	5 0	....		....	1955	....	1 10	1 10	....		1115	1 10	....	
{ Victoria.	,,	9 40	9 40	12 30	aft	aft	3 0	....		....		mrn	mrn	....			mrn	2 55	....		mrn	mrn
Carlisle............arr.		1245	1 19	3 25	3 58	4 9	6 25	7 44	8 27	1 40	2 14	4 0	5 0	5 16	5 35	6 40	6 20	2 14	4 46	5 16	6 49
		aft																			
Edinburgh (Princes St.)arr.		3 20	4 5	6 0		6 20	9X18	10 10	11 0			....		8 0	8 13		9 0			8 0	
Glasgow (Central).....	,,	3 20	4 22	6 56	30		9X15	10 10	11 0		6 55	7 40		8 0	9 35		9 0		7 16		9 35
Greenock (Central).....	,,	4938	5 28	7 25	7 25		10 37	11X31				7855	8R48		9 15	1030			8 48		1030
Gourock	,,	4952	5 41	7 39	7 39		10 51	11Y45				8R10	9 40		9 29	1042			9 0		1042
Oban	,,		9 55				4 44	4 44		9 55	9 55	....		2 50			9 55			2 50	
Perth	,,		5 37			8 10		12 35	1235	5 5	5 35	....		9 12	9 37		5 35			9 12	
Dundee (West)........	,,		7 22			8 58			11 45	6 50	6 50	....		10 5	1022		6 50			10 5	
Dunkeld	,,		8 6				2F42	2F4		6 21	6 21	....		10 6			6 21			10 6	
Inverness via Dunk'ld	,,						6F06	F0		9 25	1015	....		4 42			9 40			4 42	
ABERDEEN	,,		9 5			10 35		3 0	3 0	7 40	7 40	....		11 50	1155		7 40			11 50	
Ballater............	,,									9 45	9 45	....		5 0			9 45			5 0	
Inverness via Aberd'n	,,							8F56	sF56	1155	1155	....		6 21			1155			6 21	

Week Days.   **Sun. from Scotland.**

		mrn	mrn	mrn	mrn		mrn	aft	aft	mrn		aft		aft	aft	b	d	aft	aft	mrn	aft		aft
Inverness via Aberd'n dep.							a			7 40	b			b	1259	1250	b	d				1 10		
Ballater............	,,						6 50			9 55					3 35	3 35								
ABERDEEN	,,		6 30		8 30					12 30	aft				7 30	7 45					1 10			
Inverness via Dunk'ld	,,	h	b	b	1120	aft	8 10	a	a	10 30	mrn		4 30			4 30			a					
Dunkeld	,,				7 51	mrn	10 6			1 10	aft		T			T								
Dundee (West).......	,,				9 5	mrn	1159			2 25			9 10		9 0	9 15					3 0			
Perth	,,				9 5	mrn	1159			3 25			9 10		9 45	10 0					3 50			
Oban	,,				5 40	mrn	8 45			11 45	mrn		5 30			5 30								
Gourock	,,		8 20	8 20				1145	2 50	3 50	aft	8 0		9 5		9 59	59	5			3 15			
Greenock (Central).....	,,		8 32	8 32				1155	2 59	4 1		8 11		9 15		9 159	159	15			3 24			
Glasgow (Central).....	,,		10 0	1010				1 30	4 10	5 30		9 20		1030		1110	1110	10 0	5 30		1020			
Edinburgh (Princes St.)	,,	10 0			1016			1 30		4 10	5 30			1030		mrn		10 0	5 40		1020			
Carlisle............arr.		12 0	12 14	1252	1252			3 38	3 48	6 50	8 23		12 5		1 10	1 01	251	561	592	8 1235	8 20		1 0	
		aft		aft	a			aft	aft	aft				mrn	mrn	mrn			mrn		mrn		mrn
Manchester { Exchange arr.								7 27	7 27	1056					5 50	6 5								
{ Victoria..	,,	3 35		3 50	4 35			7 2		1055	12 18								4 15					
Liverpool { Lime St....	,,										12 45					6 6	15				12 25			
{ Exchange..	,,	3 25		3 45	4 43			7 57	5	1025														
Birmingham (New St.)	,,	5 17		6 40				9 45			2 15					6 52	7 11			7 23	2 15		6 13	
London (Euston)	,,	6 50		7 30				1030			5 0		6 55		7 40	7 30	8 0	8 20		7 30	5 0		7 30	

SLEEPING SALOONS ON NIGHT TRAINS.

a CORRIDOR, DINING, AND REFRESHMENT CAR EXPRESS.   **b** Not on Saturday nights.   **d** Saturday night and Sunday morning.   **f** No connecting Trains to these Stations on Sunday mornings.   **g** Corridor, Luncheon, and Tea Car Express.   **h** Luncheon Car Express.   **j** Leaves Birmingham 3 10 mrn. on Mondays.   **q** On Saturdays arrives Greenock 5 51 aft. and Gourock 5 45 aft.   **R** On Sundays arrives Greenock 9 15 and Gourock 9 29 mrn.   **s** Saturdays only.   **T** Calls at Dunkeld when required to pick up passengers. Notice to be given at the Station.   **V** Via Newton-le-Willows.   **X** On Saturdays arrives Edinburgh 9 23 aft., and Glasgow 9 26 aft.   **Y** On Wednesdays and Saturdays arrives Greenock 11 42 aft. and Gourock 11 56 aft.   **Z** Sunday mornings excepted.

ARTHUR WATSON, General Manager, L. & N. W. Railway.
DONALD A. MATHESON, General Manager, Caledonian Railway.

July, 1922.

Collaboration between companies before Grouping ensured that long-distance through services could be run successfully, and by this time passengers could expect corridor carriages with catering. *(Bradshaw)*

Seen at Derby in 1930 is ex-Midland Railway 118, a 4-2-2 given the power classification 1 by the LMS, with most withdrawn by the late 1930s. *(Colour-Rail 2233)*

This book starts with a brief history of each of the constituent and subsidiary companies, the joint ventures with other railways and its Irish interests, followed by details of the railway's venture into other modes of transport, including air services, examples from the comparative timetables for 1922 and 1938, the last year of true peacetime operation, as well as telling the story of the LMS itself in peacetime and at war. Tables give details of its steam locomotives.

It was not until 1927 that the public began to notice the change of ownership from the pre-Grouping companies, as organising such a disparate and widespread set of railway companies into a cohesive whole was a massive problem. Unification was not helped by the fact that from the start there were struggles for dominance between the senior managers of the former MR and their counterparts in the LNWR, while in Scotland, the Caledonian Railway (CR) established itself as the dominant force and policy setter. On the engineering side, there was also serious fractional fighting between the two major locomotive works at Crewe (ex-LNWR), and Derby (ex-MR). The MR owned the former London Tilbury & Southend Railway, which meant that the LMS was in direct competition with the LNER and under pressure from local authorities to electrify this line.

The company may have been too big to be managed efficiently, and indeed one of its directors, or vice-presidents in LMS terms, admitted as much at one stage. It constantly looked across the Atlantic to the United States for inspiration, although rejected a forward-looking suggestion from a major freight customer that it should drop wagon-load freight and concentrate on train-load freight between major centres. It standardised production of rolling stock, and experimented with diesel traction, but only in its marshalling yards did it do this wholeheartedly.

The legacy of the pre-Grouping companies was mixed to say the least. The MR was famous for its policy of small locomotives, and this contributed in no small part to the LMS having the lowest main line speeds of any of the 'Big Four', although an earlier belief on the LNWR that 45mph was good enough did not help! On the other hand, the LNWR had begun electrification of its London suburban network, while the MR's policy of centralised train control was adopted and proved successful. Both the LNWR and MR had a reputation for comfortable mainline rolling stock.

The LMS was second only to the LNER in its dependence on freight traffic, and this was to

prove to be a weakness with the years of the Great Depression worsened by the 1926 Miners'
Strike and the loss of major export markets for British coal. Nevertheless, rationalisation of freight
handling and management meant that by 1939, the company's freight business was generally
profitable. This was despite the failure to introduce large 40-ton mineral wagons other than to
supply coal to one of its own power stations, even though new Stanier 2-8-0 freight locomotives
accelerated trains. New fast freight trains were introduced, so that by 1938, there were seven
running daily more than 150 miles non-stop, and another 57 running more than 90 miles non-
stop. It was also a major operator of London commuter services, which it could not afford to
electrify beyond the original LNWR scheme, and which can hardly have been profitable.

The first step towards organising the LMS into a cohesive whole came with the creation of
three, later four, operating divisions. Sir Josiah (later Lord) Stamp was appointed president in
1926, heading a four-man executive, later increased to seven, which fulfilled the role of general
manager and an officers' committee. Stamp came from outside the industry, and his management
practices were those currently in vogue in the United States, including work study. A year later,
he also took on the role of chairman. Costs were analysed and working practices standardised,
and as funds permitted, this soon extended to new equipment.

Sir Henry Fowler of the MR became the first Chief Mechanical Engineer, and was ordered to produce
more powerful steam locomotives to end double heading. This was a tall order for a CME accustomed
to building small locomotives and the result was the 'Royal Scot' class 4-6-0, which still fell short of
what was needed. When he retired, Sir William Stanier was recruited from the Great Western. One
of his first achievements was to end the Crewe–Derby battles, and then to start a massive locomotive
rationalisation and building programme that saw the number of classes fall from 404 in 1932 to 132 by
1938, while the number of locomotives needed to operate the system fell by 26 per cent.

Similar standardisation followed in carriage and wagon design, which with modernisation of the
repair shops, also saw massive gains in productivity. For the main line services, corridor carriages
were mass produced, which have generally been regarded as the best in the British Isles for comfort,
while the later versions provided the basis for the British Railways Mk1 rolling stock. His famous
'Black Fives', the Class 5 4-6-0 mixed traffic locomotives, also provided the basis for a British Railways
standard design post-Nationalisation. Irish broad gauge (5ft 3in) versions of the locomotives and
carriages were built for the Northern Counties line. At Derby, a research laboratory and testing
facility was opened, and in 1938 this was joined by the world's first School of Transport.

Such forward thinking and a penchant for excellent publicity material nevertheless could not
disguise the fact that the entire railway did not stand up to critical appraisal. Stations reflected
the company's poverty, seldom painted and often dirty, and generally unwelcoming. Its branch
line trains were often slow and dirty, in contrast to the fast expresses such as the streamlined
'Coronation Scot', running between Euston and Glasgow. The Wirral, Mersey and Manchester
South Junction & Altrincham lines were electrified, the latter jointly with the LNER, but many
of the other electrified lines were inherited from the LYR and the LNWR.

Like the other members of the 'Big Four', the LMS operated ports, shipping and hotels, with
Europe's largest chain of hotels, and in 1938 operated 6,870 route miles on the mainland of Great
Britain alone. Its ferry services from Heysham and Stranraer to Northern Ireland and from Holyhead
to Dublin were successful, although it was less involved in port operation and management than the
LNER or the Southern. Nevertheless, despite the progress made between Grouping and the outbreak
of the Second World War, it struggled to make a profit and dividends were scarce. It was a major
owner of canals with more than 540 miles of waterways, of which 490 miles were in England.

The Second World War probably affected the LMS less than the other members of the
'Big Four', although it suffered badly in the bombing of Coventry, Birmingham, Manchester,
Glasgow and Belfast. Its regional control centres proved themselves more than adequate for
crisis management. Nevertheless, the strain of wartime operations and the shortage of skilled
manpower meant that the weaknesses of the LMS were accentuated, giving rise to the graffito
'The LMS, a hell of a mess'. There are even anecdotal stories of passengers being unable to see
station name signs because of the grime on the carriage windows.

Chapter 1

The Ancestors and the Neighbours

Many claim that the London Midland & Scottish Railway was the largest private enterprise concern in the entire British Empire. There are so many different means of assessing the size of a company, such as the number of employees, annual turnover, the value of the assets, or the stock market valuation, which on its formation was £400 million (roughly equivalent to £16 billion today) that this is difficult to judge. However, but one thing is clear, which is that the LMS was by far the largest of the four great railway companies established by the Railways Act 1921. It was also the only one to operate in all four parts of the United Kingdom, being the 'other' railway company in Wales and again in Scotland, and also inheriting the Northern Counties Committee, the former Belfast & Northern Counties Railway, from the Midland Railway.

In short, this railway extended from Thurso in the far north of Scotland to Bournemouth on the South Coast, running over S&D metals, and from Londonderry, and beyond into Donegal, to Southend and Shoeburyness in Essex.

Yet, all of this might not have happened, as the original proposals for grouping the railways envisaged seven companies rather than four, and a clue that the LMS might not have been a single railway lies in the fact that after nationalisation it was split into two British Railways' regions. The original Railways Bill envisaged Scotland having a separate railway company while the other six companies would cover England and Wales. It was only after strong objections from Scotland that a Scottish railway company would have to raise fares and goods charges more than Anglo-Scottish companies that the decision was taken to form what would eventually be the LMS and its East Coast counterpart, the London & North Eastern Railway.

This was not the only part of the legislation to attract comment, as many expected the Cambrian Railways to be included with what became the LMS rather than, as happened, the Great Western, because the Cambrian's route structure brought it closer to the old London & North Western Railway than to the GWR. The government's original plans would have seen a 'North-Western' company rather than a London, Midland and Scottish business. In many ways, the original plan for the railways was what was foisted on them on nationalisation when once again, a separate Scottish Region was introduced. The LMS extended into North Wales, and the original Bill, when first published, indicated that all of the railways in Wales would be passed to the Great Western.

Under Grouping, the plan was simply to create a 'North Western, Midland and West Scottish' railway company and it took all of 1922 for appointments and structures to be agreed, and even then, most passengers did not notice the change until 1927 as there was so much to be done. As with the other grouped companies, the companies absorbed were defined either as constituent companies, which meant that they had a director on the board of the new company, or as subsidiary companies.

The London Midland & Scottish Railway had as its constituent companies:
Caledonian Railway
Furness Railway
Glasgow & South Western Railway
Highland Railway
Lancashire & Yorkshire Railway (Which had already agreed to be purchased by the LNWR.)
London & North Western Railway
Midland Railway
North Staffordshire Railway

The subsidiaries included:
Arbroath & Forfar Railway
Brechin & Edzell District Railway
Callander & Oban Railway
Cathcart District Railway
Charnwood Forest Railway
Cleator & Workington Junction Railway
Cockermouth Keswick & Penrith Railway
Dearne Valley Railway
Dornoch Light Railway
Dundee & Newtyle Railway
Harborne Railway
Leek & Manifold Valley Light Railway (2ft 6in gauge)
Maryport & Carlisle Railway
Mold & Denbigh Junction Railway
North & South Western Junction Railway
North London Railway
Portpatrick & Wigtownshire Joint Committee
Shropshire Union Railways & Canal
Solway Junction Railway
Stratford upon Avon & Midland Junction Railway
Tottenham & Forest Gate Railway
Wick & Lynster Light Railway
Wirral Railway
Yorkshire Dales Railway

Some of the smaller lines were already leased to or worked by the larger companies. The Mersey Railway was taken over in 1938 to be absorbed into the LMS's Wirral Lines. The Irish companies were not mentioned in, or covered by, the legislation, which was confined to Great Britain.

Many of the companies absorbed by the LMS were already substantial ventures in themselves. No fewer than four of them had London termini, while the Great Western, by contrast, had just the one, at Paddington. The London & North Western had Euston, the Midland had St Pancras, the North London had Broad Street, and the London Tilbury & Southend had the smallest of all the London termini at Fenchurch Street. The first two of these railways were particularly substantial, and post-Grouping their managements were eager to come out on top, while the Lancashire & Yorkshire, despite merging with the LNWR on the eve of Grouping, also had its own ideas. North of the border, there was also rivalry between the Glasgow & South Western and the Caledonian.

If any believed that the legislation would impose some neat boundaries on the four great grouped companies, they were soon to be mistaken. Apart from the issues over Scotland and, to a lesser extent, Wales, and the LMS competing with the LNER between London and Southend, the LNER took over the Cheshire Lines Committee, of which it has often been said, ran more in Lancashire than in Cheshire, and the LMS was not without its lines further east. To be fair, the Cheshire Lines were a partnership, but the LNER provided the motive power, except for through trains by the LMS.

The Constituent Companies

Caledonian Railway

The largest Scottish company to be merged into the LMS, the Caledonian Railway, adopted the Royal Arms of Scotland as its crest and its locomotives were smartly presented in a blue livery. It was founded in 1845 to extend the West Coast main line from Carlisle to Glasgow and Edinburgh, dividing at Carstairs, and at the time it was expected to be the only Anglo-Scottish line. The engineer was Joseph Locke. Initially, grand termini were planned in both cities, as well as a cross-country line, but these plans were thwarted.

The company reached Glasgow over the metals of the Grankirk & Glasgow (later renamed the Glasgow & Coatbridge) and the Wishaw & Coltness railways to Buchanan Street station, whose wooden train sheds remained until after Grouping. Eventually, three Glasgow termini were used, including, from 1849, the South Side station accessed via the Clydesdale Junction and the Glasgow Barrhead & Neilston Direct, and also shared Bridge Street with the Glasgow & South Western. South Side was closed when Central and St Enoch were opened in the 1870s, but Bridge Street continued to be used until 1906, after Central had been extended, and eventually had 17 platforms on two levels.

The line was extended north to Aberdeen using the Scottish Central, Scottish Midland Junction and Aberdeen railways, and in 1856 the latter two merged to form the Scottish North Eastern Railway, before all three were absorbed by the Caledonian in 1865-66. From 1880, the Caledonian served the Western Highlands over the Callander & Oban Railway, which it effectively rescued and developed, and then up to 1900, built a network of lines along the Clyde to compete with the Glasgow & South Western and North British railways, giving the company a suburban and tourist network as well as serving steamer services, the growing shipyards, and the mines of Lanarkshire, for which many new lines and private sidings were built.

Seen around the time of Grouping, this is ex-Caledonian Railway 0-4-4T No. 172 on the Wanlockhead branch, with two four-wheel carriages. Wanlockhead is the highest inhabited village in Scotland. *(HMRS AAD302)*

The Caledonian's main routes were the finest in Scotland. The company moved into steamer services, including tourist vessels on Loch Lomond, with the main steamer-railway terminus being at Wemyss Bay. The further expansion of the Glasgow suburban network was cut short by the appearance of horse and, later, electric trams, with the Paisley & District line completed, but never opened for passenger trains.

Meanwhile, in Edinburgh, the unsatisfactory Lothian Road station was replaced by Princes Street, which later had the Caledonian Hotel added providing an impressive frontage. A network of suburban services was also created in the Capital. Further north, the company built its own station at Stirling and took the lead in remodelling the joint stations at Perth and Aberdeen, and opened new tourist lines from Crieff to Lochearnhead, and from Connel to Ballachulish.

The company provided railway links for all of the docks within its wide operating area, as well as owning those at Grangemouth, which it acquired with the Forth & Clyde Canal in 1867.

Intense competition arose with the Glasgow & South Western and, especially after the opening of the East Coast main line, the North British, initially for traffic between Edinburgh and London, but after the Tay and Forth bridges were completed, this rivalry extended to Aberdeen. The hotel business extended from Glasgow and Edinburgh to include the famous hotel at Gleneagles. The company became famous for good design and high standards, with a strong awareness of the importance of public image. When merged into the London Midland & Scottish Railway in 1923, it contributed 1,057 route miles.

Furness Railway

The Furness Railway not only served the shipbuilding and steel town of Barrow-in-Furness, but it also reached into the Lake District, with this 2-4-0, No. 46, at Lakeside station, Windermere. *(HMRS AAB634)*

The smallest of the constituent companies, it had its origins in an isolated line built in 1846 to move iron ore and slate from the Furness peninsula to the docks at Barrow-in-Furness. A series of take-overs and extensions resulted in a line from Carnforth to Whitehaven, opened in 1857, with branches into the Lake District and connecting steamer services on Lake Windermere and Coniston Water. In 1862, the FR acquired the Ulverston & Lancaster Railway. The company initially prospered with the steel and shipbuilding industry, but during the late 19th and early 20th centuries, its promotion of tourism brought it great benefits before it became part of the LMS.

Glasgow & South Western Railway

The G&SWR was formed in 1850 when the Glasgow Paisley Kilmarnock & Ayr Railway, authorised in 1837, acquired the Glasgow Dumfries & Carlisle Railway. The line to Ayr had been completed in 1840, and was followed in 1843 by a branch from Dalry to Kilmarnock, but this eventually became the main line to Carlisle via Dumfries. It had less severe gradients than the rival Caledonian line to Carlisle via Beattock, but was 18 miles longer. During the remainder of the 19th century, the company acquired other lines in its area, including Scotland's first railway, the Kilmarnock & Troon, dating from 1811. It built the first railway hotel for golfers at Turnberry in 1906. The main works were at Kilmarnock, completed in 1856, but a new workshop at Barassie, near Troon, was completed in 1901.

The main business of the railway was the movement of coal, and tourist and commuter traffic to the resorts on the Ayrshire coast, while it also handled a substantial volume of traffic to Ireland. It was forced to operate the 'Port Road', the lines from Dumfries to Portpatrick, and later Stranraer when that became the main Scottish port for Ireland, in partnership with the Caledonian, London & North Western and Midland railways. Financial and operational difficulties delayed completion of the Glasgow–Stranraer route until 1877 and it was not fully incorporated into the G&SWR until 1892. The problems were caused partly by competition for Irish traffic through ports in Ayrshire, and by the fact that at the time it was also possible to sail directly from Glasgow to Belfast and other Irish ports.

In Glasgow, through running to the North British became possible when the City Union Railway was completed in 1870, and through running to the Midland Railway's Settle and Carlisle line started once this route was completed. Parliament rejected plans for a merger with the Midland, but the two companies collaborated on express services from St Pancras to St Enoch, completed in 1876. Strong competition developed with the Caledonian in Ayrshire, and joint operation of a new direct Glasgow–Kilmarnock line was forced on the companies when it opened in 1873. A bid for the G&SWR by the CR was rejected by Parliament in 1890. Quadrupling of the 30 miles from Glasgow to Kilwinning was largely completed by the outbreak of the First World War.

Highland Railway

Formed in 1865 from the merger of the Aberdeen & Perth Junction Railway with the Inverness & Aberdeen Junction Railway, initially the HR had main lines to Keith, opened in 1858, and Dunkeld, opened in 1863. The latter was extended to Inverness and then further north, reaching Wick and Thurso in 1874, albeit taking an extremely circuitous route around the Beauly Firth via Dingwall, while another line went to Kyle of Lochalsh, reached in 1897. These lines included steep gradients of as much as 1 in 70, while there was a swing bridge over the Caledonian Canal at Clachnaharry, and a viaduct over the Kyle of Sutherland between Culrain and Invershin. The HR acquired the Duke of Sutherland's Railway in 1884. A plan for a direct Inverness–Glasgow line through the Great Glen, promoted in 1883, proved fruitless, but a direct line was opened to Aviemore in 1898.

The HR planned a number of branch lines, but by this time road transport was emerging as a serious competitor, especially in remote areas. Nevertheless, the North British-sponsored West Highland Railway (1894), and the Invergarry & Fort Augustus Railway (1903), threatened the HR's position.

Most of the network was single track, with passing loops and a double section between Clachnaharry and Clunes providing the total of 47 miles of double track, but efficiency improved when train staff and tablet instruments were introduced during the 1890s. The problems of heavy snowfall on isolated stretches of line led William Stroudley, the HR's first locomotive superintendent, to design a range of snow ploughs. His successor, David Jones, designed Britain's first 4-6-0 locomotive.

The HR did much for the fishing industry, especially with fast goods trains running from Buckie on the Moray coast to Liverpool and Manchester, and from Wick and Thurso to the south. There were also significant movements of beef cattle, and whisky distilleries were sited close to the railway. The company also attempted to boost tourism, even building a branch to the spa town of Strathpeffer in 1885, and building a hotel there in 1911. Nevertheless, given the low population, mixed trains were commonplace, and carriages could be behind loose-coupled goods wagons, but after a number of accidents, the Railway Regulation Act 1889 demanded continuous braking for passenger trains, although the HR was given an extended period until 1897 to adapt.

The system came under sustained heavy use during the First World War, with the famous 'Jellicoe Specials' carrying men and coal to Thurso for the fleet at Scapa Flow, while Invergordon was another major naval base along its route. Later in the war, Kyle of Lochalsh also became important, with mines for the Northern Barrage and also US naval personnel.

Lancashire & Yorkshire Railway

The Manchester-based Lancashire & Yorkshire Railway played a pivotal role in the British railway network, with its 600 route miles, which made it the eleventh largest amongst mainland railways. Belying its importance – far more impressive and reflective of its status – was the locomotive fleet, which made it the fourth largest, while its fleet of 30 ships was the largest of any pre-Grouping railway.

Much of its infrastructure was built by Sir John Hawkshaw, and the trans-Pennine routes featured steep gradients, tall viaducts and tunnels, while on the western side, much of the route mileage was relatively flat. The company emerged in 1847 on the renaming of the Manchester & Leeds Railway when it acquired the Wakefield Pontefract & Goole Railway, which opened the following year. Later, it joined the London & North Western in acquiring the North Union and Preston & Wyre, as well as the docks at Preston and Fleetwood, and also gained access to Blackpool and Lytham St Annes. Further lines were added to the system on both sides of the Pennines, before absorbing the East Lancashire Railway in 1859, with which it had had a difficult relationship earlier, and the West Lancashire, which had opened a line between Preston and Southport in 1882, followed in 1897. While these additions were important, the main LYR system was already complete by 1880.

Despite its strategic importance and the wealth of the major cities on its network, as well as the tourist and commuter potential of many destinations, the LYR was for many years notorious for trains that were dirty, slow and unpunctual. This began to change in 1883 when John Parsons replaced Thomas Barnes as chairman, and when he died in 1887, his work was continued by George Armytage, who remained in office for more than 30 years. A new locomotive works at Horwich, Manchester, replaced the two old and cramped sites at Miles Platting and Bury. A new locomotive superintendent took over in 1886, J.A.F. Aspinall, and he began a major programme of producing modern steam locomotives to replace the ageing fleet, with many elderly engines having been kept in service to meet rapidly growing traffic. The most significant of the new locomotives were 2-4-2 tank engines, which took over all passenger services other than the main line expresses, with 332 built between 1889 and 1911. Aspinall became general manager in 1899, with similar success in his new role.

Many of the LYR's routes were lengthier than those of the rival London & North Western, but in 1888–89, new lines by-passed Bolton and Wigan, allowing many services to be accelerated. Early in the new century, the best expresses took just 65 minutes for the run from Manchester to Blackpool, on which the famous club trains were introduced, with passengers having to be elected to membership of the club carriages, and while initially only first class, second class

The former MR and LYR lines ran through some bleak countryside – this is the northern tunnel portal of Blea Moor in 1938. *(HMRS ACW616)*

club carriages made an appearance later. Through workings with other companies saw trains run from Colne to Euston and from both Liverpool and Manchester to Scotland and from major cities in Yorkshire to the South Coast. Prominent in through running was the Midland Railway, which used running powers to reach the Seattle & Carlisle line, and from 1888 provided Scottish services from the LYR.

The main passenger and goods stations were also developed during this period, with new marshalling yards, while the busiest parts of the main line were quadrupled, as were many lines around Manchester and near Liverpool. Freight traffic included coal, cotton, wool, finished manufactured goods, timber, grain and fish. Jointly with the LNWR, shipping services were operated to Belfast, while the company had its own service from Liverpool to Drogheda. In the east, the company was the major railway at Goole, and ran packet and cargo ships to Denmark, Germany, the Low Countries, and France.

Nevertheless, these developments were not without cost, and as a result of the heavy capital investment, and the earlier neglect of the system and the customers, dividends during the early years of the 20th century were around 3-4 per cent.

In 1903, the LYR introduced Britain's first electro-pneumatic signalling, initially at Bolton, and then on lines near Manchester and Stockport. The signalling school at Manchester Victoria used a model layout for training. Electrification was introduced by Aspinall for the growing suburban traffic around Liverpool and Southport, using third-rail 600V dc power and electric multiple units, with the first sections operational in March 1904. The network was extended to Liverpool–Aintree in 1906. Instead of sticking with the original system, experiments followed with overhead electrification on a branch line running from Bury to Holcombe Brook in 1913, and in 1916 with 1,200V dc third-rail between Manchester, Whitefield and Bury, which must have pleased as the Holcombe Brook branch was converted to this system in 1917.

With Grouping looming, the LYR merged with the LNWR in 1922, with several LYR senior officers given senior posts with the LNWR and then with the LMS.

London & North Western Railway

Formed in 1846 by an amalgamation of the London & Birmingham, Grand Junction and Manchester & Birmingham railways, initially it consisted of 247 trunk route miles stretching as far north as Preston, with through running over other lines to Carlisle, while also serving Liverpool and Manchester. Lacking a regional base and vulnerable to competition, the LNWR immediately set about establishing alliances and also acquiring other lines along its route. The first major alliance was known as the Euston Square Confederacy, formed in 1850, and was a defensive measure against the Great Northern. This was followed by the Octuple Agreement, pooling receipts for traffic between London and points north of York, which in turn was replaced by the English & Scotch Traffic Agreement which ran from 1859 to 1869, and which gave Glasgow traffic to the LNWR's West Coast route and that to Edinburgh to the East Coast.

In the meantime, by 1859, the LNWR had added Cambridge, Leeds, Oxford and Peterborough to its network, while also leasing the Lancaster & Carlisle Railway, and concluding an alliance with the Caledonian Railway, so that the West Coast Main Line served not just Glasgow, but also Edinburgh and Aberdeen. It had also acquired the Chester & Holyhead Railway and the major share of the traffic to Ireland through both Holyhead and Liverpool, where in 1864, the company acquired the dock at Garston, which was enlarged in 1896, mainly for coal to Ireland. Later, it reached the Cumberland coast and started running through mid-Wales and established a cross-country service from Shrewsbury to Swansea and Carmarthen, largely run over its own lines. This was followed by a further cross-country service from Hereford to Cardiff and Newport, and acquiring a number of branch lines in South Wales.

In the London area, it acquired the North London Railway which retained its identity as a subsidiary, and used a number of lines in west London operated jointly with the Great Western that enabled it to by-pass the Capital and operate through to the South. In 1847, the Trent Valley line opened, by-passing Birmingham, and this was followed by another line in 1864 that by-passed major junctions at Winwick and Golborne, and in 1869, a direct line was opened to Liverpool through Runcorn.

From 1861, all locomotive building was concentrated on Crewe, while the works at Wolverton, which had built locomotives for the Southern Division before it was merged with the Northern Division, concentrated on carriage building. Crewe also included a steelworks and produced the company's rails, at the time, longer than any other railway in the British Isles at 60ft, helping to provide the smoother ride and high quality permanent way in which the company took such pride. Eventually, almost everything from soap and tickets to signalling equipment was produced 'in-house'.

Crewe became the ultimate company town, with the LNWR providing the services that would normally be provided by a local authority. The chief mechanical engineer from 1871 to 1903, F. W. Webb, took the existing stock of 2-2-2 and 2-4-0 locomotives, added many more of the latter, and then started to build compound locomotives, and the first 0-8-0 freight locomotives in Britain.

Despite collaboration with the GWR in London, competition developed on traffic to Birmingham and Merseyside. In an attempt to secure its position, the LNWR proposed a merger with the Midland Railway, but this failed and further competition resulted when the Midland managed to reach London over the GNR. A planned merger with the North Staffordshire Railway also failed. By 1869, there was heavy competition with the MR and later the Great Central for Manchester business. This extended to Anglo-Scottish traffic once the Midland completed its Settle and Carlisle line in 1875.

A far happier relationship flourished with the Lancashire & Yorkshire Railway, despite competition between Liverpool and Manchester, and in 1863 the two companies established a series of traffic pooling agreements. Parliament rejected a merger in 1872, but in 1908 the two companies and the MR agreed to send freight consignments by the shortest route. Freight was important to the LNWR, and in Liverpool, it operated no fewer than six goods depots. In 1882, it pioneered gravity-operated marshalling yards at Edge Hill. The mixture of slow freight traffic and fast expresses led the company to quadruple its tracks and when this was not possible, provide a double-track alternative, so that by 1914, 89 per cent of the 209 miles between Euston and Preston was covered in this way, as well as much of the route to Holyhead and to Leeds. Flying junctions, of which the first was at Weaver Junction, north of Crewe, also accelerated traffic and reduced conflicting movements.

Although the company invested in shipping as well as railways and ports, it did not acquire the mail contract from Holyhead to Ireland until 1920, while previously, political considerations had left this with the City of Dublin Steam Packet Company. The LNWR had worked hard for the previous 40 years to gain this business, building a new harbour and quays at North Wall, Dublin, as well as acquiring faster ships. The reward in the interval was a major share of cattle and freight traffic across the Irish Sea. Earlier, in an attempt to gain the traffic between Great Britain and Belfast, the company took a majority shareholding in the Dundalk Newry & Greenore Railway, and in 1873 had started a shipping service to Greenore. Perhaps more successful was the joint operation with the LYR from Fleetwood to Belfast and from Stranraer in Scotland to Larne with the Midland, Caledonian and Glasgow & South Western.

Despite the length of its trunk route to Scotland, Sir Richard Moon, the chairman between 1861 and 1891, believed that excessive speed used too much coal and argued that 45mph was sufficient. Nevertheless, a step forward in comfort came with bogie carriages in the late 1880s, and these were followed by all-corridor trains for the Scottish services in 1893. Another move to improve the comfort of passengers was the adoption of 'club' carriages, as pioneered by the Lancashire & Yorkshire on some of its commuter trains from Blackpool to Manchester, with the LNWR adding a service from North Wales. Passengers had to be elected to membership of the club carriages, and while initially only first class, second-class club carriages made an appearance later. With Liverpool the major port for transatlantic traffic at the time, special 12-wheel carriages were built for the boat trains, but eventually most of this traffic transferred to Southampton. Between 1914 and 1922, it electrified its suburban services from Euston and Broad Street to Watford using the third and fourth-rail system favoured by the Underground group of companies. After Grouping this was extended to Rickmansworth.

In the year before the Grouping, the LNWR finally merged with the LYR, using the LNWR name, a move intended to strengthen its influence in the eventual grouping in 1923, when the LNWR was one of the three largest railways in the British Isles, contributing 2,066 route miles to the LMS.

Midland Railway

Authorised in 1844, the Midland Railway resulted from the amalgamation of the Birmingham & Derby Junction, Midland Counties (MCR) and North Midland railways, and had George Hudson, the 'Railway King', as its first chairman. This was the first significant merger of railway companies sanctioned by Parliament. Initially, the Midland was a regional railway without its own access to London, and acted as a link between the London & Birmingham at Rugby and the York & North Midland, another Hudson railway, at Normanton. Initially, the MR had a monopoly of traffic from London to the North East, but a more direct line, the Great Northern, was authorised in 1846 and opened throughout in 1852.

Nevertheless, the MR had by this time, started its own programme of expansion, reaching Lincoln in 1846, and that year leasing the Leeds & Bradford Railway, which was authorised to extend to Skipton, where it would connect with the North Western Railway (NWR – not to be confused with the LNWR) line to Lancaster and Morecambe. The MR itself reached Peterborough in 1848, and then acquired the Birmingham & Gloucester and the Bristol & Gloucester. Nevertheless, expansion was soon checked by the stock market crisis of 1847-48, and then by Hudson's downfall in 1849 after he was discovered paying dividends out of capital to attract investors.

Hudson's successor was John Ellis, who provided the steady hand the company needed. The MR then started a period of profitable operation, and even paid a dividend in the difficult period of 1849-51, with an average of 4 per cent paid up to 1859, and then more than 6 per cent during the 1860s.

The relationship with the NWR had not worked as well as the MR had anticipated and the decision was taken to build its own line between Settle and Carlisle, which was authorised in 1866, but with poor timing as this followed a collapse in the stock market. The MR tried to abandon the project, but the North British and the Lancashire & Yorkshire railways, which had supported the measure, managed to persuade the MR to press ahead, although the line took ten years to complete because of extensive engineering works including the Ribblehead Viaduct. Meanwhile, the MR reached Manchester in 1867 running through the Peak District and with running powers over the Manchester Sheffield & Lincolnshire Railway, forerunner of the Great Central. Next, the MR headed towards London, initially with a line from Leicester to Bedford and Hitchin, where it connected with the GNR and acquired rights to run to King's Cross, but finding this far from satisfactory, built a line from Bedford to London, where it opened its terminus at St Pancras in 1868. It was intended at one time that the head office should move from Derby to London once St Pancras was completed, but this did not happen and instead, the building at the London terminus became a hotel. Derby enjoyed another innovation later, when in 1910, a central control office was created in an attempt to improve the poor punctuality of the MR's trains.

The Settle & Carlisle line and the St Pancras extension were part of a £6 million investment programme, equating to at least £350 million today, although given the high cost of property in the London area today, the real figure would probably be very much higher. This organic growth was not the sole way forward, as the MR sought to expand. In 1875, it joined the London & South Western Railway in leasing the Somerset & Dorset, enabling it to reach Bournemouth on the South Coast. The following year, running powers were acquired that enabled the MR to reach the coalfields of South Wales.

Only the LNER was more dependent upon freight traffic than the LMS, and heavy duty Class 7F 0-8-0 locomotives such as No.9626 were needed, seen at Crewe in 1936. *(Coloiur-Rail 2259)*

Rather more attractive were the Class 5F 4-6-0 locomotives such as No.2801, seen here at Stirling between duties. Note the large quantity of ash beside the track, an inescapable aspect of the steam railway. *(Colour-Rail 2260)*

In 1872, the MR announced that it would carry third-class passengers on all of its trains, a revolutionary move at the time when many railways regarded third-class as a nuisance. In 1875, it announced that it was scrapping second class, which meant that third-class passengers enjoyed the comfort of former second-class rolling stock, and at the same time, the MR cut first-class fares. While this was intended to put its competitors at a disadvantage, many other companies retained second class, in some cases as late as 1912. The MR's move had another advantage, for while it could reach Edinburgh and Glasgow by way of the Settle & Carlisle, it was a longer route, and by providing a more comfortable service, it meant that it could still compete, once through running started in 1875. A further step in ensuring the comfort of passengers followed a visit to the USA by the competitive general manager, James Allport, in 1874, which had him persuade the board to introduce Pullman cars, for which a supplementary fare could be charged. When restaurant and Pullman cars did start running on the MR, the company gained a good reputation for its food.

While the MR certainly took passenger traffic very seriously, it was also a major freight railway, and this part of its operations actually increased with the extension to London. It was amongst the first to attempt to purchase the private owners' wagons that used its rails, and while not completely successful, this was certainly a measure approved of by most railway managers.

Despite the excellence of its facilities at Derby, the MR had no hesitation in buying locomotive or rolling stock from other sources when quality, innovation or price made this attractive. Nevertheless, the company had just two locomotive superintendents between 1844 and 1903, Matthew Kirtley and S.W. Johnson. It inherited its engineer, W.H. Barlow, from the MCR in 1844, but he remained until 1857, and then continued as a consultant, building St Pancras. He was succeeded by J. S. Crossley, who was responsible for the Settle & Carlisle line. The magnificent engineering of the Settle & Carlisle and the grand St Pancras nevertheless, were in contrast to the MR's policies on locomotives, which were relatively straightforward and smaller than those appearing on other railways during the late 19th and early 20th centuries, so that double heading was a feature of MR expresses. There was some logic behind this, as the MR's routes were more sharply curved than those of the other main line companies, and it was its policy to run lighter, but more frequent, trains. Nevertheless, when one railway writer produced a 'Railway Alphabet' book for younger readers, he wrote:

M is for Midland with engines galore
Two on each train and asking for more

As the century ended, the MR was still expanding. Its partners in Scotland were the Glasgow & South Western Railway and the North British Railway, with the latter helped by the MR contributing 30 per cent of the cost of building the Forth Bridge, opened in 1890. On the other side of Scotland, it acquired a 25 per cent stake in the Portpatrick & Wigtownshire Joint Railway, which ran from Castle Douglas to Stranraer and Kirkcudbright, which took traffic that had come off the West Coast line at Dumfries on to connect with the packet service to Larne in Northern Ireland, a route later known as the 'Port Road'. It strengthened its hold on the Ulster market in 1903 when it bought the Belfast & Northern Counties Railway, the most prosperous railway in the north of Ireland. In 1904, it opened a new port at Heysham in Lancashire for packet services to Belfast. The MR helped to create the Midland & Great Northern Joint Railway in 1893 so that it could reach East Anglia. Less logical as it was isolated from the rest of its network, was the purchase of the London Tilbury & Southend Railway in 1912, which the MR promised to electrify, but never did. The company did, nevertheless, develop its existing network, separating slow freight trains from fast expresses, so that between London and Leeds, it had a higher proportion of quadrupled route mileage than its competitor, the Great Northern.

As a constituent part of the LMS, many of its ideas and practices were adopted, such as central control, but not the policy of small locomotives.

North Staffordshire Railway

Formed in 1845 by local industrialists to keep the Potteries free from incursions by the big companies that were emerging, the NSR used the Staffordshire Knot as its emblem and became known affectionately as 'The Knotty'. It developed a network of more than 200 route miles, and secured running rights over more than 300 route miles belonging to other companies. Although formed to transport coal, ironstone and quarried materials, it also became the largest railway canal owner, starting with an amalgamation with the Trent & Mersey Canal in 1846, but unlike other railway companies, it continued to develop the canals it bought.

The main lines linked Crewe with Derby and Colwich with Macclesfield, meeting at Stoke. The Macclesfield line was used by the London & North Western Railway as a cut-off to avoid Crewe and save five miles between Euston and Manchester. A loop line completed in 1875 linked all six Potteries towns, while branches connected the NSR with the Great Western at Market Drayton and another served the Biddulph Valley. With the Great Central, the NSR was joint owner of the 11-mile long Macclesfield Bollington & Marple Railway. It also worked the 2ft 6in gauge Leek & Manifold Light Railway, opened in 1904.

Before the First World War, freight and passenger traffic combined provided an average 5 per cent dividend, while demands to reduce Sunday services were resisted and instead industrial workers were encouraged to make excursions into the countryside.

Rationalisation and some decline followed the Grouping, but during the Second World War, a branch was opened to a Royal Ordnance factory at Swynnerton, near Stone, which carried three million passengers a year from 1941 on trains that never appeared in the public timetables.

Subsidiary Companies

Callander & Oban Railway

Originally intended to be provided by the ill-fated Glasgow & North Western Railway, the idea of a line south from Oban to serve the growing resort and feed passengers to the steamer services to the islands, was revived during the 1860s. The cheapest route was 71 miles to Callander, connecting with the Caledonian Railway. Engineered by Blyth & Westland of Edinburgh, the line was amongst the first to use bowstring girder bridges on the section up Strathyre. Funding ran out leaving the line to terminate at Tyndrum with a stage coach connection to Oban, and it was only after extra capital was raised that the line to Oban was completed in 1880, using John Strain as engineer. The line suffered from steep gradients and the Caledonian had to design locomotives with small wheels and low axle weights to work the line, while a system of trip wires had to be used to operate signals if rocks fell on to the line. Three branches were built, the shortest to Killin opened in 1886; the longest opened in 1903 to Ballachulish, and then there was one to Comrie and Crieff opened in 1905. The line to Comrie closed in 1964, the other branches in 1965, and the section of the line between Dunblane and Crianlarich closed the following year, leaving the remainder of the line to be reached from the West Highland line.

Cockermouth Keswick & Penrith Railway

Opened in 1864 and 1865, the Cockermouth Keswick & Penrith Railway was worked by the London & North Western Railway and the North Eastern Railway, before becoming part of the LMS on Grouping.

Dearne Valley Railway

Not opened until 1909, although incorporated in 1897, initially this line between Black Carr Junction, south of Doncaster, and Brierley Junction, east of Barnsley, running via Cadeby and Grimethorpe, was freight only and intended to serve the collieries in the area. Passenger services were introduced in 1912. Throughout its life it was worked by the Lancashire & Yorkshire Railway, so it passed into the control of the London & North Western on the eve of Grouping before becoming part of the LMS.

Leek & Manifold Valley Light Railway

A 2ft 6in gauge railway authorised by a Light Railway Order in 1899 and opened in 1904, the Leek & Manifold Valley Light Railway linked Waterhouses with Hulme End. It was worked and maintained by the North Staffordshire Railway, before becoming part of the LMS.

London Tilbury & Southend Railway

Already a subsidiary of the Midland Railway at the time of Grouping, otherwise it would probably have been a constituent company. The LTSR was originally authorised in 1852 as a joint scheme by the Eastern Counties Railway (ECR) and London & Blackwall Railway (LBR) running from Forest Gate Junction on the ECR to Tilbury and Southend, ending rivalry between the two companies to expand into the area. In many ways, this was a contractors' line as the impetus had come from G.P. Bidder, as engineer, and the contractor Samuel Morton Peto, who were joined by two others, Thomas Brassey, and E.L. Betts, who built the line. It opened in stages between 1854 and 1856, and was then worked under lease until 1875, although rolling stock was supplied by the ECR. The sponsors' ambitions were to attract the excursion traffic from Tilbury to Gravesend, and only later did the holiday market for Southend become important.

At first, trains were divided at Stratford with portions for Bishopsgate and Fenchurch Street. A branch was opened to Thames Haven in 1855 by the Thames Haven Dock & Railway Company, and this was taken over by the LTSR on opening. Traffic grew quickly, and an avoiding line had to be built to bypass Stratford, opening in 1858, which then became the main line while all trains ran to and from Fenchurch Street only. The LTSR became an independent company in 1862, although the main shareholders remained the LBR and the newly created Great Eastern Railway which ran the line until 1876. After this the line was modernised and received its own 4-4-2T locomotives and carriages, and ran its own trains from 1880, with full independence following in 1882, and the other two railways no longer appointing directors. In 1884, an extension from Southend to Shoeburyness, long delayed by War Office objections, was opened, with a shorter line from Barking to Pitsea via Upminster opened between 1885 and 1888, and in 1893 a branch opened from Grays to Romford. Meanwhile, the opening of new docks at Tilbury in 1886 provided goods traffic and also required boat trains to be operated when liners called, while the line served the new housing developments in the east of London as well as a growing commuter market at Southend.

Although acquisition of this thriving line by the GER was widely expected, in 1912 the LTSR was acquired by the Midland Railway, and under Grouping passed to the LMS, as a self-contained and isolated line away from the company's main area of operations, although the LMS was able to run boat trains from St Pancras and Manchester through to Tilbury.

Maryport & Carlisle Railway

Authorised in 1837 to extend the Newcastle & Carlisle Railway westwards to Maryport, this line was engineered by George Stephenson. The 28-mile line was opened in stages between 1840 and 1845. In 1848, it briefly became part of George Hudson's empire, but regained its independence in 1850. Traffic consisted mainly of coal from the northern part of the Cumberland coalfield, but there was also iron ore, passengers and grain. Two branches were built, one through Mealsgate in 1866, which failed to capture the anticipated traffic, but the second, to Brigham and known as the 'Derwent branch', opened the following year, providing a link to Cockermouth and with it, the company reached a total of 43 route miles. It was an early convert from coke to coal as a fuel, and one locomotive is believed to have had the first all-steel boiler in 1862. Another distinction was the absence of any serious accident throughout its history.

The line achieved an average dividend of 6.6 per cent between 1850 and 1922, while between 1870 and 1882, it reached 11.1 per cent. It remained independent from 1850 until absorbed by the LMS.

Mersey Railway

Not part of the Grouping but acquired later in 1938 when it was integrated into the newly electrified Wirral lines of the LMS. The line originated as the Mersey Pneumatic Railway, authorised as early as 1866, which became simply the Mersey Railway two years later. Nevertheless, it did not open its first section of 2¼ miles underground between James Street, close to the Liverpool docks, and Green Lane, Birkenhead, until 1886. In 1888, a further section opened to a surface station at Birkenhead Park, shared with the Wirral Railway. Later extensions were between Green Lane and Rock Ferry, with a junction with the Birkenhead Joint Railway, opened in 1891, and then between James Street and Liverpool Central (Low Level) in 1892, making a total route mileage of just 4½ miles.

Although it was originally planned as a pneumatic railway, conventional steam locomotives with powerful condensing apparatus were used once it opened, but the result was extremely unpleasant with tunnels, stations and carriages filled with smoke and soot, so that the Birkenhead ferries advertised themselves as the 'health route', with the result that passenger traffic was so bad that the company was in receivership between 1897 and 1900. This was the first railway in the British Isles to convert from steam to electric traction when, in 1903, it was electrified using third-rail 650V dc. Electrification was just what was needed and proved to be the company's salvation, to the extent that by 1930, it was carrying 17 million passengers annually. Notable features were the steep gradients on the line and the use of US-style clerestory carriages with stable half-doors.

North & South Western Junction Railway

Opened between 1853 and 1857, the North & South Western Junction Railway linked Willesden on the London & North Western Railway to Old Kew Junction on the London & South Western Railway, and had a branch from South Acton to Hammersmith and Chiswick. It was worked by the LNWR and LSWR, while the passenger service was provided by the North London Railway. Between 1871 and 1922, it was leased jointly by the LNWR, NLR and the Midland Railway, so under Grouping it passed to the LMS. It was mainly used by freight trains between the South and the Midlands and the North West, avoiding central London.

North London Railway

Somewhat surprisingly, this important railway was not a constituent company under the Act. Authorised in 1846 as the East & West India Docks & Birmingham Junction Railway, running 13¼ miles from Camden Town on the London & North Western Railway to Blackwall, it opened in stages between 1850 and 1852. It was renamed the North London Railway in 1853. Its promoters naturally enough saw freight traffic as its main business, but passenger trains operated quarter-hourly from its opening. Initially, Fenchurch Street on the London & Blackwall Railway was the terminus, but the approach was indirect and time consuming, but after a two-mile stretch of line was opened from Dalston to Broad Street in 1865, passenger traffic grew quickly. Much of the business was generated by trains running over 54¾ miles of track belonging to other companies. By 1907, the NLR's revenue was split 50:50 between freight and suburban passenger traffic.

William Adams built the NLR's locomotives from 1863 at its own works at Bow. The locomotive stock was highly standardised, with 4-4-0Ts for passenger services and 0-6-0Ts for freight.

The major shareholder was the LNWR, which managed to keep Great Northern trains out of Broad Street, although after 1875, NLR trains were able to work to GNR stations, including High Barnett, Potters Bar and Enfield, by using a curve at Canonbury. NLR trains ran over the London & South Western to Richmond. The NLR also provided the services on the North & South Western Junction Railway line between Willesden and Kew after it opened in 1853, which was jointly leased by the NLR, LNWR and the Midland in 1871, as well as the Hampstead Junction Railway, which ran for 6½ miles from Camden Town to Willesden and opened in 1860, which was another LNWR venture. In short, the NLR was the strategic link that was far more important than its route mileage suggested, and connected the railways running to the west, north and east of London – only the London Brighton & South Coast Railway and the two South Eastern companies were not directly linked to it. An idea of its importance was that it had no fewer than 123 locomotives and 620 carriages by 1908. At Kentish Town Junction, Camden Town, the NLR installed the first completely interlocked points and signals, made at its own works at Bow. In 1874, the lines between Broad Street and Camden Town were quadrupled. An interesting feature was that the NLR only provided first and second class accommodation until 1875.

Generally a highly efficient and well-run railway, as it needed to be, given the traffic coming off other lines, it nevertheless suffered a spate of accidents with trains running into one another on the connecting curve with the GNR at Canonbury Tunnel in 1881. The cause was found to be GNR signalmen not understanding NLR bell codes.

By 1880, the railway had settled into a steady business which lasted until the turn of the century, and except for two years when dividends were 6¾ per cent, it paid 7½ per cent. Nevertheless, it was also one of the first to suffer the impact of electric tramways, and this forced it to consider electrification. The LNWR took over operations from 1909, although the NLR remained as a separate company, and electrification was approved in 1911 as part of the LNWR's scheme for its London suburban services. Electrification was completed between Broad Street and Richmond in 1916, and then between Broad Street and Watford in 1922, using the third and fourth rail system.

The NLR was one of the few railway companies to suffer enemy air attack during the First World War, and occasionally had to close its passenger services.

Portpatrick & Wigtownshire Joint Railway

Completed as the Portpatrick Railway in 1862, it was designed to link the Castle Douglas & Dumfries Railway, completed in 1859, with Portpatrick, the Scottish port for the packet service to Donaghdee, shortest of all the sea crossings to Ireland. The line ran through Creetown and Newton Stewart to both Portpatrick and Stranraer, and the two railways combined became known as the 'Port Road'. Despite its potential, the railway was cheaply built to minimise costs on the heavy civil engineering works needed because of the heavily undulating terrain traversed, with many tall viaducts. The Glasgow & South Western Railway ran to both Dumfries and Stranraer, but it was the Caledonian Railway that bought traffic rights for trains coming off the West Coast Main Line.

Port Patrick lacked sufficient space for expansion either of the port or the railway terminus, so in 1874, the western terminus was moved to Stranraer, where a new port and long pier were constructed, with a branch line to the harbour, while Larne became the Irish ferry terminus. A branch to Garlieston and Whithorn, known as the Wigtownshire Railway, was opened in 1877, but neither this nor the line to Portpatrick prospered, and in 1885, the Caledonian, Glasgow & South Western, London & North Western and Midland railways jointly acquired the line. A further branch was constructed from Tarff to Kirkcudbright.

Local traffic along the 80-mile line was never significant as the area was, and remains, thinly populated, but it did carry expresses with boat train traffic, although for passengers from London, the Midlands and the North West, the Lancashire ferry ports were far more convenient.

Shropshire Union Railways & Canal

Following the merger of the Ellesmere & Chester and Birmingham & Liverpool Junction canals in 1842, consideration was given to converting part of the system into a railway. In 1846, the Shropshire Union Railways & Canal Company was authorised, largely based on the Ellesmere & Chester, while the Shrewsbury, Shropshire and Montgomeryshire canals were added between 1847 and 1850, making an inland waterway system of 190 miles. In 1849, the company built a 19-mile railway from Stafford to Wellington. At this time, the intention was to create an integrated canal and railway system.

The London & North Western Railway had leased the company from 1847, although the canal directors retained responsibility for the infrastructure and often resisted the railway interest, and the company was not absorbed by the LNWR until 1922, before being absorbed again by the LMS.

Solway Junction Railway

Opened between 1869 and 1873 with running powers over the North British Railway line from Silloth, the Solway Junction linked Kirtlebridge, Annan, Bowness and Brayton. It was transferred to the Caledonian Railway in 1873. Its main structure was the Solway Viaduct, over which traffic closed in 1921, although it continued to be used by pedestrians as on Sundays thirsty locals trekked from 'dry' Scotland to 'wet' England. The remaining parts of the SJR were absorbed into the LMS.

Stratford upon Avon & Midland Junction Railway

Created by the amalgamation of four small railways, the SMJR was connected to no fewer than four of the major railways, the Midland, Great Central, London & North Western and the Great Western. Its main route ran off the MR at Ravenstone Wood Junction, on the Bedford–Northampton line, to Broom Junction on the Barnt Green–Ashchurch line. Branches were built from Towcester to the LNWR at Blisworth and Cockley Brake Junction. Despite its strong connections, the line ran through sparsely populated countryside and did not prosper, only showing its worth for freight during the two world wars. When it entered receivership, no other company was interested in buying it, but it struggled on after a reorganisation in 1908. It was absorbed into the LMS.

Tottenham & Forest Gate Railway

Jointly owned by the Midland Railway and the London Tilbury & Southend Railway, the Tottenham & Forest Gate Railway opened in 1894. Control passed to the Midland in 1912, but kept its separate identity to be grouped into the LMS.

Wirral Railway

The Wirral Railway (WR) was formed in 1891 from a number of short lines, one of which was the Hoylake Railway which had opened in 1866 to link Hoylake with the docks at Birkenhead. Eventually, the WR had 13½ route miles with connections to the Great Western and London & North Western joint line at West Kirby and extensions to Birkenhead Park, New Brighton and Seacombe, where passengers could transfer to a ferry service to Liverpool. The line was mainly used by passenger trains.

  Although powers to electrify the line were obtained in 1900, electrification on the third-rail system did not come until 1938, by which time it was part of the LMS, and its operations were linked with those of the Mersey Railway.

Yorkshire Dales Railway

Opened in 1902, the original Yorkshire Dales Railway connected Skipton with Grassington and was worked by the Midland Railway until it was absorbed into the LMS. The title lives on as the operating company of the Embsay & Bolton Abbey Steam Railway, a heritage line, opened in 1979.

Joint Ventures

Cheshire Lines Committee

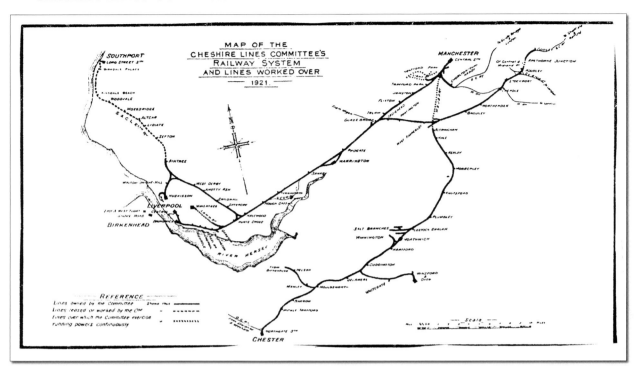

The Cheshire Lines were operated jointly by the LMS and the LNER.

Despite the name, most of the 143 route miles of this railway, operated as the Cheshire Lines Committee (CLC), were in Lancashire, as were the largest of its 70 stations, including Liverpool Central and Manchester Central, connected by punctual expresses taking just 40 minutes, while most of its revenue came from the same county. In 1865–66, the Manchester Sheffield & Lincolnshire Railway (which was later renamed as the Great Central Railway, ready for its extension to London Marylebone), the Great Northern and the Midland railways formed a committee with the intention of breaking the London & North Western Railway's monopoly in Manchester.

Companies were formed to build lines in the Manchester and Stockport areas that linked to the MSLR, while the company also gained access to Liverpool docks, and reached Birkenhead docks over the Wirral Railway. A line was built to Chester Northgate to connect with the GCR lines to Bidston and North Wales. Highly profitable, it was estimated that at one time the CLC took almost a fifth of the trade of the port of Liverpool. Locomotives were provided by the member companies, and after Grouping in 1923, mainly by the LNER, although through trains from the LMS were hauled by its own locomotives, while the CLC also had its own rolling stock, including four Sentinel railcars.

Dearne Valley Railway

Opened in 1909, although incorporated in 1897, the Dearne Valley Railway, running between Black Carr Junction, south of Doncaster, and Brierley Junction, east of Barnsley, running via Cadeby and Grimethorpe, was initially freight only and intended to serve the collieries in the area. Passenger services were introduced in 1912. Throughout its life it was worked by the Lancashire & Yorkshire Railway, but it passed into the control of the London & North Western on the eve of Grouping and then became part of the LMS.

Kilsyth & Bonnybridge Railway

An extension of the Kelvin Valley Railway (KVR), which opened in 1879, the Kilsyth & Bonnybridge Railway (KBR) opened in 1888. While the KVR was operated by the North British Railway, the KBR was operated jointly by the NBR and the Caledonian Railway, and although it passed to the London & North Eastern Railway in 1923, joint working with the LMS continued until Nationalisation.

Manchester South Junction & Altrincham Railway

Formed in 1845 to provide a link between its owners, the Liverpool & Manchester Railway and the Sheffield Ashton & Manchester, a predecessor of the Manchester Sheffield & Lincolnshire Railway (later renamed the Great Central Railway), it ran for its 1½-mile length on a brick viaduct on the south side of the city, but with an eight-mile branch from Castlefield to Altrincham, which soon became far busier than the connecting line, as it encouraged the development of suburbs. Both shareholding companies provided frequent suburban trains to Altrincham, initially from Oxford Road and then, in 1879, from London Road, by which time they had developed into the London & North Western and Manchester Sheffield & Lincolnshire railways.

Despite having come together to build the MSJAR, the two proprietors had an increasingly unhappy relationship, to the extent that a further Act in 1858 ensured that an arbitrator should attend their meetings. The MSJAR had its own carriages and wagons, but most locomotives came from the MSLR. In 1931, by which time the owners had become the London Midland & Scottish and London & North Eastern railways, the line was electrified using a 1,500V dc overhead system.

Midland & Great Northern Joint Railway

The longest of the joint railways at 183 route miles, the MGNJR was an attempt by the Midland and Great Northern railways to penetrate East Anglia, bringing Midland and Yorkshire coal to Norfolk and fish and agricultural products to the industrial centres of the Midlands and the North. Initially, the route used four short contractors' lines, promoted by Waring Brothers, to get from Peterborough to Bourne, Spalding and King's Lynn, which were opened between 1858 and 1866, and worked by the MR and GNR. Later, other lines were opened beyond King's Lynn with the Lynn & Fakenham, opened in 1882 and a line between Yarmouth and North Walsham, opened throughout in 1888, which combined to form the Eastern & Midlands Company, running across Norfolk. A branch to Norwich was added later, followed by one to Cromer in 1887.

Nevertheless, the EMR passed into receivership in 1890, when the MR and GNR purchased it and added the earlier sections to it to form the Midland & Great Northern Joint Railway in 1893. The following year, a branch was opened westwards from Bourne to meet the MR at Saxby, adding through services to Nottingham, Leicester and Birmingham. The new owners also doubled some of the line, but even so, 77 per cent remained single track, while operations were much improved after new tablet-exchange equipment was introduced in 1906. Although the two owners had operating rights, the line also pursued an independent existence with its own locomotive works at Melton Constable. With the wide range of destinations served by

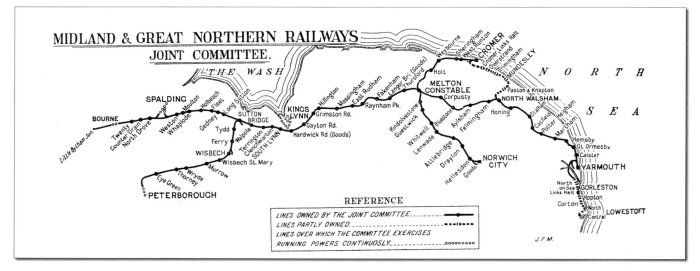

The need to take East Anglia's agricultural produce and fish to the Midlands and the North of England, and to transport coal into East Anglia from the Midlands and Yorkshire, resulted in the creation of the Midland & Great Northern Railways Joint Committee.

this time, cattle and fish traffic alone required five trains daily during the summer, while the line also brought holidaymakers to Cromer and Yarmouth. The GNR even ran through trains between London and Cromer, but this was a lengthy route at 174 miles, 35 more than on the Great Eastern.

Rivalry with the GER was left behind in 1896, when the three companies agreed to develop the Norfolk & Suffolk Joint Railway, but only two sections were completed, between Cromer and North Walsham in 1898, and Yarmouth and Lowestoft in 1903. Nevertheless, this meant that the MGNJR and its owners could reach Lowestoft. On Grouping, the line remained jointly operated, passing to both the LMS and LNER, but in 1936, administration and control was taken over completely by the LNER, through whose home territory the line ran.

Shrewsbury & Hereford Railway

Authorised in 1846 and planned by Henry Robertson, work did not start until 1850, when Thomas Brassey was appointed contractor and also agreed to lease the line for eight years once opened. The 51-mile line opened in stages during 1852–53. At Shrewsbury, a joint station was built with the Shrewsbury & Chester and Shrewsbury & Birmingham railways, while at Hereford it connected with the Newport Abergavenny & Hereford Railway (a predecessor of the West Midland Railway). The line supported and later worked an eight-mile line to Tenbury Wells, opened in 1861.

Both the London & North Western and Great Western saw the line as a link between the Midlands and the expanding coal fields of South Wales, and when Brassey's lease expired in 1862, they took over, paying the shareholders a guaranteed 6 per cent dividend.

Somerset & Dorset Joint Railway

The Somerset & Dorset Joint Railway was created by the amalgamation of the Somerset Central Railway (SCR), which had opened during 1854–59, running from the Bristol & Exeter Railway at Highbridge to Glastonbury, Wells and Burnham-on-Sea, and the Dorset Central

Railway, which opened during 1860–62, running from the London & South-Western Railway at Wimborne through Templecombe to meet the SCR. The new company almost immediately went into receivership for four years, and in 1874 nearly managed to do so again after opening an extension from Evercreech to Bath, although this then became its main line. Salvation came when the Midland Railway and LSWR leased the line in 1875, realising the potential of a link between the Midlands and the South Coast.

The new ownership was marred by a head-on collision in 1875 at Radstock in which 13 people were killed.

The SDJR consisted of 102 route miles, including the Bridgwater Railway, opened in 1890, with a 64-mile main line, parts of which were double track, but 26 miles were single track and these, with the hilly section through the Mendips near Bath, made working difficult. The line retained its own works at Highbridge and used Midland locomotives, while carriages were painted blue. The line passed to the Southern Railway and London Midland & Scottish Railway on Grouping. The new owners made economies, with the SR taking responsibility for carriages, track and signalling, and the LMS for locomotives, closing the workshops at Highbridge, but the line never made a profit. The locomotives were not officially absorbed into LMS stock until 1930. Despite carrying expresses such as the Bournemouth–Manchester 'Pines Express', the line did not have a good reputation, earning the nickname 'Slow and Dirty'.

The rural traffic of the Somerset & Dorset Joint Railway, which retained its identity after Grouping, required vehicles such as this large cattle truck, No. 1238. *(HMRS AAC401)*

South Yorkshire Joint Line Committee

The importance of the vast South Yorkshire coalfield was such that all of the railway companies bordering the area wished to, and needed to, become involved. In 1903, an Act of Parliament authorised the South Yorkshire Joint Line Committee (SYJLC), the members of which included the Great Central, Great Northern and North Eastern railways, all of which became constituent companies of the London & North Eastern, as well as the Midland Railway and the Lancashire & Yorkshire Railway, which passed into the London Midland & Scottish.

The core of the SYJLC was the line from Kirk Sandal Junction on the old Great Central line between Doncaster and Barnby Dun, which led to an end-on junction with the GCR and Midland Joint Line which in turn led to the GCR's Retford to Sheffield main line at Brancliffe Junction. Each company worked its own traffic over the SYJLC, although the trading title for the network was the 'South Yorkshire'. Excluding sidings, the system had a total route mileage of just over 38 miles.

The line opened for mineral traffic on 1 January 1909, but it was almost two years before passenger traffic started on 1 December 1910, with four trains daily between Doncaster and Shireoaks. This started as a joint venture between the GNR and GCR, but the Great Northern withdrew after a year. Passenger trains were suspended except on Saturdays during the First World War, and again during the General Strike and Miners' Strike of 1926, and not reinstated afterwards.

Under Grouping, the line became a joint LMS and LNER venture.

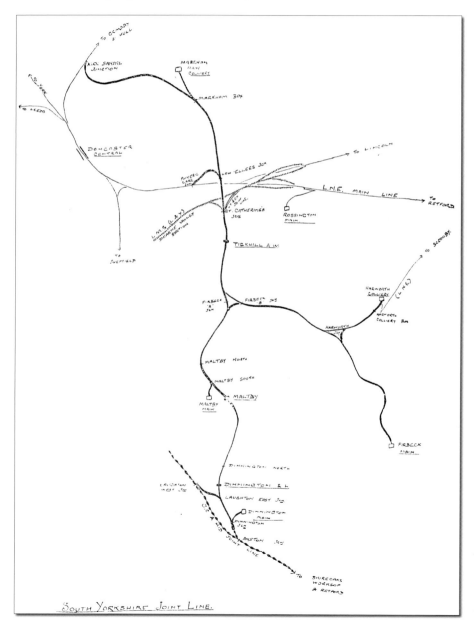

No fewer than five of the pre-Grouping companies were involved with the South Yorkshire Joint Lines, which remained a joint operation after Grouping, with the LMS and LNER working together.

Irish companies

Ballycastle Railway

Supported by the Belfast & Northern Counties Railway , this 3ft gauge line ran for 16¼ miles from Ballymoney, on the BNCR main line, to Ballycastle. It opened in 1880 and was absorbed by the Northern Counties Committee, successors to the BNCR, in 1924, making it a subsidiary of the LMS.

County Donegal Railways Joint Committee

Formed in 1892 as the Donegal Railway when the Finn Valley Railway, originally opened in 1861, using 5ft 3in gauge and running between Strabane and Stranorlar, merged with the 3ft gauge West Donegal Railway opened in 1889 and ran between Stranorlar and Donegal. The system underwent further work between 1893 and 1905, including conversion of the former Finn Valley line to 3ft gauge and construction of branches to Killybegs, opened in 1893; Glenties, 1895; and Ballyshannon, 1905. The County Donegal Railways Joint Committee was formed when the railway was taken over by the Great Northern Railway of Ireland and the Midland Railway in 1906, and while the line from Londonderry to Strabane was actually owned by the MR, and later the LMS, all services were worked by the Joint Committee. The CDRJC also worked the Strabane & Letterkenny Railway, which opened in 1909. In all, the system amounted to around 125 miles of narrow gauge railway, the largest such system in the British Isles.

On Grouping, the MR's interest passed to the London Midland & Scottish Railway. The company worked through a sparsely populated area of Ireland, with Donegal being one of the three counties of Ulster left out of Northern Ireland in 1922, so that the line ran mainly in what became the Irish Free State, but had its terminus just over the border in Londonderry. In order to economise, it became one of the pioneers of petrol and diesel railcars, which proved popular with passengers although whether the fortunes of the line were completely transformed seems doubtful. In 1934, the first of what eventually amounted to eight articulated diesel railcars, constructed by Walker Brothers of Wigan, entered service so that post-war, virtually all passenger services were operated by diesel railcar. The railcars were sufficiently powerful to be capable of hauling a trailer or freight wagon, enabling economies to be made in freight working and continuing the Irish tradition of the mixed train. A steam locomotive was converted to diesel for freight use and named *Phoenix*.

Dundalk Newry & Greenore Railway

Originally incorporated in 1863 to run from Dundalk to Greenore, while in 1873, the year that the line was opened, an extension was authorised to Newry, giving a total route mileage of around 26 miles of Irish 5ft 3in gauge line when this opened in 1876. The driving force behind this short line was the London & North Western Railway, which operated a steam packet service between Holyhead and Greenore, and which supplied locomotives and carriages of its own standard design, but modified for the 5ft 3in gauge, and also appointed six out of the eight directors. On Grouping in 1923, it became part of the LMS, but from 1933, the LMS, while retaining ownership, passed management and operation to the Great Northern Railway of Ireland.

Northern Counties Committee/Belfast & Northern Counties Railway

Formed in 1860 by the merger of four smaller railways: Belfast & Ballymena Railway, Ballymena Railway, Coleraine & Portrush Railway, and the Londonderry & Coleraine Railway, all of which were on the Irish 'standard' gauge of 5ft 3in. In 1884, the Belfast & Northern Counties acquired the 3ft gauge Ballymena, Cushendall & Red Bay Railway. In total, it had 201 miles of 5ft 3in gauge and 48 miles of 3ft gauge, with a main line, single in places, 92½ miles from Belfast to Londonderry, as well the line from Belfast to Larne, packet port for Stranraer in Scotland, and a branch off the Londonderry line to Portrush, which was important for summer holidaymakers.

The company faced direct competition with the Great Northern Railway of Ireland between Belfast and Londonderry, but had the faster line.

In 1903, it was taken over by the expansive Midland Railway, whose livery it adopted, and which paid lip service to local control by establishing the Northern Counties Committee (NCC), which became its name. When it became part of the LMS, it used re-gauged versions of its standard steam locomotives and carriages.

An unusual feature of the main line to Londonderry was that at one point, the line ran across the runway of a military airfield at RAF Ballykelly, built during the Second World War and subsequently used by the United States Navy. The trains had the right of way.

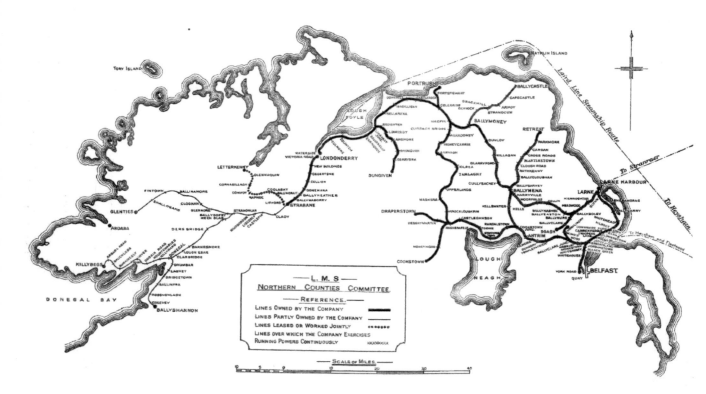

The network of the Northern Counties Committee, the former Belfast & Northern Counties Railway, was substantial with more than 200 route miles. It also served the most prosperous and industrialised part of Ireland.

The Neighbours

The LMS was present in Ireland, a country where the railways had a distinctive feel not least because of the different gauge of 5ft 3in, and a substantial mileage of 3ft gauge lines. Yet, if Ireland seemed to be a case on its own, so to some extent was Merseyside, with the Merseyside Railway not incorporated into the LMS until 1938, while the Liverpool Overhead Railway was also a unique operation that escaped integration with the LMS, despite being linked to the lines of the former Lancashire & Yorkshire Railway.

To give a better perspective of Ireland, the other railway in County Donegal, the Londonderry & Lough Swilly, as well as the LMS's partner in the County Donegal and eventual operator over the Dundalk Newry & Greenore Railway, the Great Northern Railway of Ireland, GNR (I) is covered here, as is the Liverpool Overhead Railway. As we have already seen, railway operation was never confined to the extent of a company's own lines, although through working or inter-working was not practised on the narrow gauge systems which were always feeders to the broad gauge, or existed to serve areas with a sparse population.

Grouping in what was known as the Irish Free State following partition in 1922, came in 1925, but was incomplete as no action was taken on those companies that ran across the border into Northern Ireland, and there was no similar grouping north of the border. The most significant company to emerge from the Grouping was the Great Southern Railways, which included the former Great Southern & Western Railway; the Cork Blackrock & Passage Railway, the Cork Brandon & South Coast Railway, the Midland Great Western Railway, and the Dublin & South Eastern Railway.

Great Northern Railway of Ireland

Usually referred to as the GNR (I), it was incorporated in 1876 as the Great Northern Railway of Ireland, but more usually known as the Great Northern Railway (Ireland). It began operations in 1877. The company consisted of a merger of the Dublin & Drogheda Railway, opened 1844, with the Dublin & Belfast Junction, the Irish North-Western and the Ulster railways, opened 1839 and which had a 6ft 2in gauge, as well as a number of branch lines. It operated from both Dublin and Belfast to Londonderry, the latter in competition with the Belfast & Northern Counties, as well as to Bundoran and Enniskillen and a branch to Newcastle, Co. Down, eventually creating some 616 route miles built, and later rebuilt to the Irish gauge of 5ft 3in. It became one of Britain's first international railways with the creation of the Irish Free State in 1922, and customs posts were established at Dundalk and Goraghwood, while a police presence was maintained at many stations close to the frontier.

During the Second World War, locomotive crews working from Northern Ireland would often pass coal to their Dublin-based counterparts to help the steaming of their locomotives forced to burn peat, because of the shortage of coal in Eire. The main line was 112½ miles between Dublin Amiens Street and Belfast Great Victoria Street, although the secondary main line from Dublin to Londonderry Foyle Road was slightly longer at 121½ miles.

The international nature of the operation ensured that it avoided nationalisation in 1948, but this followed the bankruptcy of the company in 1953.

Liverpool Overhead Railway

Running 16ft above street level for the 6½ miles from Dingle to Seaforth, the Liverpool Overhead Railway (LOR) was built during 1893–96 and was the world's first elevated electric railway. Third-rail 500V dc electrification was used. Elevated construction keep the line clear of the entrances to the many docks along its route, and it was nicknamed the 'Dockers' Umbrella'. In 1905, it was connected to the Lancashire & Yorkshire Railway's Ormskirk and Southport electrified lines. Notable firsts also included Britain's automatic semaphore signals and, in 1921, colour light signalling.

The creation of such a line was only possible because the Liverpool docks were not carved out of the land, but built out from the shoreline, so that the landward end of the dock systems was more regular than that in London.

The LOR was closed in 1956 because the heavy cost, estimated to be around £2 million at the time, of replacing the steel decking could not be justified in the light of declining traffic.

Londonderry & Lough Swilly Railway

Authorised in 1853, initially the line was to be 14 route miles linking Londonderry and Letterkenny, with a branch to Buncrana. It was the Buncrana to Londonderry section that first opened in 1863, and initially this used Irish gauge of 5ft 3in, but it was converted to 3ft gauge in 1885 and all the subsequent lines were built to this gauge. It acquired the Letterkenny Railway, opened in 1883; the Cardonagh Railway, opened in 1901; and an extension opened to Burtonport in 1903, running 50 miles from Letterkenny through sparsely populated and mountainous country.

The company was unprofitable for much of its life, but before the First World War, efficiency improved and it even managed to pay a small dividend. Lough Swilly was a major anchorage and naval base for the Royal Navy and during the war years, traffic to the base at Buncrana was heavy. Post-war, traffic declined to its old level and the situation was made worse by growing competition from motor bus services and road haulage, while partition of Ireland in 1922 helped to separate Londonderry from its hinterland which lay mainly in County Donegal, so that the LLSR became heavily dependent on subsidies from the then Irish Free State to continue.

It eventually became a road haulage and bus operator.

Chapter 2

London Termini

Only the Southern Railway had more termini in London than the LMS. As with the Southern, which had two large termini at Waterloo and Victoria, and many much smaller, the LMS had a large terminus at Euston, with a grand frontage behind which the terminus grew into a muddle created over many years, and a medium-sized terminus at St Pancras, across the road from King's Cross. This showed what an important terminus should look like with its large single span roof. The LMS also had two much smaller stations: the former North London Railway's terminus at Broad Street, sitting next to Liverpool Street in the heart of the City of London, while on the edge of the City lay Fenchurch Street, the smallest of all the London termini. This handled just the former London Tilbury & Southend Railway's line to Southend and Shoeburyness.

If the termini differed in size, their business was different as well. Broad Street and Fenchurch Street were commuter stations, and that was that. Euston and St Pancras were long-distance stations, built for lengthy expresses, although both had commuter traffic, and this was especially so at Euston with its electric trains to Watford. Not all of the old LNWR commuter services were electrified, and many years later, even after Nationalisation, Euston still had most of its suburban traffic handled by steam locomotives.

Broad Street

No longer in existence, Broad Street was built as the City terminus for the North London Railway, which opened in 1850 as the East & West India Docks and Birmingham Junction Railway, dominated by the London & North Western Railway. The name of the original company showed that goods traffic was the aim, but by the time the simpler title of the North London Railway was adopted in 1853, it was clear that passenger traffic was of growing importance. At first the NLR used Fenchurch Street on the London & Blackwall Railway, but this involved a four-mile detour around East London.

The small NLR could only afford a terminus – sited at the junction of Broad Street and Liverpool Street – because the LNWR agreed to meet most of the cost as it needed a goods station in the City. To obtain Parliamentary approval for its extension, which was in doubt because of the number of homes that needed to be demolished, the NLR promised to provide workmen's trains from Dalston for a return fare of just one penny. Design and construction of Broad Street was entrusted to the LNWR's first chief engineer, William Baker. Three tracks connected the station with the rest of the NLR network. The platforms were approached by an external staircase on the eastern side of the station frontage, itself showing a mixture of styles, and no record can be found of an architect.

Broad Street operated as a joint station with two booking halls, one for the NLR and the other for the LNWR, on either side of the clock tower. At platform level, there were two train sheds, initially having just four tracks between them. Opened on 1 November 1865, the initial service was a train every 15 minutes to Bow, and another service every 15 minutes to Chalk Farm, as well as a service every half-hour to Kew via Hampstead Heath. In 1866, a service to Watford was introduced and in 1879, some Chalk Farm workings were extended to Willesden, but were cut back again in 1917. The LNWR goods yard was below the passenger platforms and wagons were raised and lowered by hydraulic lifts, but the goods sidings were to the west of the passenger station.

Although having been built as cheaply as possible, the NLR and Broad Street proved to be a great success. The NLR's traffic doubled and increased still further when, from January 1875, trains ran through to Broad Street from Great Northern Railway suburban stations. For a short time in its early years, Broad Street was one of the busiest of the London termini, handling 712 trains daily with 80,000 passengers in 1906. A fourth track into the station had been completed in 1874, while the station had eventually grown to have eight stone platforms, although tracks were laid over engine pits, while each pair of platforms shared a coaling stage, an indication of the intensity of suburban working. In 1912, a booking hall was built beneath the forecourt of the terminus for the Central London Railway's extension from the Bank to Liverpool Street.

Before 1910, Broad Street handled local trains only, but to compete with the Great Western Railway's improved service to Birmingham, the LNWR introduced a weekday restaurant car express between Wolverhampton and Birmingham and Broad Street, and which had as a special feature, a typist who would type letters for passengers during the journey. This service only lasted until the outbreak of the First World War and was never reinstated.

Despite the promising first 40 years or so, by its very nature Broad Street's traffic was amongst the first to be seriously affected by the electric tram, the growth of the London Underground network and then the arrival of the motor bus. This first started to become noticeable in 1901, and by 1911 traffic was falling steadily. The answer lay in electrification, and although considered as early as 1904, it was not until after the LNWR took over the operations of the NLR in 1909 that progress began to be made. The LNWR's 1911 scheme used the third and fourth rail system and electric trains started operations to and from Broad Street in October 1916, when services to Kew Bridge and Richmond were converted from steam. Rush hour services to Watford followed in 1917, but the off-peak service was not introduced until 1922, by which time there were also electric trains to Dalston.

By the time of Grouping an intensive electric service was being operated, but steam trains continued to run to Poplar, Tring and a number of stations on the London & North Eastern Railway. The LMS lengthened Platforms 1 and 2 and, in a curious switch, introduced services to Grays, Tilbury and Southend from 1923, duplicating those from Fenchurch Street. Even so, this traffic continued to decline, and the LNER service became rush hour-only, while enlargement of Fenchurch Street saw the Southend and Tilbury services disappear in 1935. The appeal of the services was not helped by the LMS still using old NLR four-wheeled carriages up to 1938 on the Poplar service, at a time when most railway passengers had come to expect the superior ride of bogie carriages.

Broad Street suffered some air raid damage during the First World War, with a thousand panes of glass being shattered, a wall demolished and horses wounded by bomb explosions in September 1915. This was nothing compared to the Second World War, when the terminus was put out of action on the night of 3/4 October 1940, and remained closed for several days. It also had to close on 13 October and 11 November following further enemy action. Services to the LNER were cancelled to make way for war traffic, but reinstated post-war. Heavy air raids on London's East End and the evacuation of many of the local residents also meant the withdrawal of services east of Dalston Junction, which were not reinstated after the war.

Post-war, Broad Street once again saw longer-distance trains as services to Cambridge were diverted to ease the pressure on King's Cross. It was closed completely on 30 June 1986 and subsequently demolished.

Euston

The starting signals outside Euston in 1935. Despite being the busiest terminus on the LMS, with congested approaches, the signalling was poorer than at less-busy stations such as Belfast York Road. *(HMRS ABJ205)*

London's first main line railway terminus, as with so many, was a joint effort between an engineer and an architect, in this case Robert Stephenson and Philip Hardwick. The station was built for what was then the London & Birmingham Railway (LBR), predecessor of the London & North Western Railway, and opened to the public on 20 July 1837. The station buildings were built on a grand scale, unlike many of other London termini, distinguished by Hardwick's famous Doric portico, while his son Philip Charles designed the Great Hall. Unfortunately, this grandeur, which included the famous Great Hall, an unnecessary and costly extravagance used for shareholders' meetings and little else, did not continue beyond the buildings, and the interior, until rebuilding for the Liverpool and Manchester electrification, was gloomy and it was not possible to view the platforms as a whole from what passed for a main concourse, which was in any case above platform level.

Originally, it had been intended that the terminus would have been at Islington, stopping close to the Regent's Canal, to allow easy transhipment of freight to barges heading for the London docks. Stephenson proposed a site further west, close to Marble Arch, but this was regarded as unsuitable for freight. The third suggestion, a site near Maiden Lane, close to King's Cross, was rejected by the House of Lords. When the LBR board asked for economies to be made, Stephenson proposed a stop at Camden Town, again close to the Regent's Canal. This received Parliamentary approval in 1833, but in 1834 the LBR decided to go closer to London and sought approval for a 1¼-mile extension to Euston Grove. This was clearly the right idea, but after crossing the Canal, the new site for the terminus could only be reached by a severe gradient that varied between 1 in 68 and 1 in 77. This meant that at first trains were intended to be hauled up by stationary engines, but in fact until these were completed, locomotives had to move trains up the gradient with one locomotive at the head of the train and another as a 'banker' pushing from behind.

As was usual at the time, tickets were collected before the train reached the terminus, and in the case of LBR trains, this was at Camden Town, after which the trains were attached to the cable and descended the bank to Euston controlled by 'bank riders'. Cable working only lasted until 1844, and the stationary locomotives were then exported to Russia. Afterwards, steam locomotives often needed assistance in the climb out of Euston so for some years a pilot locomotive was used and this was disconnected near the bridge over the Canal until the LNWR returned to having a banking engine at the rear of the train, eliminating the delay while the pilot locomotive was uncoupled.

From the start, the line into Euston was quadruple, with the two eastern lines used for trains working to and from the terminus, and only these were fitted with the cable. The most westerly of the four tracks was used for locomotive workings, while the remaining line was effectively a carriage siding. The station itself had four roads, but only two of these had platforms, known as the 'arrival stage' and the 'departure stage'. Railway offices were built on the eastern end of the large site that had been bought, for the western end was reserved for the Great Western Railway's London terminus, as the main line from Bristol was planned to meet the LBR at Kensal Green. The seemingly inevitable arguments between the two companies over tenancy at Euston were compounded by the GWR's insistence on the broad gauge, and it was as well that it changed its mind and built its own terminus at Paddington. Although this left Euston distinctly out of balance at first, the fast growing traffic at the terminus eventually required all the land to be used by the LNWR, so having the GWR as a tenant, no matter how amicable, would have led to problems. The GWR's own growth soon resulted in expansion at Paddington.

Another big 'first' for Euston was the first railway hotel, or indeed hotels, as two were built and opened in September 1839. Both four-storey buildings were designed by Hardwick; they were placed on either side of the portico and some way ahead of it. On the west, there was the Victoria Hotel, a 'dormitory and coffee room', unlicensed and cheerless. To the east, there was the more comfortable and up-market Euston Hotel, aimed at first-class passengers. In 1881, these were linked by a French-style hotel by another architect, which completely obscured the view of the portico, but compensated for the visual damage by earning itself a good reputation with travellers. Damaged by enemy action during the Second World War, the hotel was demolished in 1963 to enable work to start on reconstruction of the terminus.

The land that had been reserved for the GWR was soon taken over, in 1846, when growing traffic led the company to use it for trains to and from Yorkshire, leaving Lancashire trains with the original station. The change only lasted until the Great Northern Railway provided a more direct route to Yorkshire from 1850.

The enlarged hotel was not the only development in 1881, when further offices were found to be necessary, and so the steady development of Euston as a dark and dreary terminus with the architect's original vision increasingly dominated by mundane extensions began.

The LNWR was growing into one of Britain's leading railways, and Euston also had to expand further, even beyond the site that had been reserved for the GWR. Between 1887 and 1892, the station expanded westwards so that Cardington Street had to be diverted over a cemetery. Once completed, the enlarged Euston had 15 platforms and two booking offices reached from different entrances, effectively having a station within a station, which caused considerable confusion and even comparison with the old Waterloo. Eventually, a cab yard extension and a new booking office put matters right.

Fifteen platforms was the maximum extent of the old Euston. Main line arrivals used Platforms 1 to 3; suburban trains 4, 5 and 7; 6 handled arrivals and departures, as well as Royal trains; while 8 to 10 were used for parcels and peak-period local trains; 11 was used for parcels,

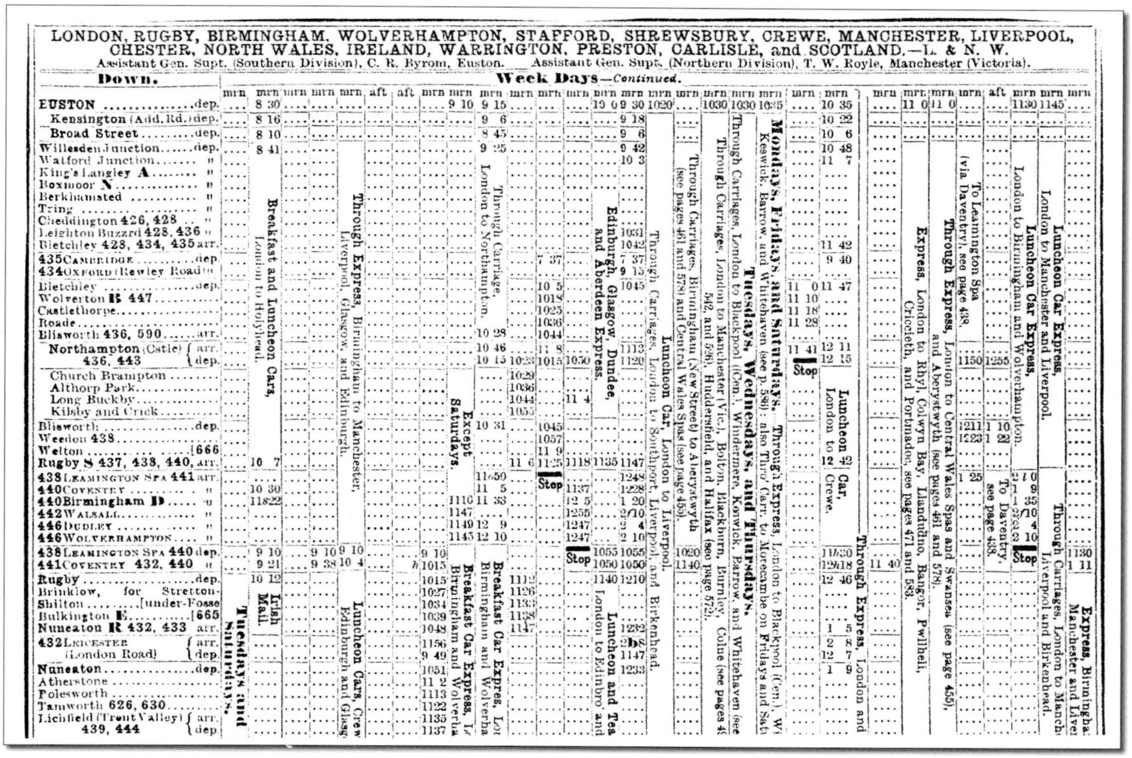

LONDON, RUGBY, BIRMINGHAM, WOLVERHAMPTON, STAFFORD, SHREWSBURY, CREWE, MANCHESTER, LIVERPOOL, CHESTER, NORTH WALES, IRELAND, WARRINGTON, PRESTON, CARLISLE, and SCOTLAND.—L. & N. W.

Assistant Gen. Supt. (Southern Division), C. R. Byrom, Euston.   Assistant Gen. Supt. (Northern Division), T. W. Royle, Manchester (Victoria).

Down. — **Week Days**—Continued.

[Timetable, 1922]

The mainstay of the services out of Euston station were those to the Midlands, the North-West and on to Scotland, as shown here in this timetable for 1922, above, but by 1938, below, the last year before the massive cuts and deceleration of timings of the Second World War, services from Euston were more frequent and much faster. Many of the trains had also acquired names. *(Bradshaw)*

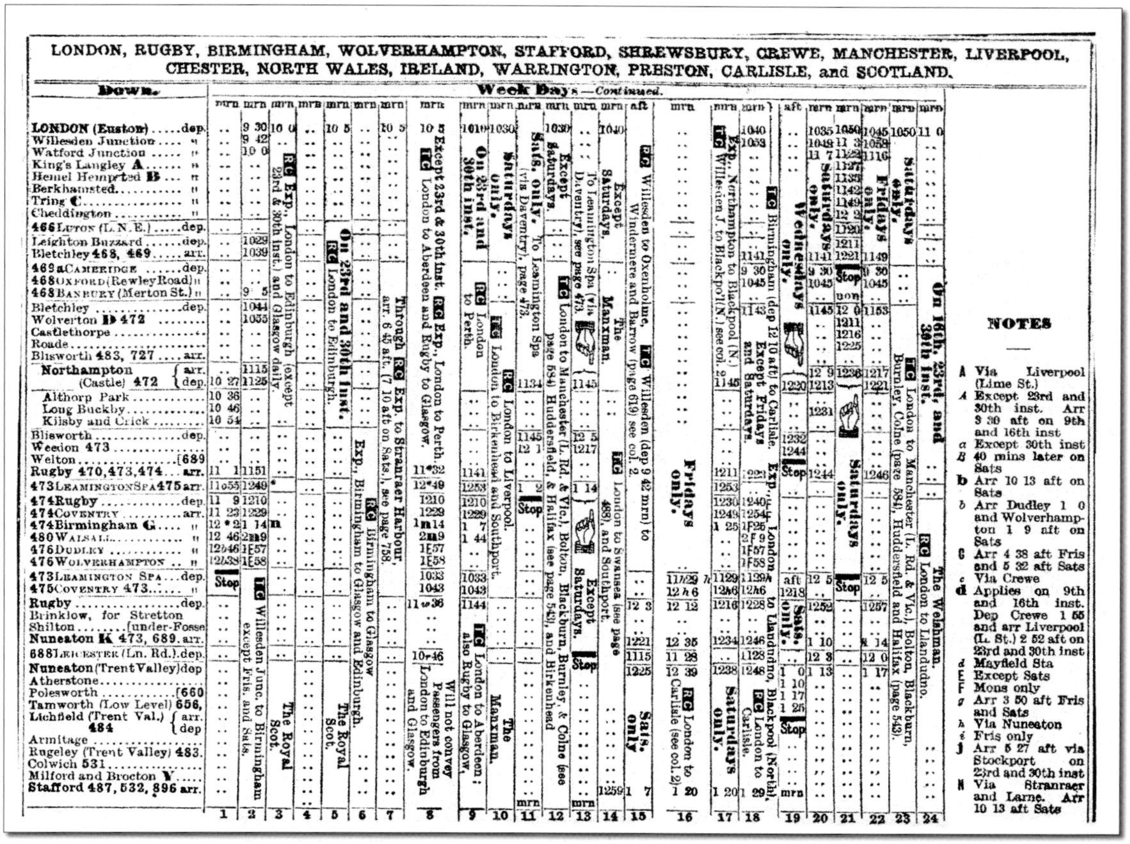

LONDON, RUGBY, BIRMINGHAM, WOLVERHAMPTON, STAFFORD, SHREWSBURY, CREWE, MANCHESTER, LIVERPOOL, CHESTER, NORTH WALES, IRELAND, WARRINGTON, PRESTON, CARLISLE, and SCOTLAND.

Down. — **Week Days**—Continued.

[Timetable, 1938]

fish and milk; and 12 to 15 were used for main line departures. Inserted between platforms 5 and 6 was a road known as the 'horse box' line. Behind the Great Hall were reception sidings, known as 'the field', and at the outer end of 10 and 11 was a carriage dock and a locomotive siding. There were also sidings between 10 and 11, 13 and 14, and alongside 15; while an engine turntable was at the outer end of 15.

Eventually, the LNWR decided that this altogether unworthy mess should be rebuilt and obtained Parliamentary approval in 1900, but the Boer War had unsettled financial markets and so Euston continued to develop piecemeal. Nevertheless, between 1901 and 1906, the cutting between Camden and Euston was widened to allow an additional down line, and carriage sheds were built, eliminating the 5½–mile trip to Willesden depot. This meant that there were two up and two down lines in and out of the terminus. Before the outbreak of the First World War, the LNWR built a new booking concourse south of the Great Hall and the old booking offices were converted to refreshment rooms.

Earlier quadrupling of the line north of Camden enabled Euston to start its first suburban service in 1879, running to Watford. The station was, and remains, predominantly a main line terminus. The connection with the London Underground that commuters find so convenient did not come until May 1907, when the City & South London tube was extended from the Angel, and a little over a month later the Charing Cross, Euston & Hampstead Railway also provided a link. Earlier plans to extend the surface railway from Charing Cross to Euston had never come to fruition, but the tube was a workable substitute. The Metropolitan Railway responded in 1909 by renaming its nearest station Euston Square, even though it was at the northern end of Gower Street, but this was, and remains, some distance away, a good five minutes brisk walk even without heavy luggage!

Meanwhile, the LNWR clearly decided that there was value in suburban traffic. In 1906, it announced plans to build a new electrified line alongside the existing lines between Euston and Watford. In 1909, the LNWR assumed the management of the North London Railway, and agreed with the Underground companies that the new outer suburban line would include LNWR electric trains to Euston and Broad Street, and Bakerloo tube trains running from Watford to the West End and Waterloo through a new tube connection from Queen's Park to Paddington. Plans for the LNWR electric trains to use an underground loop at Euston to reverse were dropped, and instead these ran into the existing station where Platforms 4, 5 and 7 were electrified on the third and fourth-rail dc system. To avoid interference with main line traffic, the new electric lines ran in twin tubes at Primrose Hill and through burrowing junctions at Chalk Farm. A new single track tunnel was also provided for a new line for empty carriage workings. The First World War delayed completion of these plans until 1922, the eve of Grouping.

On 26 April 1924, a serious accident occurred when, at 7.53am, a six-car electric train ran into the back of a Cup Final excursion train from Coventry, waiting at the up slow home signal. Five passengers in the excursion train were killed, and the motorman of the electric train was trapped in his cab for five hours. The inspecting officer found that the signalman had intended giving 'train out of section' for an up Glasgow express standing on the fast line next to the excursion train, but had instead used his up slow instrument, so that the electric train was cleared to enter the section. The unfortunate motorman on the electric train did not see the waiting excursion train until he was within 16 yards of it because smoke and steam under Park Street Bridge had obscured his view.

No major changes or improvements were made to the terminus by the new company until 1935, when it proposed to demolish the entire station and build a new one using low-cost government loans. This would have created a far more attractive and welcoming terminus, and more efficient as well, but it was to take another three decades with another war and nationalisation before this dream was realised. Some limited installation of colour light signalling was introduced, but overall, signalling, as with so much else at Euston, remained inadequate for such a great terminus and many have pointed out that the signalling on the much less busy

Northern Counties Committee terminus at Belfast York Road was far better.

The Second World War left Euston comparatively unscathed compared with other major London termini. In 1940, at the height of the Blitz, a bomb damaged the roof of the Great Hall, while another bomb landed between Platforms 2 and 3 and wrecked offices and damaged part of the hotel.

Fenchurch Street

The smallest railway terminus in London, it was originally built for the London & Blackwall Railway in 1841, but rebuilt in 1854 by George Berkeley. The growth of the docks at Tilbury acted as a spur for what became the London Tilbury & Southend Railway, although many of the boat trains originated at the Midland's London terminus at St Pancras. Originally it had four platforms, but after the railway was acquired by the Great Eastern, a fifth was added, while later, to the surprise of many, the LTSR company was acquired by the Midland Railway. The London & North Eastern Railway remodelled the station between 1932 and 1935, but most of the trains were operated by the Midland's successor, the London Midland & Scottish Railway. The inconvenient site with difficult access from the rest of London and the small size of the station meant that boat trains for liners docking at Tilbury had to run from St Pancras.

St Pancras

The most impressive of London's railway termini, with the tower of the Midland Hotel dominating the skyline and the much lower and meaner structure of King's Cross just across the road. St Pancras was built for the Midland Railway's extension to London after the original arrangement, originating from early 1858, that saw trains running from Hitchin to King's Cross, had proved expensive. The heavy excursion traffic for the Great Exhibition of 1862 also showed the limitations of capacity at King's Cross, and the growth in the Great Northern Railway's traffic in the years to follow would only have seen the problems repeated. It was clear that to be a railway with London amongst its destinations, the MR needed its own terminus and its own approach route.

The MR already had its own goods yard in London at Agar Town, between the North London Railway and the Regent's Canal. It was decided to extend this line to the Euston Road, at the boundary set by the Royal Commission on London's termini, which effectively barred further incursions by railways into the centre of London. A 4½-acre site was found for the terminus, separated from King's Cross by a road, and the eastern part of Lord Somers' estate was acquired for a modest price. Even so, when work started in 1866, the extension required the demolition of thousands of slum dwellings in Agar Town and Somers Town, with some 10,000 people evicted without compensation. The line also infringed the cemetery of St Pancras Church, with successive layers of corpses having to be removed and re-interred, but it took complaints in the press for this to be done with any sense of reverence. The disruption to the cemetery was largely due to a double track link being constructed to the Metropolitan Railway on the east side of the extension, with a tunnel down to the Metropolitan lines having a gradient of 1 in 75.

Despite these problems, the line to the terminus itself had to pass over the Regent's Canal which meant both a falling gradient towards the terminus and a platform level some 20ft above street level. Ironically, the widening of the Metropolitan (City Widened Lines) did not go further west than King's Cross and so was of more use for GNR trains than those of the Midland until further widening in 1926, but then the spur from the Midland main line was closed in 1935!

Initially, when William Barlow designed the station, he proposed filling the space under the tracks and platforms with soil excavated from the tunnels, but James Allport, the MR's general manager, saw the potential for storage space, especially for beer from Burton-on-Trent. This led Barlow to design a single span train shed, which not only allowed greater freedom in planning

No other London terminus has such an imposing façade as St Pancras, due largely to the Midland Hotel. An open-top bus can just been seen in the lower right of this 1925 view. *(HMRS AAD905)*

the storage space beneath the station, but also meant that the layout of the tracks and platforms could be altered as needed in the years to come. A large Gothic hotel was constructed in front of the station, giving it the most impressive frontage of any London terminus. Initially, the interior of the roof was painted brown, but Allport later had this changed to blues and greys to give the impression of the sky. While trains from Bedford to Moorgate started using the tunnel under the terminus to the Metropolitan Railway from 13 July 1868, the terminus itself was not opened to traffic until 1 October 1868, without any ceremony.

The Midland Grand Hotel was still at foundation level when the station opened, but this was intended to be the most luxurious of its kind, and a monument to its architect, Sir Gilbert Scott. The hotel also included offices for the MR in its upper storeys. Meanwhile, in the terminus itself, even the handsome booking hall was not completed until the following year.

When opened, the station had eleven roads and five platform faces. One of these, later Platform 1, was a short local platform facing the west wall, while the other face of this platform was the long main line departure platform, after which there were six carriage roads, occupying the space later used by Platforms 2 to 5, and followed by the two arrival platforms, later 5 and 6, with a 25ft wide cab road running between them. Against the east wall was the excursion platform, later Platform 7.

In 1892, a wooden platform was inserted in the carriage roads, later becoming Platforms 3 and 4, leaving two sidings between Platforms 4 and 5. A hoist provided access to the beer vaults. In this form, Platforms 1 and 2 were used for arrivals and departures, including local trains; 3 and 4 were used for departures, and 5 to 7 were used by arrivals.

The approaches consisted of four tracks, although further out these became an up line and two down lines. After Cambridge Street Junction, the line became simple double track until St Paul's Road Junction, where the lines from the Metropolitan surfaced. The main locomotive depot was at Kentish Town, 1½ miles from the terminus. Despite not being as busy as Waterloo, Victoria or Liverpool Street, the approaches were congested, almost from the beginning, and difficult to operate, especially when working empty stock to and from the station. Improvements during 1907-8 helped, but the problem was never resolved during the age of steam, although in later years, diesel multiple unit working with trains turned around in the station helped considerably.

The station was meant to serve the MR's long-distance ambitions. The company saw its main market as the East Midlands, but while that was the basis of its traffic, its services to Scotland that started in 1875 were also important. Despite having a local platform, there was almost no suburban traffic for many years with the MR's suburban trains, never plentiful, working through to Moorgate. Even in 1903, there were just 14 suburban arrivals between 5am and 10am. It was not until 1910 that the Midland Railway began to encourage suburban traffic at St Pancras.

The MR needed running powers into the London Docks over the Great Eastern, and in return the GER was able to claim that St Pancras was its West End terminus, which required some stretch of the imagination, and ran trains from Norfolk and Suffolk into the station. The GER trains were eventually suspended in 1917 as a First World War economy measure and, with the exception of a daily train to Hunstanton during the summers of 1922 and 1923, never reinstated. Nevertheless, it was St Pancras that was used by the Royal Family when travelling to and from Sandringham.

From 1894, the London Tilbury & Southend Railway ran boat trains for passengers catching ships at Tilbury to Scandinavia and Australia. These services survived nationalisation and did not revert to Liverpool Street until 1963.

During the First World War, St Pancras had the unwanted distinction of being the worst affected of all the London termini. On 17 February 1918, a German Gotha bomber dropped five bombs across the station, and one of these exploded in the cab court outside the booking office, killing 20 people and wounding many others. Train services were not disrupted.

Under Grouping, St Pancras passed to the LMS, which put the MR in the same group as its old rival, the London & North Western Railway. Despite the sway held by the ex-Midland engineers over locomotive design, post-Grouping the emphasis was on Euston, the largest of the LMS termini, and the company has been accused of neglecting its other main line London terminus. Nevertheless, the company suffered greatly from the Miners' Strike of 1926 and the years of the Great Depression, and struggled to modernise.

The Second World War saw St Pancras suffer bombs and land mines, but the station's structure, despite being built over cellars and vaults, proved resilient. During the night of 15/16 October 1940, at the height of the blitz, a land mine wrecked much of the train shed roof, closing the station for five days. As the blitz drew to a close, on the night of 10/11 May 1941 the station had to be closed for eight days after a bomb passed through the station floor at the inner end of Platform 3, and while no serious structural damage occurred, there was considerable damage to trains.

Chapter 3

Destinations

The sheer size and scale of the LMS meant that it covered many of the major cities in Great Britain as well as the two largest in Northern Ireland. It reached into Yorkshire to Leeds and indeed, went as far east as Goole on the River Humber, and across Scotland to the three largest cities of Glasgow, Edinburgh and Aberdeen, as well as to Inverness and the Far North. Cities more usually associated with other railways were also served, including both Bristol and Cardiff in Great Western territory and Bournemouth on the Southern, through joint operation of the Somerset & Dorset. Some of these cities can be discounted not because they are unimportant, far from it, but because they were off the main network. Dublin was less important than Belfast to the LMS, despite having a railway in the docks, and was served by railway steamers from Holyhead on Anglesey operating to Dun Laoghaire rather than to the city itself. An alternative was for passengers to travel to Liverpool and catch the British & Irish, or B&I*, ferry – at the time a subsidiary of Coast Lines, but later taken over by the Irish government – to Dublin.

The busiest resort on the LMS was, of course, Blackpool, as the company had to share the traffic for its other major resort, Southend-on-Sea, with the LNER services from Liverpool Street, but Llandudno in North Wales was the second most important. All three resorts were also the source of substantial commuter traffic, with Blackpool and Llandudno having the famous club carriages for regular travellers prepared to pay a premium for their daily journey to Manchester. Birmingham and Glasgow were other cities with substantial commuter traffic.

Contrary to popular opinion, the old railway companies often sent through trains over each other's tracks, and this happened even before Grouping. Services such as that between London and Glasgow depended on collaboration between companies before the LMS was created, and even afterwards trains such as those between Aberdeen and Penzance, ran through on the London & North Eastern Railway and the Great Western Railway thanks to collaboration with the LMS.

While Londonderry, or 'Derry' to Irish nationalists, was the 'country' terminus for the Northern Counties Committee, and also the main terminus for the County Donegal Joint Railway, in which the LMS had a 50 per cent stake with the Great Northern Railway of Ireland, it was not a large town by mainland standards. The amount of traffic handled was relatively low, despite it being home to four railway termini, with a terminus for the GNR(I) services from Belfast and Dublin and the fourth terminus being that of the Londonderry & Lough Swilly Railway. Portrush and Coleraine as well as the ferry port at Larne probably rivalled Londonderry for passengers.

Belfast

Belfast developed as an extension of the shipbuilding industries in the North West of England and the South West of Scotland, and amongst its industries were those producing mill machinery

*Not to be confused with BI, British India, taken over by the Peninsular & Oriental Steam Navigation Company, P&O, in 1914.

for the production of linen. The city achieved a political and legal importance on the division of Ireland in 1922 into what was then known as the Irish Free State, or in general use, Southern Ireland, and Northern Ireland, still an integral part of the United Kingdom and of which Belfast became the capital.

The early railways in Belfast included the Ulster Railway, which opened in 1839 connecting Belfast with Lisburn, a distance of 12½ miles, the Belfast & Holywood Railway, incorporated in 1846 and opened in 1848, later extended to the coastal resort of Bangor, and was the predecessor of the Belfast & County Down Railway, which also reached Donaghdee and Newcastle, Co. Down. In 1860, four railways, including the Belfast & Ballymena Railway, merged to form the Belfast & Northern Counties Railway, the largest railway to run wholly within Northern Ireland. Northern Ireland's second largest railway was created in 1876, the Great Northern Railway of Ireland, usually referred to the GNR(I), whose constituent companies included the Dublin & Belfast Junction Railway and the 6ft 2in gauge Ulster Railway, which was soon rebuilt to the Irish 'standard' gauge of 5ft 3in. This meant that there were two companies operating between Belfast and Ulster's second largest city, Londonderry.

On Grouping, the LMS reached Belfast both by its ferries from Heysham, inherited from the Midland Railway, and Fleetwood, also in Lancashire, the former LNWR and LYR joint ferry port. It was also reached by a combination of the Northern Counties Committee trains from Larne, reached by ferries from Stranraer in Scotland, itself reached by the Glasgow & South Western Railway with its direct line to Scotland's largest city, and the Portpatrick & Wigtownshire Joint Railway, which brought traffic from the West Coast Main Line at Carlisle and the branch off the main line at Dumfries. Nevertheless, the LMS and its predecessors also fed traffic into Liverpool for the Belfast Steamship Company's sailings and to Ardrossan for the Burns & Laird sailings to Belfast.

The LMS acted quickly to rationalise its ferry services from the North-West, concentrating on Heysham.

Birmingham

It was not for nothing that the London & Birmingham Railway was the original name for the London & North Western, as unlike many of the major centres nurtured by the advent of the railway age, Birmingham was already a growing industrial city, and like Glasgow was sometimes described as the 'workshop of the world', while Birmingham was also known as the 'home of 1,500 trades.' Before the railways arrived, Birmingham was already the hub of a canal network that served the Midlands and beyond, with the Grand Union Canal linking the city with London. Many of the canals were to pass into railway ownership. Birmingham was linked to London by rail in 1838 when the London & Birmingham Railway opened its line from Euston with a Birmingham terminus at Curzon Street. It seems strange that the city did not become a borough until that year. As with the canals earlier, Birmingham became a 'grand junction' for the railways, and indeed the Grand Junction Railway (GJR) linked the city with Liverpool and Manchester and provided an important link in the network that was eventually to see London and Scotland linked from 1858.

The GJR's original terminus at Vauxhall was soon connected with Curzon Street, and of course it was one of the railways that merged with the LBR to create the LNWR. Such was the growth of traffic to and from Birmingham and through the city that congestion was an early problem until relieved by the Trent Valley Railway's by-pass route between Rugby and Stafford in 1847. Curzon Street was replaced by New Street in 1854, which the LNWR guide books of the day noted as 'a fine structure close to the centre of the best street in Birmingham.' The railway companies all built substantial goods yards and depots as well as passenger stations, while many factories had their own private sidings.

The Great Western Railway's advance on Birmingham was checked abruptly when the Midland Railway acquired the Birmingham & Gloucester and Bristol & Gloucester companies, to the relief of the London & North Western Railway, as the LBR had become by this time, as the LNWR had been concerned about the disruption that would be caused by broad gauge lines running into the city if the Great Western was welcomed by the Midland into its terminus at New Street.

The GWR was determined to serve Birmingham, however, and indeed aimed to go further north to Merseyside. Its ambitions were to be satisfied by the acquisition of first the Birmingham & Oxford Railway, which opened in 1852, followed in 1854 by the acquisition of the Birmingham, Wolverhampton & Dudley Railway. Unable to enter New Street, a new terminus was built for these broad gauge companies at Snow Hill, which was also in the central district of Birmingham but, as with some of the London termini, was approached through a tunnel to avoid demolition of valuable properties. All of the companies serving Birmingham, which included the Grand Junction as well as the GWR, LNWR and MR, were slow to develop a suburban network for the growing city, and it was not until the 1860s that suburban branches started to open.

The MR was if anything more active in this respect than the LNWR, and also built lines through to the East Midlands and the Vale of Evesham between 1859 and 1868, which also served to ensure that agricultural produce could reach the city more easily and cheaply. By this time, a Paddington–Banbury direct route had been opened, in 1910, and the GWR's timings from Paddington were now competitive with those of the LNWR, whose route was in fact slightly longer. Great Western expresses were then able to cover the 110½ miles between the two cities in two hours.

Blackpool

The railways projected Blackpool from being a small seaside resort to one of the leading resorts in the British Isles. Expansion started when the Preston & Wyre Railway reached the town in 1846. A little more than half a century later, the number of visitors annually had soared from a mere 3,000 to more than 3 million. A second line running along the coast reached the town in 1861, although this was not connected to the line to Preston until 1874, by which time both lines into the resort were owned and operated jointly by the Lancashire & Yorkshire Railway and the London & North Western Railway, but both companies used separate termini, with the LYR using Talbot Road, which later became Blackpool North, and which was rebuilt in 1898 with 15 platforms, and the LNWR using Central, rebuilt in 1900 with 14 platforms. In 1903, the 1861 coast line had an avoiding line built that shortened the distance from Preston by five miles.

Between the world wars, motor coaches made inroads into the summer excursion traffic, and this increased post-war with the added competition from private cars. Up until the outbreak of the Second World War, it was not uncommon for works outings to be by speciallychartered train rather than by coach. Nevertheless, the main factor in the decline of Blackpool as a resort and the reduction in railway services has been the growth of foreign package holidays.

Crewe

Originally a small hamlet, in 1837 Crewe found itself at the junction of three important railway lines, with the newly authorised Chester & Crewe Railway (CCR) and Manchester & Birmingham Railway (MBR) meeting the newly completed Grand Junction Railway, all predecessors of the London & North Western Railway. In 1840, the GJR acquired the CCR, and acquired large areas of land to which it moved its locomotive and carriage works from Birmingham's Edge Hill. When the MBR opened in 1842, it was worked by the GJR. Crewe's expansion was rapid, for by 1843, the GJR had built 200 houses and was moving workers into these and the rapidly expanding works. The LNWR continued the expansion of Crewe, although carriage building was moved several times, eventually finding a permanent home at Wolverhampton.

The town's role as a junction was no less important, and both the North Staffordshire Railway in 1848 and the Great Western Railway in 1863 and 1867, sent new lines into Crewe. Meanwhile, the LNWR had to rebuild the station twice, in 1849 and again in 1867, to accommodate growth. By 1900, the LNWR employed 10,000 people in the town, where it had provided utilities and its first police force, while more than a thousand trains a day passed through and additional land had had to be purchased to the south to accommodate expansion. After Grouping, there was intense competition between Crewe and Derby to become the leading locomotive works for the new London Midland & Scottish, and although at first Derby was in the ascendant, the company eventually moved its locomotive department from Derby to Crewe in 1932.

In 1938, with war in Europe looming, Rolls-Royce built an aero-engine factory, so that Crewe was no longer exclusively a railway town. Post-war, RR moved its car production to Crewe.

The years after the war also brought nationalisation and contraction, with the works eventually slimming down to a quarter of its peak size.

Derby

Unlike Crewe, Derby was an important county and market town with a long-established silk manufacturing industry before the railways came. It was well-located as a centre for the new railways, but also an important traffic generator in its own right. During 1839 and 1840, three railway lines met at Derby: the Midland Counties, the Birmingham & Derby Junction, and the North Midland. Nevertheless, they only accepted an offer from the council of land on the outskirts – on condition that they agreed to a joint station – with reluctance. Each company built its own engine sheds and workshops, but in 1844 they merged to form the Midland Railway. The railway area of Derby remained just outside the town, rather than the town springing up around the railway, as at Crewe and Swindon.

There was no need to build more lines into Derby, but the expansion of the MR to London increased the company's and the town's importance, and the company based its headquarters in the town, refusing to move to London even after St Pancras opened. An impressive station was built and a large marshalling yard just outside the town at Chaddesden eventually coped with 2,500 wagons daily. The MR combined the works of its main constituent companies, and the total area occupied quadrupled over the next three decades. It was not until 1851 that locomotive building began, and by the turn of the century almost 5,000 were employed in this activity, aided by the relocation of the carriage works. Eventually, by 1900, the MR employed 12,000 people, 12 per cent of the local population, in every kind of railway activity. After Grouping, Derby played an important role in the London Midland & Scottish Railway's development of diesel traction, but in 1932, the steam locomotive department was moved to Crewe. Nevertheless, the LMS located its first research department and then the new School of Transport in the town.

The railway works provided a skills base that attracted Rolls-Royce to Derby as early as 1907, and by 1945 this company was Derby's largest employer.

Edinburgh

Scotland's capital was already a tightly built-up area by the time the railways arrived, while the topography included high ridges running from east to west. There was substantial passenger traffic to be had from the affluent areas around the city centre, but goods traffic depended on being able to reach the port and industrial area of Leith to the north, and the coal mining areas to the south. The first railway was the horse-drawn Edinburgh & Dalkeith, which was extended to the docks at Leith, but which was effectively a tramroad. When the first steam railway, the Edinburgh & Glasgow, reached the city it stopped in the West End, then under construction, at Haymarket, with strong local opposition to any further advance eastwards, and it was not until the North British Railway arrived in 1846 that a short connecting line was built under the shadow of the Castle to a new joint station at Waverley, situated out of sight in a valley that divided the medieval Old Town from the Georgian New Town. The Edinburgh Leith & Granton Railway, next to be built, had its platforms at right angles to those of the NBR at Waverley and ran in a tunnel under the New Town.

History repeated itself in 1848 when the Caledonian Railway reached Edinburgh, having to stop at the bottom of Lothian Road, close to the western end of Princes Street, which it took as the name for its Edinburgh terminus. Nevertheless, by 1850, the NBR provided a link to the north of England and eventually this became the East Coast Main Line, and the opening of a branch to Hawick later led the way through the Border Union Railway to Carlisle, giving the NBR a second route over the border and Edinburgh a second route to Carlisle, and south via the Midland Railway. The last major link in the network of railways in and around Edinburgh followed in 1890 with the completion of the Forth Bridge, which meant that the city sat astride the most direct route between Aberdeen and London.

Included in the Edinburgh network were a number of suburban and country branches, with lines opened to Polton and North Berwick in 1850, Peebles in 1855, Dolphinton in 1864, Penicuik in 1876, and Gullane in 1898. There was also a link line to Galashiels, while a light railway was opened to Gifford in 1901. Eventually, a number of routes of varying degrees of directness linked Edinburgh and Glasgow. In 1884, the NBR opened the Edinburgh & District Suburban Railway (EDSR). The inner suburban railways soon suffered from competition from electric trams, and this was especially so with the EDSR, which was laid out as an oval and so often did not provide the most direct route between two points.

Most of these lines terminated at Waverley, which became very congested and needed rebuilding in 1890, and has been rebuilt again since. A new station at Leith was opened to ease the pressure on Waverley, but Leith Central was not convenient for most of the passenger traffic, and especially not for the first-class traveller looking for an express. Both the NBR and the Caledonian built branches into the docks at Leith. The Caledonian's Princes Street terminus eventually had an impressive frontage created by the construction of the Caledonian Hotel.

The NBR had two locomotive sheds in Edinburgh, at Haymarket and St Margaret's, but after merging with the Edinburgh & Glasgow, it transferred most of its heavy work to Cowlairs Works in Glasgow.

Seen in 1935 after exchanging identities in 1933 with No.6100 *Royal Scot*, is Royal Scot-class 7P No.6152, originally named *The King's Dragoon Guardsman*. The locomotive is seen near Lancaster with an Anglo-Scottish express. (*Colour-Rail 12257*)

The approach tracks of Glasgow Central High Level in 1946 with an 0-4-4T in charge of a suburban train with LMS suburban carriages, which appear to be in good condition. *(HMRS AAL407)*

Glasgow

Variously known as the 'Workshop of the British Empire' and the 'Empire's Second City', Glasgow, the largest city in Scotland, with more than twice Edinburgh's population before the Second World War, was one of the world's leading industrial cities during the 19th century, with a substantial proportion of the world's merchant shipping built on the Clyde. This was not a one-industry city, however, and its engineering activities included several major railway locomotive works, some of which were independent, and later commercial vehicles were also built at the Albion factory, while lighter engineering included the Singer sewing machine factory, and there were also cotton mills and breweries. These industries and the surrounding coal mines were served by a rudimentary network of tramroads developed during the 18th century.

Glasgow's first railway was the Glasgow & Garnkirk, opened in 1831, which soon built an extension to a temporary wooden terminus at Buchanan Street, which was taken over by the Caledonian Railway, initially for its services to Aberdeen, but it later also became the terminus for services to London Euston. The city soon became a focal point for a growing number of railways, with the next being the Glasgow Paisley Kilmarnock & Ayr, which shared a terminus at Bridge Street, south of the Clyde, with the Glasgow Paisley & Greenock. North of the river was the Edinburgh & Glasgow Railway's (EGR) Queen Street station, reached by a cable-working from Cowlairs in its early days.

Initially, the Clyde proved to be a major barrier with the north and the south of the city kept separate, partly because of Admiralty objections to a fixed bridge. The river was not bridged until 1876 when the Glasgow & South Western sent its line into St Enoch, also the terminus for Midland Railway services from London St Pancras. In 1879, the CR opened Glasgow Central Station. The North British Railway was able to use land vacated by the university as it sought more suitable premises, and also had the support of the City council in demolishing some particularly bad slums, in building its sidings and sheds, while it used Queen Street, acquired with the EGR. Between 1885 and 1910, the rival companies each built their own competing lines into the docks and many industrial areas. Suburban and even urban routes proliferated, and included the Glasgow Subway, a circular route initially worked by cable.

GLASGOW, PAISLEY, DALRY, KILMARNOCK, KILWINNING, and AYR.—Glasgow and South Western.

Week Days only.

Down.

Miles	Station			
	Glasgow (St. En.) dep.			
	Eglinton Street			
7¼	Paisley (Gilmour St.)			
9½	Elderslie			
11¼	Johnstone North			
12½	Kilbarchan			
17	Lochwinnoch			
20¼	Kilbirnie			
11	Johnstone			
12½	Milliken Park			
13½	Howwood			
16½	Lochside			
18¼	Beith			
20½	Glengarnock 853			
22¼	Dalry			
28¼	Montgreenan			
30¼	Cunninghamhead			
32¼	Crosshouse [820			
34¼	821 Kilmarnock arr.			
26¼	Kilwinning arr. / dep.			
29	Bogside			
30½	Irvine			
32	Gailes			
34	Barassie 820			
35	Troon 20			
37½	Monkton			
38½	Prestwick			
40½	Newton-on-Ayr			
41¾	Ayr 818 to 823 arr.			

A Arrives at 7 57 mrn.
a Runs to Kilmarnock, arriving at 12 32 aft. see page 815.
c Calls at Shields Road 5 minutes after leaving Glasgow (St. Enoch).
h Via Irvine.
l Canal Station.
x Saturdays only.

For Local Trains and intermediate Stations BETWEEN
Glasgow, Johnstone North, and Johnstone.......................... PAGE 822

For Notes and Continuation of Trains, see opposite page.

The South of Scotland was shared between two railway companies, the Caledonian and the Glasgow & South Western, with the latter operating along the Clyde coast and down into Ayrshire. The 1922 timetable, above, was much less impressive than that for 1938, below. *(Bradshaw)*

GLASGOW, KILWINNING, TROON, and AYR

Down — **Week Days**

Miles	Station
	Glasgow (St. E.) dep.
1½	Shields Road
7½	Paisley (Gilm'r St.)
8½	" (Canal)
26¼	Kilwinning arr. / 755 dep.
29	Bogside
30½	Irvine 757a
32	Gailes
34	Barassie 768
35	Troon 768
38½	Prestwick
40½	Newton-on-Ayr [771
41¾	Ayr 757, 770, arr.

Down — **Week Days—Continued**

Down — **Week Days—Continued** | **Sundays**

A Takes up for Stranraer (see below).   a 3 mins. *earlier* on Sats.   Bb Stop when required.   C Calls Ibrox 6 38 aft.
e Conveys Restaurant Car Passengers only.   D Calls Dalry 6 27 aft.   g Sats. only: on other days stops as when required
E or Ɛ Except Sats.   F The Fast Belfast.   G On 10th & 24th inst   H Calls Ibrox 7 49, 9 52 & 1057 aft. respectively.
h Stops on notice to the Sta Master at Irvine J Calls at Johnstone at 10 20, 11 1, & 11 38 mrn, 12 noon, 2 7, 2 40, & 9 15 aft
J Weds. only.   L Stops to take up.   ∟ Stops to take up.   N Except Sats and 18th inst.   ᴏ Stops when required to take
up for Ireland.   P Calls at Johnstone 2 35 aft.   ᴘ Stops when required to set down 4 or more Passengers on notice to
Station Master at Glasgow (St. E.)   R Thro Train from Edinburgh (P. St.), p 753   RC Restaurant Car   S or § Sats only.
W On 17th & 31st inst.   X Calls Ibrox 10 44 mrn.   z Tues. only.   Y Dep Ibrox 11 42 mrn. except on Sats. Thro' Train
from Edinburgh (P. St.), see page 753.   y Calls Monkton 5 mins. after leaving Troon.   Zz Calls at 5 6 aft. on Sats. Also
on other days as note ᴘ.   † Does not convey Passengers from Glasgow or Paisley to Ayr on Sats.   ‡ The Irishman
and Restaurant Car, except Sats.

Glasgow was the only other city apart from London to have a Royal Commission on its railways, but unlike that in London, which imposed an inner limit on construction of new surface lines and termini, that in Glasgow had no effect. The city's industry contributed much, and the CR in particular was predominantly a freight railway, but even so, passenger numbers at Central station rose from 4.75 million in 1880 to reach 15.75 million in 1897. The termini included hotels, such as the St Enoch Hotel, which when opened was the largest hotel in Scotland. Suburban lines developed on a scale second only to London, including the famous 'Cathcart Circle', albeit never a true circle, which operated out of Glasgow Central. The expansion of Central between 1901 and 1905 took it over Argyll Street, which famously became a meeting place for exiled Highlanders, known as the Highlandman's Umbrella, or *Hielanman's Umbrella*.

As with other major cities, passenger numbers began to fall as the urban and inner suburban networks soon proved vulnerable to competition, first from the electric tram, and then after the First World War, from the motor bus. Cathcart Circle or not, traffic at Central began to decline from 1905 onwards. Glasgow also began to lose its competitive edge, with heavy industry beginning a slow decline, while the 1926 Miners' Strike hit demand for coal particularly hard. To counter this, new stations were opened, close to new residential or industrial developments. The Glasgow Subway was taken over by the City and electrified between the wars. Known locally as the 'Clockwork Orange' because of the orange livery applied at one time, it remains the only true tube railway outside of London.

Grouping had little impact on the pattern of railway services. There was some rationalisation of the networks to the south-west, mainly favouring the former G&SWR lines over those of the rival CR, but plans to rationalise the four termini – Buchanan Street, which would have been enlarged, Central, Queen Street and St Enoch – into two failed, for regardless of the economies that could have been achieved and the greater convenience of passengers, the money was simply not available. Another plan never implemented was to expand the Glasgow Subway, although this could have been difficult given its unusual 4ft gauge and the relatively small bore of the tunnels, all of which would have made through running with other lines difficult.

Liverpool

At the dawn of the railway age, Liverpool was already one of Britain's major ports, and the fact that the Liverpool & Manchester Railway (LMR) was amongst the country's first railways was simply a reflection of this. The city's ocean trade expanded rapidly throughout the 19th century and the railway age naturally coincided with that of the steamship and the firm establishment of the British Empire. The LMR opened in 1830, while in 1840 Samuel Cunard introduced regular steamship sailings to the United States and Canada. Even before this, with a grant of £2,000 (worth £150,000 today) from the City, Lime Street replaced the original LMR Crown Street terminus in 1836, and by 1838, the city had good railway links to both Birmingham and London. Initially, Lime Street had to have its approaches worked by a cable, while the station was rebuilt and expanded in 1849 and again between 1867 and 1874. The LMR and the London & North Western Railway, which absorbed it, had reached the docks through long tunnels opened in 1839 and 1849.

The LNWR did not have a monopoly in Liverpool for long, for the Lancashire & Yorkshire Railway reached the city, initially stopping at Great Howard Street, but had a new terminus, Exchange, close to the docks. By 1859, the LYR connected Liverpool with Manchester, Preston, what was then the small village of Southport, and Wigan. Nevertheless, a duopoly was soon established which other railways could not break, although the Great Northern, Manchester Sheffield & Lincolnshire (later Great Central Railway) and the Midland Railway formed the Cheshire Lines Committee in 1865, and in 1874 opened a third line between Manchester and Liverpool. Meanwhile, the LNWR had shortened its approach to the city by building the Runcorn Bridge and opening a direct line in 1869, prompted by competition for traffic to and from the Midlands following the arrival of the Great Western across the Mersey at Birkenhead in 1854.

Other developments that followed before the end of the 19th century included the 500V dc

Even as late as 1938, a clerestory carriage seems to have found its way into this train from Bournemouth to Liverpool and Manchester, headed by 5MT 4-6-0 No. 5302 on the Lickey incline. It is not recorded whether this was actually the 'Pines Express'. *(HMRS AEU317)*

Liverpool Overhead Railway, opened completely in 1896, running more than six miles between Dingle and Seaforth.

The Mersey Docks & Harbour Board built an extensive network of lines serving 38 miles of quays.

While the railway network changed little after Grouping, electrification of the lines to Ormskirk, Southport and the Wirral was completed, and integrated with the Mersey Railway.

Manchester

Like Birmingham, at the start of the 19th century Manchester was already an important industrial centre and was well served by the canal network. The opening of the Liverpool & Manchester Railway in 1830 was a reflection of the city's importance as a centre for the cotton industry in particular, for which it needed access to the docks at Liverpool, both for the import of raw materials and for the export of finished goods. Nevertheless, that not all was well in relations between the two cities was demonstrated by the opening of the Manchester Ship Canal in 1894 to avoid the high harbour dues at Liverpool. In the meantime, there had been considerable growth in Manchester's railway network, along with the Lancashire & Yorkshire Railway, the Midland Railway and the Great Central Railway.

The start of the city's links to London were in 1838 from Liverpool Road station, but these were considerably shortened with the opening of the Manchester & Birmingham Railway in 1842, running from London Road station to Crewe and connecting with the London & Birmingham Railway, with which it merged in 1846 to form the London & North Western Railway. Before this, the opening of the Manchester & Leeds Railway in stages during 1839–40 provided a route across the Pennines, while there were lines radiating out from the city to other parts of Lancashire, including Bury, as well as to York and to the East Midlands.

One feature of Manchester's railways was that many of them were running on viaducts, so that by the middle of the 19th century the city was almost enclosed by a horseshoe of railway viaducts. Yet, despite this, the city's early railway stations were outside the centre so that north–south travel through the centre of the city was impossible and it was not until 1880 that the Cheshire Lines Committee completed Central station, which was also used by the Great Northern and the Midland railways, while another station in the centre was Victoria, built by the Lancashire & Yorkshire Railway, which refused to let the London & North Western share it

MANCHESTER, SALE, BROOKLANDS, and ALTRINCHAM.—Cheshire Lines, Great Central, and London and North Western.

Manchester was important to several railways, and it had an extensive suburban network. The service between Manchester, Sale and Altrincham doubled in frequency between 1922 (above), and 1938 (below). *(Bradshaw)*

MANCHESTER, SALE, BROOKLANDS, and ALTRINCHAM.—G. C. and N. W. Joint and C. L.

Down. Week Days.

Stations: London Road A ..... dep., Central, Oxford Road, Knott Mill and Deansgate, Old Trafford, Warwick Rd. (O. Trafford), Stretford, Dane Road, Sale, Brooklands, Timperley, Navigation Road B, Altrincham C ..... arr.

A South Junction Platform.
B Navigation Rd. (Altrincham).
C Altrincham and Bowdon.
E Except Sata.
N Mons., Weds., and Sata.
P 3 mins. *earlier* on Sata.
S Sats. only.

Where the MINUTES under the Hours change to a LOWER figure and DARKER type it indicates the NEXT HOUR

so the latter opened Exchange station next to it, in 1884. It was not until the LMS came into being that the two stations were united by the construction of a through platform, Britain's longest, at 731 yards.

Most of Manchester's growing suburban traffic was carried by the LYR, which electrified its line to Bury on an overhead system in 1916. Electrification was prompted by the inroads into railway traffic made by tramway electrification, and jointly the LMS and the LNER electrified the Manchester South Junction & Altrincham Junction Railway. The city and the surrounding area also became home to a number of major locomotive builders, while the Manchester Ship Canal Company also operated an extensive railway system serving its dock facilities.

Preston

An important port and centre for the cotton trade before the arrival of the railway, Preston was boosted still further by the Lancaster Canal, and a horse-drawn tramway was built to link the northern and southern sections of the waterway. In 1836, a local railway, the Preston & Longridge, linked the town with nearby quarries, while in 1838, the North Union Railway connected Preston with London, Liverpool and Manchester. A link with Carlisle and Scotland followed between 1840 and 1849, as well as lines to Fleetwood and Blackpool, while more direct lines were built to Manchester and Liverpool, while a branch was built to the docks on the River Ribble. Until restaurant cars appeared, Preston was a refreshment stop on the West Coast Main Line.

The various railway lines around Preston soon became part of either the London & North Western Railway or the Lancashire & Yorkshire Railway, which shared the main station with the two companies operating the Ribble branch jointly. Between 1836 and 1900, the population grew from 14,000 to 115,000. The railway station was extensively rebuilt and extended between 1873 and 1913, but a much-needed avoiding line for holiday and excursion trains to Blackpool was never built. The original Longridge line closed to passengers in 1930.

Sheffield

An old centre for the iron industry, the coming of the railways enabled the industry and the new steel industry to grow rapidly and the city became famous for its cutlery, the population tripling between 1843 and 1893. The railways performed the double act of not only improving transport for raw materials and fuel and for the finished articles, but also of being a major market for steel plate and rails.

Strong competition developed between the Midland Railway and the equally ambitious Manchester, Sheffield & Lincolnshire Railway, which later renamed itself as the Great Central, ready for its advance on London. Yet, at the outset, George Stephenson planned the North Midland Railway in such a way that the city was by-passed and was served by a branch line. A direct rail link to Manchester was delayed by the massive engineering feat needed to take the railway through the Pennines, with the need for a three-mile-long tunnel under the watershed at Woodhead, and despite being authorised in 1837, this and the inevitable funding difficulties for such a costly route meant that the 35-mile line was not completed until 1845.

The city's early railway termini were shabby and cheaply built, with that for Manchester having to make do with a temporary wooden structure at Bridgehouses.

When the Sheffield, Ashton-under-Lyme & Manchester Railway was absorbed into the Manchester, Sheffield & Lincolnshire Railway in 1847, matters started to improve and an extension opened to Gainsborough and Grimsby in 1849. The MSLR opened a new terminus worthy of the city at Victoria in 1851, with a glass roof.

By 1864, Sheffield was producing 96 per cent of Britain's cast steel, and moves were made to construct a north–south railway line, largely underground, but nothing came of this, and it was not until 1870 when the Midland built a new line from Chesterfield to a new station at Pond Street that the city eventually found itself on a main line. This came at a cost, with the demolition of a thousand homes, a significant proportion for a city with a population of 200,000. The Midland developed its services with a new line through to Manchester, which required a tunnel of more than 3½ miles at Totley, while Pond Street was rebuilt and enlarged in 1906.

The LNER tried to gain an advantage over what had become the LMS route to Manchester by starting electrification of the Woodhead route on a 1,500V dc overhead system in 1936, but wartime delays meant that this was not completed until 1954, well after Nationalisation.

Southend

The other major resort served by the LMS, and the most easterly part of the sprawling network, the railways reached Southend in 1856 after delays caused by rivalry between the London & Blackwall Railway and the Eastern Counties Railway. The problem was resolved by an act of 1852 which authorised a joint line from Forest Gate via Tilbury, but the driving force was the contractor Samuel Peto, who not only built the line but operated it from partial opening in 1854 until 1875. At first, the objective was to secure the lucrative excursion traffic to Gravesend, for which the Tilbury–Gravesend ferry was hired, and Southend was only a secondary objective, although this soon changed and the town became important both for holidaymakers and, increasingly, commuters.

The ECR was merged into the Great Eastern Railway in 1862, and the LTSR became an independent company that year, although still with directors appointed by the GER. The GER continued to run the line until 1876, when over the next four years the LTSR acquired its own rolling stock and trains ran from Fenchurch Street only. Even earlier, a loop had to be built to avoid congestion at Stratford, and this opened in 1858.

The GER opened its own branch to Southend with services from Liverpool Street in 1889, seven years after the LTSR had become completely independent. Southend was the end of the line until 1884, when the War Office dropped its objections to an extension to Shoeburyness, an artillery training area.

The dawn of the new century saw the line from Fenchurch Street to Southend as one of the most profitable in the country with a growing season ticket traffic as well as summer excursions and boat trains for liners calling at Tilbury. It was widely expected that the GER would acquire the LTSR and thus establish a monopoly between London and Southend, but in a surprise move the Midland Railway acquired the LTSR in 1912. With the extensive suburban development at the London end of the line, electrification was expected, and even promised, but not delivered until some time after Nationalisation.

A mixed rake of carriages is being drawn by 4F 0-6-0 No. 4052, on its way from Fenchurch Street to Southend in 1947, running over electrified lines shared with the District Line. *(HMRS AEQ609)*

Chapter 4

Creating a
New Railway Company

It would not have been surprising if any of the directors and senior managers of the newly formed LMS thought that if they had to start creating a new railway company, they would not have started from here, or at least with such a collection of disparate companies and so scattered and unwieldy a network. How they must have envied their counterparts of the Southern Railway and the Great Western, with the latter dominating its constituent and subsidiary companies so completely, or even those at the London & North Eastern. Few were surprised when later, one of the more thoughtful vice-presidents, Sir William Wood, later to be its last president, let slip that the company was probably too big to be managed effectively.

The new company had almost 270,000 employees according to its own figures*, 6,870 route miles, more than a third of the nation's total of railways on the mainland, plus almost 300 route miles in Ireland, and consumed 6.5 million tons of coal annually, giving employment, some have estimated, to 26,500 miners. There were 10,316 steam locomotives, but less than 1,900 were superheated. While the Caledonian had some larger 4-6-0s, these 65 locomotives were spread over no fewer than ten classes!

The initial capitalisation of the new LMS was £400 million, a staggering figure for the day and equivalent to roughly £25,000 million today.

The railways were suffering from the impact of the First World War. They had suffered relatively little from bombing, in contrast to the Second World War, but the predecessors of the LMS had seen a total of 53,555 employees called up for or volunteer for military service, with a consequent knock-on effect on maintenance. Supplies of raw materials had been adversely affected, while equipment, including locomotives, had been commandeered for service overseas. Control of the railways by the government continued almost up to Grouping, and the government whilst in control of the railways had allowed wages to rise and accepted an eight-hour working day, all to the subsequent disadvantage of the companies when their property was returned to them.

While the London & North Western Railway had been the largest of the constituent companies, especially after it absorbed the Lancashire & Yorkshire, it was the Midland Railway that became the guiding hand, especially when Sir Guy Granet took over as chairman in 1924. The Midland Railway's deep red or maroon livery became that of the new company, providing a visual link between pre-Grouping and post-Grouping. On the other hand, it must be admitted that the only other contender would have been the LNWR's deep maroon and white colour scheme, which would have been much more expensive to introduce than the simpler Midland red, albeit that the Midland had very expensive lining out and detailing.

In fact, it took until 1927 for the new railway to become firmly established in the public mind. Indeed, for many years, even after Nationalisation, the names of the old pre-

*Some publications suggest that this was 233,000, but the figure quoted comes from the *LMS Magazine* in its first issue. In fact, the true figure, not rounded-up, was around 263,000, and this even increased slightly during the early years.

Grouping companies lived on in such things as lineside warning notices, where there was no commercial value and yet much cost in replacing these. The former LNWR locomotives retained their brass number plates until the late 1920s and suburban carriages remained in the old colours as late as 1933 on workmen's trains, although by that time all normal service rolling stock was red.

Another example of the enormity of the task facing the management was that it took until November 1923 before the first edition of a house magazine, the *LMS Magazine*, appeared, at a time when change was taking place and employees of all levels were struggling to identify their place in the organisation. That this was the case was borne out by the early editions of the *LMS Magazine* devoting much space to reminding employees of the companies that had come together under Grouping, as well as articles telling them that the company was the largest railway operator of hotels and steamships. There were even articles about the constituent and subsidiary companies.

The territorial ambitions of the MR and to a lesser extent the LNWR meant the new company sprawled even more than it might have done. It seemed logical that it had a substantial network in Wales, event to the extent that some believed that the new company should have included the Cambrian, and the lines north of the border in Scotland made sense as well. But there was no logic to the Midland having taken over the London Tilbury & Southend Railway, and the interests in Ireland were two unconnected lines of which only the Northern Counties Committee, the old Belfast & Northern Counties Railway, was a substantial entity in its own right, and a half share in the County Donegal Joint Railway, a narrow gauge 'no-hoper' running through sparsely populated terrain. Even there, the fact that the Midland ownership had been concealed by the change of name to the NCC told a story. The mainland railways should have stopped at the ports, as British Railways was to do later. Having a stake in a line such as the County Donegal, extremely poor territory for railways, was madness.

In view of this, it seems that the government's original idea of having seven grouped railways, with one for Scotland and one for London, might have been easier to handle, especially if the Scottish plan had been dropped. In any case, the idea of a grouped railway for London eventually materialised in one sense with the creation of the London Passenger Transport Board, although this dealt purely with the Underground lines and did not, for example, include such possibilities as the North London Railway. As mentioned earlier, Sir William Wood, later the company's last president, once admitted that the LMS was too big for effective management and that there was no example that the management team on Grouping could follow. The paradox was that he went on to serve for five years on the British Transport Commission after Nationalisation, in a still larger and much less easily manageable concern!

As with all the grouped companies, there was a pressing need for standardisation, and a management standard also had to be set. Given the number of Midland people at the top of the LMS, inevitably it was the Midland view that prevailed in the early years and while this was good news for the passenger carriages, it was bad news for the steam locomotives. It may also have been the same Midland view that gave electrification a lower priority.

Unlike the other companies, the LMS set about extending the Midland's centralised train control system. This was to become a source of considerable pride to the LMS, but it had been introduced by the Midland as a remedy for its relatively poor time-keeping. Many doubted that the LMS was taking the right course, especially as the London & North Eastern Railway took the opposite view and devolved its operations. The LMS refined its centralised control system into three, later four, operating divisions. This did not mean absolute centralisation, as even the centralised control system for freight trains was divided into four regions to make it manageable.

Perpetuating the Midland's penchant for small locomotives meant that at first there was no great acceleration of services, so that by 1929, there was little progress over 1914, and overall the LMS was at the time the slowest of the 'Big Four' despite having some of the longest distance trains.

American-style management

When Sir Josiah Stamp joined in 1926, he continued the American-style of management that had been introduced shortly after Grouping. He headed a small four-man executive, and although the numbers were later increased to seven, this replaced the traditional general manager and officers' committee that was the British practice. When he became chairman in 1927, the strength of the executive increased. The strength of such a small team was that lines of communication were kept short and coordination was much easier. What followed was a ruthless analysis of costs and productivity across the entire company. Inherent in this was a rapid move to standardise equipment and working practices, but the former proved difficult at a time when trade was depressed. The LMS was to the fore in recruiting specialists from outside the company to 'help' the company's own officers and free it from inherited ideas and practices.

An Executive Research Office was established with considerable authority, but despite its technologically exciting title, one of its roles was to control all stationery ordering and printing, with a considerable lowering of quality, it was alleged. Although this was understandable as money was short, and in any case the managements of the old companies, far away from head office in the case of the smaller concerns, could not be allowed to continue with their old habits and no doubt cosy relationships with local printers and stationery suppliers, the company ended up with the poorest quality letterheads of any substantial business. Standardising stationery and printing was one way of creating a new corporate identity.

On the other hand, despite money being short, a new headquarters was built for the company, Euston House. This may have been important for efficiency, bringing the senior management team and head office departments together, especially as the Midland Railway, alone of all the railways running into London, had persisted in maintaining its headquarters in Derby. It would have been impossible to assemble and accommodate everyone in the offices at Euston station.

Perhaps more exciting was the recruitment of a Colonel Ord to advise on the modernisation of goods depots, while marketing and publicity experts were also taken on board. Inevitably, the newcomers were not welcomed by and not understood by the traditional railwaymen, many of whom knew nothing of the outside world and of developing management techniques. Another newcomer was the company's electrical engineer, Lieutenant-Colonel Cortez-Leigh. His term of office seems to have been short as despite his identifying many lines, especially in the London area, that would benefit from electrification, little was in fact done. There can be little doubt that the state of the economy had a bearing on this, and as discussed later in the chapter on steam locomotives, there were other reasons as well, but it is also clear that the LMS did not see a long-term future in which electrification would play a part, as it allowed no fewer than three different systems of electrification to survive. What this meant in practical terms was that the LMS never enjoyed the surge in traffic and revenue and the reduced train-mile costs that the Southern experienced with its massive electrification programme.

The LMS suffered badly during the Miners' Strike and the associated General Strike in 1926, for it was heavily dependent upon goods traffic, and the loss of coal traffic for many months and then the reduced demand afterwards had a severe effect on the company's finances. This was only part of the story, for from the end of the First World War onwards, road competition for both goods and passengers substantially increased. Much of this was down to the war years having produced many more men able to drive and maintain road vehicles, combined with a glut of cheap army-surplus vehicles, but even without this short-term stimulus it was inevitable as the reliability and size of road vehicles began to increase. The steam age was giving way to the age of the internal combustion engine.

The need for more power

Despite the Midland's grip on locomotive development, the sheer waste of double heading the main expresses was too obvious to ignore. The executive instructed the chief mechanical engineer,

Sir Henry Fowler, to produce a more powerful locomotive. Despite this, his most ambitious proposals were abandoned due to the innate conservatism of the management, and his 4-6-0 'Royal Scots' proved only just adequate for the task, more a locomotive for secondary main lines rather than for the heavy Irish boat trains, the Anglo-Scottish expresses and those linking London with the Midlands and the North-West. Fowler was also inhibited by the internecine warfare between the Midland workshops at Derby and those of the LNWR at Crewe.

The differences between Derby and Crewe ran much deeper than matters of locomotive design.

'At Derby, the nice little engines were made pets of,' recalled D.W. Sanford. 'They were housed in nice clean sheds and were very lightly loaded. There must have been a Royal Society for the Prevention of Cruelty to Engines in existence... At Crewe they just didn't care so long as their engines could roar and rattle along with a good paying load, which they usually did.'

In fact, the former LNWR engines were anything but nice. The goods 0-8-0 locomotives in particular were so filthy that they often had their numbers chalked on the side of the cab as the originals were covered by layers of grime.

After Ernest Lemon, another ex-Midland man, took over from Fowler in 1931, Stamp resolved the situation by looking outside the LMS for the next CME, bringing in Sir William Stanier from the Great Western in 1932. Movement between companies by CMEs and even senior operating managers was nothing new for the railways at a time when many stayed with the same employer for life. Stanier's appeal was that the Great Western was the most standardised railway of all, and had moved quickly to standardise the other companies brought under its sway by Grouping. Belatedly, the LMS needed the same approach.

Stanier proved to be a wise choice. His standardisation programme swept through the LMS so that by 1938, the number of locomotive classes had been reduced from 404 to 132. Workshops were modernised with equipment and working practices standardised so that costs and the length of time rolling stock spent under repair were both reduced. The net result was a 26 per cent cut in the number of locomotives required each day, a saving of £2 million at the time, or around £120 million today. The standardisation even extended to Ireland, with the NCC receiving standard LMS locomotives and carriages re-gauged for 5ft 3in.

Mass production techniques were introduced for new corridor carriages, which many regarded as being the most comfortable and spacious on Britain's railways, with just four seats in LMS first-class compartments, and six in third-class compartments, although these were also meant to take eight passengers, at a pinch. Improved non-corridor rolling stock was also built for branch lines and suburban services. Many believe that the peak of his achievements for passenger rolling stock came with the very non-standard 'Coronation Scot' express with its streamlined locomotives and carriages; but to show just what could be achieved with electrification, he built lightweight monocoque rolling stock for the modernisation of the Liverpool and Southport line that entered service during 1939–40, immediately before the wartime restrictions began to bite.

Stanier's most enduring legacy were his 4-6-0 Class 5 mixed traffic locomotives, the famous 'Black Fives', which provided the basis for a post-Nationalisation standard mixed traffic locomotive, but he also accelerated goods trains with his 2-8-0 locomotives, many of which were also built during the Second World War for service abroad, while others were built as a wartime standard locomotive by the other railway companies.

Operationally, the LMS also rationalised and mechanised the coaling of locomotives and freight handling, following another American idea, a work study programme carried out during 1933. By 1939, the company's freight services were generally regarded as profitable. In 1938, seven daily goods trains ran more than 150 miles non-stop, and another 57 ran non-stop for more than 90 miles. Despite this, the LMS refused to follow the Great Western by investing in large, 20-ton mineral wagons, which many consider strange, but perhaps the LMS was aware that the GWR had considerable difficulty in getting colliery owners and others to accept and use the new wagons, and did produce even larger, 40-ton wagons to supply coal to its own power station. There was some sense in the colliery-owners' attitudes as the bigger wagons were more difficult to work on the tight radius curves and often restricted loading gauges of many pithead areas.

On the debit side, the LMS was notoriously slow at mechanising collection and delivery of its goods traffic. Nevertheless, with the other railway companies it did much to rationalise these services with inter-company cooperation. There was competition and overlap in many areas with the Great Western Railway on the one hand and with the London & North Eastern Railway on the other, so an agreement was reached with these two companies that they should coordinate their activities as far as the goods business was concerned. The fourth grouped company, the Southern Railway, was not a party to these arrangements as it was a comparatively minor player in the goods business. The coordination of the collection and delivery operations were to prove their worth, especially once wartime restrictions began to bite, although in central London, the parcels and sundries collection and delivery traffic was so linked into the different company termini that in the capital it was probably at its least effective.

Modernisation

The four grouped railway companies were not allowed to act as true businesses and if they seemed to be lacking in enterprise at times, this was because their operations were strictly controlled by the legislation that had created them. The Railway Rates Tribunal ensured that they could not charge what they wanted, or what the market might bear, or even what was needed to cover their costs. The Common Carrier Obligation meant that they could not refuse traffic, even if it was difficult or expensive to accommodate. The road haulage industry, on the other hand, could carry whatever it wanted for whatever price the customer was prepared to pay.

There was also an element of personal service with road haulage as the vehicle collecting the consignment would often carry it through to its destination, with no transfer between road and rail, and then between rail and road, and no waiting for a stopping goods train to be assembled. Transhipment not only added to time and cost, but it also increased the likelihood of damage to goods or even of theft, although the inter-war period was one of considerably low levels of crime.

The late 1920s saw intense lobbying by the railway companies for restrictions on road transport, and for the right to operate buses and lorries in their own right, other than just for conveying passengers and goods to and from their stations.

The one gift to the railways by the government came in 1929, when the then Chancellor of the Exchequer, none other than Winston Churchill, relieved the railways of the duty levied on all fares of more than an old penny per mile. This was a tax first introduced as early as 1832. Churchill was not thinking of the railway balance sheets, or even of the passenger, but wanted to relieve unemployment by enabling the railways to invest in modernisation programmes, and the relief from the levy was conditional on the sums saved being capitalised and up to 90 per cent of this invested. The measure was followed by the Development (Loans, Guarantees and Grants) Act that provided low interest 'soft' loans for capital investment. The LMS was also able to raise capital on its own account.

With such funding behind it, the LMS started a major modernisation programme. Unlike the Southern, it did not embrace wholesale electrification, but the LMS was different from the Southern, which was predominantly a passenger railway and except for the lines to Weymouth and those beyond Exeter, that were a small part of its operations, overwhelmingly dealing with shorter distances. The electric trains of the day could beat steam on services with many stops, but were hard-pressed to match steam on long, non-stop, fast services.

In addition to electrification inherited from the LNWR and the North London, the LMS electrified the Wirral lines and with the LNER undertook the Manchester South Junction & Altrincham overhead electrification. Most of the available funding was devoted to new rolling stock, modernisation of depots and marshalling yards, and the early installations of automatic warning systems to improve safety. As we will see later, the company also became a leader in the use of diesel shunters and built a prototype articulated diesel multiple unit.

In 1930, doubtless inspired by American ideas yet again, the LMS appointed a director of scientific research, Sir Harold Hartley, already a distinguished scientist. A new research laboratory was established at Derby to test and develop new products. Existing products were not spared the attentions of the research people, even to the extent that a 'mechanical bottom' was introduced, bouncing up and down testing upholstery and springing of carriage seats to destruction. Hartley later became chairman of Railway Air Services when it was founded in 1934.

In common with the other railway companies, line closures were few, and it could be argued far fewer than they should have been, but while Grouping had given many of the companies duplication of routes, more often these were needed to cope with the traffic, and as a diversionary route. The days of complete line closures and the transfer of passengers to buses was still some way off. One line that was closed was the main part of the Solway Junction, but this was in 1921 when the viaduct across the Solway Firth was declared unsafe, and so was before Grouping. The viaduct was eventually demolished, taking twelve months in 1934–35, to the dismay of the Scottish drinking men who had used it on Sundays to walk from 'dry' Scotland to 'wet' England for a drink. The first actual line closure after Grouping was the Carmyllie branch near Arbroath in Scotland, operated jointly by the LMS and LNER, five miles long and running from Elliot Junction, 1½ miles from Arbroath; this had just two passenger trains daily taking 25 minutes for the journey.

On the other side of Scotland, there was some rationalisation of competing routes in Ayrshire, but despite the company north of the border being dominated by former Caledonian Railway managers, it was often the old Glasgow & South Western Railway routes that survived.

Unlike the Southern, there were no new lines opened however, and few new stations. The places where additional stations actually were built were on the electrified Manchester and Bury line, as well as on the Euston–Watford line, at South Kenton, and on the very much steam-operated Fenchurch Street and Southend line, as well as a number of new stations to serve housing developments in the Glasgow commuter area.

Competing for investment were powers gained in 1929 to allow the railway companies to invest in road transport and the following year in air transport. Hitherto, the railways had only been allowed to be involved in road transport that served their stations, with feeder bus services and collection and delivery haulage. The provision for air transport was inevitable and spared the railways a repeat of the problems they had suffered before being allowed to engage

At first, what the railway companies were limited to until 1929, when they were allowed to invest in bus companies and road haulage contractors, was the operation of services feeding passengers and goods to and from their stations. This is a new bus service introduced between Newark, Southwell and Mansfield in 1929. *(LMS)*

in shipping in the middle of the 19th century. For most of the railway companies, air transport was a natural extension of their operations, and in the case of the LMS, this meant that it became primarily occupied with air services across the Irish Sea, and with the GWR and SR, the LMS became involved with Railway Air Services (RAS), while there was collaboration with another airline on services to the Scottish islands.

One of the most far-sighted moves by the LMS was to found a School of Transport, and this was first announced in late 1936 and opened at Ormaston Park, near Derby, in 1938. This was a boarding college, not just because distance would have rendered a day school useless, but also because it was felt that the new breed of LMS men would need to make a break with not only different departmental attitudes, but also with the various traditions of the past.

A mini-Beeching

As we will see later, Lord Stamp, the far-sighted president of the LMS from 1926 to his death in an air raid in 1941, was forced by his management to enter into a row with one of the company's largest non-coal freight clients, Unilever, when the latter suggested that the future in railway freight lay in trainload business between major railheads. This was one of the proposals made by Dr, later Sir and subsequently Lord, Beeching, who has remained more famous for his proposed cuts to the system.

The grouped companies were slow to make cuts to their networks, and despite their poverty and the restrictions imposed upon them under Grouping, struggled to keep their systems intact. Many believe that had not the Second World War intervened, with a second spell of state control under the Railway Executive Committee, the LMS would have been forced to consider a more radical programme of line closures, not least in Ireland where substituting bus services for many of the branch lines and for all of the County Donegal would have made sense. Elsewhere, in North Wales and in Scotland, in the Lake District and in Herefordshire and Shropshire, many lines could have been closed. Others could have been rescued by using diesel railcars or multiple units, but the LMS was slow to implement such new ideas, even though it did experiment.

Perhaps sanity would have prevailed and many smaller goods depots could have been closed and a move made from wagonload freight to trainload freight. On the other hand, the mainstay of these small goods yards was coal for domestic heating, and also for smaller businesses and offices where a coal fire or a coke stove provided heating in the days before central heating became commonplace.

The trouble was that closures required the approval of the Minister of Transport in Great Britain, by his counterpart, the Minister of Commerce, in Northern Ireland, and in fact a parliamentary bill south of the border in the Irish Free State. The procedures were costly and time-consuming. In Great Britain, the LMS had offloaded its bus services and followed the other railways in merging these into the bus companies in which it acquired an interest, so providing what is now known as 'bustitution' would not have been too difficult, but in Northern Ireland, road transport was nationalised, and the same happened in the Irish Free State. As we will see later, the LMS favoured this move by the governments of the two different parts of Ireland, and one wonders why they did not push further and propose nationalisation of the railways. This would have set an unhealthy and unwelcome precedent, sending the wrong signal to the political left on the mainland of the United Kingdom, but it would have relieved the LMS of the burden of its involvement with the CDJR and the NCC's branch lines.

The LMS was famous for its great expresses, but it also had branch lines and on some mixed goods and passenger trains were operated, as seen at the Highland resort of Strathpeffer worked by this 2P No.15199 in 1936. (Colour-Rail 2921)

Chapter 5

The Managers

It was no easy undertaking merging so many railway companies, and especially since several of them were very large. In addition, personalities came into play. The railway companies had strong personalities of their own, which was usually reflected in the style of their managements. The London & North Western management was regarded as somewhat aristocratic and also autocratic, especially when compared with its new colleagues from the Midland Railway and the Lancashire & Yorkshire railways.

While the LNWR was the oldest and largest of the eight constituent and 27 subsidiary companies that came together to form the LMS, during the early days it was the Midland philosophy that always seemed to win through, giving Hughes, for example, continued difficulties and frustration in his plans for larger and more powerful steam locomotives. The Lancashire & Yorkshire also had its own way of doing things, while in Scotland there was rivalry between the Caledonian, which emerged triumphant, and the Glasgow & South Western.

Fortunately, Parliament had allowed a year for the new structures to be put in place and for key appointments to be made. Subject to the agreement of the Amalgamation Tribunal, companies within the same grouping could merge before the Act took effect, and the LNWR and LYR did just that, doubtless expecting to gain extra muscle in the grouped company. The situation was not made any easier by the vast array of ancillary activities in which the railways were involved, and the LMS inherited the largest network of canals in England, as well as 27 hotels and important ports such as Barrow-in-Furness, Fleetwood, Garston and Heysham, and more than a hundred steamships of all sizes, including a Thames ferry. How often those involved must have envied the Great Western, which so dominated the rest of its constituent companies, but in this respect the GWR was unique.

The Midland brought with it two things, a reputation for passenger comfort and a centralised train control system that was in every respect far ahead of its time. Against this, it also had the drawback of having too many small and underpowered locomotives so that double heading (for which also read double manning) was a necessity. The LNWR nevertheless also lacked high speed trains as a former general manager had believed that 45mph was fast enough.

One problem which the Midland also provided was that it was the largest British railway company not to have its head offices in London, remaining loyal to Derby even after it broke through to St Pancras. The LMS believed that its senior management should be concentrated in London, close to the departments of state and Parliament itself, as well as the financiers of the City of London and, of course, bodies such as the Railway Rates Tribunal. This meant that there was a certain amount of upheaval.

It was, in the circumstances, not surprising that the first general manager of the LMS, Arthur, later Sir Arthur, Watson retired in 1924 because of ill health. Watson had been general manager of the LYR and on the merger with the LNWR, became GM of the enlarged LNWR. On 1 January 1923, he found himself under a board, of which he was not a member, but which included two former general managers of constituent companies, Sir Guy Granet of the Midland Railway and his predecessor at the LNWR, Sir Thomas Williams, who had stood down on the merger with the LYR.

The new company was the largest in the British Empire, at least on formation, by stock market valuation. But this was a time of major industrial mergers, creating Imperial Chemical Industries (ICI), and Amalgamated Electrical Industries (AEI), and so the age of the giant conglomerate was already taking shape, and there were emerging sectors that showed more promise than the railways. The LMS was to be distinguished by its wholehearted adoption of American management techniques, with a president and vice-president instead of chairmen and directors. Just how much difference this made is hard to say, even with hindsight, as the economic situation made real progress difficult.

What is clear is that the company was a large sprawling organisation with many far-flung operations that made effective control difficult, and that a smaller and more compact organisation, with some of the outposts of the old Midland Railway empire set free, could have been much easier to manage, and probably more likely to have ensured that the core businesses would have become viable.

The LMS could have done without the Irish railway and road transport operations, the Somerset & Dorset, and the London Tilbury & Southend. Nevertheless, these were the men who were entrusted to make it work, for the travelling public, the goods customer, the investor and the workforce of around 270,000. They endured a decade of infighting, a decade of progress amidst the years of the Great Depression, and six years of war.

Fairburn, Charles Edward

Fairburn studied under Henry Fowler at the Midland Railway's Derby works from 1910 to 1912, before joining Siemens, where he worked on the electrification of the North Eastern Railway's Newport–Shildon freight line. He moved in 1919 to English Electric to establish an electric traction department and became general manager of its works at Preston and Stafford.

He joined the LMS in 1934 as chief electrical engineer and in 1937 he was appointed Stanier's deputy, before finally becoming chief mechanical engineer in 1944, but the following year he died suddenly, widely regarded as a great loss to the industry. His achievements at the LMS included the large-scale introduction of diesel-electric shunting locomotives and he started work on designing a fleet of 1,500hp diesel-electric locomotives for main-line use. Of more immediate use were his 2-6-4T locomotives which he introduced in 1945 and which many regard as the outstanding example of a tank locomotive.

Fowler, Sir Henry

After serving an apprenticeship at the Lancashire & Yorkshire Railway's Horwich Works under John Aspinall, Fowler joined the Midland Railway in 1900, and was promoted to assistant works manager at Derby in 1905, before becoming works manager in 1907. He became chief mechanical engineer in 1909 and retained this position until Grouping, being knighted for his services to the railways during the First World War. In 1923, he became deputy CME for the London Midland & Scottish Railway and became CME from 1925 until he retired in 1930.

At the LMS, he struggled to integrate the design, locomotive and carriage construction and repair policies of six major companies. Nevertheless, he

Sir Henry Fowler, the first chief mechanical engineer for the LMS, was frustrated by the refusal of the directors to authorise the construction of more powerful steam locomotives. But he did press ahead with the development of diesel shunters. *(Institution of Electrical Engineers)*

had considerable experience in workshop management and in improving productivity in both railway and government workshops. He had already organised line production for locomotive overhauls, reducing the time needed, while standardising components and eliminating small locomotive classes or those that offered reliability or maintenance problems, and also boosted productivity and reduced costs. His plans for 4-6-2 passenger and 2-8-2 freight locomotives were overruled by train operators because of the need for larger turntables. Nevertheless, he was responsible for the 'Royal Scot' 4-6-0s built between 1927 and 1930, although Sir William Stanier, his successor, had them rebuilt.

In retirement, he was a consultant to the LMS vice-president (research) and authorised the introduction of prototype diesel shunting locomotives, with the LMS producing these on a large scale by the time the Second World War broke out in 1939.

Granet, Sir Guy

Originally trained and qualified as a barrister, Granet was appointed secretary to the Railway Companies Association in 1900, where he was credited not only with expanding its scope and influence, but also with developing his skills for a senior management role in the industry. Despite not having the traditional experience gained in an operating department, he became assistant general manager of the Midland Railway in 1905, clearly destined to become its next general manager as he assumed this role the following year, when he was just 39 years old. He received a knighthood in 1911. During the First World War,

Sir Guy Granet became chairman of the LMS in 1924, and more than anyone else was responsible for the LMS adopting American-style work practices and even job titles, with vice-presidents instead of directors.

he was one of three railway general managers seconded to the War Office, becoming deputy director-general of military railways in 1916, and then of movements and railways in 1917.

On returning to the Midland in 1918, he became a board member and in 1922 was the company's last chairman. On Grouping, he became the LMS's first deputy chairman and then chairman in 1924. Over the next three years, almost single-handedly, he introduced the LMS to an American management style, even extending this to adopt such titles as 'president' and 'vice-president'. He retired in 1927.

Hughes, George

Unusually, George Hughes worked for two of the predecessor companies of the LMS, starting with an apprenticeship at Crewe in 1882 under F.W. Webb of the London & North Western Railway, before joining the Lancashire & Yorkshire Railway in 1895, where he became principal assistant for carriages and wagons. He rose to works manager at Horwich in 1899 before becoming chief mechanical engineer in 1904, a position he retained until the merger with the LNWR, when he became CME for the combined company during its existence until assuming the same role for the LMS on Grouping in 1923.

He was one of the leading British pioneers of firetube superheaters, which he first applied to 0-6-0 goods locomotives in 1906 and then to 4-4-0s in 1908. This innovation saved his 4-6-0s of 1908, which were costly in their consumption of coal, but after rebuilding with superheating showed a 25 per cent improvement in economy, leading to many more being built. He also favoured building larger and more powerful locomotives, but his plans were thwarted on at least two occasions. The first time was at the LYR where his 1913 proposal for a large, four-cylinder 2-10-0 freight locomotive was overruled by the operating department. Again, at the LMS he saw clearly the need for more powerful locomotives, having designs prepared for 4-6-2 Pacific passenger locomotives and 2-8-2 goods locomotives, but these were never built, although his successful mixed traffic 2-6-0s did go ahead with 245 built, but only after he had retired in 1925.

Lemon, Sir Ernest John Hutchings

Apprenticed to the North British Locomotive Company, one of the leading independent steam locomotive builders, Ernest Lemon then worked for the Highland Railway before moving to Hurst Nelson and finally in 1911, at the age of 27 years, he joined the Midland Railway as its chief wagon inspector. In 1917 he was made carriage works manager at Derby, after Grouping being promoted to divisional carriage and wagon superintendent in 1923, when he developed production-line methods for the construction of wagons and carriages. Lemon was appointed to the post of chief mechanical engineer in 1931, replacing the retiring Henry Fowler. After less than a year as CME however, Lemon was again promoted to vice-president railway traffic, operating and commercial, where he was responsible for modernisation of the LMS's motive power depots. This seems to have been a move sideways to allow Stanier, who had been head-hunted from the Great Western Railway, to take over as CME, leaving him free to revolutionise the company's locomotive policy.

In addition to his duties with the LMS, Lemon was a member of the Territorial Army's Engineer and Railway Staff Corps which he joined as a Major in November 1929, and was promoted to Lieutenant-Colonel in April 1932. He resigned his commission in August 1943, as during the Second World War he was Director-General of Aircraft Production, for which he received a knighthood in the 1941 New Year's Honours list. Post-war, he returned to the LMS, but retired from the railway in 1948. He died in Epsom in 1954.

Stamp, Sir Josiah Charles/ Baron Stamp of Shortlands

After an early career with the Inland Revenue, in 1919 he became secretary and a director of Mond Nickel Company, which later became part of Imperial Chemical Industries (ICI). He became first president of the executive and later chairman of the London Midland & Scottish Railway in 1926. The LMS organised itself on US lines with a committee of vice-presidents, but suffered from over-centralisation, tight financial controls, and in-fighting between the old London & North Western and Midland Railway factions, which also showed itself in disputes over locomotive design and

Lord Stamp was president of the LMS at the outbreak of the Second World War, and was heading the negotiations between the railway companies and the government over the terms under which the state would control the railways in wartime. He was killed in 1941 in an air raid, along with his wife and eldest son.

procurement. To break free from some of the infighting between the MR and LNWR factions, Stamp recruited a new chief mechanical engineer, William Stanier, from the Great Western, leaving him to produce a series of classic locomotive designs, while Stamp established a research department and a School of Transport.

Stamp was challenged by a shareholder at one annual general meeting over his salary of £15,000 (worth about £900,000 today), which the shareholder regarded as too high. He replied that it was the equivalent of a ham sandwich from each shareholder and famously concluded: 'I'm sure that you will not grudge me my ham sandwich.' He was reputed by some to be the second wealthiest man in England, although it seems unlikely that he was quite as rich as that.

A lifelong teetotaller and non-smoker, which was unusual at a time when 80 per cent of men smoked, he was a nonconformist lay-preacher and the author of several textbooks on economics, as well as being a noted orator. In June 1938, he was elevated to the peerage becoming Baron Stamp of Shortlands. In 1940, with the country at war, the coalition government offered him the position of Chancellor of the Exchequer, which he declined.

Stamp was prominent in promoting the 'Square Deal' campaign of 1938–39, which pressed for the railways to be able to set their own freight rates, and in 1941 was negotiating with the government over terms for the state control of the railways during the Second World War, when he was killed, with his wife and eldest son, Wilfred, during the Blitz. One side effect of father and eldest son being killed at the same time was that his estate suffered double death duties when it passed to his second son.

Stanier, Sir William Arthur

Serving an apprenticeship on the Great Western Railway under William Dean from 1892, he became locomotive works manager in 1920, and in 1922 was appointed principal assistant to the chief mechanical engineer. In 1932, he succeeded Ernest Lemon as CME on the London Midland & Scottish Railway, breaking the former Midland Railway's stranglehold on locomotive design and specification as the LMS had suffered from the legacy of small locomotives inherited from the Midland Railway. Between 1932 and 1947, he produced more than 2,000 locomotives which incorporated much of GWR practice, such as tapered boilers, as well as LMS features, and these included his famous and successful 4-6-0 Class 5 or 'Black Five' mixed-traffic locomotives.

Undoubtedly the most famous LMS personality was Sir William Stanier, the chief mechanical engineer from 1932 and responsible for many of the company's finest locomotives. Many of his ideas were incorporated into the British Railways Standard locomotives, some of which bore more than a passing resemblance to Stanier's designs. *(Royal Society for the Arts & Sciences)*

Stanier also built many 4-6-2 Pacific locomotives, starting with the record-breaking 'Princess Royal' class in 1933, and 2-8-0 goods engines, with the latter also being built by other companies as a standard wartime design. His express Pacifics culminated in the streamlined 'Coronation' class of 1937. He also standardised components, and the layout and working practices in the repair shops.

Stanier was of that first generation of CMEs who also thought beyond the steam locomotive, and built some 90 diesel-electric shunting locomotives, which, along with the 'Black Fives', were adopted by British Railways after Nationalisation. He also produced a prototype diesel-hydraulic articulated three-car multiple unit in 1938. During the Second World War, he became scientific adviser to the Ministry of Production in 1942, and later a director of Power Jets, the company set up to exploit Sir Frank Whittle's jet engines. He was knighted in 1943.

Wood, Sir William Valentine

Born in Belfast, Wood first worked as a junior accountant for the Northern Counties Committee, before working for the Irish Railway Executive Committee after it was formed in 1916, mirroring the work of its mainland counterpart, which existed from the outbreak of the First World War.

Rebuilt Coronation-class No.6221 *Queen Elizabeth* post-war, waiting to take an express. *(HMRS AAL726)*

When the Ministry of Transport was formed in 1919, he became its first financial director. He moved to the newly formed LMS in 1924 as assistant to the accountant general, becoming controller of costs and statistics in 1927, where he must have impressed because in 1930 he was elevated to the much superior position of vice-president of the executive committee. It was in this role that he become renowned as a master of railway statistics and the complex pricing mechanisms that the railways were forced to use for goods traffic, but also proved to be an articulate spokesman for the company and the industry. He worked closely and well with Stamp, and between them they wrote a book, *Railways*, which was published in 1927. Wood was knighted in 1937.

That the relationship between the two men was one of friendship seems to be borne out by his distress at Stamp's untimely death in an air raid in 1941, forcing Wood to become the company's president, and also becoming a member of the Railway Executive. Post-Nationalisation, he spent five years as a member of the British Transport Commission.

Wood once let slip the fact that he considered the LMS to be far too big for effective management, and that there was no precedent for such a large and diverse company, certainly in the United Kingdom.

Chapter 6

Steam Locomotives

Despite electrification, even before the First World War, and the heavy programme of electrification being carried out by the Southern Railway, none of the 'Big Four' grouped companies was as wedded to steam as the LMS. Today, this may seem both surprising and backward looking, but there were a number of good reasons for the strong advocacy of steam by the company. Great Britain had a very strong and substantial coal mining industry, and uncertainty over supplies of fuel oil, almost all of which had to be imported in the pre-North Sea oil days*, had concerned many even before the First World War, with the Admiralty ordering a number of coal-fired ships for this reason. The electric trains of the day were far superior to steam in terms of acceleration, so showed good savings in journey times on busy suburban services, but struggled to match the performance of steam on longer services with few stops or even none at all. The LMS, with the LNER, operated the country's longest main-line services.

Some even argue that the large and powerful steam tank engines built by the LMS for services such as that from Fenchurch Street to Southend in lieu of electrification, had superior acceleration compared with electric multiple units when the rails were wet or slippery.

There was also the fact that electrification only made financial sense on routes that were heavily used, with high frequencies and the need for very short turnrounds at the termini. Frequencies were much less than today on longer distance services, with just two or three trains daily between London and Glasgow, for example, rather than regular hourly or even more frequent departures. As a result, it was also clear even for those who foresaw the end of steam traction that many lines would have to be operated by diesel because frequencies did not justify electrification.

Electrification? Who needs it? This was the implied assumption when the introduction of these new Stanier three-cylinder 2-6-4T locomotives was announced. This was the first, No. 2500, now preserved in the National Collection at York (*The LMS Magazine*)

*Great Britain was not entirely oil free as shale oil was available in a number of areas, notably in the east of Scotland

While the benefits of electrification and of dieselisation were covered in the *LMS Magazine*, and in a fair and considered manner, at one stage the financial benefits of electrification were challenged in an article on 'The Future of the Steam Locomotive' published in 1925. The author of the article foresaw a long future for the steam locomotive with increased power and operating economy benefiting from very high boiler pressures. As we will see later, higher boiler pressures were fraught with danger and after some accidents were not pursued further.

On the other hand, far from coal being king, the security of fuel supplies in fact resulted in the conversion of a number of locomotives to oil-burning in 1926 as British miners, or colliers in the language of the day, went on strike.

Conversion of locomotives to oil firing took place as early as 1897 on the Great Eastern, with the 'oil' being tar formed as a by-product of oil-gas production, but the idea was dropped when this commodity became very expensive. The Midland Railway was one of the pioneers many years later after a miners' strike in 1912 and then again in 1921, as this photograph taken around the time of Grouping shows, of 4-4-0 No. 527. *(HMRS AEW225)*

Of course, part of the problem was that the railway inherited a massive infrastructure for the construction and upkeep of steam locomotives, and the years between the two world wars were not prosperous, a situation made far worse by the miners' strike which saw many markets for coal, and especially export markets, lost for good. Money was in short supply, and industry was working at far less than its optimum capacity. The only railways that saw some good years in the 1920s and '30s were those heavily dependent upon passenger traffic, and shorter distance and commuter traffic at that. A root and branch conversion from steam to electricity was beyond the limited means of the LMS. Infrastructure problems were amongst the reasons why the Midland Railway had stuck with 4-4-0 steam locomotives as anything larger would have had difficulty using the turntables at many of its depots.

The legacy of the Midland

Officially, the first steam locomotive to join the LMS was one ordered for and built by the Lancashire & Yorkshire Railway at its Horwich Works, which joined the new railway on its first day, 1 January 1923. As No. 10433, the new 4-6-0 arrived painted dark grey before the instruction was given that it was to be turned out in the official crimson lake.

The architects of the Railways Act 1921, which provided the legal authority for the Grouping, were not railwaymen and had little consideration for or appreciation of the problems that the managements of the grouped companies would have. As mentioned earlier, in the case of locomotive power, the LMS inherited more than 10,300 steam locomotives of many different classes, but while it was an advantage that almost two-thirds were of LNWR Crewe or Midland Derby ancestry, many were elderly, and less than 1,900 had superheating. Then, of course, there was the Midland preoccupation with smaller locomotives, in part a reflection of the many curves on its longer routes, but the net result was that many heavy expresses could only be worked by double heading. Just a third of the vast collection of locomotives rated anything higher than the Midland Railway's power classification 2, a system largely adopted by the LMS.

There is some history to this, however, and the widespread assumption that the Midland was introspective and backward looking in keeping with its tried and trusted 4-4-0 locomotives bears challenging. At the time, locomotive development had still some way to go, and while many railway companies in the quest for more power had moved on from the 4-4-0s to 4-6-0s for express passenger trains, almost all of them had been plagued by problems. Some of these were created by attempts to keep the overall weight down, so that the ex-LNWR 4-6-0 'Claughtons' had undersized boiler barrels, while the other 4-6-0, the 'Princes', suffered from a shallow fire grate that made efficient firing difficult.

The 'Claughtons' had been built to a new design for smoother running, with all four cylinders driving a single axle to avoid the hammer blow effect on the track, but the chief civil engineer disagreed and it was only after Grouping, and his death in 1924, that his theory was vindicated and the locomotives were rebuilt with larger boilers. Meanwhile, the 'Claughtons' were notoriously unreliable and under-utilised, with a survey of 23 of them as late as 1930 showing they spent 29 per cent of the time under repair, and another 13 per cent under inspection, and even when running their daily average usage was just 91 miles. While the Midland Railway did not like to stretch its locomotives, imposing a limit of 240 tons on them, the LNWR had no such qualms, and its 'George V' class 4-4-0s were often given 400-ton expresses and left to get on with it, which they did. Although they had a boiler designed to give a high performance, this was at the expense of a light underframe which often fractured. The Midland, of course, ignored the 4-6-0 completely.

This is not to say that the Midland flatly refused to countenance anything bigger than a 4-4-0, for this was the same railway that built what was for some time the country's only 0-10-0 'Decapod', unofficially named 'Big Bertha' after a notorious First World War German gun. 'Big Bertha' was the banking locomotive for the notorious Lickey incline. That Derby could produce larger, more capable and exciting locomotives was also in evidence, however, in the form of 7F 2-8-0s for the Somerset & Dorset Joint Railway.

Of the need for standardisation, no better instance existed than the fact that former LNWR and Midland steam locomotives had regulators that worked in the opposite directions. The Midland practice was the standard for most railways, and when an ex-Midland driver found himself in a former LNWR steam locomotive cab, he had to remember that the regulator worked in the opposite direction. Many forgot, and locomotives ended up being reversed through the shed wall of a roundhouse! This might have been understandable, but there were in addition too many cases of carelessness when locomotives were run into the turntable well, which put the shed out of action for several hours.

The average steam locomotive spent up to 15 per cent of its life in the works for major overhaul, with the most time-consuming work being on the boiler. The LNWR deliberately built fewer tenders than locomotives to take this into account. The Midland built a tender for every locomotive and went as far as to put the locomotive number on the tender. After Grouping, the LMS picked up this Midland practice, but only for a while, as cases began to emerge of tenders carrying a different number from the locomotive. Eventually, engine numbers appeared on the side of the locomotive cab and the letters 'LMS' appeared on the tender. Tank engines had the opposite practice, with the engine number on the side of the coal bunker, and 'LMS' on the side of the water tanks.

Only the English companies could really offer sufficient locomotives of performance suitable for system-wide use and capable of handling the heavy and fast expresses. The Caledonian's ten different classes, totalling 65 4-6-0s, have already been mentioned, and there was also the Highland Railway's 'River' class, but there were just six of them!

Goods locomotive development had been happier, and instead of the troublesome 4-6-0s, both the LNWR and the LYR had succeeded in developing very capable 0-8-0 freight locomotives from the 1890s onwards. The LNWR's G2s handled much of the heavy freight during the 1930s, and many of them outlasted later designs and were still working during the twilight years of the steam age during the 1960s. The Caledonian also adopted the 0-8-0, but with less success, and for the most part the Scottish companies favoured the 0-6-0 for goods work, as did the Midland. Unfortunately, many of the Midland's 0-6-0s were elderly with more than 400 of them at least 50 years old on Grouping. There were more recent locomotives, but even the Midland's Class 4F 0-6-0 goods engines had to be used in pairs.

Not all of the railway companies that came together to form the LMS had good locomotives, the Glasgow & South Western for example, having a motley collection. Amongst the other companies, some, such as the Furness Railway, were too small to make an impression on the LMS.

It was not just the range of locomotive classes that was wanting. Partly due to the age of many of them, modern refinements were rare. Super-heating was not the only omission – inside cylinders and cumbersome mechanisms meant that vital components were often over-stressed. Problems such as hot axleboxes were viewed as a fact of life, while there was poor provision for lubrication. The design of boilers and fireboxes was also far short of what could be expected at the time. The Midland had produced fine locomotives for their day, but it became increasingly obvious that their day had passed and it was time to move on.

The 'Claughtons' and 'Princes' were soon rebuilt and proved competent if costly locomotives. The 'Claughtons' became known as the 'Patriots', nicknamed 'Baby Scots' although in fact there was very little of the original locomotive left as the rebuilding was so extensive. The moral was clear, rebuilding was not the answer, but if the LMS wanted to cut down its 400 or so classes of steam locomotive, the only way forward was a policy of scrap and build: costly, but less expensive than rebuilding, and more satisfactory.

The need for power

Obviously, no one locomotive could meet all the needs of such a diverse railway as the LMS, but there was a pressing need for standardisation and there were some serious omissions in the range of locomotives available to the operating departments.

It should have been clear from the outset that the new LMS needed a large and powerful passenger express steam locomotive that could operate unaided as it handled the long gradients in the North of England and Southern Scotland. This was a massive challenge as no railway company possessed anything like it in 1923, so any designer would be working in uncharted territory. The grip of the Midland during the early days of the LMS was such that proposals to build such a large and powerful locomotive were blocked time and time again. The LMS did not follow the usual railway practice of having the chief mechanical engineer managing the locomotives, but instead a motive power superintendent was appointed reporting to the chief general superintendent. J.E. Anderson, formerly of the Midland, was the motive power superintendent until he retired in 1932.

Next, a capable mixed traffic locomotive was also needed for the lighter expresses and for fast fully fitted goods trains, either a 2-6-0 or a 4-6-0 that actually worked well. There were also the ancient LNWR 0-8-0s, the oldest of which dated from 1858, that needed to be replaced even more urgently than their Midland counterparts if the heavy coal trains between the Midlands and London, and other places in the south, as well as in Scotland, were to be handled efficiently. This called for an update of the 0-8-0 concept.

Nevertheless, a policy of scrap and build was introduced. There was some rebuilding, using Caledonian boilers to improve the performance of some of the ex-Highland Railway locomotives

LONDON, TILBURY, SOUTHEND, and SHOEBURYNESS.—Midland (L. T. & S. Section).

Down. — Week Days.

Miles	Down.	mrn	mrn	mrn	mrn	mrn	mrn	mrn	mrn	mrn	mrn	mrn	mrn	mrn	mrn	mrn	mrn	mrn	mrn	mrn	mrn	mrn	mrn
	646 ST. PANCRAS dep.	4 15	5 5					5 48				6 48				7 53	8 50		9 30				
	646 Moorgate Street "															7 54	8 43		9 18				1013
	646 Kentish Town "	4 22	5 12					5 57				6 55			7 38	8 15	9 0		9 39				1040
—	FENCHURCH ST. dep.	5 5	5 45							6 52		7 30	7 42		8 11	9 5	9 18	9 39		1017		1045	1113
1¾	Stepney	5 11	5 51							6 58		7 37	7 48		8 17	9 10	9 23	9 48		1022		1050	1119
2¼	Burdett Road	5 13	5 53							7 0		7 40	7 50		8 19			9 50		1024		1052	1121
3¼	Bromley		5 57						6 55														
4½	Plaistow		6 2				6 50		7 0			7 48	7 58		8 26		9 36	9 57					1127
5½	Upton Park		6 5				6 54		7 4			7 51	8 2		8 30		9 39	10 0					
—	382 Ealing dep.				5 33	5 43	5 52	5 59		5 59	6 27	6 50	7 6	7 28	7 28	8 15	8 34	8 53	9 19	9 26	9 36	9 56	1029
—	382 Mark Lane "		5 28		6 13	6 21	6 33	6 36		6 47	7 6	7 30	7 47	8 7	8 7	8 55	9 15	9 37	9 57	10 3	1013	1036	11 4
—	382 Aldgate East "		5 30		6 15	6 23	6 35	6 38		6 49	7 8	7 32	7 49	8 9	8 9	8 57	9 17	9 40	10 0	10 6	1015	1039	11 6
6½	East Ham	5 23	6 9			6 50		7 4		7 13	7 27	7 55	8 6		8 34	9 20	9 43	10 4			1033	11 1	1132
7½	Barking	5 29	6 16		6 40	6 55	7 1	7 8	7 13	7 20	7 35	7 59	8 15	8 40	8 41	9 25	9 50	10 8	1029	1034	1041	11 5	
11¼	Dagenham	5 37			6 47						7 43		8 23	8 48			9 58					1113	
13¾	Hornchurch	5 43			6 53						7 48		8 29	8 53			10 4					1119	
15¾	Upminster 649	5 47			7 1						8¶24		8 37	8 57			1011		1043			1126	
19¼	East Horndon	5 55											8 45				1019						
22¾	Laindon	6 4											8 57				1028						
10¼	Dagenham Dock		6 23						7 20	7 27		8 6			8 48	9 31		1015					
12¾	Rainham ¶		6 29						7 26	7 33		8 12			8 54	9 36		1021					
16	Purfleet		6 36					7 24	7 33	7 42		8 20			9 3	9 45		1030					
20	Grays		6 46	7 12	7 27	7 17	7 23	7 33	7 41	7 51	8 46	8 29			9 13	9 55		1039		1054			1154
21½	Tilbury Docks		6 51	7 15	7 31	7 20	7 27	7 36	7 46	7 56	8 50	8 34			9 19	10 1		1044		1059			1159
22½	Tilbury arr.		6 54		7 34		7 30		7 49	7 59	8 53	8 37			9 22	10 4		1047		11 2			12 2
—	Gravesend (Town Pier) arr.		7 4		7 44				7 59	8 9		8 49			9 32	1014		1057		1115			1212
	Gravesend (Town Pier) dep.		6 47							7 50		8 32				9 58				1054			
—	Tilbury dep.		6 59							8 2		8 45				1010				11 6			
24	Low Street		7 6							8 9		8 52				1017				1113			
27¼	Stanford-le-Hope		7 14							8 16		9 2				1026				1122			
32¼	Pitsea	6 12	7 25							8 29		9 14	9 5			1043	1036			1133			
35¼	Benfleet	6 19	7 32							8 35		9 23	9 12			1052	1043		11 8	1140		1150	
39	Leigh-on-Sea	6 27	7 40							8 43		9 33	9 21			11 0	1051		1116	1148	1126	1159	
40¾	Westcliff-on-Sea	6 31	7 45							8 47		9 38	9 26			11 4	1055		1120	1152	1130	12 4	
41¾	Southend-on-Sea	6 38	7 52							8 53		9 44	9 34			11 9	11 1		1125	1157	1135	1210	
44	Thorpe Bay	6 49	8 2							9 3			9 44			1117	1110			12 5	1144	1221	
45¼	Shoeburyness arr.	6 53	8 6							9 7			9 48			1121	1114			12 9	1148	1225	
																			Through Train, St. Pancras to Southend.		Through Train, Ealing to Shoeburyness.		

Down. — Week Days—Continued.

Down.	aft	mrn	mrn	mrn	aft	aft	mrn	mrn	aft	aft	aft	aft	aft	aft	aft	aft	aft	aft	aft	aft	aft
646 ST. PANCRAS dep.								11 40					12 20						1 4		
646 Moorgate Street "																					
646 Kentish Town "		1130						11 53					12 29				1 0		1 10		
FENCHURCH STREET dep.			1135	1157		12 10		12 25	1243	1255	1 0	1 5		1 11	1 15	1 25		1 35	1 48	1 48	1 56
Stepney			1140			12 16		12 31						1 17	1 21	1 31		1 40	1 54	1 54	
Burdett Road			1142			12 18		12 33				1 12		1 19	1 23	1 33			1 56	1 56	
Bromley																			2 0		
Plaistow			1149		1213			12 40										1 48	2 4		
Upton Park			1152		1216			12 43							1 30				2 7		
382 Ealing dep.			1053			11A20	11A20	11V50					12c20	1220	1226			1244	1255		
382 Mark Lane "			1131			12K0	12K0	12V30					1c0	1 1	1 7			1 28	1 39		
382 Aldgate East "			1133			12K2	12K2	12V32					1c2	1 3	1 9			1 30	1 41		
East Ham			1156		1220			12 49							1 34			1 54	2 11		
Barking			12 3		1223	12 28	12 34	12 57					1 25	1 30				1 58	2 15		
Dagenham							12 41							1 38							
Hornchurch							12 46							1 43							2 22
Upminster 649						12 41	12 51					1 33	1e38	1 46		1 54	2 0			2 16	
East Horndon							12 59										2 8				
Laindon							1 9						1e51				2 17				
Dagenham Dock			1210					1 4										2 5	2 22		
Rainham ¶			1216					1 10										2 11	2 28		
Purfleet			1225					1 19										2 20	2 37		
Grays	1216		1234					1 28							2 1			2 28	2 47		
Tilbury Docks	1221		1239					1 32							2 5			2 32	2 51		
Tilbury arr.	1224		1242					1 35							2 8			2 35	2 54		
Gravesend (Town Pier) arr.			1255					1 45							2 18			2 45	3 4		
Gravesend (Town Pier) dep.			1235												2 3				2 48		
Tilbury dep.	1227		1247												2 15				3 0		
Low Street	1232		1253												2 22				3 6		
Stanford-le-Hope	1239		1 0												2 30				3 13		
Pitsea	1248		1 10				1 16								2 53		2 24		3 23		
Benfleet				1245		1 3	1 23								3 1	2 18			3 30		
Leigh-on-Sea		1 0	1822	1253		1 11	1 31		1 40	1 48	1 57	2 4	2 10	2 18	3 9	2 26	2 36		3 38	2 45	2 52
Westcliff-on-Sea		1 5	1826	1257		1 15	1 35		1 44	1 53	2 1	2 9	2 14	2 22	3 13	2 30	2 41		3 42	2 49	2 56
Southend-on-Sea		1 12	1831	1 3		1 20	1 40		1 49	1 58	2 6	2 14	2 20	2 27	3 18	2 35	2 46		3 47	2 54	3 1
Thorpe Bay				1 11		1 28	1 47		1 57		2 14	2 22			3 26				3 56	3 2	
Shoeburyness arr.				1 15		1 32	1 51		2 1		2 18	2 26			3 30				4 0	3 6	
	Saturdays only.	Saturdays only. Through Train to Southend.		Saturdays only.					Saturdays only.	Saturdays only.	Saturdays only.	Saturdays only.	Through Train, St. Pancras to Southend.	Saturdays only.	Saturdays only.	Saturdays only.	Saturdays only.	Saturdays only.	Except Sats.	Saturdays only.	Saturdays only.

For Notes, see page 652; for Continuation of Trains, see pages 651 and 652.

Southend may not have got its electric trains, even though these were promised, but the 1938 timetable, opposite, was still an improvement on that for 1922, above. *(Bradshaw)*

LONDON, TILBURY, SOUTHEND-ON-SEA, and SHOEBURYNESS.

Down. — Week Days.

Miles.	Miles.	Down.	mrn (Monday morns. only.)	mn	mn	mn	mn Z (Calls at Bromley at 5 49 mrn)	mn	mn	mn	mn	mn	mn	mrn (Calls at Bromley 6 55 mrn)	mn	mn	mn	mn	mn	mn	mn	mn	mrn		mrn	mrn
		678 St. Pancras ..dep.	..	.	410	.	5 0	.	.	.	6 5	.	.	..	.	.	648	.	.	B	715	.	..	..	..	..
		678 Kentish Town .. "	...	...	416	...	5 7	...	...	...	611	...	...	...	...	...	654	...	...	.	734	...	...	...	...	...
—	—	FENCHURCH ST. ...dep.	1215	425	5 0	.	537	.	615	.	.	.	.	6 45	652	.	730	742	.	.	758	812	8 24	..	..	8 40
1¾	1¾	Stepney (East)	...	...	5 6	...	543	...	621	...	...	...	...	...	658	...	735	748	...	...	8 4	818	8 30	...	...	8 47
2¼	2¼	Burdett Road	..	.	5 8	.	545	.	.	.	.	.	.	..	7 0	.	737	750	.	.	8 6	821	8 32	..	..	8 49
4¼	4¼	Plaistow	..	.	515	.	554	.	.	.	.	648	.	7 1	.	720	744	.	.	.	812	827	..	..	.	8 57
5¼	5¼	Upton Park	..	...	...	...	557	...	...	...	...	652	...	7 4	...	...	747	...	...	...	815	830	...	...	...	9 0
6½	6½	East Ham	...	.	520	.	6 2	.	.	.	649	.	7 3	..	713	726	751	759	.	.	819	834	8 42	..	..	..
7½	7½	Barking	1230	440	527	530	610	625	640	.	654	7 1	7 7	7 14	721	731	756	.	814	.	825	839	8 47	..	..	9 8
9½	—	Becontree		...	...	...	...	...	...	...	...	...	...	...	...	...	...	...	...	...	830	...	...	...	...	...
11½	—	Dagenham		.	536	.	.	.	647	.	.	.	.	..	.	739	.	.	..	.	835	.	..	..	..	..
13¾	—	Hornchurch		...	541	...	...	...	652	...	...	...	...	...	...	744	...	...	...	...	840	...	...	...	...	...
15¼	—	Upminster 681		.	547	.	.	.	7 1	7 4	.	.	.	..	.	748	.	815	.	829	845	.	9 1	..	9 12	9 22
19¼	—	East Horndon		...	555	...	...	...	...	712	...	...	...	...	...	...	...	...	...	...	853	...	...	...	...	...
22¼	—	Laindon		5 4	6 3	.	.	.	.	721	.	.	.	..	.	.	.	828	.	.	9 1	.	..	..	..	..
—	10½	Dagenham Dock		...	...	536	617	631	...	...	7 0	7 7	713	7 20	727	...	8 2	...	820	...	...	846	...	...	...	...
—	12½	Rainham ¶		.	.	.	622	636	.	.	.	.	.	7 25	732	.	8 7	.	.	.	.	851	..	..	..	..
—	16	Purfleet		...	...	...	630	643	...	...	...	...	724	7 32	739	...	814	...	...	...	...	9 2	...	...	...	...
—	19¾	Grays		.	.	.	639	650	719	.	714	725	732	7 40	747	.	822	.	.	847	.	911	..	..	9 30	..
—	21½	Tilbury Town B		...	...	...	646	654	724	...	717	729	735	7 45	752	...	827	...	...	851	...	916	...	...	9 34	...
—	22½	Tilbury C ...arr.		.	.	.	649	657	727	.	.	732	.	7 48	755	.	830	.	.	854	.	919	..	..	9 37	..
—	23	Gravesend (Town Pier) arr.	...	...	...	...	7 2	710	737	...	...	746	...	8 1	8P7	...	842	...	...	9A5	Y	933	...	...	9Y50	...
		Gravesend (Town Pier) dep.	..	.	.	.	640	.	.	.	.	.	.	7 40	.	.	821	.	.	.	.	.	..	..	..	..
—	—	Tilbury C ...dep.	...	...	...	...	653	...	...	...	...	...	...	7 53	...	...	834	...	...	...	...	...	...	...	...	...
—	24¼	Low Street	..	.	.	.	658	.	.	.	.	.	.	7 59	.	.	839	.	.	.	.	.	..	..	..	..
—	27¼	Stanford-le-Hope	...	...	...	...	7 8	...	...	...	...	...	...	8 6	...	...	846	...	...	...	...	...	...	...	...	...
26½	32¼	Pitsea, for Vange	..	514	610	.	719	.	.	729	.	.	.	8 24	.	.	858	.	.	.	9 8	.	..	..	..	..
29¼	35	Benfleet A	1259	521	616	...	725	...	...	735	...	...	...	8 30	...	...	9 4	839	...	...	914	...	9 21	...	...	...
32½	38¼	Leigh-on-Sea	1 6	532	624	.	732	.	.	742	.	.	.	8 37	.	.	911	847	.	.	921	.	9 28	..	..	9 48
34	39½	Chalkwell	1 10	537	628	...	736	...	...	746	...	...	...	8 41	...	...	915	851	...	...	...	...	9 32	...	...	9 52
34¾	40¼	Westcliff-on-Sea	1 14	545	632	.	740	.	.	750	.	.	.	8 45	.	.	919	855	.	.	926	.	9 36	..	..	9 56
35¾	41½	Southend-on-Sea	1 18	549	638	...	746	...	...	755	...	...	...	8 49	...	...	924	9 0	...	...	931	...	9 40	...	...	10 1
36¾	42½	Southend East	.	557	645	.	753	.	.	8 0	.	.	.	...	.	.	.	9 6	.	.	937	.	9 45	..	..	10 6
38	43¾	Thorpe Bay	...	6 1	649	...	757	...	...	8 4	...	...	...	8 57	...	...	...	910	...	...	941	...	9 49	...	...	1010
39½	45¼	Shoeburyness ...arr	..	6 7	653	.	8 1	.	.	8 8	.	.	.	9 1	.	.	.	914	.	.	945	.	9 53	..	..	1014

Down. — Week Days—*Continued.*

Down.	mrn T	mrn (Calls at Bromley 9 25 mrn.)	mrn	mrn S (Kentish Town to Southend-on-Sea.)	mrn (St. Pancras to Southend-on-Sea.)	mrn (Ealing (dep. 9 40 mrn., page vii) to Shoeburyness.)	mrn T	mrn	mrn	mrn	mrn (Saturdays only.)	mrn (Except Saturdays.)	aft Z (Saturdays only.)	aft	mrn Y	mrn (Saturdays only.)	non (Saturdays only.)	mrn S (to Southend-on-Sea.)	mrn (Saturdays only.)	aft (Saturdays only.)	mrn (Except Saturdays.)	aft (Except Saturdays.)
678 St. Pancras ...dep.	8B0	8B50	..	..	9 30	..	..	..	..	10B4	..	..	..	..	..	..	..	..	..	..	..	..
678 Kentish Town ... "	8 15	9 1	...	9 28	9 40	...	...	...	...	1030	...	...	...	...	...	...	...	1126	1126	..	1126	...
FENCHURCH STREET ..dep.	9 4	9 12	9 40	..	..	..	1017	1045	..	1113	1125	1142	..	..	1135	1156	12 0	..	12 4	12 8	1210	..
Stepney (East)	9 11	...	9 47	...	...	...	1022	1050	...	1119	...	...	...	...	1140	...		...	1210	1214	1215	...
Burdett Road	..	..	9 49		..	..	..	1052	..	..	..	..	..	..	1142	..		..	1212	1216	1217	..
Plaistow	..	9 30	9 57		..	1028	..	..	..	..	..	..	..	..	1150	..		..	..	..	..	..
Upton Park	...	9 34	10 0		...	...	...	...	...	...	...	...	...	...	1153	...		...	...	...	...	...
East Ham	9 25	9 39	10 4		..	1033	..	..	..	1129	..	1155		..	1157			..	..	.	..	..
Barking	9 32	9 47	10 8		1026	1045	1034	11 3	11 8	...	...			...	12 3			1218	1222	1227	1228	1234
Becontree	...	9 53	...		...		...	...	1113	...	...			...	...			...	...	...	...	...
Dagenham	..	9 58	..		..		..	..	1118	..	..			..	..			..	..	..	..	1241
Hornchurch	...	10 4	...		...		...	...	1123	...	...			...	...				...	...	...	1246
Upminster 681	..	1011	..		1040		..	..	1127	..	1149			12 2	..				1235	1240	1240	1250
East Horndon	...	1019	...				...	...	1135	...	...			...	...				...	1248	...	1258
Laindon	..	1031	..				..	..	1143	..	..			..	..				..	1256	..	1 6
Dagenham Dock	9 38		1014				...	...	...	...				...	12 9		...					
Rainham ¶	9 43		1019				..	..	..	..				..	1214		..					
Purfleet	9 52		1028	...			...	...	...	1145				...	1223		...					
Grays	10 0		1036	..			1053	..	..	1153		1214	1213	12 20	1232		..					
Tilbury Town B	10 5		1041	...			1053	...	...	1158		1218	1217	12 25	1237		...					
Tilbury C ...arr.	10 8		1044	..			11 1	..	..	12 1		1221	1220	12 28	1240		..					
Gravesend (Town Pier) arr.	1020	Y	1056	Y			1115	...	Y	1213		1233	1235	12P45	1252	...	...					
Gravesend (Town Pier) dep.	9 55		..	..			1051	..	..	..		..	1212	..	1233	..	..	..				
Tilbury C ...dep.	1012		...	...			11 6	...	...	...		...	1224	...	1246	...	...	...	...	...	...	...
Low Street	..		..	..			..	..	..	..		..	1229	..	1251	..	..	..	..	..	.	..
Stanford-le-Hope	1024		...	...			1119	...	...	...		...	1238	...	1258	...	...	...	...	...	...	...
Pitsea, for Vange	1034	1040	..	..			1133	..	1150	..		..	1247	..	1 9	..	..	..	1252	..	..	1 15
Benfleet A	1040	1046	...	1058	11 1		1139	1131	1156	...		...	...	...	...	...	1241	...	1258	...	1259	1 21
Leigh-on-Sea	1047	1053	..	11 5	11 8	1119	1146	1138	12 3	..	1212	..	..	..	1S22	1241	..	1252	1 5	1 10	1 7	1 28
Chalkwell	...	1057	...	11 9	1112	1123	1150	1142	12 7	...	1216	...	...	...	1S26	...	1250	1256	...	1 14	1 11	1 32
Westcliff-on-Sea	1052	11 1	..	1113	1116	1127	1154	1146	1211	..	1220	..	..	..	1S30	1246	..	1 0	1 10	..	1 15	1 35
Southend-on-Sea	1056	11 5	...	1119	1122	1132	1159	1151	1215	...	1224	...	...	...	1S34	...	1256	1 5	1 14	1 20	1 19	1 40
Southend East	11 1	1110	..	..	..	1137	12 4	1157	1220	..	1229	..	..	..	..	..	1 1	..	..	1 24	1 24	1 45
Thorpe Bay	11 5	1114	...	...	...	1141	12 8	12 1	1224	...	1233	...	...	...	...	1256	1 5	...	...	...	1 28	1 49
Shoeburyness ...arr.	11 9	1118	..	..	..	1145	1212	12 5	1228	..	1237	..	..	..	..	1 0	1 9	..	..	..	1 32	1 53

for example, but in the main rebuilding centred on getting a much improved performance from the 'Claughtons'. Unfortunately, the way forward was seen as updating Midland locomotive designs rather than introducing new and more powerful classes. Three of the Midland classes were chosen for the new construction programme: the Deeley/Fowler 4-4-0 compound; the freight class 4F 0-6-0, and the Johnson class 3F 0-6-0T shunter. These were augmented by the Fowler class 2P rebuild. From 1924 until Anderson retired in 1932, no fewer than 1,265 locomotives of these classes were built, despite none of them being suitable for the growing needs of the LMS.

Midland attitudes prevailed in other ways as well, with ex-LNWR locomotives that had managed to handle heavy loads being forced to take a pilot locomotive. The new railway was being run with scant regard for what people would now call the 'bottom line'. Drivers without a pilot waiting to start could be challenged by ex-Midland officials. Grudgingly a compromise was reached, which was that the best of the old LNWR locomotives could exceed the stipulated loadings in what was known as the 'S' scheme. Even so, when the 'Royal Scot' express was launched in 1927 with up to 15 carriages, it had to be double-headed.

Not everything that the Midland produced was bad. The 4-4-0s could be outstanding examples of their type. In late 1923, one of the first completely new classes expected of George Hughes and designed at the former LYR works at Horwich, was a 2-6-0. Naturally the design had to be adapted to fit Midland preconceptions of what a locomotive should be, but when it finally entered service in 1926 the design proved to be economical and free-running, with wide route availability. A number were re-gauged to 5ft 3in and sent to Northern Ireland for the Northern Counties Committee's boat trains and expresses.

With the heavy coal trains between Toton and Brent in mind, consideration was given to a 2-8-2 goods locomotive, but Hughes decided that a Beyer-Garratt articulated locomotive would be the answer to double heading, and wanted to order a 2-6-2+2-6-2 from Beyer Peacock for £10,000, more than £600,000 by today's prices. Anderson intervened, ordering a 2-6-0+0-6-2 instead and using standard Midland axleboxes that were for ever running hot after they entered service in 1927.

There were other locomotives being built at this time, including 4-4-2T tanks for the heavy suburban workings on the London Tilbury & Southend line, and which remained in production until 1930 despite the design being out-of-date. The locomotives were completely underpowered for such a demanding route with trains forever stopping and starting. Once it had its first three classes of 'standard' locomotives in production, Derby was asked to produce a replacement, and broke away from tradition by designing a 2-6-4 tank. On this, Fowler introduced a redesigned Walschaerts valve gear with long lap and long travel, with the result that the locomotive was an outstanding success and capable of speeds in excess of 80mph. The LT&S should have been electrified, but it wasn't, and the stalwarts amongst the drivers maintained that in wet conditions, this locomotive was superior to the electric trains of the day. Whether this was true or it was simply the traditional railwayman's dislike of electric multiple units, which many scornfully referred to as 'trams', is another matter.

The solution to the need for a powerful express locomotive was seen as being a 4-6-2, or 'Pacific', tender locomotive, and indeed, the LYR at Horwich had worked on such a design pre-Grouping. Hughes put the idea forward, but it was instantly blocked by Anderson. The same reaction occurred in 1926 when Fowler's team, which had worked on a three-cylinder compound 4-6-0 the previous year, also proposed a Pacific as the solution to the problem. The Midland-inspired mood was that a 4-6-0 could do all that was required. The main advocate of the 4-6-0 on Britain's railways was the Great Western, and so to prove themselves right, the 4-6-0 faction borrowed No. 5000 *Launceston Castle* from the GWR in September 1926 for trials between Euston and Carlisle. What resulted was the design for a large, three-cylinder 4-6-0 known within the company as 'an improved Castle', which was rushed through with Fowler ordering enough of these locomotives to be built to take over the West Coast service to Scotland for the 1927 summer timetable.

Officially known as the 'Royal Scot' class, the contract for the first 50 was given to the North British Locomotive Company in Glasgow in December 1926. It was no mean achievement that the first of the class was delivered in June 1927. 'Design in haste and repent in service' should have been the outcome, but in fact the design was basically sound and capable of handling 420-ton trains without assistance over Shap and Beattock. This was due in part to Fowler again insisting on the same valve gear that had been introduced with the 2-6-4Ts for the Fenchurch Street services. As it was, the design soon showed that it had weaknesses in its coupled axleboxes and suspension, as well as in bogie control, which had to be modified after a derailment at Weaver Junction in 1930. There were also piston valve leakages, but all of these problems were eventually solved through modifications, leaving just one serious fault that could not be modified, frame failures.

The new locomotives were able to handle the first major acceleration of LMS services in 1927, while the re-boilered 'Claughtons' ('Patriots') were relegated to the Irish mail expresses and services to Scotland from Manchester and Birmingham. The new boiler was at least a success even though the resulting locomotive was greedy in its consumption of coal and thirsty in its demand for water. The boilers were placed on what was essentially a 'Royal Scot' frame, of which 52 were built after the first appeared in 1930. Although officially still 'Claughton'-rebuilds, the original content was very low indeed.

Meanwhile, in an attempt to show what higher steam pressure could provide in terms of enhanced performance and reduced fuel consumption, an experimental locomotive was built in 1929, No. 6399 *Fury*, by the North British Locomotive Company, to the LMS's specifications. Using a high-pressure cylinder between the frames and two larger, low-pressure cylinders outside, it incorporated a Schmidt-Henschel high-pressure water-tube boiler system which provided high-pressure steam at 900psi, with a sealed high pressure circuit filled with distilled water to transfer heat from the firebox to the high-pressure boiler.

In original form, *Fury* never entered service but remained experimental, not being shown on the LMS stock list. On 10 February 1930, during trials, an ultra-high pressure tube burst, killing an engineer from the Superheater Company. As usual the accident was thoroughly investigated and trials resumed after repairs, continuing until 1933, after which the locomotive was laid up until 1935 when it was rebuilt by Stanier, becoming 'Royal Scot' class No. 6170 *British Legion*.

High pressure proved to be an enigma, as any economies in fuel consumption were outweighed by the extra maintenance needed.

Less adventurous, but not very successful, was an attempt to update the LNWR G2 0-8-0s with a new locomotive, the 7F 0-8-0, which despite being highly efficient, suffered from a weakness in the axleboxes that meant they were retired before the G2s! After the success with the 2-6-4Ts, there was a series of 2-6-2Ts which did not live up to their power classification of 3 because their boilers were too small due to weight restrictions. This seems to have been a recurring weakness in locomotive design.

Despite these problems, the locomotive fleet was reduced to around 9,032 by 1932, with many of the older types scrapped so that standardisation and modernisation were proceeding hand in hand. Productivity increased, with much less need for double heading and locomotives spending more time in service and less in the shed, or as the LMS was to call it, motive power depot.

In 1932, Anderson retired after William Stanier was recruited as CME from the GWR, bringing experience of the GWR approach rather than having the LMS designers simply copy and attempt to build 'improvements' of the GWR originals. D.C. Urie took over from Anderson, but Stanier was undoubtedly the more powerful figure in the company.

The Stanier revolution

The LMS had admired and envied the products of Swindon, and now they had what almost amounted to a Swindon-émigré aboard. While the preceding years had seen a lack of direction and indecision, as well as a Midland-orientated approach, Stanier laid down firm design guidelines, which in practice meant that the GWR way was the right way. In came handsome tapered boilers and Belpaire fireboxes, with low superheating and top feed, a circular smokebox on a saddle, with straight steam ports and direct exhaust passages to a jumper blastpipe,

On Great Western territory, Stanier 5MT 4-6-0 No. 5302 takes a passenger train out of Bristol Temple Meads in 1936. *(Colour-Rail 2896)*

Swindon-style axleboxes with large axle journals, cylinders with large valves. The footplatemen were not forgotten either, with better grouping of controls in a comfortable cab.

Three of the existing LMS classes were selected for incorporation of these features in new versions, with the first being the 2-6-0 in 1933, followed by the three-cylinder 'Jubilee' class 4-6-0 and three-cylinder 2-6-4T in 1934, with the latter having reduced hammer blow for use on the Fenchurch Street services. A two-cylinder 2-6-4T appeared in 1935 for more widespread use, but again, a 2-6-2T proved a disappointment and as before it was the boiler that let the design down.

Adapting existing designs meant that Stanier could also turn his attention to much needed new classes. The need for a powerful express locomotive for the demanding West Coast route emerged yet again, with the weight to be drawn increased to 500 tons without assistance, but there was also a desperate need for a new heavy freight locomotive, and for a mixed traffic 4-6-0 locomotive.

The GWR had had but one Pacific locomotive, *The Great Bear*, which had been more loved by the directors as a status symbol than by the managers, and eventually was converted to a 'Castle' class 4-6-0. Stanier was a product of Swindon, but he showed that he was not a slave to his origins. Only a Pacific could provide the power needed, and he immediately set about creating a locomotive that owed much to a 'King' class 4-6-0, but with a 4-6-2 wheel arrangement. The result was No. 6200 *The Princess Royal*, and she appeared in 1933. Next came the new 4-6-0 mixed traffic locomotive in 1934, owing much to the GWR's 'Hall' class, while the next year came the third engine, the 2-8-0 heavy freight locomotive. The last two locomotives were effectively mass-produced, with 842 4-6-0s and 852 2-8-0s built. Stanier's designs were to prove to be locomotive classics, but they had two weaknesses, the jumper blast pipe which had to be abandoned by 1936, and the low level of superheating, a GWR failing, which Stanier eventually put right.

One of the 'Princess Royal' class, No. 6201 *Princess Elizabeth*, soon showed that Stanier was right, and earned the LMS the kudos of setting its first speed record, as we will see in Chapter 12.

This is to leap ahead by a few years. The removal of the Railway Passenger Duty in 1929 on condition that the sums saved were capitalised by the railway companies and the money used for new investment to help reduce unemployment, and the availability of low-interest loans backed by The Treasury in the years that followed saw the LMS do its best to modernise. In 1934, new works amounted to £8.4 million, well over £525 million by today's prices, and a proportion of this was devoted to new rolling stock providing 232 steam locomotives, 159 new boilers for rebuilding of older locomotives, 674 new carriages and 5,365 new wagons, as well as 80,000 tons of steel for 500 miles of permanent way to be relaid.

There was also the opportunity to experiment. The earlier forecast in the company magazine that higher boiler pressures would help the steam locomotive to have a bright future was not idle speculation. As already mentioned, the LMS had built an experimental steam locomotive

Fury with a high-pressure three-stage Schmidt-Henschel boiler, but it been very disappointing. More exciting was the collaboration with Metropolitan-Vickers (MetroVick) in which a 'Princess Royal' class Pacific was built as a geared turbine locomotive, which became known throughout the company as the 'Turbomotive'.

The logic was impeccable; geared turbines had displaced pistons for fast steamers at sea, so why not on the rails as well? Unfortunately, the experiment was not a success, and although the Turbomotive ran for 450,000 miles and remained in service until 1950, she was a liability and spent long periods in the workshops with lubrication problems and gear train failures. One problem in transferring marine technology to the railways is that ships generally do not have the constant changing of power output that is necessary on the railways, and even fast non-stop expresses are not immune to this due to permanent way slacks, or the impact of rising gradients.

Successful though they were, especially once fitted with a decent standard of superheating, the 'Princess Royal' class was in danger of being overtaken by the steady rise in train weights, meaning that something still more powerful was needed. The LNER was pressing ahead with streamlined locomotives, so the LMS had no option but to follow or appear to be backward and less glamorous. In fact, the company hedged its bets with the 'Duchess' or 'Coronation' Pacifics, many of which were streamlined, although those with the streamlined casing had it removed in the immediate post-war period.

The streamlined locomotives were truly impressive, but those without the streamlining, and the rest once it was removed, were still very attractive locomotives, and some would say that they were even more so than with the streamlining. Given the largest boiler and firebox that the loading gauge would allow, with a grate area 11 per cent larger than on the 'Princess Royals', and with the inside valve gears removed, the result was the most powerful steam locomotive ever to run in the British Isles. With scant regard to corporate identity, initially the streamlined locomotives used on the 'Coronation Scot', of which more in Chapter 10, were painted blue with white stripes, with the theme running along the rake of carriages, something that the GWR would not have allowed, one feels, but the colour scheme was changed to red with gold stripes in 1939.

This combination of steam locomotives gave the LMS what it needed, especially once the 'Royal Scots' were rebuilt.

The importance of streamlining was not purely aesthetic. The shape of a conventional steam locomotive was scarcely aerodynamic, and the railway locomotive designers were as aware as any aeroplane designer of the impact on performance of what the latter would refer to as 'drag'. It was also well known that high winds could also affect performance. The LMS Research Centre at Derby included a wind tunnel, albeit only large enough to test models, but the 'Coronation' design was tested in the wind tunnel with artificial winds and gales blasted at the model head-on from the front, sideways and at various different angles across the track.

The LMS never managed to electrify its line from Fenchurch Street to Southend, with some maintaining that the powerful tank engines used on these services were fully up to the task. This is Stanier 3MT 2-6-2T No. 99 heading a Southend train on tracks shared with the District Line at Upminster. *(HMRS AEQ608)*

This is the famous 'Turbomotive', the unofficial name of the Stanier 7P 4-6-2 No. 6202, an experimental variant of the successful 'Princess Royal' class. This attempt to harness developments in marine technology to the railways proved unreliable. She is seen here bringing an express into Crewe in 1937. Seldom photographed, and this one leaves something to be desired. *(HMRS AAL716)*

'In the result, virtually all projections and protuberances have been smoothed away, the only visible parts which are reminiscent of an orthodox locomotive being the wheels and motion,' reported the *LMS Magazine*, announcing the start of 'The Coronation Scot' expresses on 5 July 1937. It explained that the streamlining could not be extended over the motion because this would cause it to overheat. The new streamlined locomotives were to set a speed record of their own and earn the LMS much-needed good publicity. Many believe that they may in fact have been capable of higher speeds than the famous LNER Gresley A4 Pacific No. 4468 *Mallard*, but without an official record attempt, this can never be verified.

The Second World War saw Stanier called away to work for the government in 1942, and he was replaced by first Fairburn and, after he died early, by H.G. Ivatt, but in his short period in office, Fairburn produced a highly successful short-wheelbase version of the Stanier 2-6-4T which also was built in large numbers. He also did much to reduce the time locomotives spent 'on shed' being serviced.

Ivatt took over as CME in late 1945, at a time when the wartime restrictions on building new locomotives were being eased and scrapping resumed. The priority was to build new mixed traffic locomotives, and Ivatt developed Stanier's earlier designs with Class 2 2-6-0T and 2-6-2Ts, which first appeared in 1946, and the following year the last steam locomotive design to be built by the LMS, a new 2-6-0 to replace the Class 4F 0-6-0, but the prototype had a utility specification and was hardly the handsomest steam locomotive, even if it didn't quite justify the epithet of the 'Flying Pig'.

On the eve of Nationalisation, the LMS locomotive stock had shrunk from 10,316 to 8,084 steam engines, plus 54 diesels. These locomotives were far more capable and powerful, and more reliable, than those that had been replaced, and showed the steam locomotive at the peak of its powers. The reduction in numbers also showed a massive increase in productivity.

Chapter 7

Electrics, Diesels and 'Ro-Railers'

The LMS inherited the electrification work of the LYR, the LNWR, which had taken over the management of the North London Railway, although the company remained as a separate entity, and the Midland Railway. But this was in a difficult economy, and wholesale electrification was hard to justify for a railway that was primarily longer distance and goods rather than passenger. The one major electrification scheme was between Manchester and Bury, but attention was also paid to diesel shunters and later to a diesel multiple unit passenger train, as well as to diesel locomotives for high speed expresses.

The inherited electric railways had all been a reaction to the competition from electric street tramways that had made substantial inroads into the traffic for suburban steam railways, with electrification seen as the only effective counter-measure. The first such conversion from steam to electricity was the Mersey Railway in 1903 using a third-rail system. In 1904, the Lancashire & Yorkshire Railway electrified the first sections of its Liverpool–Southport line for the growing suburban traffic using third-rail 600V dc power and electric multiple units, with the first sections operational in March 1904. The network was extended to Liverpool–Aintree in 1906. Instead of sticking with the original system, experiments followed with overhead electrification on a branch line running from Bury to Holcombe Brook in 1913, and in 1916 with 1,200V dc side-contact third-rail between Manchester, Whitefield and Bury, which must have been successful as the Holcombe Brook branch was converted to this system in 1917.

The next stage was the Midland Railway on its Lancaster–Morecambe–Heysham electrification in 1908, using 6,600/6,700V ac overhead electrification.

One of the original Morecambe electric railcars, around 1935. These operated with trains of standard carriages, as can be seen here. *(HMRS AEP131)*

In the London area, the North London Railway was one of the first to suffer the impact of electric tramways, and this forced it to consider electrification. The LNWR took over operations from 1909, although the NLR remained as a separate company, and electrification was approved in 1911 as part of the LNWR's scheme for its London suburban services. Electrification was completed between Broad Street and Richmond in 1916, and then between Broad Street and Watford in 1922, using the third and fourth-rail system as adopted by the Underground Group. After Grouping, the system was extended to Rickmansworth.

There were distinct advantages and disadvantages to the different systems. Third, or even third and fourth-rail direct current (dc) required less infrastructure work as bridges and tunnels could remain unchanged, but needed many more additional sub-stations. Overhead alternating current (ac) required fewer sub-stations, but overbridges and tunnels needed higher headroom while the trains themselves lost space having to incorporate transformers. At this time, many railways using overhead electrification did so with direct current. Putting the power supply overhead had safety advantages for those working at track level, and even third-rail systems often had overhead wires in goods yards.

Apart from extending the LNWR/NLR system to Rickmansworth, the only two electrification schemes actually carried out by the LMS were the Manchester South Junction & Altrincham (MSJ&A), operated jointly with the LNER, and the Wirral lines. The eight-mile long MSJ&A was completed in 1931 and used 1,500V dc overhead collection, but for the Wirral lines, completed in 1938, 650V dc was used with third-rail to ensure efficient through working with the Mersey Railway, and the LMS trains could operate on either third or third and fourth-rail systems. This was another part of the problem as the system used not one, two or even three methods of electrification, but four. The ideal solution would have been to evaluate which system was best and convert them all, but this would only really have been justifiable if a far wider and more comprehensive scheme had been planned, and it wasn't. Even today, the Mersey Railway remains third rail.

As on other railways, electrification was accompanied by an increase in the frequency of trains, although not on the scale enjoyed by passengers elsewhere, with the average weekday service of the MSJ&A increased from 99 trains to 124, while on Saturdays the increase was from 96 to 127, but on Sundays 38 trains were replaced by 44.

The original Liverpool and Southport electrification of the LYR received new multiple unit rolling

By contrast, new rolling stock in 1939-40 for the Southport third-rail electric system were three- car electric multiple units of modern design, which compared favourably with the design of rolling stock used on the Southern Railway or the District Line. This is No. 28683 which was amongst the first railway carriages to employ monocoque construction. *(HMRS AEL125)*

stock with sliding doors in 1939–40, before wartime stringency clamped down on carriage production. These carriages were not just novel for a surface railway in having sliding doors, they were amongst the first to have monocoque construction, with bogies attached directly to the bodies.

One attempt was made to introduce a more widespread electrification scheme, and a main-line scheme at that. When H.E. O'Brien took over as the company's electrical engineer in 1924 he worked on a scheme to electrify the West Coast main line between Crewe and Carlisle at 1,500V dc using overhead wiring. This section was busy and included the massive climb over Shap. There were even tests and a design was produced for a 2-D-2 electric engine based heavily on Swiss practice. He presented the theme in a paper to the Institution of Electrical Engineers in 1924, and aroused such fury at Euston that he felt obliged to resign. Just how much the fury was that of a board and senior management that had been kept in the dark and not given a chance to approve his presentation, or that of old-guard steam railwaymen is not clear. Certainly going public without first letting his superiors know was most unwise and few companies, even today, would tolerate such behaviour.

There was one other legacy from the predecessor companies of the LMS, the battery electric shunter. Battery electric locomotives were rare in Britain, mainly used by deep-level tube railway maintenance trains, but the LMS inherited one each from the Midland, the LYR and from the North Staffordshire Railway. The fact that each of these had just one says much about the feasibility of this form of traction, but that of the Midland survived from 1913 to 1964, spending its entire life working at West India Dock, Poplar. The NSR example survives today, in preservation, in the National Collection.

The diesel

Anxious to look for improved productivity and economy, the LMS first took an interest in its shunting operations. In March 1930, four shunting engines were purchased from Sentinel that were steam-powered, but could be operated by one man. In 1932, seeking to improve the economics of sparse branch lines, trials began with a 'Ro-Railer', a bus that could run on the railway line and which would cost far less to run than a steam train that required a crew of three, while the bus would also have been able to divert into the centre of villages to pick up passengers.

This is the futuristic end of the prototype articulated diesel multiple unit, seen at Bletchley, leaving on a trip to Cambridge in 1938. The front is reminiscent of the original design for the Northern Line 1937 stock. The train was painted Post Office Red and silver. (HMRS AEU227)

The 'Ro-Railer' was based on the French Micheline, a petrol-engined bus which had solid rubber tyres fitted to the flanges of flanged wheels and could run on rails, in many ways similar to an articulated lorry in that the low-slung passenger cabin was separate from the cab and engine, with which trials were conducted in Great Britain during 1932. Later, three modifications of standard four-wheel 40-seat buses were supplied to the LMS in 1934 by Leyland. While these had basic buffers and drawgear, they lacked the power to pull a trailer. In 1936, the LMS bought two Micheline vehicles built in the UK by Armstrong Siddeley, and these achieved modest success before being withdrawn in 1939.

Far more practical was a three-car diesel unit with articulated carriages and with futuristic bow-ended driving cabs designed by Stanier at Derby. Using hydraulic transmission and six Leyland diesel engines, the train was designed to operate on secondary main lines and operate at 75mph, although on trials almost 80mph was reached. The carriages were all open, while a luggage compartment was located behind the driver's cab at each end. Seating capacity was 24 first class and 138 third class, with most of the seats reversible to allow passengers to face in whichever direction they wished. The colour scheme was described in the *LMS Magazine* as 'a distinctive exterior livery of aluminium and Post Office red.' The red was confined to the lower half of the carriages. On a trial run between Tring and Euston, the diesel unit reached King's Langley, 10.8 miles from Tring, in 10 minutes 50 seconds, while it reached almost 80mph near Hemel Hempstead.

This would hardly please the advertising authorities today – claiming diesel-electric traction to be 'electrification in its latest form'.

While the LMS maintained that it wished to discover how diesel multiple units compared with steam trains in terms of 'working costs under similar and suitable conditions', it seems that the experiment was not successful enough to justify extending the trials or converting a number of routes to this type of unit. Suitably re-gauged, it seems that it would have been ideal for the NCC main line between Belfast and Portrush and Londonderry, and for the line to Larne which was much shorter, as the double-ended dmu could have been turned round so much more quickly. Weight compared favourably with steam and conventional carriages, at 73 tons compared with 173 tons for a similar steam train, although much of this consisted of the locomotive's weight.

Arriving at the right design for a diesel shunting locomotive took some time, as this photograph of the 1936 Derby prototype shows. No doubt the design was also compromised by using a steam locomotive frame! *(HMRS AAK810)*

Meanwhile, an early experiment with diesel-powered shunting occurred in 1932 when a Midland 0-6-0T was rebuilt from steam to diesel, using hydraulic drive, but it was not a success and was abandoned. The LMS was not disheartened by this failure as it had already ordered eight diesel-mechanical shunters from independent builders, but these also proved a failure when used on general shunting duties, almost certainly because they were underpowered and

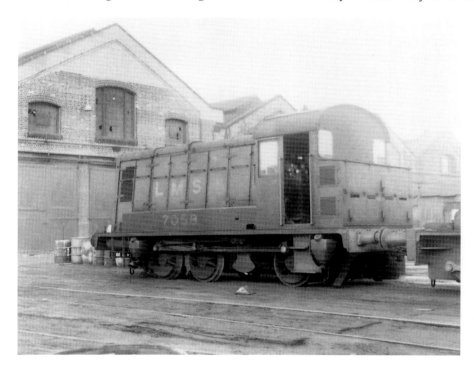

Rather more like the modern idea of a diesel shunter was this 0-6-0 prototype, No. 7058, built by Armstrong Whitworth using a 250hp Sulzer diesel engine and seen at Derby in November 1947, shortly before Nationalisation. *(HMRS AES728)*

One of the suppliers of diesel locomotives was the Vulcan Foundry, which built this 275hp 0-6-0 as a demonstrator. It is seen here being used by the LMS in 1937 handling a freight train.
(*HMRS AAW001*)

in the 150–180hp range. Far more successful was a 250hp 0-6-0 diesel-electric ordered from Armstrong Whitworth in late 1932 and delivered in 1934, when it was soon joined by a 300hp English Electric shunter.

The two more powerful shunters soon proved their worth, not only being able to work around the clock, but they also carried sufficient fuel for a week. They needed just a driver as the LMS had secured a single-manning agreement with the unions the previous year. At Willesden's Brent Yard, up to 1,000 tons could be moved by one of these shunters, using just 60 gallons of fuel in 24 hours. The difference in manning and fuel costs, as well as in availability, compared with a traditional steam shunter, was impressive. Another 20 were ordered from Armstrong Whitworth, with increased engine power.

This was not the end of the story as experience with this large batch of locomotives led to a standard 0-6-0 diesel-

Sentinel was another manufacturer of diesel shunting locomotives, although it also built steam railcars, or railmotors, for the LNER.

THE
L.M. & S.R^Y
and
"Sentinel" Patent Locomotives

Reproduced from "Modern Transport." 15/2/30.

Write for full particulars to:

The "Sentinel" Waggon Works, Limited,
Railway Department,
20, Iddesleigh House, Westminster, S.W.1.

electric shunting engine with a 350hp English Electric power unit, a cab with duplicated controls so that the driver could work with equal ease from either side, and including a supplementary speedometer with a scale graduated from 0 to 3mph for precise speed control when shunting over the hump in the modernised marshalling yards. The 600-gallon fuel tank was more than adequate for a week. Maximum speed was 20mph. The first of these was introduced in 1939, and they were clearly a great success, as despite the shortage of materials and fuel during the Second World War, another 50 were built and in service by the end of 1947.

Throughout its history, the management of the LMS was always keeping an eye on developments elsewhere in the world, and especially in the United States. The magazine included articles on operating practice on the American railways (and elsewhere as well as we shall see later). It was only a matter of time before main-line diesel locomotives were introduced, and no doubt had it not been for the Second World War, this could have happened much earlier.

The first three diesel-electric locomotives were ordered during 1946–47 when severe weather worsened the severe shortage of coal. Two were built at Derby and of Co-Co configuration with 1,600hp English Electric diesel engines, while the third was a Bo-Bo built by the North British Locomotive Company using an 800hp Paxman diesel and was intended for secondary main lines and cross-country services. The first of the two main-line locomotives, which could be used in tandem, was No.10000 and was completed just before Nationalisation so appeared with the raised letters 'LMS' on her side casing, but the second, No. 10001, appeared after Nationalisation. As prototypes, both performed reasonably well given that there was no infrastructure for their maintenance and much work was done in the less-than-satisfactory surroundings of a steam shed, but the third, which appeared in 1950, well after Nationalisation, was underpowered and had a short operating life. In fact, British Railways, which learned so much about steam locomotives from the LMS, failed to learn the lessons for diesel-electric main-line locomotives, and its first generation of these contained far too many types that were underpowered, and even followed the LMS in ordering many that were too small, once again for secondary services.

While this advertisement for 'Oil Electrification of Railways' was hardly much better. This was a time when Britain was the major exporter of railway locomotives and rolling stock.

Chapter 8

Carrying the Goods

Only the LNER was more heavily dependent on goods traffic than the LMS. The fast expresses might have had the glamour and the fame, and the suburban and branch line services the face of the LMS to many people, along with the holiday excursion trains, in terms of effort this was primarily a goods railway, or to be more precise a freight* railway. When it was first formed, the LMS gained 60 per cent of its turnover from freight, which amounted to about a million tons per route mile annually, but as the years of the Depression took their toll this figure began to drop, and it was then that the massive effort put into modernisation and standardisation began to show rewards.

Looking back over the literature of the period, one gets the impression that the railways were very much caught on the back foot by the tremendous growth in road haulage following the First World War. There is a lot of truth in this, and in the fact that the railways were hampered first by their 'common carrier' obligation that ensured that they had to carry any freight offered, and then by the Railway Rates Tribunal, which governed how much they could charge for any of the railways' traditional traffic. The range of goods carried by the railways at the time was far wider than today, when the railways have been able to cherry pick and have lost traffic such as parcels and sundries, for example. If you wanted to move house, or even move a whole farm, you contacted your local station. There were even instances, not at all uncommon, of a circus including the animals being moved by train. New forms of traffic, often requiring express freights, were more profitable. The railway companies employed salesmen, at the time known as 'canvassers', to sell their freight services. Incentives were offered to customers, including a number of free passes for their directors or senior managers, with the number dependent on the volume of business provided.

Giving the road competition a hand? Goods vehicles included many specialised types to handle the wide variety of traffic carried by the railways, with well wagons ideal for these single-deck buses being delivered in 1938. *(HMRS AEU225)*

*While most of us consider 'freight' to be an American term and 'goods' British, not only the LMS, with its penchant for American practices and terminology, but also the GWR used the term 'freight'. The LMS, some have pointed out, always seemed to be unsure about which to use as its official publications and advertising could speak of goods depots and freight vehicles.

The period after the Grouping coincided with growing industrial instability while traffic fell from the artificial peaks of the war years. Anxious to stimulate traffic, in 1923 freight rates were reduced from 112 per cent to 75 per cent above the pre-war rate. Nevertheless, costs had risen considerably during the period of state control, and traffic was falling. Estimates for Britain's railways as a whole suggest that the total of railborne freight reached 367 million tons in 1913, and then went on to peak at more than 400 million tons during the First World War, and then, except for a recovery during the Second World War, went into steady decline from 1919 onwards.

For most of Britain's railways freight was the main business, with the only exception amongst the 'Big Four'

A rear view of the goods yard at Settle, where, no doubt, the opportunity to unload vans and wagons while sheltered from the Pennine weather was appreciated in winter. The loading gauge outside was there to check there were no over-height loads being despatched on to the system. *(HMRS ACW323)*

being the Southern Railway. The LMS came second only to the LNER in the ratio of freight-to-passenger turnover and this would have been even higher in 1936 had it not been for the years of recession and also the loss of many export markets for coal during the Miners' Strike of 1926. Oddly, the LMS, which prided itself on being efficient and forward-looking, and in the van with new ideas, could also refuse to countenance change. It was to the fore in the introduction of containers so that loads could be transferred easily from road to rail and then back again, but the concept of abandoning wagonload freight in favour of trainload freight between railheads was, as we shall see, a step too far.

Freight problems

Freight brought many problems to the railways, which had gained a 'common carrier' obligation, which meant that they were forced by law to accept any traffic offered to them, provided that it could be carried by rail. There was nothing so simple as a charge of X per ton per mile travelled, as different rates applied to different categories of goods. This obligation was to become an increasing burden as road transport competition developed, able to charge what it liked and carry whatever suited that mode of transport most, often leaving the railways with the less economic loads. It is hard for us today to fully understand the importance of freight to the railways and of the railways to freight. Virtually every railway station (halts were another matter) had its own goods yard, often shared by one or more of the local coal merchants who would bag and distribute coal to their customers from the premises. These were the days when the dominant form of household heating, and in some cases cooking as well, was coal. Offices would have coal fires, so would schools. Even larger establishments would have a coal-fired boiler room for the central heating. Most households that had an electric supply only had one strong enough to provide lighting, but not for cooking or heating, let alone the range of electrical appliances to be found in the modern home.

If a farmer wished to move farms, his entire stock of animals and equipment would travel in a train specially hired for the purpose. People moving house over anything other than a short distance would often have their belongings loaded into a demountable container aboard a lorry,

A 20-ton double bolster wagon, No. 725740, just out-shopped from the works. *(HMRS AAS012)*

which would take it to a railway station where it would transfer to a flat truck for the rest of the journey. The circus usually arrived by rail rather than by road, with the final procession from the railway station being through the streets.

Freight, or goods, traffic was classified either as 'full load' taking a whole wagon or goods van, and what was variously known as 'smalls' or 'sundries', smaller consignments but different from parcels, which were often carried by passenger train and charged at a higher rate. The smalls traffic suffered delays while waiting to be consolidated into mixed loads, in which a van or wagon full of these smaller consignments would be grouped together, all travelling to the same goods station or depot, but for a number of different consignees. Bulk traffics such as coal often provided a full train-load rather than just a wagon or two; a huge number of goods wagons were owned by industrial customers of the railways and could be seen around the system carrying their owners' names and in some cases their colours as well. The coal mines were major owners of goods wagons, but so too were many of the larger coal merchants.

Private-owner coal wagons could not be used for other traffic when being returned to their home base, so they ran empty back to their collieries. The location is not known in this 1934 view of a train hauled by a Fowler 0-6-0. *(HMRS AEV127)*

Private-owner wagons were the bane of many a railway manager's life. They could not be used for other traffic and had to be returned to the premises of the owner, as well as being generally looked after by the railway while away from their owners' premises. Long trains of empty coal wagons that could not be used for anything else did little for railway productivity, the railwaymen would argue, although having sent a train of fifty or more empty coal wagons to a coal merchant, it is hard to see what could have been carried on the return.

There was another problem with private-owner wagons, which was that they were built to the often limited and outdated specifications of the owners, rather than the railway. So while the railways, including the LMS and GWR, might want to increase the size of its goods wagons and introduce continuous braking to permit higher speeds, a typical wagon owner such as a coal mine would want to persist with short-wheelbase two-axle wagons because of the tight curves on their premises. Many wagon owners wanted the cheapest and simplest wagon possible. Handling in many industrial sites, and especially collieries with tight curves and limited clearances above the mines (the surface goods wagons were too big to go underground), was often primitive and only the unbraked wagon, operated loose coupled, was acceptable. When larger coal wagons were introduced, the mine owners largely ignored them as they were too big for the lines in their collieries, leaving the LMS to use its new fleet of 40-ton wagons for coal deliveries to its own power station.

While special arrangements were made for whole trains for a particular freight customer, and some of these had regular timetables, for wagon-load and less than wagon-load freight a steam locomotive and guard's van would operate what was known as a pick-up freight, calling at station sidings and collecting whatever wagons or vans that were ready to move. There were also other goods trains that went from one station to another dropping off wagons and vans. Unless the station was busy enough to justify its own shunting locomotive, the locomotives of these goods trains would spend much of their time shunting wagons, something that was made more difficult and time-consuming as they always had to ensure that the guard's van was at the back of the train before continuing with their journey. This was just in case a wagon coupling failed so that guard would have time to alert the nearest signalman and place detonators on the track to protect the train.

The collieries were not the only users of private-owner wagons, as shown in this 1927 view of a Shell tanker wagon used by one of its distributors, the Lisbon Coal & Oil Fuel Company. *(HMRS ABP312)*

One of the most satisfactory locomotives for mixed traffic was the Stanier 5MT 4-6-0, such as No. 4869, seen here with a train of goods vans in 1947. Unlike many photographs taken at this time, the locomotive is reasonably clean and the number is clear to see. Post-war, a number of these locomotives were converted to burn oil, until a balance of payments crisis led to the programme being abandoned. *(Colour-Rail 12079)*

Obviously the wagons collected by the pick-up freight would need to be sorted and sent onwards to their destinations. This was done in marshalling yards, and the LMS was to the fore in introducing a new style of marshalling yard, with humps so that wagons could role down the slope using gravity and be directed into different sidings depending on their final destination. In the older yards, locomotives would push the wagons into sidings, often letting them roll away. Wagons were stopped by simply bumping into another wagon, or by shunters running alongside to apply the brakes, but this was usually when running on the level. Damage to wagons was often severe, and their contents often fared badly as well, but measures were put in hand between the wars to minimise this damage, with growing use of steel wagons and even shock-absorbing underframes.

Goods trains were classified as either fully fitted, that is with many of the vehicles having vacuum-brakes that could be controlled by the locomotive driver, or unfitted, that is with no continuous braking system. On unfitted goods trains, each wagon had only a simple handbrake that could be applied in a siding or if the train was checked on a steep gradient, otherwise braking was left entirely to the locomotive and, in an emergency, the guard's van. Such trains ran at speeds of around five or ten miles per hour. Stopping would be accompanied by a clatter as the wagons ran into one another. Fully fitted freight trains were allowed to travel much faster, provided that the rolling stock could do this safely, and the permitted speed depended on the proportion of wagons or vans fitted with the vacuum brake, which automatically applied the brakes once the vacuum was broken, as would happen if the wagon became uncoupled from the rest of the train. Not all wagons were necessarily fitted with vacuum brakes on express goods trains, and there were some variations with those trains having between one-third and one-half of the wagons fitted with vacuum brakes allowed to run at speeds of up to 45mph, while with less than one-third of the wagons fitted with vacuum brakes, the speed was reduced to 35mph. This was still an improvement over the speed of an unfitted goods train.

Many smaller customers had their goods collected or delivered from the goods station or depot by the railways' own fleet of road vehicles, and even between the wars many of these were still horse-drawn although petrol and diesel vehicles were steadily taking over. Two of the most practical of the new vehicles were designed with handling railway work in mind. These were the Scammell Mechanical Horse and the Karrier Cob, both of which were three-wheeled tractors with incredible manoeuvrability introduced in 1930. On Nationalisation, the new British Railways inherited some 6,000 of these vehicles from the 'Big Four' railway companies. Other vehicles introduced at this time were 10cwt (or half-ton) light vans supplied by the Yorkshire car and van manufacturer Jowett, as well as 6-ton Albion lorries. By 1934, the collection and delivery motor fleet was covering 20 million miles annually.

In common with the other railways, the LMS employed salesmen, known as canvassers, who sought business from firms that were likely to become freight customers. Through running of trains or wagons between the different companies produced a fair volume of accounts to be settled, and as with passenger traffic, this was done by the Railway Clearing House. There was overlap and competition at various points on the LMS's network with the GWR in particular, and also occasionally with the LNER, and so an agreement was reached between these companies that they should coordinate their activities as far as goods business was concerned. The Southern Railway was not a party to these arrangements, but as already mentioned, was a comparatively minor player in the freight business.

The Railways Act 1921, which created the 'Big Four', laid down what it described as 'standard revenues', or what would be described as profits, which each of the companies could make each year. For the LMS, its standard revenue was fixed at £20.6 million, a 4.8 per cent return on its capital value. By 1937, the actual standard revenue earned was just £14.4 million, a shortfall of £6.2 million. The Railway Rates Tribunal was in theory supposed to be able to remedy this by allowing the company to adjust its charges, but was unable to do so adequately given the weakness of the economy. Sir Josiah Stamp, the chairman, was always an eloquent and effective advocate of the case for the railways, but even he failed to make a difference.

There were four ways in which the railways could re-establish their competitive edge. The first was to speed up the longer distance goods trains, which also required them to increase the number of vehicles that could be braked by the locomotive, with trains either being unfitted or unbraked (except by hand), partly fitted with a number of wagons having vacuum brakes, or fully fitted, meaning that most and ideally all vehicles could be braked. The second was to introduce containers that could be easily and quickly transferred between road and railway vehicles. The third was to modernise the goods yards, creating large marshalling yards with a hump, so that wagons could be sorted as they ran down from the hump on to different tracks so that longer distance goods trains could be assembled. The fourth way was to improve the collection and delivery of goods, and from its inception until the outbreak of the Second World War the LMS made massive strides in the mechanisation of this activity, which in 1923 was for the most part dependent upon horse-drawn vehicles: magnificent, but hardly productive.

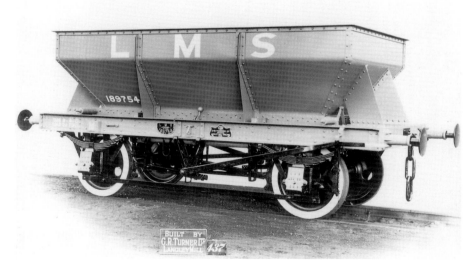

A new 20-ton steel hopper wagon, No. 189754, for aggregates and similar loads, supplied by an independent builder in 1929. (HMRS AAY309)

The LMS started life with 9,100 heavy horses, many of which won prizes for their presentation at agricultural shows, where no doubt they also helped to keep the name of the company before the audience. By comparison, there were just 1,350 motor vehicles or, in the language of the day, 'road motors'. The LMS handled 12,350,000 tons of freight annually, and 43 million parcels. The freight figure excluded bulk shipments such as coal, of which the company was carrying 85 million tons annually by the early 1930s. The collection and delivery service cost the LMS £3,250,000 to provide, equivalent to about £220 million today, and in its staff magazine, the company pointed out that on the other side of the Atlantic, the US railroads expected the customers to bring their consignments to the goods depot and collect them as well.

In one year, 1934, the company built no fewer than 5,365 goods wagons, and also bought another 2,000 specifically for express freight.

While the more glamorous passenger trains were accelerated at intervals, the LMS did not ignore its freight trains. An entirely new category of train was introduced for longer distance freight, known as the 'Maltese Cross', each of which included at least four vacuum-braked vehicles, improving braking and so allowing higher speeds. Of course, alongside the major innovations were many smaller improvements all of which contributed to the progress that was being made. New oil axleboxes eliminated the need to inspect wagons every 80 miles or so, and more powerful locomotives were introduced for goods under the 'scrap-and-build' policy mentioned earlier. A new freight locomotive was introduced in 1924, but this was a 4-6-4T version of the LYR's 4-6-0, and was ordered before the Grouping. Ten of these 'Baltics' were built at Horwich.

With the benefit of hindsight, the single most important development for which the LMS can take credit was the introduction of containers, the first of which appeared in 1926. By the following year, the company had no fewer than 400 containers, a number which rose steadily to 3,713 by mid-1933, so that by the time of Nationalisation more than half the 19,358 containers received by British Railways came from the LMS. These, of course, were not the container that we are used to seeing today, being much smaller, and looked more like an enclosed goods wagon body, so that they could not be stacked.

The first major goods yard to be mechanised was Toton 'Down', near Nottingham, but operations at many smaller yards were also analysed with the objective of reducing shunting movements. By 1933, the LMS was able to boast that 70 per cent of all consignments were delivered the following day, and 94 per cent by the second day after despatch.

The LMS was a strong supporter of the use of containers to ease transhipment between road and rail, although the containers were much smaller than those of today and could not be stacked. This is 4-6-0 No. 25791 with flat wagons carrying a container on the first wagon and a trailer on the second. *(HMRS ABT908)*

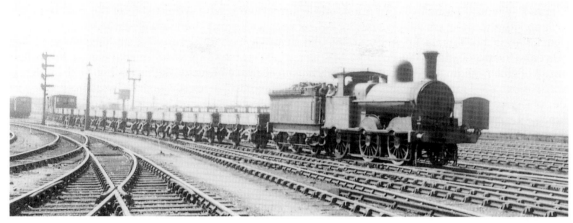

Not all goods workings are revenue-earning, and this is a ballast train being headed by Webb 'Cauliflower' 2F 0-6-0 No. 8518 in 1935. *(HMRS AEP135)*

This is not to suggest that the LMS was ever in the van of progress and always forward looking. It may have looked across the Atlantic for inspiration and imported American management techniques, but it could also be very ingrained in its ways and even backward looking. One of the company's largest freight customers was Unilever, the manufacturer of washing powders, soap and very much else, and the director responsible for its transport was one Frederick Smith. It was Smith who suggested that the future of railway freight and the only way to make it both efficient and profitable, was for the railways to concentrate on trainload business between major railheads. An unseemly row followed, with Stamp adopting the LMS line. Smith was to be proved right in the long term as this was one of the conclusions drawn in the early 1960s by none other than Dr Richard Beeching. Had Stamp listened to Smith, such concepts as Freightliner might have emerged some thirty years earlier.

King coal

The LNWR was struggling to cope with paths north of Carlisle, and especially with the long steep ascent to Shap summit. Long, slow freight trains did not mix well with the fast expresses hurrying towards their destination, and even in LMS days a fast goods train was normally booked to run at 30mph, and sometimes much more, while the expresses aimed for at least twice that speed. At one time, building a relief line, or even a tunnel under the summit of Shap, was considered. Either would have been costly. With Grouping came the second route, the Midland, which with the LYR lines over which the Midland had gained running powers, provided the necessary relief.

The figure of 85 million tons of coal mentioned earlier included 9 million tons of coal either for export, often through the company's own loading equipment at its ports, or as bunker coal to power merchant ships. Coal merchants were the main tenants at goods yards, while coal was taken away from around 800 collieries.

The long, slow through goods train carrying coal to a major customer, or perhaps for the railway's own use, or building materials including aggregates, such as ballast, again for the use of the railways, was bottom of the pecking order. Fast, scheduled goods trains were at the top of the pecking order, with many scheduled to run overnight.

In late 1929 the LMS did, nevertheless, introduce 30 40-ton wagons for coal for its own power station at Stonebridge Park, providing power for the electrified lines of the former LNWR.

The coal trains had open wagons, and were slow moving, so they were the ideal target for the dishonest in British society. Coal was stolen from wagons if they stopped, or from the sidings, and in some cases the lines were greased so that the locomotive struggled and as it came to a crawl, it would be boarded by men, and even women, who would shovel the coal over the wagon sides to their associates waiting below with sacks and even wheelbarrows!

The impact of this traffic on the shape of the railway is hard for anyone under the age of, say, 50 years, to appreciate today. For the LMS, its biggest marshalling yard for coal was at Toton, just south of Nottingham, where coal was bought from almost a hundred collieries, before the wagons were marshalled into long trains for onward movement to power stations, railway motive power depots, gasworks, heavy industry such as iron and steel works, and to hundreds of goods yards, large and small, where the coal merchants waited. The busiest route for the long coal trains from Toton was that to Brent, in north-west London close to Hendon and Cricklewood, and at Brent the trains would be broken up and shorter trains would then work through to the LMS depots in and around London, at Brockley Lane, Clapham Wharf, Knight's Hill and Walworth Road, and, of course, to the yards of other railways, of which the most important were Acton on the GWR and Brixton, Feltham and Hither Green on the Southern.

Long-standing agreements also meant that the LMS had goods yards well away from its own network. The long coal trains often had to be moved off the main line, and at Wellingborough there was a massive set of holding sidings and a large engine shed where many of the locomotives used on the coal trains were kept, and even a hostel for the footplatemen firing and driving the coal trains. The Midland had been far-sighted enough to build a special route for the Toton–Brent coal trains for part of their journey, separating them from the express passenger lines, and this ran from just south of Wellingborough to just north of Bedford and avoided Sharnbrook Summit which had a 1-in-120 gradient, by using a tunnel. Even so, from Bedford to Hendon the coal trains were using the same lines as outer suburban stopping trains and often had to be diverted into a siding to allow the passenger trains to pass. Until the centralised control system was introduced, there were tales of footplatemen being relieved by a fresh crew while their train was stationary in a siding, and eight hours later the new crew being relieved without their train having moved an inch, but, of course, it was still consuming coal and water as the fires were kept ready for the off! South of Hendon, at Silkstream Junction, the goods lines diverged away from the passenger lines and arrived at Brent via a flyover.

At the outset, the LMS was faced with using a variety of often ancient locomotives on this and on other major freight routes. In an attempt to accelerate the coal trains, the Lickey 0-10-0 banker, 'Big Bertha', was tried, but was not a success. Then the LMS ordered massive Garratt articulated locomotives from Beyer Peacock, but instead of allowing this company – experienced in the design of these locomotives, most of which were exported – to produce a standard design, the LMS insisted on using standard Midland parts, so that the resulting locomotives produced a fairly mundane performance and were little better than a double headed 0-6-0. In the end, a solution came from the much less exotic and more economical new Stanier 2-8-0s, and these really made a difference.

A humble goods train but with dramatic lighting and smoke effects as Stanier Class 5 4-6-0 pulls hard through Stainforth cutting in 1939. (HMRS ACW525)

6004 ex-LNWR 'Claughton', rebuilt, had power classification 5XP, but is seen here looking in need of some attention taking a freight train out of Crewe in 1946. Typical of the condition of many locomotives after wartime neglect she is so dirty that her number cannot be seen. *(Colour-Rail 12475)*

Fast freight

Not all goods trains were slow; carrying relatively low value items such as minerals and coal, there was a growing market for fast goods trains for perishable items. As the great cities grew, milk had to be brought daily over longer distances, while fish and meat were other foodstuffs that justified faster workings and insulated wagons. Special wagons were included in the fleet for fruit, including bananas. Interspersed with these items was another perishable traffic, but not one that could be digested, at least in the usual way, and that was newspaper traffic. Often the newspaper trains ran in the opposite direction to the milk trains, but there were instances of both types of commodity on the same train.

Efficient handling of freight requires not only fast running and a lack of delays on the line, but also attention to transhipment at each end of the journey. Special loading docks were used for items such as milk, often using platforms in passenger stations, while newspapers were usually handled in passenger stations and often the special vans would be part of a passenger train. The LMS's espousal of containers capable of being lifted from road trailer to railway wagon and back within minutes undoubtedly helped as well.

The LMS is generally regarded as having made impressive strides in improving the productivity of its freight operations by the outbreak of war in 1939. The control systems and the improved locomotives it placed in service from Grouping onwards contributed much to the war effort. Through running of trains or wagons between the different companies produced a fair volume of accounts to be settled, and as with passenger traffic, this was done by the Railway Clearing House. As already mentioned, there was overlap and competition at various points on the LMS's network with the GWR and the LNER, and so an agreement was reached between these companies that they should coordinate their activities as far as goods business was concerned.

One advantage of using locomotives rather than diesel or electric multiple unit working was that the same locomotive could work a Manchester to Blackpool commuter express, and then switch to working a fish train from Fleetwood, just to the north of Blackpool, to Broad Street in London. This was just the sort of work the famous Stanier 'Black Fives' were designed for. Such traffic was profitable and most of it was regular, worked daily, while there were, of course, seasonal markets for freshly-picked fruit or vegetables 'in season' or when a cargo of bananas or oranges arrived at a port. Many of these trains ran over long distances, with a regular milk train from Carlisle to London, with many of its wagons having come to the line from Stranraer or others from the line to Maryport. Further still was the Aberdeen to Broad Street fish train, with its load for Billingsgate.

Such trains did not crawl along at the 5mph or 10mph of the coal trains and unlike the coal trains did not have to wait in a siding while a passenger express raced past. These trains, or rather their loads, were so important that they were scheduled as tightly as a passenger express, and one ran at 46mph between Crewe and Willesden. Others were not quite so fast, running at around 30mph. The centralised control system inherited from the Midland was a major feature, and while originally intended to make sense of the chaos on the lines in the South Yorkshire and East Midlands coal fields, it became system-wide and was based on telephonic communication between district offices and all signalboxes, stations, yards and engine sheds. Under the LMS, the system grew with four divisions: Midland, which extended down to London and Bristol; London & North Western, which reached Workington at one end and London at the other, and went as far east as Huddersfield; Lancashire & Yorkshire, which was centred on Manchester; and Scottish, which included Carlisle, although strangely did not extend north of Glasgow or Edinburgh. The Midland Division had 24 district control offices, the London & North Western had 18, the Lancashire & Yorkshire just one, while Scottish had six.

The standard of operation varied considerably between these divisions, with Manchester being up-to-date with the technology of the day, with a large display of miniature track plans with coloured lights to show the position of trains. As a result, the Lancashire & Yorkshire division really was centrally controlled. At some of the district offices in the other divisions, the system could be primitive, with coloured cards, an absence of displays, and controllers telephoning signalboxes or engine sheds and goods yards using telephone booths.

To run safely at such speeds, the trains had to be 'fitted', with most or even all of the wagons vacuum-braked.

The LMS took sufficient pride in this control system to publish a booklet on it in time for the British Empire Exhibition at Wembley in 1924–25.

The 'Fair Deal' campaign

The pressure by the railways to be released from their onerous restrictions on charges and the common carrier obligation contributed to a growing interest in transport by the government, but when restrictions on competition occurred, they were aimed more at restricting road transport than liberating the railways. The first step was the Road Transport Act 1930, which required road haulage to be licensed, with a system of 'A' licences for hauliers, 'B' licences for manufacturers and traders who also wished to be able to hire out their vehicles, for example after making a delivery so that they did not run home empty, and 'C' licences for manufacturers and retailers to deliver their own goods to customers. The 'C' licences were granted automatically, but a case had to be made for the 'A' and 'B' licences after the initial issue to existing operators under grandfather rights.

Passenger transport legislation and licensing came next, in 1933, with only private hire coaches exempt from the need for a road service licence, which was necessary for stage carriage work, express services and excursions and tours. Again, after grandfather rights had been granted to existing operators, these had to be applied for and objectors could seek a hearing. The objectors were often competitors, who would argue that existing bus or coach services were adequate, or even not making enough money, but they could also include the railways. All in all, this was a system of transport rationing.

Finding that the Road Traffic Acts 1930 and 1933 had not helped the situation very much, the 'Big Four' launched a 'Fair Deal for the Railways' campaign arguing against the restrictions. War intervened and state control of the railways for the duration put an end to the campaign, so we will never know for sure what the outcome might have been. The omens weren't good. The public opinion poll to end all public opinion polls was Mass Observation, which started to survey public opinion before the outbreak of war and continued for some years afterwards. One of its first surveys was on public reaction to the 'Fair Deal' campaign, and it found that many were either completely uninterested or believed that the railways were, in effect, protesting too much.

As always, there was scant public sympathy for railway management.

Chapter 9

The Best Railway Carriages

The LMS was predominantly a goods, or freight, railway, but it also had a substantial long-distance traffic being the railway for passengers to Northern Ireland, and competing with the GWR between London and the Midlands, and between England and the newly formed Irish Free State, and with the LNER on services between London and Scotland, as well as between London and Southend. The great cities, already almost conurbations, of Birmingham, Manchester and Liverpool were firmly in its area. Not only in London, but in these other cities and in Glasgow, the LMS also had a substantial suburban traffic.

The relative importance of the different traffic handled by the LMS can be gained from a 'receipts barometer' published in the *LMS Magazine* early in 1934. In 1933, passenger turnover amounted to almost £24 million, while that for general merchandise totalled £23.5 million and for coal and coke the figure was £11.5 million, meaning that the total for all goods was £35 million. In other words, 40.7 per cent of the business was passenger and 59.3 per cent goods of all kinds.

An idea of the importance of the LMS to London's railways can be gained from the fact that when the London Passenger Transport Board was established in 1933, and all passenger transport operators within its area, which stretched out as far as Watford and beyond Tilbury, had to pool their receipts after deducting costs, the LMS share was 5.1 per cent. This was almost five times that of the GWR, but only a fifth of the Southern Railway's share, and a percentage point below that of the LNER. So the LMS was important, but not by any means the biggest.

Services from St Pancras to the East Midlands improved in speed and frequency between 1922, above, and 1938, next page. (*Bradshaw*)

LONDON, LEICESTER, NOTTINGHAM, DERBY, SHEFFIELD, LEEDS, and SCOTLAND.

Down. — **Week Days**—Continued. — **Sundays.**

	aft	aft	aft	aft	aft	aft	ngt.	ngt.	ngt.	mrn	mrn	mrn	mrn	mrn	mrn	mrn	mrn	mrn	mrn	aft
LONDON (St. Pancras)..dep.	..	9 30	..	..		1120	1150	12 0	12 5	1220	..	..	8 0		9 0	9 30	9 45	10 0	1015	1030
Luton ...."	..	..	..	..		..	1233	12 45			..	..	9 11		9 49			1043	1058	..
Bedford (Midland Rd.)..."	..	..	..	..		..	1 2	1 13	1 19	1 29	..	..	9 53		1016	..		1111	1134	..
Oakley	..	..	..	..		..					..	..	9 59		..	..				
Sharnbrook	..	..	..	..		..					..	..	10 7		..	..				
Irchester ....[685, 690	..	..	..	..		..			1 41	1 51	..	..	1018		..	..				
Wellingboro' A 472, arr.	..	1045	..	..		..					..	..	1022		1038	1047			1153	
Northampton B.... {arr.	F	1120	..	..		1123					..	..	1059		F					
412, 470, 472, 685 {dep.	8V30	..	..	..							..	..	9 42		V					
Wellingboro' A.........dep.	..	1047	..	..		1145			1 49	1 56	..	..	1028		1040	1050			1159	
Finedon	..	..	..	..		..					..	..	1035		..	..				
Burton Latimer, for Isham..	..	..	..	..		..					..	..	1035		..	..				
Kettering 692 ......arr.	..	1058	..	..		1156			2 0	2 7	..	..	1040		1051		11 8		1210	
677 Cambridge ....dep.	..	..	..	..		Stop					..	..								
Kettering ....dep.	..	11 0	11 5	1116					2 3	2 12	..	..	1045		1054		1111		1213	
Glendon and Rushton C..	..	..	..	1123							..	..								
Desborough and Rothwell D	..	..	..	1130							..	..	11 7							
Market Harboro' 470, 471,	1043	..	..	1137					2 21	2 30	..	..	11 5		1116				1233	
East Langton ....[895	1050	..	..	..							..	..	1125							
Kibworth	1057	..	..	..							..	..	1132							
Great Glen	..	..	..	..							..	..								
Wigston (Magna)	11 7	..	..	..							..	..	1143							
Leicester (Lon. Rd.) { arr.	1116	1135	..	..			2 6	2 17	2 43	2 51	..	..	1126		1151		1213	1254	1250	
688, 690 {dep.	..	1142	..	..			2 14	2 24	2 50	2 58	8 55	..		1142				1250	1235	
Humberstone Road......	..	..	..	..							8 58	Stop		Stop						
Syston 690	..	..	..	..							9 5									
Sileby F	..	..	..	..							9 11									
Barrow-on-Soar and Quorn ..	..	..	..	..							9 17									
Loughboro' (Mid.) 844 ...	..	..	..	..					3 9	3 17	9 24		12 0					1 18		
Hathern	..	..	..	..							9 32									
Kegworth	..	..	..	..							9 37									
Trent 680, 696 ......arr.	..	1212	..	..					3 21		9 43		1213				1 29	1259		
Nottingham 692, { arr.	..	..	1234	aft			2 10		3 48		10 0	mrn	1231		12 5	1225		2 8	1 20	
696, 698, 700, 900 {dep	..	..		12 5			2 18				6 17	9 20	9 55		1215	1230				
Trent ....dep.	..	1215	..	1222					3 23		9 48	10 9					1 31	1 3		
Derby 656, 664 ......arr.	..	..	..	1239			2 52	2 59	3 38	3 41	1011	1025					1 46			
528 Stoke-on-Trent ...arr.	..	..	..	Stop							1135									
664 Buxton .... "	..	..	..	..							Stop	12 8								
664 Manchester (Cen.) .. "	..	..	..	..					5 25	5 25										
664 " (Victoria) "	..	..	..	..					6 12	6 2										
664 Liverpool (Central). "	..	..	..	ngt.					7 7	9 35		mrn								
Derby ....dep.	..	..	..	1235			3 10	3 22			6 55	11 2			1115				1136	F
Chesterfield 697, 701	..	..	..	1t10			3 21	4N2	4N14		8 c3	1139			1154	1 21	1 17			
Sheffield 669, 699, {arr.	..	..	..	1 35	mrn		3 50	4 23	4 37		8 44	12 8			1219	1 27	1 42			
704, 904, 911 {dep.	..	1 14	..	2 10			3 55	4 37	4 49		9 20				1225			1 59		
Rotherham (Masboro')	..	..	..	Pf			4 5	4 47	4 59		9 35				1235			2 5		210
Parkgate and Rawmarsh	..	..	..	..							9 42									223
Kilnhurst	..	..	..	..							9 47									233
Swinton 695, 704	..	..	..	..							9 50									237
704 York ....arr.	..	..	..	..																
704 Newcastle (Central) "	..	..	..	..																
Wath-on-Dearne	..	..	..	..							9 57									243
Darfield	..	..	..	..							10 2									248
Cudworth 686	..	..	..	..			4 23	4 30	5W7	5W20	1011									350
Barnsley P 686, {arr.	..	..	..	..			5 40	4056	5 40		1045									240
904, 918 {dep.	..	..	..	..							9 58									
Royston and Notton......	..	..	..	..							1017									3 2
Sandal and Walton	..	..	..	..							1025									310
Normanton 554, 945	..	..	..	3 10	4 42		5 23	5 36			1031		1 10					2 41		318
554 Wakefield (K'kgate) arr.	..	..	..	3V15			5 41	9 31			1126		2 21							
554 Huddersfield ...... "	..	..	..	5Y26			7d33	6 40	10 17		1235		2 59							
554 Halifax .... "	..	..	..	3Y58			5d30	6 54	10 50		1235		3 27							
945 York 947 .... "	U 2L55	..	..					8 12	9Q5				2 6							
826 Newcastle (Central) "	U 5L10	..	..				1047	12 4					4 20							
Altofts and Whitwood	..	..	..	..							1040									322
Methley 616	..	..	..	..							1045									327
Woodlesford	..	..	..	..							1050									332
Hunslet ......[934, 947, 952	..	..	..	..																
Leeds ♦ 706, 712, 933a, arr.	..	1 59	..	3 27	5 5		5 58	6 1			11 3		1 35					3 0		343
952 Harrogate ....arr.	..	..	..	L 4 38			8 15	8 2					3 1					5 12		512
712 Ilkley 952 .... "	..	..	..	t6 53			8r30	8K47			2r36		2X54					6r9	6r9	
706 Bradford R ...... "	..	2 49	..	j 4 36	5 38		6 57	7 9			1 39		2 35					4 10		521
706 Carnforth .... "	..	..	..	..			8 55	9 26										8 12		812
706 Morecambe T ..... "	..	..	..	..			9 0	9 35										8 16		820
706 Carlisle.......... "	..	4 38	..	..			1044											5 50		
714 Glasgow (St. Enoch). "	..	7 31	..	..			1A34	s										8 32		
714 Edinbro' (Wav.)..... "	..	..	..	..			1r31	s										8c35		

Typical of the rolling stock inherited by the LMS, is this rake seen at Saltley in 1934, by which time clerestory carriages were out-of-date. The end carriage is a brake third, and the next two are composites. *(HMRS AAG235)*

The Midland's inheritance that had proved so limiting in terms of the locomotive power available to the LMS was quite the opposite when it came to passenger rolling stock. The Midland was the railway that was first to care for *all* of its passengers. The process started in the mid-1870s when the bold decision was taken to abolish second class and withdraw all of the relatively small number of third-class carriages. This meant that third-class passengers suddenly found themselves enjoying the delights of second-class carriages for the same fare. This may seem illogical today when the question that springs to the lips of many would be 'why didn't the Midland abolish third class' instead? It couldn't, as it had to use third class for its Parliamentary trains and in any case, with other railways still offering three classes it would have been a move too far, although second class started to disappear generally from this time onwards.

Midland conservatism did have an impact on carriage design, nevertheless, as it was one of the first to introduce carriages with clerestory roofs, and one of the last to stop building them, so it was not until just before the outbreak of the First World War that semi-elliptical roofs appeared. The Midland was also slower to provide corridor connections between carriages, so if you wanted to take advantage of their excellent dining cars, you needed to move carriages at a station, or one could spend the entire journey wining and dining in the dining car. One did not have to wait until joining the train to reserve a seat in the dining car, on the prestigious two-hourly expresses between London and Manchester one simply telephoned St Pancras or Manchester Central the day before to reserve a seat, and there was no booking fee!

The last carriage built by the Somerset & Dorset Joint Railway, a lavatory composite, before Highbridge Works closed in 1929 and the Southern Railway took over responsibility for carriages. The LMS did the same for locomotives. *(HMRS AAC408)*

Midland carriages were comfortable, had more coats of paint than a Rolls-Royce motorcar, but were still wooden-framed on a steel underframe.

The LNWR provided the most carriages for the LMS on Grouping, more than 5,000, but these were a mixed bag. On the plus side were the West Coast Joint Stock, which included magnificent 12-wheeled dining and sleeping cars, and the 12-wheeled corridor coaches built for the appropriately named 'Corridor' train that ran from Euston to Aberdeen, Edinburgh and Glasgow, and back. There were also the boat train sets for Euston-Liverpool, then the Cunard Line's port for its sailings to and from the United States and Canada. On the debit side were the very many elderly carriages built during the 1880s and 1890s, which the LNWR saw no reason to scrap so long as they could still move. In between, there were some reasonable corridor and non-corridor sets for secondary expresses and suburban traffic.

The Lancashire & Yorkshire Railway had a number of unexciting corridor carriages for its longer services, plus the club cars for the services between Manchester and Blackpool, but for the most part its rolling stock consisted of non-corridor carriages of varying ages. Of the other English railways, the only one to have any corridor carriages was the Furness Railway for use on through trains operating onto the LNWR, but for the most part this company, and the North Staffordshire as well as the London Tilbury & Southend, catered for a predominantly local traffic.

North of the border, the Caledonian Railway also contributed a very mixed bag of rolling stock to the LMS pool. The company had its share of the West Coast Joint Stock, but instead of dining cars provided Pullman cars on its principal trains. While the Glasgow–Aberdeen service had excellent 12-wheel 'Grampian' corridor coaches, passengers on many branch lines and suburban services, had to make do with four or six-wheel non-bogie stock. This was conservatism carried to the *nth* degree as in 1922, just before Grouping, new four-wheeled suburban carriages were introduced to Edinburgh's Balerno branch. The Glasgow & South Western also had a varied collection of carriages, but did at least have some restaurant cars, unlike the Highland Railway, which despite the length of some of its routes, such as those to Inverness and Wick, had no restaurant cars and just a few corridor carriages, suggesting that north of the border one was expected to have a strong bladder.

Looking as if it belonged on the other side of the Atlantic, this is a former LNWR sleeping saloon, No. 297238, dating from 1898 but converted by the LMS as staff sleeping quarters, was based 'somewhere in Scotland' in 1936. (*HMRS AAH227*)

The traveller to the Highlands of Scotland enjoyed a more frequent and faster service in 1938, bottom, than in 1922, top, but true high-speed running was inhibited by much single-line working north of Perth. *(Bradshaw)*

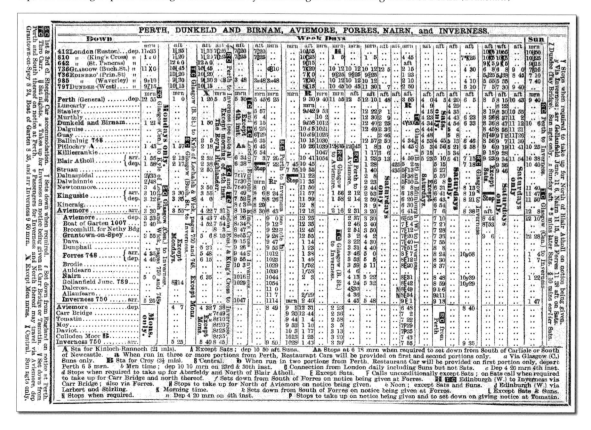

Today, when there are basically just two lengths of passenger carriage, 20 metre and 23 metre, equating to 65ft 8in and 75ft, it is strange to note that the LMS had carriage lengths ranging from 26ft for a four-wheel carriage up to 65ft, while widths varied between 8ft and 9ft. The lack of bogies on the four-wheeled carriages meant that the ride was very much rougher, even on good track.

As with the steam locomotive fleet, there was no standardisation and the policy once again had to be one of 'scrap and build'. The passenger rolling stock policy was left in the hands of R.W. Reid, who had been the Midland's carriage superintendent, and took up the same position with the LMS.

Towards a standard carriage

Standardising rolling stock could only go so far. Non-corridor carriages might seem like an anachronism, even in the 1920s, but they were, and remain, the best means of getting the maximum number of seats into any one carriage, and have the advantage that they are very quick to load and unload. At the time, even corridor carriages were built with side doors to each compartment and indeed the Southern Railway persisted with this kind of design even as late as 1938. This arrangement also increased seating capacity, despite the corridor and lavatories, but there was another reason for the enduring popularity of a side door on to the platform, which is that many passengers did not like having to move luggage along corridors. Nevertheless, as large picture windows became more popular by the end of the 1920s, the LMS was building carriages of this pattern having built ones with side doors shortly after Grouping. These had small opening windows above the main picture window, which itself could be dropped, with rotating vanes that could be set by passengers to either face or trail the passing airstream – no doubt the true reason for the adjustment was that the carriage could be moving in either direction.

As an example of the capacity of non-corridor carriages, those on the eleven-carriage trains on the Southend services from Fenchurch Street could accommodate more than 900 third-class passengers and another 120 first-class. As the overall journey time was more than an hour, two of the carriages had toilets, but as they were non-corridor, they could only be reached from a compartment on either side, so that just 14 first-class and 20 third-class passengers were able to use the lavatories.

Another question was that of open saloons versus compartments. Despite its admiration for much that was American, the LMS maintained that many of its passengers preferred to have the privacy of a compartment rather than an open saloon, but both types were built for both first and third-class passengers. On many trains the open saloons were marshalled next to the kitchen cars to allow them to be used as dining cars.

The first step forward was to standardise the dimensions of new rolling stock, with the LMS opting for 57ft in length and 9ft in width, as favoured by the LNWR and, latterly, by the Midland, although earlier it had built its rolling stock at 54ft. Despite this move and the centralisation of LMS decision-making, the standard was not set rigidly, and the company produced a few 54ft carriages when this was seen to be necessary, and even some 51ft carriages for Glasgow's Cathcart Circle line.

In addition, Reid moved quickly to modernise the basic design of the carriages and also the means of production. At Derby and Wolverhampton, carriage parts were prefabricated to speed production, so that the main production line was engaged in final assembly only and the more detailed work was handled away from it. 'All-steel' carriages were the next step, except that the roofs and window frames were still made of wood. These eased mass production, but also, from 1929 onwards, reduced the demand for mainly imported timber and provided work for the steel industry, which was hard pressed by the Depression years. This, after all, was what Churchill had in mind when he removed the passenger duty and then provided low interest Treasury loans. Considerable orders for new carriages were placed outside the company with independent carriage builders, as the company's own works could not keep pace with the demand. As a sop to conservatism, the new all-steel carriages were still lined out, even to the extent that panels, which no longer existed, were picked out, making painting an expensive business, but by this time the LMS was to build only carriages with end doors for its longer distance services.

All-steel was an apt description, but unlike the bleak rolling stock of utility design that appeared during the Second World War and immediately after, the interiors were trimmed with wood, and in later years the LMS had a small notice advising passengers of the type of wood used and its place of origin, which was always within the British Empire. Comfort was of a high order, with seats padded and sprung, which was a step forward as some of the older pre-Grouping companies had used horsehair. The new first-class compartments had just four seats so that everyone had the prized corner seat, but the first-class open carriages had one and two abreast seating, as one would find today. In 1930, windows were made deeper, while the overall carriage length was stretched to 60ft, not to increase capacity but to improve comfort, so that third-class compartments went from 6ft between partitions to 6ft 6in, while first-class went up to 7ft 6in.

The improvement was temporary, and clearly too expensive at a time of financial hardship, so that carriage lengths soon reverted to 57ft, and the third-class compartment was reduced to 6ft 3in, a compromise. This amount of room was also provided on suburban trains, unlike some of those on the LNER at King's Cross and Liverpool Street, which provided just 5ft 3in, which was uncomfortable even with all passengers seated, but intolerable if there were standing passengers as well.

An unusual feature of LMS corridor carriages was that the doors from the corridor into the compartments were twin doors which had to be pulled apart, unlike the single door used by most railways, although the Southern also had some of its main line electric multiple units with double doors. The double doors were often more difficult to handle than the single doors, and, of course, needed both hands, which was inconvenient if one was carrying luggage.

When Stanier became CME in 1932, the changes continued. In contrast to his work on locomotives, he did not bring GWR ideas with him for carriages, which would have been a backward step. No longer were window frames and roofs made of wood, but these too were made of steel and window frames were rounded, while sliding window ventilators were placed in the upper part of the main window for the first time. Comfort for the third-class passenger on the main line expresses was improved when compartment carriages had their accommodation reduced from eight seats to six, with armrests and reading lights, so that they almost rivalled first-class on some companies. In theory, the armrests could be lifted to allow two more passengers to sit, but once comfortably seated, few were kind enough to do this.

Carriages became completely flush-sided, enhancing the 'modern' look and no doubt contributing something to reducing drag. At first, the lining still tried to convince the casual observer that this was a traditional carriage, but by the mid-1930s this was also much simplified, with simple lines above and below the windows and below the roof, while in some carriages for more humble trains, gold paint was replaced by deep yellow. Even Stanier, the architect of even greater standardisation, produced some non-standard carriages of 54ft, 60ft, 62ft and 65ft as well as 68ft kitchen cars and sleeping cars, and 69ft sleeping cars.

All of this seems like progress, but the task facing the LMS was immense. Even under Stanier, some 50ft-long kitchen cars were built with gas lighting and cooking as some of the constituent companies had not the infrastructure to handle dynamos and batteries.

Until 1928, sleeping cars were only available for first-class passengers. That year, the three railway companies operating sleeping car services, the GWR and LNER as well as the LMS, introduced third-class sleeping cars. These accommodated four passengers to a compartment but in reality they were more akin to the couchettes found on Continental railways as the compartments could be converted back to day use, when they could accommodate eight seated passengers. They lacked the amenities such as a hand washbasin that first-class passengers were accustomed to. By the mid-1930s, purpose-built third-class sleeping cars were introduced with permanent berths, but still four to a compartment.

The 'Coronation Scot'

A 'Royal Scot' class 6P
4-6-0 *The Lancer* heads
an Anglo-Scottish
express at Carstairs
in 1947.
(Colour-Rail 12200)

The LMS had its prestigious expresses, especially those between Euston and Liverpool or Manchester, with the latter departing every two hours, and which could load to as many as 16 carriages and have four dining cars and two kitchen cars. The club trains inherited from the LYR between Blackpool and Manchester, and from the LNWR between Llandudno and Manchester, and later introduced between Windermere and Manchester, were an achievement in their own right. An opportunity to create a truly prestigious train came with the Coronation of King George VI in 1937.

The 'Coronation Scot' was in many ways the LMS answer to the LNER's rival, named simply the 'Coronation'. New streamlined steam locomotives were built, but locomotives of the same class were also built in unstreamlined form. Initially, standard LMS carriages were used, but repainted into the blue with silver stripes of the locomotives, with the lining continued down the train. Later, these were joined by specially-built carriages, which had pressure ventilation and articulation, and in 1939 the livery of the train changed to red with gold stripes. The special carriages were sent with a locomotive to the 1939 New York World Fair, spending the war there, although the much-needed locomotive was repatriated shortly after the start of hostilities.

The LMS did not ignore articulation, but did not pursue it with the enthusiasm of the LNER. As well as the articulated carriages built for the 'Coronation Scot', pairs of articulated carriages were built for excursion trains, and there were some three-carriage sets for suburban use, as well as the prototype diesel multiple unit.

Suburban electrics

While the LMS provided little new electrification itself, it did not ignore its existing electrified lines and these also received new rolling stock when the time came. Instead of sticking to a version of its standard passenger carriages, when the Liverpool and Southport line needed new rolling stock, the LMS supplied new open carriages with high-density but comfortable seating, roller-blind destination displays, and air-operated sliding doors. A total of 59 motor coaches and 93 trailers replaced the original LYR rolling stock in 1939 and 1940. These carriages were ahead of their time, being of monocoque construction, that is without an underframe and with bogies attached directly to the integral body, giving greater strength and lightness. In appearance, they were ahead of their time and compared favourably with the more traditional image of the Southern Railway's suburban rolling stock.

Chapter 10

The Named Expresses

The practice of naming trains had its origins in the late 19th century. There were two kinds of named train, the descriptive, and the formal. The former included such trains as the Blackpool, Llandudno and Windermere club trains, while the others were inspired by marketing considerations and included the 'Royal Scot' and the inter-company 'Sunny South Express', operated jointly with the Southern Railway. This is because, in considering titled trains, specials such as 'Excursion' or descriptive terms such as 'Limited' or 'Mail', are generally rejected. Purists also reject informal titles, but it can surely be argued that these gain credibility through constant use. In fact, early editions of Bradshaw did include a number of titled trains that were descriptive, and also justified their status with accelerated timings, and by 1877, there were already several of these, mainly mail trains.

Our interest centres on the titled trains operated by the LMS, and these follow in alphabetical order. There were a number of titled trains operated by the predecessor companies, including some in Scotland prompted by the strong competition between the Caledonian Railway and the North British Railway for the traffic between Glasgow and Edinburgh in the central belt, and Dundee and Aberdeen further north. Not all of these trains survived the First World War, with titles being dropped under wartime austerity and not revived afterwards until the late 1920s and early 1930s, when the LMS indulged in what almost amounted to an orgy of train naming, with the title of the 'Granite City' being revived for the main service between Glasgow and Aberdeen. The railway practice of describing services as 'up' and 'down' as they ran to and from London had a particular twist on the Anglo-Scottish services, as trains would run 'down' from London to the border, and 'up' to Edinburgh (or Glasgow) and then, if they continued, would run down to Inverness or Aberdeen.

On its main expresses, the LMS excelled, with many having first-class compartments that seated just four passengers, so everyone had a corner seat. In third-class compartments, there were just six seats with reading lights and armrests. Dining car service was of a high standard with freshly cooked food. Adding to the feeling of civilised travel was the facility to send one's heavy luggage in advance. This meant that the luggage could be collected from your home and delivered to your destination, with the same service available for the homeward journey, or one could have a slightly cheaper service, from departure station to destination station, or any variation of home, station and destination.

The 'Bon Accord'
- see the 'Granite City'.

'Night Mail'

Perhaps nothing sums up the glamour of the expresses, and especially those of the mail trains, than W. H. Auden's poem, 'Night Mail'. This was an age when the railways were still admired, especially by boys of all ages. There was music as well, including the piece 'Coronation Scot', which vividly conveyed the impression of a heavy steam express pulling out of a station and very rapidly (far more so than the real thing) reaching express speed. Both the poetry and the music was, of course, unmistakably LMS!

This is the night mail crossing the border,
Bringing the cheque and the postal order,
Letters for the rich, letters for the poor,
The shop at the corner and the girl next door,
Pulling up Beattock, steady climb –
The gradient's against her but she's on time.

Past cotton grass and moorland border,
Shovelling white steam over her shoulder,
Snorting noisily as she passes
Silent miles of wind-swept grasses;
Birds turn their heads as she approaches,
Stare from the bushes at her blank-faced coaches;
Sheep dogs cannot turn her course,
They slumber on with paws across,
In the farms she passes no one wakes,
But a jug in the bedroom gently shakes.

Dawn freshens, the climb is done,
Down towards Glasgow she descends
Towards the steam tugs, yelping down the glade of cranes
Towards the fields of apparatus, the furnaces
Set on a dark plain like gigantic chessmen.
All Scotland waits for her;
In the dark glens, besides the pale-green sea lochs,
Men long for news.

The Club trains

Longer distance commuting is not and never has been the preserve of the south of England. As the railways developed and Manchester grew in size, many of those who could afford it started to commute to the city from the resorts of Blackpool, Lytham St Anne's and Southport, which also became upper-class dormitory towns. What happened next was unique to Manchester commuter trains.

In the late 19th century, corridor stock was still the exception and the typical train consisted of non-corridor compartment rolling stock, although open carriages were known on the London Underground and in some countries abroad, notably the United States. The commuters from the Fylde Coast resorts to Manchester seem to have been a gregarious bunch as in 1895, they approached the Lancashire & Yorkshire Railway proposing that in return for a guaranteed number of first-class season tickets between Blackpool and Manchester paid for at above the standard rate, they should be provided with modern saloon accommodation. The LYR agreed and provided two,

Letters of thanks, letters from banks,
Letters of joy from the girl and boy,
Receipted bills and invitations
To inspect new stock or visit relations,
And applications for situations,
And timid lovers' declarations,
And gossip, gossip from all the nations,
News circumstantial, news financial,
Letters with holiday snaps to enlarge in
Letters with faces scrawled in the margin.

Letters from uncles, cousins and aunts,
Letters to Scotland from the South of France,
Letters of condolence to Highlands and Islands,
Notes from Oversees to the Hebrides;
Written on paper of every hue,
The pink, the violet, the white and the blue;
The chatty, the catty, the boring, adoring,
The cold and official and the heart's outpouring,
Clever, stupid, short and long,
The typed and the printed and the spelt all wrong.

Thousands are still asleep
Dreaming of terrifying monsters
Or a friendly tea beside the band at Cranston's or Crawford's
Asleep in working Glasgow, asleep in well-set Edinburgh,
Asleep in Granite Aberdeen.
They continue their dreams
But shall awake soon and long for letters.
And none will hear the postman's knock
Without a quickening of the heart,
For who can bear to feel himself forgotten?

later increased to three, comfortable saloons complete with an attendant serving light refreshments. The saloons were positioned in the train so that on arrival at Manchester they were close to the station exits. The homebound saloons were placed in a train that left Manchester at 5.14pm.

Not to be outdone and with upmarket resorts and dormitory towns such as Llandudno on its network, the LNWR also introduced the 'Llandudno Club Train' before the First World War. This had the longest journey of any club train, running over 87¾ miles in 2 hours 8 minutes homeward, while the morning train ran in two hours.

Much later, a third club train was introduced for passengers from Windermere, and as this ran over part of the route originally built for the Great Central Railway's Wigan branch, it ran over LNER metals for some distance. In the winter months, it travelled on lines seldom used by regular passenger trains.

The LMS continued the tradition and even replaced the original saloons of the Blackpool trains with two of more up-to-date rolling stock while the Llandudno train received the two massive 12-wheel first-class saloons originally built for the LNWR's Liverpool transatlantic boat train services. Membership of the club cars was subjected to certain rules, including the availability of a space and new members had to be elected by the existing members, to avoid anyone deemed unsuitable. A third-class club saloon was eventually introduced as well. The tradition continued up to the outbreak of the Second World War and the removal of catering facilities on most routes. Although the trains were never officially named, they were known as the 'Manchester Club Trains' and to this day commuter trains from the resorts of the North West and North Wales are known as 'Club trains', but the modern diesel multiple units have little to distinguish them, or attract passengers, let alone encourage them to offer to pay more.

The 'Comet'

Replacing an earlier up evening express running from Manchester to London Euston, the 'Comet' was first named in 1932, leaving Manchester London Road at 5.40pm initially, but this was soon put back by five minutes, with an arrival at Euston at 9.20pm. It bypassed Crewe and stopped only at Stafford, with the run onwards over the 133.6 miles to London taking just 128 minutes, making it one of the fastest trains on the LMS. Not surprisingly, the train proved to be very popular, to the extent that a relief had to be run on Fridays, leaving Manchester at 5.40pm and reaching Euston non-stop at 8.57pm.

The train was a heavy burden for its 4-6-0 'Royal Scot' locomotive with a minimum of eleven carriages, and sometimes, if extra vehicles were attached, a 4-4-0 compound was provided as a pilot.

The down train was not as deserving of the name 'Comet', leaving Euston at 11.50am and arriving at Manchester at 3.20pm. This had a six-carriage formation, but a seven-carriage rake was attached for Liverpool as far as Crewe, again making 13 vehicles, but there was usually a through composite brake for Birkenhead as well, which comprised the fastest train of the day between London and Birkenhead!

The name was dropped during the Second World War, but reinstated afterwards albeit with an overall up journey time of 3 hours 46 minutes, leaving Manchester at 5.50pm and arriving at Euston at 9.36pm, no doubt largely due to the poor state of the track after the hard use and neglect of the war years.

The 'Coronation Scot'

Although the crazy days of the railway 'races' of 1888 and 1895 were long past and since then, through Grouping, the East and West Coast companies had co-existed peacefully, the LMS could not be expected to ignore the announcement of the LNER in autumn 1936 that it would celebrate Coronation year in 1937 with a streamlined express between London King's Cross and Edinburgh. The result was the 'Coronation Scot'. The LMS did not dither, but instead, on 7 November 1936 staged a high-speed run from London Euston to Glasgow Central with the non-streamlined 4-6-2 No. 6201 *Princess Elizabeth*, handling a rake of seven carriages and covering the 401.4 miles between the two cities in 5 hours, 53½ minutes. Despite heavy rain and high winds the following day, the up journey was made by the same locomotive but with eight carriages in 5 hours 44¼ minutes, an average speed throughout of 70mph.

Although one of Great Britain's leading main lines, the West Coast route has the twin summits of Shap, 915ft above sea level, and Beattock, 1,015ft above sea level, while in between them the line drops virtually to sea level around Carlisle.

Not to be outdone by the LNER's striking Gresley A4 Pacifics with their streamlining, the LMS produced its own streamlined Pacifics for the train. Despite the outstanding timings set by the non-streamlined locomotive on the test runs, the through journey time for the 'Coronation Scot' was set at 6½ hours, including a two-minute stop at Carlisle. Many believe that even if six hours, as on the LNER service to Edinburgh, was regarded as too tight and not robust enough to allow for delays, 6¼ hours might have been attempted. An example of what could be achieved came when a test trip was conducted between Euston and Crewe on 29 June 1937. The timetable was adhered to between Euston and Stafford, but the locomotive, No 6220 *Coronation,* was then given her head, reaching 114mph past Maddeley. On the return, the 270-ton train covered the 158.1 miles in just 119 minutes, giving an average speed of 79.7mph start-to-stop. This compared with a booked time of 144 minutes for the Crewe–Euston leg. In a sense, the scheduled timings for the entire journey between Euston and Glasgow almost seem a triumph of streamlined imagery over substance.

The 'special' rolling stock for the train in fact consisted of a streamlined locomotive, but the carriages were standard modern LMS vehicles, but painted blue to match the locomotive with the white lines extended back along the carriage sides from the engine. Northbound, the rake from the locomotive consisted of a corridor third-class brake, open third class, kitchen car, two open third-class carriages, kitchen car, open first, corridor first and corridor first brake. Naturally, the reverse arrangement applied southbound.

Specially built rolling stock was introduced in 1939, with the carriages and locomotives painted LMS red, but with gold stripes replacing the earlier white. This was so logical, given the corporate identity of the LMS, to the extent that one wonders why blue and white was ever considered, let alone applied! The new carriages also included a first-class buffet lounge. The entire train was sent to the New York World's Fair that year, but although the locomotive *Coronation* was brought home during the war, the shortage of shipping space and the risks of attack by U-boats meant that the carriages were left in the US as an officers' rest train until the war ended, when they were finally brought home.

Operationally, the train replaced the 'Midday Scot', which despite its name had a 1.30pm departure in each direction, and arrival at 8pm at both Glasgow and London, with the up and down trains passing at Preston.

To travel on this 'high speed train', which did at least have an average speed over the 299.1 miles between Euston and Carlisle of 63.4mph, passengers were charged an extra 2s 6d (12.5p), regardless of class. This was probably good value as the LMS compartment stock had just four passengers instead of the more usual six in first class, and six instead of the more usual eight in third class. On the other hand, in the open carriages, it was two and four-abreast facing in first and the same in third class!

A guide book, *The Track of the Coronation Scot*, was published for passengers so that they could look out for places of interest along the route.

The train was withdrawn during the war years, and not reinstated afterwards, but in any case, the title was one that had to be short-lived.

The 'Devonian'

One of a number of trains on the old railways that happily and smoothly moved between different company operating areas, the service between Bradford and Paignton showed that even competing railway companies in the pre-Grouping days could collaborate when the market needed it. The origins of the service pre-dated Grouping, and it was not until 1927 that the 'Devonian' was finally named, and in 1937 the service was accelerated so that it provided a fast service between the important intermediate stops of Birmingham and Bristol. Although a cross-country service, the train included restaurant cars.

The southbound train left Bradford at 10.25am and ran to Leeds, where it reversed and departed at 10.52am to run to Sheffield, taking 50 minutes, stopping for 5 minutes before running to Derby in 53 minutes. At Derby, a through carriage for Bournemouth was dropped and one from Newcastle to Bristol added to the train, after which it left for Birmingham, covering the 41.3 miles in an unexciting 47 minutes. After spending six minutes in Birmingham, the train left for Cheltenham, for which it was allowed 53 minutes for the 45½ miles, which included a service stop at Blackwell before descending the Lickey incline, then running at more than a mile a minute to Cheltenham, where the stop was followed by one at Gloucester, before the 37 miles from Gloucester to Bristol was covered in 44 minutes, arriving at 3.32pm. This was one of the best cross-country timings for the day, covering the 206 miles from Bradford to Bristol in 4 hours 40 minutes, and the timings could possibly have been improved had the dwell times at some of the stations been reduced.

In winter, the three carriages being sent through to Paignton spent 18 minutes at Bristol before being taken on by a Great Western train at a much slower pace*, reaching Paignton after many stops at 6.51pm, making a through journey of 323 miles in 8 hours 26 minutes. During the summer, from May to September, the entire train continued to Kingswear, and on summer Saturdays it ran in several parts, or, as non-railway people would describe it, had one or more relief trains.

Northbound passengers spent the morning in the care of the GWR, leaving Paignton at 9.15am and not reaching Bristol until 12.13pm. The wait in this direction was even longer, at 22 minutes, before the 'Devonian' departed. The first leg of the journey to Gloucester involved a steep climb of two miles to Fishponds with gradients varying between 1 in 69 and 1 in 90, and the need to pick up a banking' locomotive for the Lickey incline. The main difference between northbound and southbound services was the additional call northbound at Burton-on-Trent, with the train finally reaching Leeds at 5.24pm and Bradford at 5.54pm. From Paignton, the northbound schedule was even longer than the southbound, taking 8 hours, 39 minutes.

Initially, the service used 'Jubilee' class locomotives between Leeds and Bristol, but before the Second World War, Stanier 'Black Fives' started to appear.

While the service was suspended during the Second World War, it was restored in October 1946, although slower by some 20 minutes, but the following year it became slower still, taking almost ten hours southbound in the summer, while the winter trains lost their name and terminated at Bristol.

The 'Fast Belfast'
– see the 'Irishman'.

The 'Granite City'

Based on a Caledonian express linking Glasgow and Aberdeen that was first launched in 1906, but lost its name during the First World War, the 'Granite City' was relaunched by the LMS in 1933, and at the same time the Pullman restaurant car that had been used in the hitherto unnamed train was also taken over as the contract with the Pullman Car Company had expired, and it was repainted in Midland red. Later, the LMS substituted its own more modern catering vehicles for those originally provided by Pullman.

The train left Glasgow Buchanan Street at 10.05am each morning for Aberdeen, returning from Aberdeen at 5.35pm every day. The LMS steadily reduced the northbound schedule to 3½ hours, which called for some tight timing as the train made eight intermediate stops over the 153 miles, including a five-minute wait at Perth. The fastest stretch was between Coupar Angus and Forfar, with 16.7 miles run in just 18 minutes, start to stop. The southbound train was allowed an extra nine minutes.

A further enhancement of the service came in 1937, with the launch of two new named expresses over the same route, 'The Bon Accord' and 'The St Mungo', which reduced the overall journey time between the two cities to just three hours and for the first time the mid-morning departure from Glasgow was balanced by a working from Aberdeen. The morning departure of the 'Granite City' was advanced and the 'Bon Accord' took its departure time of 10.05am. The departure of

---

*Much of the problem probably lay in the GWR's tendency to have leisurely stops at stations, which countered any high-speed running. In any case, by this time the fastest trains to Devon and Cornwall no longer ran via Bristol.

the 'St Mungo', named after a Scottish saint, was earlier, at 9.35am. The return workings were at 3.20pm for the 'Bon Accord' from Aberdeen and at 1.30pm from Glasgow for the northbound 'St Mungo'. Clearly these were days when few people made a return business trip between such cities all within the one day. The performance was impressive, with five minutes still spent at Perth, but the number of stops was reduced to just that city and Stonehaven for 'The Bond Accord', and Perth and Forfar for the 'St Mungo', with the 'Bon Accord' covering the 73.7 miles from Stonehaven to Perth in just 76 minutes, while even more sparkling was the 'St Mungo' running over the 32.5 miles between Forfar and Perth in just 33 minutes. Neither train ran on Saturdays.

Such performance meant that both trains were limited to just eight carriages, meaning around 260 tons empty, and were usually worked by 4-6-0 'Jubilee' locomotives.

Wartime saw the names of both trains dropped, and the dining cars were removed in 1940 with the general reduction in onboard facilities and to allow for a larger passenger load. Nevertheless, while the timings were extended by 23 minutes northbound and 28 minutes in the opposite direction, in general Scotland's internal railway services were not slowed as much as journeys south of the border, and at times the booked point-to-point timings of many trains were amongst Britain's fastest.

Post-war, the restaurant cars returned on 1 October 1945, but the names were not taken up again until after Nationalisation.

The 'Hebridean' and the 'Lewisman'

Far from being crack expresses, the 'Hebridean' and the 'Lewisman' ran well away from the main lines, and over a route that was largely single track with passing places, accompanied by tight curves and steep gradients. Both trains ran over the 63½-mile Dingwall and Skye branch built from Inverness by the former Highland Railway for passengers for the Kyle of Lochalsh, where they could catch the ferry to Kyleakin on Skye and also the packet ships to Stornoway.

It seems to have been usual for the crack named expresses to have departed when the day was well advanced, often late morning or even during the afternoon or early evening, but the 'Lewisman' pulled out of Kyle at 5.5am each morning. There was no restaurant or buffet for the traveller to seek comfort in breakfast, but there was a through coach attached for Glasgow, so that when the train reached Inverness at 8.10am, and this was shunted to the 8.35am for Glasgow, it did at last offer refreshments. This arrived at Glasgow Buchanan Street at 1.44pm, with the through passengers having travelled 263 miles in 8 hours 39 minutes, an average speed of 30.4mph! The return 'Lewisman' left Inverness at 10.15am and arrived back at Kyle at 1.40pm, and on this journey had a restaurant car.

A slightly later start was accorded the 'Hebridean' which departed from Inverness at 7.25am and which included a through carriage for Kyle that had run overnight from Glasgow, departing at 10.45pm. The 'Hebridean' reached Kyle at 10.31am, and after a short wait, started its return journey to Inverness at 10.45am, with arrival at Inverness at 2pm.

The strange pattern of these workings included using just one restaurant car for the two trains, so that the vehicle had to be transferred between trains at 12.13pm when the down 'Lewisman' reached Achnasheen, where there was a passing loop. It was as well to have an early lunch and finish quickly, otherwise one might not finish at all!

Both trains disappeared during the war, and it was not until after Nationalisation that the name of the 'Hebridean' was revived.

The 'Irish Mails'

Not a single train but usually two trains a day in each direction, and noted more for their considerable weight than for speed, with, even in peacetime, trains of up to 16 or 17 carriages being pulled along the

North Wales main line between Holyhead and Chester by a single 4-6-0 'Royal Scot' class locomotive. Pacific locomotives were used for a time during the 1930s, but the service soon reverted to the 'Royal Scots', possibly because of the demand for the more powerful Pacifics, which were really a small stud of high-performing locomotives compared to the overall size of the LMS. Departure time from Euston varied between 8am and 9am each morning, and at around the same times each evening, with arrival at Euston at about 5am and 6am and between 5pm and 6pm daily.

The morning departures were of day trains for which the restaurant cars were, reputedly, outstanding for their food and service. The night trains included both first and third-class sleeping cars, but whether the extra cost of travelling in these was worth it must be questionable, as on the down journey passengers had to leave their snug berths at 2.20am when the train reached Holyhead, and walk to the waiting ferry. Far happier was the up passenger, who could be off the ferry and in his berth by midnight, and could remain in it for some time after reaching Euston. All four trains daily included two Post Office sorting cars, with their mail bag apparatus used at Nuneaton, Llandudno Junction and the Menai Bridge, before the trains crossed over, or perhaps it should be through, the Britannia Tubular Bridge into Anglesey.

In 1939, the morning departure from Euston was at 8.45am, and the train headed northwards with a one-minute stop to pick up passengers at Watford, from which it reached the next stop at Rugby in 68 minutes for the 65.1 miles, before stopping for three minutes at Rugby. The next stop was 75.5 miles away, at Crewe, reached in 83 minutes for a nine-minute stop, largely to allow carriages to be added northbound. The last stop was at Chester, where the train spent eight minutes. It eventually arrived at Holyhead at 2.05pm. Summer Fridays saw a non-stop relief run from Euston at 8.30am, which arrived at Holyhead at 1.45pm.

The evening service left at 8.45pm officially, but the working timetable allowed an extra five minutes, and did not stop at Watford. Timings were slower, and station stops even longer, so that Holyhead was not reached until 2.20am. On summer Friday evenings, a relief ran non-stop from Euston to Holyhead, which was reached at 1.55am.

The up morning service left Holyhead at 12.40pm, took 94 minutes to cover the 84.4 miles to Chester, where it stopped for ten minutes, and later it stopped at Crewe for eleven minutes. There was no corresponding stop at Watford for the up trains, which in the mornings managed to pass the magic mile-a-minute mark between Rugby and Euston, covering the 82.6 miles in 82 minutes. Arrival at Euston was at 5.50pm. As with the down train, there was also an up relief on summer weekends.

The up night service left Holyhead at 12.13am, and reached Euston in 1939 at 5.30am. It used its postal apparatus at Bangor, Rhyl, Stafford, Tamworth, Nuneaton, Bletchley, Hemel Hempstead and Harrow.

Throughout the Second World War, the day service continued in both directions, but the night service was suspended. The wartime deceleration of railway services hit the 'Irish Mail' as much as any other, with carriages for Manchester attached between Euston and Crewe, and so despite an 8.15am start, the train did not arrive at Holyhead until 2.34pm. The timings on the up service were better, with a 1.45pm departure from Holyhead and a 7.40pm arrival at Euston, but in addition to stopping at Chester and Crewe, this train also stopped at Watford.

The night service resumed in October 1946, but later the day service had to be dropped due to competition from the airlines, and from the motorcar once drive-on/drive-off ferries were introduced.

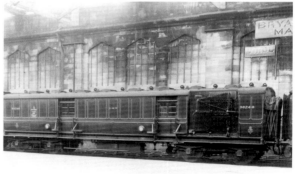

Many of the fastest night trains were those carrying the mails, with mail picked up and dropped off at speed while sorters worked through the night aboard the train. This is a daytime view of LMS mail carriages No. 30240 in the carriage shed at Whitehaven.
(HMRS AAJ315)

The 'Irishman' and the 'Fast Belfast'

The 'Irishman' and the 'Fast Belfast' both operated between Glasgow St Enoch and Stranraer, a difficult route after the long level stretch of just over 41 miles between Glasgow and Ayr, which was followed by 37 miles of steep gradients with the line for ever climbing or descending. Both trains normally included a restaurant car and were usually limited to six carriages as a heavier train required a pilot engine between Ayr and Stranraer. The more important train was the 'Irishman', an all-year-round service, while the 'Fast Belfast' was a summer-only schedule.

An oddity of the 'Irishman' service was the variation in through journey times between Belfast and Glasgow. The passenger travelling to Glasgow could leave Belfast York Road on the NCC service to Larne at 6.25pm, and be in Glasgow at 11.55pm. On the return journey, the same passenger would leave Glasgow St Enoch at 8.5pm and reach Stranraer at 10.57pm, where he had to wait all night until the ferry sailed at 6.30am, although those who could afford it could spend the night aboard in a cabin.

This was the all-year schedule, but in summer the ferry service between Larne and Stranraer doubled, and the 'Fast Belfast' was added to the timetable, leaving St Enoch at 3.50pm, with an evening crossing to Larne and arrival in Belfast just before 10pm. Travelling from Belfast, departure was at 9.28am and arrival at St Enoch at 3.28pm.

The service was popular because of the strong connections between Scotland and Ireland, and especially Northern Ireland, and in any event, the crossing between Stranraer and Larne was, and remains, the shortest sea crossing between Great Britain and Ireland, but it is also one of the roughest.

The 'Lakes Express'

The origins of this train are unclear, and there is no mention of it as a named train in the 1922 timetable, but it emerged as a summer-only service before becoming a year-round service at weekends, running from Euston to Windermere on Fridays and Saturdays, and up on Saturdays and Mondays. The summer daily service included carriages for Keswick. The service was accelerated by the LMS in 1932, and was certainly no laggard, even if not amongst the crack mile-a-minute plus brigade. The down through journey from Euston to Windermere took 5 hours 25 minutes for the 259½ miles, and ten minutes longer in the up direction, but much time was spent detaching carriages in the down direction and picking them up again in the up direction.

The service left Euston at 12 noon, reaching Rugby in 88 minutes for the 82.6 miles, where it waited for eight minutes, before departing and running non-stop to Wigan, taking 117 minutes for the 111.4 miles. At Wigan, carriages for Preston and Blackpool were detached, while there was also a connecting service to Southport. Leaving Wigan at 3.37pm, the train continued to Lancaster which it reached at 4.30pm and detached yet more carriages for Barrow-in-Furness and for the leisurely journey by the coastal route to Maryport, which could be reached more quickly by staying aboard the train or, even quicker, by catching the 'Coronation Scot' and changing at Carlisle.

At Oxenholme, the train made its final division, with a Keswick portion first away, followed by the main part of the by now much-reduced express, for Kendal and Windermere.

The up train left Workington at 9.05am, while other portions left Keswick at 9.59am and Penrith at 10.47am, with the main portion leaving Windermere at 11.15am. The complete train left Oxenholme at 11.53am and ran to Lancaster and Preston, where there was an eight-minute wait while the Blackpool carriages were added. It then ran non-stop to Crewe and made just one further call, at Bletchley, before running on to arrive at Euston at 4.50pm.

The train included three catering vehicles – an open first and an open third with a kitchen placed between them – all of which were in the Windermere portion, with a first-class corridor brake and a third-class corridor brake, and two other third-class corridors. It was normally worked by a 'Jubilee' class 4-6-0 locomotive. In wartime, while the name was dropped, the service survived, but as carriages attached to other trains, while the through journey took 7 hours 20 minutes to Windermere.

Post-war the service was revived, but curiously it made an unannounced call at Crewe to drop the carriages for Barrow and Whitehaven, which then repeated the main train's calling pattern with stops at Wigan, Preston and Lancaster.

The 'Lancastrian' and the 'Mancunian'

The 'Lancastrian' and the 'Mancunian'' were the two sides of a railway express balancing act, and both were unnamed until 1928.

The 'Lancastrian' evolved out of an unnamed LNWR evening express from Euston to Manchester and Liverpool, but as traffic grew, both these destinations gained a train of their own rather than the portioned working that sufficed at first. By the time of the LMS accelerations of 1932, the train departed from Euston at 6pm and ran non-stop for the first 176.9 miles to Wilmslow, reached in 176 minutes. Arrival at Manchester London Road was at 9.15pm, not quite a mile-a-minute for the 188½ miles. The train was formed from the London end as a first-class brake, first-class corridor, open first, first-class restaurant car, kitchen car, third-class restaurant car, followed by six or seven third-class carriages that were a mixture of open and corridor stock. Initially, the train was worked by 4-6-0 'Royal Scot' class locomotives, but before the Second World War, 4-6-2 Pacific locomotives started to take their place.

The balancing working up to Euston was the 12.05pm from London Road, but this used a different route, running via Stoke-on-Trent, on which the axle load restrictions meant that the locomotive power was limited to a 4-6-0 'Patriot' or 'Jubilee' class, while the first stop was at Stockport where carriages from stations in East Lancashire were attached, after which the train continued to the next stop at Macclesfield, after which a steep climb followed for which a banking engine was provided. The train then continued to its last call at Stoke-on-Trent. Arrival at Euston after a mile-a-minute run of 145.9 miles in 145 minutes was at 3.40pm, so that the up train was considerably slower overall than the down, but the train was also heavier, at around 14 or 15 carriages, while the locomotive power was less.

For those wanting a faster service south, the up 'Mancunian' was the train. Departing London Road at 9.45am and running non-stop from Wilmslow, the express started its journey behind a 2-6-4 tank engine, with the express locomotive taking over at Wilmslow having previously collected through carriages from Colne, Huddersfield and Rochdale. Despite a heavy load, the 176.9 miles from Wilmslow to Euston were completed in just 172 minutes, giving a 1pm arrival, a 3¼-hour journey. This train was also the preserve of the 'Royal Scots' until the Pacifics took over.

As with the 'Lancastrian', the return journey of the 'Mancunian' was slower, with a 'Patriot' or 'Jubilee' for motive power and running via Stoke-on-Trent, but unlike its counterpart, the train was lighter and carriages for Northampton were removed at Bletchley. Leaving Euston at 4.10pm, after Bletchley the train called at Rugby and Lichfield, then Stoke-on-Trent, Congleton, Macclesfield and Stockport, with arrival at Manchester London Road at 8.05pm.

The lack of true balance between the up and down trains seems odd to us today, and especially to those more familiar with routes with highly standardised calling patterns. Once again, we can see that business trips were spread over a longer period than today, and no doubt the passengers were not too concerned.

During the Second World War, the trains continued but unnamed and with different departure times, and much slower running as the trains were heavier, sometimes having to draw forward at stations so those in the rearmost carriages could alight, and the state of the track made true high-speed running difficult. Even when the 'Lancastrian' was reinstated on 7 October 1946, with a 6pm departure from Euston, it took 3½ hours to reach Manchester.

The 'Lewisman'
see the 'Hebridean'.

The 'Mancunian'
see the 'Lancastrian'.

The 'Merseyside Express'

Originally, the LNWR had an express departure from Euston each evening that included portions for both Liverpool and Manchester, and usually some through carriages for other destinations in Lancashire. This left at 5.30pm, but as traffic grew and restaurant cars increased in popularity, it became necessary to provide Liverpool and Manchester each with its own train. Initially, the Manchester departure was put back to 6pm and the 5.30pm became a train for both Liverpool and Fleetwood. It was not until 1905 that Liverpool gained its own train at 5.55pm, running non-stop to Edge Hill, although before long a stop was added at Mossley Hill.

The train ran for more than two decades without a name, and it was not until 1927 that the LMS named it the 'London–Merseyside Express', shortening this the following year to the 'Merseyside Express'. In 1932, it swopped departure times with the accelerated 'Lancastrian', departing Euston at 6.05pm with a 3 hours 20 minutes schedule for the 189.7 miles to Mossley Hill, and reaching Liverpool Lime Street at 9.40pm. At Edge Hill, two carriages were detached for Southport, which they reached at 10.30pm.

In the opposite direction, the train left Liverpool at 10am and arrived at Euston at 1.30pm, but later was accelerated to arrive at 1.20pm. The Edge Hill stop was cut out for the up train as the carriages that had left Southport at 8.50am were run into Liverpool and attached to the front of the 'Merseyside Express'. The train ran from Mossley Hill to Euston, 189.7 miles, in 189 minutes.

By the late 1930s the train was heavy, with 15 or more carriages, including two sets of dining cars and a kitchen car between two first-class dining cars and a third-class restaurant kitchen car with a third-class dining car, plus a first-class open lounge brake of the kind built for the 'Royal Scot'.

Wartime saw the usual slowing down of the service, an earlier departure, the dropping of the name, and a reversion to Manchester and Liverpool-portioned working. The train took an hour longer than in peacetime.

The return of peace saw the train depart from Euston at 5.45pm from 7 October 1946, and the journey time cut to 3 hours 55 minutes. It was not until after Nationalisation that the train reverted to its old departure time of 6.05pm.

The 'Midday Scot'

Although the train was introduced in 1889, it was not until 1927 that the 'Midday Scot' gained its official title. An earlier title used by railwaymen, and enthusiasts, was 'The Corridor', marking the fact that from 1893 it became one of the first LNWR expresses to consist entirely of corridor stock. In any case, at this time the train did not leave Glasgow until 2pm. On the other hand, this remained one of the LNWR's finest trains with the original corridor rolling stock replaced as early as 1908 with a set of 12-wheel carriages described by many as the most magnificent seen in Great Britain up to that time, or indeed for many years afterwards. The train included, from the Glasgow end, a brake third-class, composite restaurant car, composite carriage and brake third for Glasgow; composite restaurant car, composite carriage and third-class brake for Edinburgh; a composite brake for Aberdeen, and two more, one for Whitehaven and one for Altrincham. The last mentioned was detached at Crewe and worked via Sandbach over the Cheshire Lines.

The train survived the First World War and towards the end of the conflict it was the only day working between London and Glasgow.

The 'Midday Scot' streaks through Stafford in March 1938 headed by Fowler 6P 'Royal Scot' class 4-6-0 No. 6103 *Royal Scots Fusilier. (HMRS AEU 219)*

Post-Grouping, the development of the service was at first hindered by an agreement between the pre-Grouping West Coast and East Coast groups of companies that Anglo-Scottish trains should take a minimum of 8 hours 15 minutes, a throwback to the races of the late 19th century. 'The Midday Scot' was one of the services to enjoy an accelerated schedule, with the timings coming to eight hours southbound, although northbound the train required an extra five minutes, and these timings were later reduced by a further five minutes despite adding a stop at Lancaster to those at Symington, Carlisle and Crewe in the up direction. When the Pacifics replaced the 'Royal Scots', which had to be changed at Crewe, the locomotives were able to run through unchanged.

In May 1936, the train's departure time from Euston was moved back to 2pm, with another express taking its post-Grouping departure at 1.30pm and allowing the 'Midday Scot' to run non-stop over the 158 miles to Crewe in 163 minutes, with a new stop at Penrith. The train continued to divide at Carlisle for Glasgow and Edinburgh, while Edinburgh and Aberdeen portions parted company at Lockerbie. The Glasgow portion arrived at Glasgow Central at 9.35pm, while Edinburgh Princes Street was reached at 9.55pm.

When the 'Coronation Scot' was launched in 1937, 'The Midday Scot' ceased to provide a through London–Glasgow service, although a Glasgow portion remained for passengers joining at intermediate stations, and the train was reduced to six carriages at Euston, although a Great Western carriage was picked up at Crewe and, later, through carriages from Manchester to Glasgow and Edinburgh were marshalled into the centre of the train to make division easier. While Edinburgh passengers arrived earlier, at 9.45pm, those to Glasgow arrived later than before, at 9.55pm, and did not have a restaurant car after Carlisle.

The train continued to run, unnamed, for most of the Second World War, although there were lengthy periods when it was cancelled. It became a very long London to Glasgow train with 15 or more carriages, but no catering vehicles. It left Euston at 1pm and reached Glasgow at 9.58pm. An additional stop was made at Watford in the up direction.

Post-war, the train received its restaurant cars on 1 October 1946, and from 7 October 1946 the departure from Euston was changed to 1.15pm, but it did not reach Glasgow until 10.05pm.

The 'Night Limited'/'Night Scot'

Strangely, while the East and West Coast groups had agreed not to cut their day services to less than 8¼ hours between London and Glasgow or Edinburgh, there were no such restrictions for overnight services. So there arose the peculiar situation, which may well have been unique, that the overnight trains were actually faster than the day trains. The East Coast companies reduced their times to Edinburgh to 7¾ hours, but the LNWR allowed eight hours to Glasgow. Following the First World War, the West Coast train became much more popular and heavier, so the timings were slackened yet again, and an 11.45pm departure from Euston meant a 9.35am arrival at Glasgow. However, to some extent this was compensated for by the insertion of a couple of restaurant cars at Carlisle, so that the Glasgow-bound traveller could at least arrive having breakfasted. He would also have had a chance to read the morning newspapers, picked up during the stop at Symington.

Overall, the train stopped at Rugby, Crewe, Preston and Carlisle, where it was overtaken by a train that had left Euston at 12.20am. It was a heavy train with upwards of six 12-wheel first-class sleeping cars, a couple of third-class sleeping cars, a composite carriage and two corridor third-class carriages, as well as two brake vans, plus the two-car restaurant and kitchen set that ran between Carlisle and Glasgow. No restaurant vehicles were included on the southbound train. The up 'Night Scot' had the distinction of running non-stop from Glasgow to Crewe, a distance of 243.3 miles, a remarkable achievement for the 4-6-0 'Royal Scots' working the train because it also had to contend with the summits of Beattock and Shap, between which the line descended to sea level around Carlisle. Not surprisingly, by the late 1930s the train was gradually handed over to Pacific locomotives.

Along with other trains, the name was dropped in wartime, and the departure from Euston was moved forward to 9.15pm and the train lengthened, often to as many as 15 carriages and sleeping cars. It was so popular, not least because of the absence of most of the day trains, that often three trains were needed to meet the demand, but most of the carriages were standard day vehicles with just a few sleepers. The train did at least arrive earlier at Glasgow, at 6.15am, meaning that this was that rarity, a wartime train that was actually faster than its peacetime equivalent. The earlier departure from Euston was, of course, to give the train a better chance of being away from London before the nightly Blitz started.

The train reverted to its peacetime schedule and formation in May 1946.

The 'North Atlantic Express'

Not to be confused with the Southern Railway's 'Atlantic Coast Express', the 'North Atlantic Express', surely one of the most ambitious titles ever coined for a named train, was operated by the Northern Counties Committee of the LMS. The construction of a loop line and new viaduct at Greenisland meant that trains between Belfast and Portrush or Londonderry, the NCC's main line, no longer had to reverse. The new Class W 2-6-0 locomotives also provided the power that an accelerated service required and so the 'North Atlantic Express' was introduced between Belfast and the resort of Portrush, on the north coast of County Antrim. To match the new

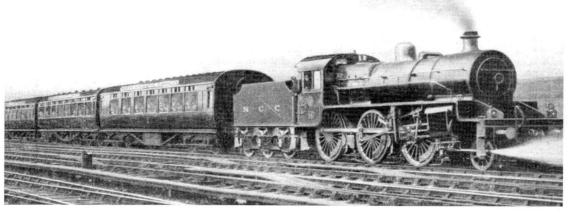

One of the grandest names for a British express was the 'North Atlantic Express' which ran from Belfast to the resort of Portrush along the Northern Counties Committee line. The LMS lost little time in sending some non-standard 2-6-0 locomotives to improve the locomotive stud of the NCC, where they were Class W.

locomotives, the LMS built three new carriages with the first picture windows on NCC rolling stock, with one of the coaches being completed as a buffet car. A year after its introduction, two additional carriages were built.

The new service was launched on 1 June 1934, and at first covered the 65¼-mile run in 80 minutes with a stop of just one minute at Ballymena, but in the years that followed, timings were tightened so that by 1938, the service took just 73 minutes, despite half the route being on a single-track railway. Between Ballymena and Belfast, the service met the 'mile-a-minute' standard with the 31 miles covered in 31 minutes. From 1935 onwards, with the additional carriages in service, when the morning service arrived at Belfast these were detached and quickly connected to the boat train for Larne Harbour.

As with most named trains, the service was discontinued on the outbreak of the Second World War.

The 'Northern Irishman'

While the most direct route for the railway and ferry passenger from London, the Midlands and the North West of England, has been via Heysham, with non-railway alternatives from Liverpool and Fleetwood, the short sea crossing between Stranraer and Larne has always had the appeal that it was shorter. This was just two hours against eight or more on the routes from England, even though the hour or so outside the sheltered waters of Loch Ryan tended to be the roughest stretch of water between the mainland and Ireland. The route was not at its most attractive to passengers until the completion of the Port Patrick & Wigtownshire Railway in 1862, which provided a direct route between Dumfries and first, Port Patrick and then, later, Stranraer. Before that, journeys involved travelling via Glasgow and the traveller completing two sides of a triangle.

BELFAST, ANTRIM, PORTRUSH, and LONDONDERRY.—Midland (Northern Counties of Ireland).

Sec. and Man., James Cowie, Belfast.

(Bradshaw timetable — Down, Week Days and Sundays — station list: Belfast (York Road), Greencastle, Whitehouse, Whiteabbey, Jordanstown, Greenisland, Mossley, Ballyclare Junc. 896, Doagh, Templepatrick, Dunadry, Antrim 887, Cookstown Junction 893, Kellswater, Ballymena 896, Cullybackey, Glarryford, Killagan, Dunloy, Ballymoney 898, Macfin, Coleraine 896, Portrush 893, Coleraine, Castlerock, Downhill, Magilligan, Bellarena, Limavady Junction, Broighter, Limavady 895, Limavady, Broighter, Limavady Junction, Ballykelly, Carrichue, Eglinton, Culmore 902, 904, Londonderry 887.)

a Stops when required. b Stops to take up on informing Station Master. † Waterside Station.
¶ "Halts" at Monkstown, between Greenisland and Mossley; and Muckamore, between Dunadry and Antrim.
☞ For OTHER TRAINS between Belfast and Antrim, see page 837; between Belfast and Greenisland, see page 897.

The Northern Counties Committee shared in the improvements introduced by the LMS between the wars, with faster and more frequent trains, helped by the new viaduct at Greenisland. The 1938 timetable on the opposite page compares favourably with that for 1922 above. *(Bradshaw)*

BELFAST, ANTRIM, PORTRUSH, and LONDONDERRY

Down — Week Days

	mrn	mn	T	mn	mrn		T	mrn	mrn	mn		T		aft	aft	aft	aft	S	aft	aft	aft	aft	T	aft
Belfast (York Road)...dep.	..	625	7A25	8 0	9 20			9A45	9 55	1045	1150	1200	1250	1 15	1 25				1 40	2 25	2 35	255	3 25	3 45
Whiteabbey	..			8 9							3 cl.								1 50		3 cl.			
Monkstown Halt ¶	..										Aa								V		Aa			
Ballyclare Junc	..	640																	3 cl					
Doagh	..	645																	Aa					
Templepatrick	..	651																				Aa		
Dunadry	..	656		826					1020	Aa									2 9			Vv		
Muckamore	..	7 1		830					1024	Aa									2 12			Vv		
Antrim 1109	..	7 6		835				1015	1029	1117		1230		1 52					2 16		3 8		412	4
Cookstown Junction 1120	..	715		842					1037	Aa									2 22		Vv			
Kellswater	..			850					1045										2 29					
Ballymena arr.		7278	0	857				1030	1052	1131		1245	1125						2 36			427	5	
Ballymena dep.		7298	2					1034	1055			1248	1126	2 7		2 25			2 36		3 23	430	5	
Cullybackey		736		Stp					11 2	Stop				2 16		Stop						437	5	
Glarryford		744							1110													445		
Killagan		749							1115													450	Stop	
Dunloy		754							1120													455		
Ballymoney 1120	8 5	8 31					11 0	1133		1 21				2 17	2 37						4 1	5 8	
Macfin	816	8 42									1 32												
Coleraine arr.	816	8 42					1111	1145			1 32			2 48							4 42	519	
Portstewart	828	8 54		1034			1128	1248		1 46		B			3 14		3 39			423	4	533	
Portrush 1120 arr.	833	9 0	mn	1040			1134	1254		1 20	1 52	2	52	353	4		3 20	aft	3 45		429	4	539	aft
Portrush dep.	7 45		8 20	910			1055		mrn		1 15				2 20						430	5	
Portstewart	7 54		8 28				11 3		G		1 23			S		2 29			Stop		437	5	
Coleraine dep.	8 5		8 45	922			1116			1150		1 45		2 55		2 37					524		
Castlerock	8 15		8 55				1127			12 6		1 55		3 4							5 46	535	
Downhill Halt	8 19		8 59							1210		1 59									5 50	Stop	
Magilligan Halt	8 25		9 5							1217		2 5									5 56		
Bellarena			9 11							1224		2 11									6 6	aft	
Limavady Junction ¶ arr.			9 19				1142			1233		2 19									6 14	550	
Limavady ¶ arr.			9 33				12 2														6 33	6*6	
Limavady ¶ dep.			9 5				1133														*535	6	
Limavady Junction ¶..dep.			9 20				1145			1234		2 20									556	6	
Ballykelly Halt										1239											6	
Carrichue Halt										1242											6	
Eglinton										1253		2 31									6	
Culmore Halt										1 1		2 37									6	
Londonderry (W.) arr.	8 55		9 40				12 5			1 12		2 45									616	6	

Down — Week Days—Continued. / **Sundays.**

	aft		aft	aft	aft	T	aft	aft	S	S	aft	aft	aft	mn	mrn	T	mrn	aft	aft	aft	aft	aft	aft
Belfast (York Road)...dep.	5 15		5 15	5 45	555	620	633	8 50	9 0	8050	1030	1040	845	9 30	9A45	11 0		225	315	530	7 0		845
Whiteabbey							A	3 cl										3 cl	3 cl				3 cl
Monkstown Halt ¶							Aa					Aa						Aa	Aa				Aa
Ballyclare Junc																							
Doagh															10 4								
Templepatrick															1010								
Dunadry			6 11			657	Aa	9 26			11 6				1015			341	556				911
Muckamore			6 14			7 0	Aa	9 29			11 9							344	559				914
Antrim 1109			6 18			7 49	22	9 33	9 17	922	1057	1114	912		1023			349	6 47	27			919
Cookstown Junction 1120			6 24			710	9 29			927		Aa	918		1031			356	611	7 33			995
Kellswater			6 31			716	9 37								1039				7 41				
Ballymena arr.	5150		5 50	6 38		658	723	9 44	9 32		1112	1131		10 9	1046			4 7	622	7 48			977
Ballymena dep.	5152		5 52			7 0	724		9 34		111?			1010	1047			220		7 49			
Cullybackey						7 7	733				1120				1054			227		Stp			
Glarryford							746								11 2					Vv			
Killagan							750								11 7					Vv			
Dunloy							754								1112					Vv			
Ballymoney 1120						729				10 0	1141			1035	1124			250		8 26			
Macfin															Aa								
Coleraine arr.						740				1011		1152		1046	1135					8 37			
Portstewart			6 31	710	754					1023		12 0		1054	1146	1213	3 7	330					
Portrush 1120 arr.		6 35	6 37	716	8 0	aft				1029		12 6		11 0	1152	1219	313	345	aft				820
Portrush dep.			6 40		745					9 10	10 10	0								730	Stop		820
Portstewart			6 48		755					9 18	10 8									738	aft		822
Coleraine dep.			6a54		7448	6				9 27	1019				1143					750	8 10	843	
Castlerock					754	817				9 39	1029				1153					8 18	8 20	851	
Downhill Halt						829				9 44					1157					8 58	8 24		
Magilligan Halt						835	Stop			9 51					12 3					811	8 30		
Bellarena					8 9	843	aft			10 2	1044				12 9					817			
Limavady Junction ¶ arr.					822	856				1018					1217					825	8 42	9	
Limavady ¶ arr.					755	830				9 50										3 54	921		
Limavady ¶ dep.																							
Limavady Junction ¶..dep					811	843	8 56			10 6	1045				1218					826		9	
Ballykelly Halt						9 1									Aa					830			
Carrichue Halt						9 4									Aa					833			
Eglinton						9 15									Aa					844			
Cu'more Halt						9 23									Aa					852			
Londonderry (W.) arr.					831	9 59	34	1026	11 5					1245					9 1				

A Refreshment Car to Londonderry.   Aa Sets down when required.   s Rail Bus 3rd class.   a Arrive.   ß By Bus
Bb Sets down when required on Sats. only.   d' Thro Carr. Dublin (dep 9 20 mrn Sats) (via Antrim) to Portrush, page ...
G Refreshment Car to Portrush.   Cc Sets down when required except on Sats.   d Depart.   G Stops at Public Crossings
when required.   J Thro Carr, Larne Harbour (dep 9 20 aft) to Portrush in connection with Stranraer Steamer, page 113a.

The LNWR was not convinced that the route had any merit, worse still, it competed with its own services. It was the Midland Railway that introduced a sleeping car express between London St Pancras and Stranraer. On Grouping, the LMS transferred both the Heysham and Stranraer Irish services from St Pancras to Euston. During the Second World War, the service became so popular that often two sleeping car trains were sent in each direction nightly. This was because the short crossing meant that the packet ships were exposed to possible U-boat attack for a shorter period than the longer crossings, while in any case, there was a shortage of ships as many ferries had been taken up from trade to augment the war effort, many serving as hospital ships.

Nevertheless, the wartime service often left Euston as early as 4.50pm instead of the peacetime 7.40pm, again to reduce the exposure to the nightly Blitz.

The 'Palatine' and the 'Peak Express'

Before the Grouping, competition for the lucrative traffic between London and Manchester was intense between the LNWR at Euston and Manchester London Road, and the Midland at St Pancras and Manchester Central. There was a difference of just a mile between the LNWR route via Crewe and that of the Midland via Derby, at 189 miles to 190 miles, but the LNWR route was reasonably level, once clear of Euston, while that of the Midland was tortuous and hilly with tight bends and heavy gradients. Despite this, by 1904, the Midland was able to run trains at 3 hours 40 minutes for the best, compared with the 3½ hours of the LNWR.

After Grouping, the competitive pressures eased with both companies absorbed into the LMS, but while logic suggested that the LMS should concentrate on the quicker and easier LNWR route, it was clear that the Midland route could ease the pressure on the already congested Western Division main line. Also, both Derby and Leicester were sufficiently important to be major calls on the St Pancras service. Some trains even included carriages for Liverpool.

It was not until 1938 that the LMS decided to name the main trains on the St Pancras route. The 'Peak Express' was the name given to the 10.30am from St Pancras while the 4.30pm became the 'Palatine'. In the up direction, the 'Palatine' left Manchester at 10am and the 'Peak Express' at 4.25pm. The down 'Peak Express' was the fastest of these trains, managing a through St Pancras to Manchester timing of 3 hours 35 minutes, which included completing the 99.1 miles to Leicester in 99 minutes, and then the next 29.4 miles to Derby in 30 minutes. Between Derby and Manchester the line was severely graded over the Peak Forest summit, but even so, the train managed the 61½ miles in 77 minutes. This sparkling performance was slowed down in 1939 with four stops inserted between Derby and Manchester, adding 21 minutes to the through London to Manchester journey.

These trains usually had a standard formation that included a third-class brake, two corridor third-class carriages, a third restaurant/kitchen car and an open first-class dining car, with a first-class brake, making just six carriages, but often an additional two carriages would be added for either the Liverpool portion or for Manchester Victoria. Invariably the motive power would be a Class 5 4-6-0..

The services between St Pancras and Manchester were especially badly affected by the Second World War and no recognisable timings for similar or replacement trains can be found, but through journey times were extended to between 5¼ and 5¾ hours.

Post-war, timings improved from October 1946, but the trains were unnamed.

The 'Pines Express'

As early as 1904, the LNWR and the London Brighton & South Coast Railway (LBSCR) began running through carriages between Liverpool, Manchester and Brighton. This inspired other companies to consider new North–South services, including a restaurant car express by the Great Western Railway and the London & South Western (LSWR) between Birkenhead and Bournemouth, which in 1910 was

An important point on the West Coast Main Line is the summit at Beattock, one of two that placed great demands on motive power. This is the signal box at Beattock Summit. *(Colour-Rail 20710)*

extended via Crewe or Warrington to Manchester London Road. The LNWR responded sharply to this development, and with the Midland introduced a train between Manchester and Bournemouth, which coincidentally gave the fastest journey between Manchester and Birmingham of 1¾ hours, running over LNWR lines, before switching to the Midland Railway at Birmingham New Street and using Midland track for the onward journey to Bath. From there, the Somerset & Dorset Joint Railway, a joint venture between the Midland and the LSWR, took over, although the final stretch of 7¾ miles from Broadstone through Poole to Bournemouth was on LSWR track.

The service was suspended during the First World War, but reinstated with the return of peace. It was not until 1927 that the LMS named it the 'Pines Express', a reflection of the fact that Bournemouth was famed for its pine trees. In 1929, in an attempt to improve the operation of the SDJR and also to cut costs, the SDJR no longer provided locomotives and these became the responsibility of the LMS, allowing the works at Highbridge to be closed, while the Southern took responsibility for the track.

In 1939, the southbound train, complete with restaurant car, left Manchester London Road at 10.10am, picking up a four-coach portion for Birmingham at Crewe, along with through carriages from Liverpool for both Bournemouth and Southampton. Between Crewe and Wolverhampton, with the 'Pines' on the slow line and the 'Merseyside Express' on the fast line, a race would often develop between the two trains. In Birmingham, the train ran into New Street where the Liverpool carriages were detached, by which it consisted of six carriages for Bournemouth, one for Southampton, to be dropped at Cheltenham, and a carriage from Bradford. The train had to reverse at Bath Queen Square.

After Bath, the train ran through the difficult gradients of the Mendip Hills, but by 1939 it was in the hands of the capable Class 5s. An idea of the difficulty of the route was that, with four intermediate stops, the 71½ miles between Bath and Bournemouth took 2 hours 17 minutes. Arrival at Bournemouth was at 4.37pm, meaning that the 252 miles from Manchester had been completed in 6 hours 27 minutes. The timings were not made any easier by the fact that 26 miles of the line were single track, while the number of stops also extended the through timings.

Heading what seems to be a mixed rake of passenger carriages is 'Patriot' 5XP 4-6-0 No. 5523 *Bangor*, caught near Lancaster in 1938. *(Colour-Rail 12530)*

The northbound 'Pines Express' left Bournemouth West at 10.35am and, despite six intermediate stops, reached Bath in 2 hours 5 minutes. It arrived at Manchester London Road at 4.51pm, 6 hours 16 minutes from Bournemouth.

On summer weekends, the train took a circuitous route to avoid both Wolverhampton and Birmingham, but a further relief train covered both these stations.

The train was withdrawn during the Second World War, but was restored on 7 October 1946, but with extended timings so that it took seven hours southbound and 7¼ hours northbound. Although later accelerated slightly, the southbound schedule was soon slowed to 7 hours 12 minutes.

The 'Robin Hood'

An unnamed express that did not receive a title until some years after Nationalisation, the train had its origins in a Midland Railway service introduced between St Pancras and Nottingham before the First World War. The LMS continued the service, but also failed to give it a name. By 1939, the train was leaving Nottingham at 8.23am to arrive at St Pancras at 10.35am.

The 'Royal Highlander'

Although a train that approximated to the 'Royal Highlander' first appeared in 1895, when it set a record for the journey between Euston and Aberdeen in the final races between London and Scotland, it was not named by the LMS until 1927.

The LMS train was far heavier than the racing train of the 1890s, and far more sedate, while it also served Inverness as well as Aberdeen. It left Euston at 7.30pm in winter, calling at Bletchley,

Rugby, Crewe, Wigan, Carlisle and Stirling before reaching Perth at 5.24am, where the Inverness and Aberdeen portions were separated, with Aberdeen reached at 7.40am. The Inverness portion had to await the LNER's rival 'Aberdonian' from King's Cross and take on a restaurant car before its onward journey, meaning that it sat at Perth for a whole hour, and finally reached Inverness at 9.50am.

The train included three pairs of sleeping cars, each first-class and third-class, for Inverness, Aberdeen and Perth, with a composite carriage for each of these cities, and either third-class brakes or long luggage-only bogie brakes. The carriage furthest from the locomotive was a restaurant car to enable passengers to take dinner before it was detached at Crewe. As demand for the service proved to be highly seasonal, no train carried the 'Royal Highlander' name between Scotland and London during the winter months.

At the height of the summer, the train ran in three portions as three separate trains because of the vastly increased demand. The first train left at 7.20pm and carried the name the 'Royal Highlander', calling at Crewe and Perth on its way to Aberdeen and Inverness, while at 7.25pm a second train ran to Inverness and Oban, and a third train left Euston at 7.40pm. The first train reached Aberdeen at 7am. The return workings during the summer were even more complicated than the down* workings, and no train carried the 'Royal Highlander' name.

Even with the introduction of the famous Class 5s, the workings through the Highlands were usually handled by two of these capable locomotives double-headed.

During the Second World War, the route was of such importance that two trains were required each evening in both directions, with one leaving Euston at 7.20pm for Inverness and the second leaving at 7.30pm for Perth. Neither carried a name. Inverness was more important than Aberdeen in wartime as it was the route to the naval bases at Invergordon and Scapa Flow.

The train was one of the first on the LMS to be accelerated post-war, starting on 1 October 1945, and its through journey time was actually cut to less than the pre-war schedule, leaving Euston at 7.20pm and reaching Inverness at 8.37am, a whole 1¾ hours earlier than in 1939.

The 'Royal Scot'

Rival to the East Coast 'Flying Scotsman', this train had an even longer history, although the 'Royal Scot' name was not introduced until 1927. Like its rival, the name was used both for the train and for a locomotive, to the confusion of the man in the street, and especially the media, ever since. In common with other Anglo–Scottish expresses, its predecessor had been hampered by the 8¼-hour minimum schedule originally agreed between the East and West Coast groups of companies, which increasingly, as railway speeds rose overall, became the railway equivalent of the motoring 'White Flag Act'. This became even more ridiculous after Grouping into what had come down to two companies, the LMS and LNER, which started with a competition to see which could operate the longest non-stop stages. As stops equated to time lost, actual running speeds fell!

The summer of 1927 saw the train limited to through passengers from Euston to Edinburgh and Glasgow only, with a 'Claughton' 4-6-0 piloted by a 4-4-0 taking the train non-stop the 236 miles north to Carnforth. There, it stopped south of the station for examination while two 4-4-0 compounds took over for the summits of Shap and Beattock before stopping at Symington, where the Edinburgh and Glasgow portions parted company. When the LNER countered with non-stop running from King's Cross to Newcastle, the LMS extended the non-stop run to Kingmoor, just north of Carlisle. At this point, the LNER played an ace, running non-stop from London to Edinburgh, something the LMS could not do because of the need to stop to divide its train. The LNER run was at the time the longest non-stop journey in the world, but the Friday before the

---

*The term 'down' is used in its Euston context as trains run 'down' from London and 'up' to London, but in Scotland, naturally enough, they run 'down' from Edinburgh and 'up' to Edinburgh. This means that a London–Scotland train on the West Coast runs down to Carlisle, and then 'up' to Edinburgh or Glasgow.

new schedule was introduced, the LMS pre-empted the record by running both sections of the 'Royal Scot' separately non-stop from Euston to Edinburgh and Glasgow. The 4-6-0 'Royal Scot' class locomotive No. 6113 *Cameronian* handled the Glasgow train over its 401.4 miles, while an unnamed 4-4-0 compound set its own record by taking the Edinburgh portion on what was the longest non-stop run by a 4-4-0 ever in Great Britain.

Far more useful for the passenger was the acceleration of 1932, after which the journey time was steadily reduced for the rest of the 1930s. By 1939, on that last summer before the Second World War, the down train left Euston at its customary hour of 10am, and took 299 minutes to reach Carlisle Citadel, and for those travelling through to Glasgow the journey time was just seven hours. The available traffic did not justify so few stops, so in winter additional stops were made at Rugby and Crewe, adding 20 minutes to the schedule. Nevertheless, Euston to Rugby took just 80 minutes for 82.6 miles and was followed by 75 minutes for the 75½ miles to Crewe, where a portion for Aberdeen was dropped to be attached to a Birmingham to Glasgow express.

In the reverse direction, the Carlisle stop was at a signalbox to change the footplatemen, so there was no chance for passengers to alight or join the train at Carlisle and it carried through Glasgow–London passengers only. The Edinburgh portion ran separately, stopping at Symington to attach a portion that had left Aberdeen at 6.50am and ran via Perth, before continuing to call at Carlisle Citadel, and then ran non-stop to Euston. In winter, the Edinburgh and Glasgow portions were joined at Symington. Despite having an extra stop, the up winter train needed 7 hours 25 minutes for the through journey between Glasgow and London.

As the service accelerated throughout the 1930s, its progress was helped by the arrival of the first of Stanier's 4-6-2 Pacific locomotives, and not before time as the Midland's legacy of small locomotives made developing the service to its full potential impossible. The summer train, from the locomotive, comprised a third-class brake, two compartment and two open third-class carriages, kitchen car, open first-class carriage, a corridor first-class carriage, and a first-class brake, all for Glasgow, while for Edinburgh there was a first-class brake, open first-class carriage, kitchen car, open third-class, a corridor third-class carriage, and a third-class brake. In winter, the Edinburgh portion was just four carriages and that for Glasgow eight, but there were also two carriages for Aberdeen.

A guide book, *The Track of the Royal Scot*, was published for passengers so that they could look out for places of interest along the route.

During the Second World War, the name was dropped but a train approximating to the 'Royal Scot' was run in both directions and, unusually, the load was limited to 17 carriages, including a portion for Perth. The need to restrict the load and the popularity of the Perth section with service personnel travelling north, eventually saw this portion become a separate train in its own right, running through to Thurso with naval personnel bound for Scapa Flow in Orkney. The run, one of the longest in Great Britain, although not quite as long as Aberdeen–Penzance, took from 10.05am until 7.20am the following morning, and the railwaymen nicknamed it unofficially the 'Jellicoe' after the 'Jellicoe Specials' coal trains run over the Caledonian Railway to Grangemouth and the Highland Railway to Thurso during the First World War.

The up train in wartime attracted so many passengers that the queue at Glasgow Central often extended out of the station for more than a hundred yards, which must have been depressing for those at the end with no hope of a seat. Even so, the non-stop run from Carlisle was usually kept, but arrival at Euston was at 6.56pm having left Glasgow at 10am.

Post-war, restaurant cars were restored on 1 October 1945, a reflection on how important this amenity was on such a long journey. On 15 October, non-stop running returned, at least in the timetable as the trains initially stopped in both directions for examination and changing the footplatemen. Even so, the down train took 8½ hours while the up train took 8¼ hours. The 'Royal Scot' did not return to anything like its former glory for many years, even after Nationalisation and the introduction of diesel locomotives.

The 'St Mungo'
see the 'Granite City'.

The 'Sunny South Express'

The other major inter-company train operated by the LMS in conjunction with the Southern Railway, the 'Sunny South Express' was aimed purely at the holiday market whereas the 'Pines Express' could claim to cater for both business travellers and the holidaymakers.

 The train had its origins as early as 1904 and reflected the desire of passengers from the North West and the Midlands heading for the south coast to avoid crossing the centre of London. The LNWR and the LBSCR arranged a through service of carriages between Manchester and Brighton, which proved so popular that in 1905, a through restaurant car express was introduced, running from Liverpool and Manchester at one end, and Brighton and Eastbourne at the other. The service developed, with carriages for Kent, while carriages were also run through from the Midland Railway and the Great Northern Railway, using the Metropolitan Railway, so that by 1914 carriages of the LNWR, MR and GNR could be found on one train.

 There was also through running of locomotives between Brighton and Rugby by the LNWR and LBSCR, whose 4-4-2 tank locomotives managed to achieve a round trip of 264 miles with a seven-carriage train on a single heaped-up bunker of coal, estimated to be around 3¼ tons. Many credit the outstanding performance of the Marsh Class I3 tank of the LBSCR to the fact that it was fitted with a Schmidt superheater, and so impressed was the LNWR that it commissioned its own Schmidt-fitted 'George the Fifth' class, an outstanding 4-4-0 series.

 It is not clear at which stage the service was given its name, but it seems to have been in use before the First World War. After being suspended for the war, the service resumed afterwards, although for much of the year it ran at weekends only, but daily service was restored during the summer months, when several trains had to be run to cope with demand.

 Liverpool and Manchester continued to be the northern termini, with departures at 10.35am and 10.40am respectively, with the two portions combining at Crewe, leaving there at 11.46am to call at Nuneaton, Rugby, where carriages from Birmingham, Northampton and Willesden were added. Willesden was reached at 3.11pm and there the Southern Railway took over, leaving by way of the West London Line at 3.24pm. The problem that then arose on reaching Clapham Junction in the years after 1933, was that the steam-hauled train had to fit into the intensive electric train service from Victoria to the Sussex coast, so arrival at Brighton during the 1930s was at 4.55pm, which was a quarter of an hour slower than before the First World War. Brighton was far from the end of the line, moreover, and at 5.04pm, the train would be pulled out with a locomotive on the other end, heading for Eastbourne non-stop, which took just 41 minutes. A further reversal took place at Eastbourne with the train taken further eastwards along the coast to Bexhill, St Leonards and Hastings, where it arrived after a 7¾-hour journey at 6.25pm. No attempt seems to have been made to divide the train at Haywards Heath, which would have saved time for passengers to Eastbourne and beyond.

 The northbound train left Hastings at 11.10am, Eastbourne at 11.49am, and Brighton at 12.35pm and reached Willesden at 2.02pm, where the Birmingham portion was taken off. The train was then taken over by a LNWR locomotive to run non-stop to Crewe, which it reached at 5.15pm having taken 106 minutes for the 94.6 miles, and where it was divided. The run north was faster than the southbound service by 36 minutes, with the train arriving at Manchester at 6.19pm and Liverpool at 6.24pm.

 From time to time, the destinations at both ends were augmented by carriages from Sheffield or Leicester, while other resorts were added at the southern end.

 The service was suspended during the Second World War, and post-war, although the service resumed, the trains were no longer named.

The 'Thames-Clyde Express'

The Midland Railway had wanted to compete on the Anglo-Scottish routes, even though the line from St Pancras was not only much longer but also more heavily graded. To Glasgow, it was 424.5 miles, or even two miles more if via Sheffield, compared with 401.5 miles from Euston, but it served important intermediate points such as Leicester, Nottingham, Sheffield and Leeds, and it was also the scenic route.

The morning departure in both directions received the apt title of the 'Thames-Clyde Express' from the LMS in 1927, and was included in the service improvements of 1932, and was accelerated again later in the 1930s. While it might be regarded as being a secondary express, after leaving St Pancras at 10am the service had some fast running, including the first 72 miles between St Pancras and Kettering, which was completed in just 71 minutes despite the early stages with a difficult uphill start and the mounting of several banks. The next 27.1 miles to Leicester took a further 32 minutes, while the 47.2 miles to Chesterfield took 57 minutes. The train usually avoided Sheffield itself and instead took the old route to Leeds, taking 60 minutes for the 49.7 miles.

Reversal at Leeds meant that the 'Jubilee' class 4-6-0 that had worked the train from London was left behind, and by 1939 the locomotive, usually another 'Jubilee', took over at Leeds and completed the journey to Glasgow. Leeds to Hellifield took 45 minutes for the 36 miles, but the express then had just 51 minutes for the 46 miles to Appleby, including 15 miles at 1 in 100 from Settle Junction to Blea Moor. What followed was an easy down gradient from Appleby to Carlisle, covering 30.8 miles in 35 minutes, and reaching Carlisle at 4.09pm.

On crossing the border, the express stopped at Annan, Dumfries, Mauchline (with a connection to Ayr), and Kilmarnock. With several severe climbs still ahead of it, it took just 2 hours 23 minutes for the 115.5 miles to Glasgow St Enoch, reached at 6.38pm, 8 hours 38 minutes from St Pancras.

The southbound train left St Enoch at 9.30am and did not stop at Mauchline, so the first stage to Carlisle took just 2 hours 20 minutes, where a connection was offered on to the 'Royal Scot', saving London-bound passengers an hour. Leaving Carlisle at 11.55am, the express then ran non-stop to Leeds, which it reached at 2.20pm. After reversal and locomotive change at Leeds, there were calls at Sheffield, Trent and Leicester, before taking 99 minutes for the 99.1

A view through the tunnel at Blea Moor. (HMRS ACW618)

miles from Leeds to St Pancras, with a 6.25pm arrival. Until 1937, a carriage was dropped at Trent for Nottingham.

The rake consisted of eight carriages for most of the year, which northbound from the locomotive, consisted of a third-class brake, third-class compartment and third-class open, a third restaurant car, kitchen car, composite restaurant, a composite carriage and a first-class brake.

Wartime saw the dropping of the name, but the train continued to run, but with a rebuilt 'Royal Scot' struggling to cope single-handed with trains of up to 15 carriages, so it was not surprising that the through journey to Glasgow took until 9.32pm, almost three hours longer than in peacetime. The southbound journey started at 10am rather than 9.30am, and reached St Pancras at 9.40pm, 3¼ hours later than in 1939. The extra weight of the train was not the sole reason for the extended timings, as the route was extended to 444 miles by a wartime diversion to include both Nottingham and Derby, which also gave the train the distinction of running through more tunnels northbound than any other, 40 in all!

The train did not regain its name until after Nationalisation, but restaurant cars were reintroduced on 1 October 1945, although through carriages to Edinburgh were not provided. Eighty minutes were cut from the southbound schedule. The following year, the departure times were changed to 9.55am from St Pancras with a 7.23pm arrival at St Enoch, and 9.50am from St Enoch, with arrival at St Pancras at 7.24pm.

The 'Thames-Forth Express'

The poverty-stricken North British Railway had a line running from Edinburgh to Carlisle, and the Midland Railway, one of the NBR's partners in the Forth Bridge, was able to use this to reach the Scottish capital along with its own arduous and lengthy Settle and Carlisle Railway, opened in 1875. The through services from London were operated jointly with the Midland supplying carriages of its own design, but marked as 'M&NB' for Midland & North British. Post-Grouping, such joint rolling stock was no longer needed, and some of the M&NB stock ended up with the LNER.

The Midland ran a number of trains departing at different times over the years between St Pancras and Edinburgh, but the LMS imposed some uniformity with a departure from London at 9.5am, and in 1927, the train became the 'Thames-Forth Express'. The late 1930s saw this train accelerated so that it could connect with the LNER 'Flying Scotsman' at Edinburgh Waverley for passengers travelling onwards to Dundee and Aberdeen, but this useful connection was severed in 1938.

The 'Ulster Express'

The Midland Railway's ambitions extended beyond Scotland to include Northern Ireland, and for many years it shared ownership of the Barrow to Belfast ferry with the Furness Railway. Through carriages were provided off its trains to connect with ferry sailings, while it also had a share in the Port Patrick & Wigtownshire Joint Railway, which provided the direct route between Dumfries and Stranraer through Castle Douglas, which had a through overnight sleeping car service from St Pancras.

It was not until 1904 that the company's own harbour was completed at Heysham, near Morecambe, and a through express was run nightly leaving St Pancras at 6pm to run the 267.7 miles to Heysham, which it reached at 11.52pm after stops at Sheffield and Leeds. The up express initially left Heysham at 4.55am, but later this was at 6.15am, and reached St Pancras at 12.05pm. The LNWR offered a competing through service between London and Belfast using Euston and the port of Fleetwood.

Post-Grouping, the LMS decided that the duplication of services was unnecessary and chose Heysham as the more modern packet port for Belfast, but transferred the service from St Pancras to Euston as this provided the more direct route to the Lancashire port, reducing the distance to 239 miles.

It was not until 1927 that the 'Ulster Express' name was conferred on this boat train, although at first the service was actually running from Euston to Fleetwood. The train left Euston at 6.10pm, running non-stop to Crewe covering 158.1 miles in 167 minutes, and leaving Crewe at 9.5pm, it arrived at Preston, 51 miles away, at 10.03pm, leaving Preston at 10.08pm to arrive at Heysham at 10.52pm after reversal at Morecambe Promenade.

The late 1930s saw the summer journeys of the 'Ulster Express' depart at 7pm, running 234.3 miles to Morecambe Promenade non-stop in 4 hours 12 minutes, with a reversal so that Heysham was reached at 11.30pm. The up train left Heysham at the more civilised hour of 7am, and arrived at Euston at 11.35am, with a seven-minute stop at Crewe. The express became a through locomotive working between Morecambe Promenade and Euston, usually with a 'Royal Scot' class 4-6-0.

During the Second World War the train lost its name, then its restaurant cars, and after much tinkering with departure times and intermediate stops, the departure time was put forward to 3pm to avoid the worst of the Blitz, and remained at this time until 1 January 1946, when it was eased just slightly to 3.35pm. On 7 October 1946, the departure from Euston was put back to 4.55pm, reaching Heysham at 10.15pm. In the up direction, the train left Heysham at the comparatively late hour of 8.25am in January 1946, but by October, this was brought forward to 6.30am with arrival at Euston at 11.35am.

The 'West Coast Postal Express'

An inheritance from LNWR days, the official title of the 'West Coast Postal' was 'North Western Night TPO' (for 'travelling post office'). It had 12 long-bogied vehicles, including five travelling post offices in which sorters handled the mail en route, and the vehicles themselves had equipment for dropping and picking up mail bags at speed. On its platform at Euston from 7pm, and receiving mail not only from a succession of Post Office delivery vans, but also from individuals who paid a 1d surcharge to drop their letters directly into one of the carriages, the train departed at 8.30pm. This was never a high speed train, but the emphasis was on punctuality.

The first stop northbound was at Rugby, with the 82.6 miles covered in 94 minutes, and after four minutes the train was on its way again to Tamworth, 27.4 miles further on and taking 32 minutes, where the train stopped for seven minutes for a frantic loading of mail from both the West Country and from the East Midlands. Mail picked up by the train's apparatus was offloaded for the following 'Irish Mail'. The up 'West Coast Postal' then ran non-stop to Preston, with a ten-minute pause, then onward to Carlisle, covering the 90 miles in 99 minutes. Many of the onboard sorters left at Carlisle to be replaced by Scottish sorters.

Between London and Carlisle, the onboard apparatus was used 14 times to pick up mail, and nine times to deliver mail, with simultaneous dropping and picking up taking place at Wembley, Watford, Bletchley, Blisworth, Nuneaton, Warrington, Lancaster, Carnforth and Penrith. At one time, two postal vans were detached at Carlisle for Edinburgh, but in later years two sorting coaches for Edinburgh were added at Carlisle. Just 73.6 miles further on at Carstairs, the train divided into Aberdeen and Glasgow portions, with the latter reaching its destination at 5.15am, while Aberdeen was reached at 7.52am. Certainly in the case of Aberdeen, much of the mail must have reached the addressees in the second post of the day.

The London-bound train had the Aberdeen portion leave at 3.30pm as part of a passenger train, with the mail vehicles detached at Perth and taken onwards on their own to Law Junction, where they awaited the arrival of the main portion that had left Glasgow Central at 6.35pm, to reach Law Junction at 7.03pm. Marshalling the different portions of the train took eight minutes, while there was a further stop at Carstairs to pick up the Edinburgh portion that had departed the Scottish capital at 6.38pm. Additional vehicles were also added at Carlisle, and a change of sorters also took place. The train eventually arrived at Euston at 3.55am.

While the train continued to operate during the Second World War, the onboard apparatus was not used and onboard sorting was abandoned. The need to make additional stops saw the scheduled extended by 71 minutes northward and 76 minutes southward. Nevertheless, the train was so important that post-war it was one of the first expresses to return to its pre-war schedule, and on 1 October 1945 onboard sorting and the use of the apparatus to pick up and drop mail bags was restored. It seems that punctuality became a problem post-war, for although additional minutes were added to different sections, given the state of the track and often the poor state of the motive power – all neglected during the war as the railways workshops were engaged in military work – as well as indifferent coal, the train could not keep to its timings. Attempts to improve the situation took place after Nationalisation.

The 'Yorkshireman'

A new train introduced by the LMS in March 1925, the 'Yorkshireman' ran between London St Pancras and Bradford Exchange, avoiding Leeds, leaving the Yorkshire city at 9.10am and St Pancras at 4.55pm. The 'Yorkshireman' was the first LMS express to consist entirely of open carriages, and running from the northbound locomotive back these included a third-class brake, then a third, first, kitchen car, two thirds and a third-class brake. The train took 4¼ hours between St Pancras and Bradford, or 3 hours 10 minutes between London and Sheffield, with just one stop at Leicester.

The 1937 accelerations saw the stop at Leicester dropped, so that 18 minutes were cut from the timetable for Sheffield, and 14 from the through run to and from Bradford. This did not produce the extra traffic expected, no doubt because 1938 was a bad year for the railways that had experienced a boost in passenger traffic in 1937 fuelled in part by the Coronation, so 1939 saw the stop at Leicester reintroduced. Even so, the train was still faster between London and Sheffield, at 3 hours 5 minutes, but Bradford became much slower at 4 hours 20 minutes.

The service ended with the outbreak of the Second World War.

'Royal Scot' 4-6-0 No. 6106 *Gordon Highlander* heads a train of six elderly carriages near Shap in 1936. (*HMRS AAK225*)

Chapter 11

Travel LMS – 'The Best Way'

The 'Big Four' railway companies were all acutely aware of the power of advertising, and mounted campaigns many of which have come to be regarded as classics both individually and jointly. However, one has to admit that the joint advertisements were much less memorable than those produced by the individual companies. Anxious to develop tourism into the UK, the grouped companies even collaborated in setting up offices in New York and Paris, using the title 'British Railways', which must have come back to haunt them! Oddly, their joint advertising, on matters such as sending luggage in advance or taking one's dog on the journey, did not use the term 'British Railways', but instead had the initials of all four companies.

For its visit to the United States, 'Royal Scot' 4-6-0 No. 6100 *The Royal Scot* had to be equipped with a bell and headlight, as well as a cow catcher, which was left off on her return, but she kept the other 'souvenirs' of her trip. It is seen here at Castle Bromwich carrying the label for the train, 'The Royal Scot', on the front of the smokebox. *(HMRS AEQ835)*

For its own advertising and promotion, the company adopted the slogan early on of *Travel LMS –'The Best Way'*.

In common with the other companies, the LMS also had an employee magazine. Again in common with the others, this was only available in return for payment, either per copy or by annual subscription, all of which seems odd today when such items are provided free, but even more so when one looks at the content which shows that the LMS was anxious for its staff to promote the business. In fact, the magazine was just one small part of its internal communications programme, which included a number of other publications such as the purely business-orientated *Quota News*. The LMS, as always awake to developments on the other side of the North Atlantic, believed in the hard sell!

Employees were expected to promote the company, and stationmasters, in addition to their other responsibilities, were presumed to know the local hoteliers and boarding house keepers in their area and sell advertising in the LMS guide books to them. No doubt this was done with varying degrees of effectiveness, but the stationmaster of a major station was still an important member of the local community at this time.

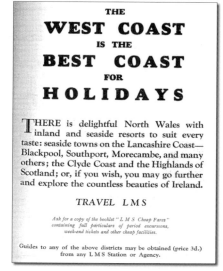

THE
WEST COAST
IS THE
BEST COAST
FOR
HOLIDAYS

THERE is delightful North Wales with inland and seaside resorts to suit every taste: seaside towns on the Lancashire Coast—Blackpool, Southport, Morecambe, and many others; the Clyde Coast and the Highlands of Scotland; or, if you wish, you may go further and explore the countless beauties of Ireland.

TRAVEL LMS

Ask for a copy of the booklet " L M S Cheap Fares" containing full particulars of period excursions, week-end tickets and other cheap facilities.

Guides to any of the above districts may be obtained (price 3d.) from any LMS Station or Agency.

The LMS even considered it worthwhile advertising services to its own staff so that they could tell their friends. All four grouped companies maintained that they served the best resorts with the best weather. (*LMS*)

GO BY RAIL WITH A
CHEAP
"MONTHLY RETURN"

That's the Ticket!

Cheap " Monthly Return " Tickets are issued all the year round between most stations and are available by any train any day.

Full particulars from any Railway Station Office or Agency

G.W.R   LMS   L·N·E·R   S.R

The 'Big Four' grouped companies collaborated on advertising and other matters when necessary, and this is an advertisement for cheap monthly return tickets, which meant that the return journey could be made up to a month after the outward journey.

"I'M READY"
TAKE YOUR DOG
WITH YOU BY RAIL
Return Tickets at Single Rate

DRINKING WATER FOR DOGS CAN BE OBTAINED FROM STATION REFRESHMENT ROOMS, OR ON REQUEST TO A MEMBER OF THE STATION STAFF.
G.W.R.   LMS   L·N·E·R   S.R.

Another joint poster advertising campaign was to encourage passengers to take their dog with them at what was effectively half the adult fare, with the promise that refreshment rooms or station staff would provide water.

The *LMS Magazine*

While its predecessor companies, including the LNWR, had employee publications and a whole year was available for the railway companies to organise themselves ready for Grouping, it was not until November 1923 that the first issue of the *LMS Magazine* appeared. From the start, a regular feature was the 'General Manager's Notes'.

'The manager of a small firm is fortunate in being in contact with the whole of his staff, and there are still cases where he knows every member personally,' wrote Arthur Watson, still to be knighted. 'With a huge undertaking like ours employing as it does a total of nearly 270,000, scattered throughout the length and breadth of Great Britain and Ireland, this personal touch is obviously missing but I think, by that very fact, important.'

The magazine tried to take into account the vast geographical spread of its readership by having four-page regional inserts, which were initially for London and the Home Counties, South Midland, North Midland, Northern, Wales and Ireland, and Scotland. These dealt with personal issues such as marriages, deaths and retirements, with the Scottish insert even substituting the Scots word 'retirals' for retirements. Even so, circulation peaked at 75,000, showing that almost three quarters of employees did not buy the magazine, and in fact the number could have been less as the magazine was also available to the public. The regional inserts survived until 1936, when a completely integrated approach took over.

The magazine was an odd combination of *The Meccano Magazine* and an employee newspaper. For the latter, it included details of gardening and other societies, as well as a page for women with recipes and seasonal advice, a page for junior staff and even a page of stories for employees' children with a cartoon strip featuring a tabby cat. The former included articles with diagrams on new locomotives, or other innovations such as coaling plants, and articles on overseas railways. The pieces on overseas railways did sometimes look at the operational practices, and even show differences between practices in the United States, for example, and those of the LMS, but they also included articles on railways of much less importance, including the Malta Railway and the Cyprus Railway. London's main airport between the two world wars was at Croydon, very much in Southern Railway territory, although some distance from any railway station, but the 'Meccano' aspect of the magazine included an article on 'The Airport for London', while there was also one on Railway Air Services in another issue, although at least the LMS was involved in this venture, unlike the LNER.

To us today, some of the features appear odd, such as one on building a crystal radio set.

Inevitably, there were items which covered various departments or company news, such as the setting of a speed record, and especially interesting to us today were those with employees writing about their jobs, which ranged from locomotive and wagon inspectors, passenger guards, hotel head waiters and booking office clerks, as well as the operator of a steam pumping machine who reminded his readers that steam power was used for pumping long before it was used for locomotion. There were also items on the company's progress and new developments, and perhaps one reason for the relatively small readership could have been that the latter included informative pieces that may have been well above the heads of some.

The urge to improve the business in what was a very difficult economic climate was there. There was some desperation in a column that appeared first in 1931 entitled 'Tell Your Friends', which was aimed at getting employees to tell their friends about new services, special fares, such as the 1d a mile summer holiday tickets, or even about improvements to the LMS goods services. One wonders how many would have read the pieces by the chief commercial manager on how to improve business. American practice in employee communication seems to have crept in here with a degree of moralising about customer service that might not have gone down too well with the more cynical British reader.

The *LMS Magazine* was augmented by two other publications, both of which were issued free to relevant staff. These were *On Time*, for the operating department, and *Quota News*, for their counterparts in the commercial department. The latter was the inspiration of a new chief

ASHTON DAVIES SAYS: "WE MEAN TO RING THAT BELL!"

The LMS was alone in setting a quota for business, and the staff magazine even included a cartoon of Ashton Davies, the chief commercial manager, encouraging people to hit the £60 million target for 1934. (*The LMS Magazine*)

commercial manager, Ashton Davies, who introduced a quota system under which targets were introduced for every station and district, all of which were grouped in leagues with trophies for the best performance. He also had a regular column in the *LMS Magazine*.

The story is told of a small goods station which, by sheer chance, was landed with a lucrative traffic in pipes, which far surpassed the quota allocated to it, resulting in the bemused goods agent being summoned to Euston to receive a trophy, a handsome shield.

On Time also reflected a league table approach, but in this case to punctuality and locomotive failures.

Self improvement was a recurring theme, and so too was safety, and the record of accidents amongst the company's personnel at first was not good. Strangely, the LMS did not seem to have an equivalent of the GWR's first aider scheme. On the other hand, while safety statistics were trotted out, there seems to have been a reluctance to tackle major incidents head on, with only a passing reference to the loss with all hands of one of the company's cargo ships, and nothing much about accidents on the line.

Reading the early issues one is also aware of just how difficult it was for the employees to grasp the extent of the upheaval that had hit the railways under Grouping. There were articles explaining just which companies had been merged to form the new LMS, followed by features on each one. Other features explained that the LMS was the world's leading railway operator of hotels, and had the world's largest railway steamer fleet.

Most employee publications do not carry advertisements, but the *LMS Magazine* was one that did. There were advertisements for tea, and another that promised that readers could furnish a complete house for just £46, but of more immediate interest to employees was one by the Abbey Road Building Society, predecessor of the Abbey National (now Santander), offering mortgages for LMS employees by special arrangement with the company. Strangely, there seems to have been no supporting or explanatory article in the magazine.

The most unusual advertisements were those by the manufacturers of railway locomotives and, after the railways gained powers to run road transport, buses. Some of these might have those concerned with advertising standards raising their eyebrows today, and especially the one that proclaimed that diesel-electric was the best route to electrification! Clearly, manufacturers thought that by supporting the magazine, they would be in the good books of the directors of the LMS.

All in all, one gets a sense of terrific upheaval and that the grouping into four companies was several steps too far and that the only companies to emerge from the Grouping in a reasonable state and a manageable size were the Great Western and the Southern.

A more severe tone followed when, without warning, in September 1939 the last issue of the *LMS Magazine* appeared, not even mentioning its demise, to be replaced by a new publication, *Carry On*, which ran up to Nationalisation.

Publicity

Publicity really consists of two different channels, the first being advertising and the second being media relations, to which the wise company will also add community, investor and political relations. In this, as in employee communications, the LMS was slow off the mark and did not seem at first to appreciate the importance of good relationships with the press, and when it started, not only was there no television but radio was in its infancy.

The first LMS advertising and publicity officer was T.C. Jeffrey, a former Midland man as were many occupying key posts in the company. He was not based in London, close to the national press, but in the chief general superintendent's office in Derby, and the post was not moved to Euston until 1927, after Jeffrey retired. His successor was his deputy, G.H. Loftus Allen.

Although the Southern Railway showed that it would take press relations seriously as early as 1925, with the appointment of John (later Sir John) Elliott, a Fleet Street journalist, it was not until 1932 that the LMS followed suit, with the appointment of D.S.M. Barrie, who had the advantage that not only did he write for the national press but was also a contributor to the railway press as well.

Barrie had been appointed by a new vice-president for commerce and operations, Ernest Lemon, whose team included Ashton Davies, chief commercial manager and a regular contributor to the *LMS Magazine*. It was Lemon's recognition of the value of good publicity that also led to the appointment of Leonard Croft, who took responsibility for railway photography, and much of the work he oversaw appeared on the front pages of the national daily press while also creating a strong archive of railway photographs.

From the beginning, the LMS offered lantern slides for clubs and societies promoting tourist resorts, but in keeping with the times, attention soon turned to the production of cinema films, including many intended for employee and training purposes, but also others intended for showing to the general public. Once again the company sought outside assistance, and the photo agency Topical Press established a film production subsidiary that recorded a total of 150 films for the LMS by the outbreak of the Second World War. A film theatre with editing and cutting facilities was created in the basement of the new headquarters in Euston House, and two old LNWR carriages were converted into mobile cinemas so that instruction could be carried to staff without them having to travel to Euston, Crewe or Derby.

Advertising and marketing

Strangely, despite the emphasis on selling and achieving preset quotas for business, much of the LMS advertising was what would today be regarded as either corporate or generic. Surely, only railway enthusiasts and students of art would have appreciated such famous poster advertisements as 'The Day Begins' showing a fine locomotive in an engine shed being prepared for the day's work. Other locomotives are gathered around, and the sun is shining through the windows. The famous railway artist Terence Cuneo was commissioned for this work, and artistic licence extended to showing a 'Duchess' Pacific in Willesden shed, where it normally would not have been.

Others showed British industry, with an illustration of a major steelworks, and with no caption or message other than 'British Industries' and 'Steel'.

The LMS concentrated much of its advertising on showing the railway behind the scenes being prepared for the train, or the customer. This poster depicts tracklaying, the company taking great pride in the standard of its permanent way. Others were less to the point, including a series showing great British industries such as steel. (*LMS*)

The reason for all of this was that the LMS advertising and publicity officer from 1927, before which he had been deputy since Grouping in 1923, was G.H. Loftus Allen, who had good connections and has been described as having varied talents. However, his taste for the arts probably did the company few favours as he pursued art for the sake of it and not for the impression it would make on consumer or industrial decision-making. At a time of economic difficulty, the LMS employed Norman Wilkinson as its art adviser and sponsored Royal Academicians to paint its posters. At one time, no fewer than 17 were working on posters depicting industries, towns and historic sites.

'Beyond indicating the place or industry that they wish to advertise, the LMS are giving the artists an entirely free hand,' reported *The Railway Magazine*. 'There is another important question, that of reproduction in poster form. The company are quite alive to that, and neither money nor trouble will be spared to ensure the best reproductions possible of these notable contributions to every man's open-air picture gallery.'

So pleased with itself was the LMS that at the height of the 1924 holiday season a horse-drawn cart was converted to carry a display of its posters around Blackpool, with the posters including one showing the Aberdeenshire countryside, the Peak District, a mounted Lifeguard and a driver's cab at night. Hopefully some of the seaside landladies would have been encouraged to book an end-of-season holiday.

Perhaps more positive was the poster showing an 'LMS Express & Cunard Liner – *The* Highest Standard of Comfort in Rail and Ocean Travel', with an express alongside a liner moored at the quayside. There was licence in this as well, for although Cunard used Liverpool at the time, the LMS express locomotives were too heavy to reach the quayside, but that can be forgiven. Another message about the quality of the track was hidden in another poster 'The Permanent Way', showing gangers laying new rails. After all, the LMS also proclaimed itself as 'The Best Way'. On the other hand, nine men are bending over, breaking their backs to do a hard job, while another thirteen are standing around watching, and only one of those is the all-important look out man! No fewer than six are standing in the middle of an adjoining line, so hopefully they have their own lookout man, but out of the picture!

The best LMS advertisement was possibly '"This is your way Sir" in England, Scotland, Ireland, Wales' which ran as a poster, and stressed the one thing that the LMS could always boast, the fact that it had penetrated all four countries.

There was advertising aimed directly at the prospective passenger, including 'The West Coast is the Best Coast for Holidays', inviting newspaper readers to ask for the LMS booklet on cheap fares. Like the other railway companies, there was an attempt to stimulate passenger traffic by providing a summer fare of 1d a mile return.

The *LMS Magazine* was available to members of the public, so it was probably logical that the publication also carried some of the company's own advertising, such as that in April 1933 which made the point that the LMS had the greatest mileage in the world of trains travelling at an average speed of 55mph or more, start to stop, with 7,898 trains running daily, while the next railway, but unnamed, had just 5,810 such trains.

All of the railway companies published books but, with the GWR, the LMS was one of the more active publishers. This started with a 6d booklet published in time for the British Empire Exhibition, held at Wembley in 1924–25, on the train control system and entitled *The Magic Wand of Transport*, and published for the company by *The Railway Gazette*. When the City of Liverpool organised a centenary celebration for the Liverpool & Manchester Railway in 1930, the LMS provided strong support for the event, which included an exhibition, a railway fair and a nightly pageant, while the company commissioned the railway historian C.F. Dendy Marshall to write a booklet *One Hundred Years of Railways*, which was sold for a shilling.

The LMS also provided books on the routes taken by its main services for passengers to purchase, including *The Path of the Royal Scot* for those travelling on its prestige service. It was followed by *The Path of the Coronation Scot* in 1937. Both of these were edited by Edmund Vale, who also wrote *Ships of the Narrow Seas*. The visit of the locomotive No. 6100 *Royal Scot* to the United

Perhaps more commercial in its approach was this poster advertising Snowdonia as a holiday destination, reached via LMS stations in North Wales.

States and Canada in 1933, when it spent six months touring, specially equipped with a North American-style headlight and bell, was commemorated by a book *The Triumph of the Royal Scot*. Finally, shortly before the outbreak of the Second World War, the LMS celebrated the centenary of the London & Birmingham Railway with another 6d booklet, *A Century of Progress*.

Much of the marketing was what would be described as destination based. At the outset, the company produced sets of lantern slides for clubs and other organisations to show to their members, but as already mentioned these were later joined by films produced by the company's film unit. The LMS also contributed to advertising by holiday resorts on condition that the company's name was mentioned, and took advertisements in the resorts' guidebooks. This

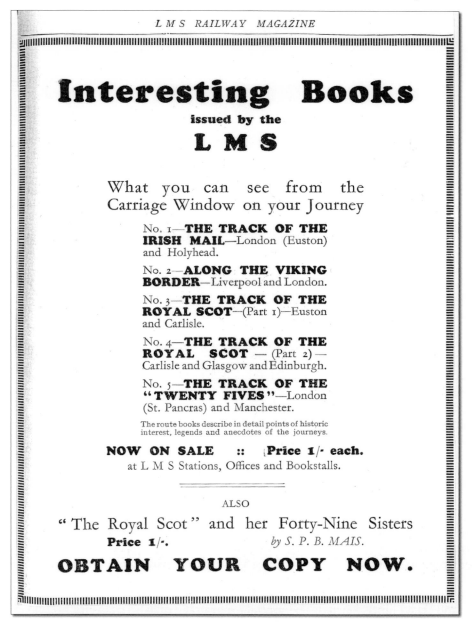

Many of the railway companies, including the LMS, sold travel books so that passengers could identify places of interest along the way. For the enthusiast, there was also a book on the *Royal Scot* and her 49 sisters! (*LMS*)

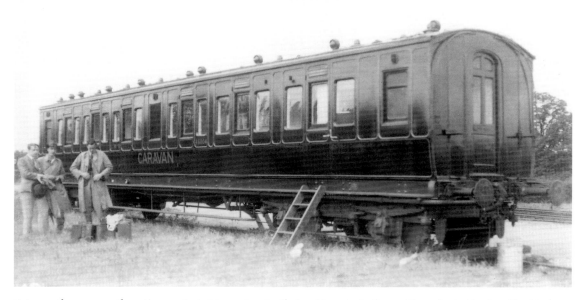

Between the wars, as the railways started to modernise their rolling stock, the problem of what to do with elderly vehicles arose. The small four and six-wheel vans and carriages were often sold off as garden sheds and summer houses, delivered free to a station closest to the purchaser. The LNER hit on the idea of converting redundant rolling stock into 'camping coaches', and during the 1930s all four companies were doing this. This LMS 'Caravan', was much larger than many. (*HMRS AAG233*)

made sense, and the LMS even mounted preview trips so that travel agents and others could visit the leading resorts. This was a question of inter-dependence, as the LMS needed the resorts as holiday destinations, but the resorts were dependent upon the LMS to provide the principal means for holidaymakers to make their way there.

The LMS produced its own range of guidebooks, selling 1.25 million copies by 1929, with the main one being an annual *Holidays by LMS*, which was available for 6d (2.5p), and as it contained more than 700 pages, with 200 having illustrations, and listed more than 10,000 hotels and boarding houses, it was good value.

To further support the destinations, from May 1934 onwards the LMS provided camping coaches at stations in holiday areas. This was one way of utilising redundant rolling stock and all four of the grouped companies adopted this expedient. A typical camping coach would be an old four or six-wheel compartment carriage with three compartments knocked through to provide a living space with a cooking area, and another couple converted to bunk spaces, usually one with two berths and the other with four. In most cases, the occupants had to leave the camping coach to move from one compartment to another, and for washing and other personal functions, the facilities in the nearby station had to suffice.

All this came to an end following the outbreak of the Second World War. Despite being under the control of the government, through the Railway Executive Committee, the LMS, like the other railways, looked forward to summer 1940 with considerable optimism. In the spring, it published its annual guide, *Holidays by LMS*, with no fewer than 684 pages including 100 with photographs, at the beginning of May, but on 10 May the invasion of the Netherlands and Belgium, and then France, started. The special programme of extra trains for holidaymakers and for the Whitsun holiday in particular, was cancelled, along with the bank holiday itself. Soon, the rush that the LMS would have to face was not that of eager holidaymakers, but of exhausted and war-battered troops that had been lifted off the beaches at Dunkirk.

Chapter 12

The Record Setters

Today, the LMS is not remembered as a railway that set records. Its achievements have been eclipsed by the sparkling, although damaging to the locomotive run of the famous Gresley A4 Pacific *Mallard* on the East Coast Main Line, setting a record for steam that has never been broken. Others will hark back to the glory days of the Great Western 'Cheltenham Flyer', at one time, albeit briefly, the world's fastest scheduled daily express train, or even earlier, to the same company's *City of Truro*. To ignore the achievements of the LMS in setting records is to do the company an injustice. The company that overall was amongst the slowest of the 'Big Four' on Grouping, was later able to claim to be amongst the fastest and, as we have already seen, had more trains scheduled to run at 55mph or over than any other at a time when 50mph was fast!

Despite the eventual construction of powerful Pacific 4-6-2 locomotives, heavy trains still needed double-heading on some sections. Here, at Burton & Holme in 1939, 2P 4-4-0 No. 655 pilots Stanier 7P 4-6-2 'Princes Royal' class No. 6207 *Princess Arthur of Connaught* with a down express of modern rolling stock. *(HMRS ACW509)*

The problem had been that the early days of the LMS saw it caught between the former Midland Railway's fondness for small locomotives, with nothing bigger than 4-4-0 apart from 'Big Bertha', the Lickey banker, and the LNWR's resistance to scrapping its older locomotives, or anything else, just so long as it would run. While there were those within the company who wanted to see the 'scrap-and-build' policy include larger and more powerful locomotives, and especially 4-6-2 Pacifics, they got no further than 4-6-0s. It took Stanier's arrival from the Great Western to change the scene and provide not only the Pacifics, but also many workaday locomotives at home on a freight train or a suburban stopping train.

There was no attempt to return to the railway 'races' of 1888 and 1895, but the LNER forced the LMS into action when the East Coast company announced late in 1936 that it would celebrate the Coronation of King George VI with a streamlined express running between London and

The record-setting Stanier 4-6-2 7P 'Princess Royal' class was capable of handling very heavy trains, as seen here with No. 6209 *Princess Beatrice* heading the 'Midday Scot' through Rugby in 1937.
(HMRS AEU205)

Edinburgh. It took just weeks for the LMS to put one of its new, but unstreamlined, Pacifics, No. 6201 *Princess Elizabeth*, on a high-speed run from London Euston to Glasgow Central with a rake of seven carriages, far less than the locomotive would normally have handled. On 16 November 1936, *Princess Elizabeth* completed the journey in just 5 hours, 53½ minutes, for the 401.4 miles. Even better, the following day she did the return run, but with eight carriages in high winds and heavy rain in just 5 hours 44¼ minutes, giving an average speed of 70mph throughout the journey.

'Over eight hundred miles in two consecutive days at a mean average speed of 69mph with an average load of 240 tons!' the *LMS Magazine* told its readers in a story bylined, 'By One Who Took Part'. The story was in fact too late for the December issue, so while it was accorded a brief mention, readers had to wait until January 1937 for a more detailed account.

The record-setting 'Princess Royal' 4-6-2 No. 6201 *Princess Elizabeth* is partially dismantled during a major overhaul at Crewe.
(HMRS AAN702)

The record was short-lived, even though the 'One Who Took Part' saw it as a milestone in railway history.

'Six weeks after the stirring events of those two days, the achievement is one which has passed into railway history, and which now comprises a mass of dynamometer-car and other records in course of analyses. Yet those who were privileged to take part in these epoch-making journeys from London to Glasgow and back in less than six hours for the 401½ miles, and those who saw the train flashing through the countryside, will long treasure memories and incidents serving vividly to recall this wonderful demonstration of speed on the steel highway. Not, indeed, since the famous "Races to Scotland" of the eighties and nineties has the West Coast Route known such a drama as that of this racing train and her gallant crew pitted against the clock – and, on the return trip, against the weather too.'

Despite this, the record is not remembered as a major event in railway history, not least because even better was to follow once the first of the streamlined locomotives, No. 6220 *Coronation*, emerged from the works. On 29 June 1937, a test run was conducted between Euston and Crewe with the locomotive 'reined-in' between Euston and Stafford, leaving Euston at 9.50am and running to the timetable, but the locomotive was then given her head, reaching 114mph

Records set by steam locomotives provided popular news in the 1930s, as can be seen by the front page 'splash' in the *Daily Sketch* celebrating the 114mph obtained by the 'Coronation Scot' on 29 June 1937. The support of pro-Conservative papers such as this was also lobbying for the continuation of private enterprise on the railways.

past Maddeley to reach Crewe just before noon. On the return, the 270-ton train left Crewe at 1.55pm and covered the 158.1 miles in just 119 minutes to arrive at Euston at 3.54pm, giving an average speed of 79.7mph start-to-stop. This compared with a booked time of 144 minutes for the Crewe–Euston leg.

The achievement earned the LMS front-page news coverage, with the tabloid *Daily Sketch* giving over the whole of its front page for the story.

The newspaper photographs of *Coronation* give the impression that she had a load of just two carriages, but the official account in the *LMS Magazine* makes it clear that the load was eight carriages.

'In the down direction the 158.1 miles Euston to Crewe were covered in 129 minutes 46 seconds, at an average speed of 73mph, start to stop,' according to the report on the run. 'The maximum speed between Whitmore and Crewe was 114mph (as recorded by the speed-recorder on the engine), while speeds of 112.5mph were maintained for a full mile and 106.5mph for five miles. The maximum speed of 114mph is the highest yet recorded in this country and the highest (with steam traction) in the Empire.'

That was not surprising as none of the Empire countries had anything that would qualify as a high-speed railway. At the time, French railways did not have their reputation, gained after the Second World War, for high-speed record-setting, and it was only in Germany that speed records were being set, but with diesel traction. Perhaps more interesting was that the locomotive had a speed recorder as the LMS did not provide speedometers on its engines, something that was to come back to haunt the company.

Despite this, as mentioned earlier in Chapter 10, the LMS did not schedule the 'Coronation Scot' as tightly as it could have done. Perhaps this was to ensure a robust timetable with on-time arrivals, or perhaps it was a concern for safety with the train running at high speeds every day, or even a concern for passenger comfort, or, perhaps it was being parsimonious, with concerns over the consumption of coal and additional wear and tear on the locomotive and rolling stock. This was one weakness of the class, for there were initially just five locomotives (later ten) with streamlining, and as it was claimed that this made a significant difference in speeds of more than 70mph, tighter schedules could not have been maintained if a non-streamlined locomotive had to be substituted.

We shall never know.

The pride of the *LMS* was the streamlined Stanier 'Coronation' class 7P 4-6-2, initially painted blue with silver stripes. This is No. 6223 *Princess Alice* heading the down 'Coronation Scot' at high speed near Bolton-le-Sands in 1939, the year that many of these locomotives were repainted red with gold stripes. (*HMRS ACW507*)

Chapter 13

The LMS
in Ireland

Alone amongst the grouped companies, the LMS inherited a substantial network in Ireland. This had been divided the year before the Grouping into the Irish Free State, predecessor of today's Irish Republic and sometimes referred to as Eire, and Northern Ireland, comprising six of the nine counties of the ancient Irish kingdom of Ulster. The LMS, as we will see in the next chapter, provided the railway shipping services to Northern Ireland as well as competing with the Great Western on services to the Irish Free State.

The Midland Railway had purchased the Belfast & Northern Counties Railway as part of its ambitious plans for expansion, but first across the Irish Sea was the London & North Western Railway which not only operated ferry services between Holyhead, on Anglesey in North Wales, and Dublin, but also operated between Fleetwood in Lancashire, and Belfast. To support these routes, the LNWR built the Dundalk, Newry & Greenore Railway, which linked the harbour at Greenore with the Great Northern Railway of Ireland's main line between Dublin and Belfast at Dundalk for Dublin-bound trains, and at Newry for those heading for Belfast. The DNGR line was built to the Irish gauge of 5ft 3in, and specially regauged LNWR six-wheeled carriages and two 0-6-0 saddle tanks were shipped over from Crewe. The lines also saw operations by GNR (I) 2-4-2Ts bringing in passenger carriages and goods wagons. A hotel was built by the London & North Western at Greenore.

The port probably served the cattle trade better than passengers, for at the time and for many years after, Irish cattle was shipped live to Holyhead and Liverpool. The LNWR also built and operated the port facilities at Dublin North Wall, where again there was a short section of railway and a hotel.

Far more ambitious, the Midland Railway bought the Belfast & Northern Counties Railway in 1903, renaming it the Northern Counties Committee, usually referred to as the NCC. This was a substantial railway by any measure, with a 92 mile-long main line linking Belfast, where the terminus was at York Road, with Northern Ireland's second city, Londonderry, with a terminus at Waterside. There was a branch to the important seaside resort at Portrush, while another important route was the much shorter line from Belfast to Larne, just over 24 miles away and a major ferry port with sailings to Stranraer in Scotland. This was by far the shortest crossing between the mainland of Great Britain and Ireland. The NCC also had a number of branch lines radiating out from Belfast. All in all, this was an inter-city railway and also a commuter railway with branch lines, although a reflection of the country's sparser population density was reflected in the fact that parts of the Londonderry line were single track and to minimise delays in switching on and off the single-line sections, locomotives had catchers fitted to the cab sides for the exchange of tablets at speed.

Portrush, one of Northern Ireland's main seaside resorts, was the transfer point for the electric tramway to the Giant's Causeway which was operated by an independent undertaking and was never linked with the NCC. It was the first electric tramway in the British Isles when it opened in 1883.

The railway included the port facilities at Larne, where there was a railway-owned hotel, *The Laharna*, while the other hotel owned by the NCC at Portrush carried the rather less romantic name of *The Northern Counties*.

Given such a broad gauge as standard, Northern Ireland, rather like Spain (where the gauge on the traditional lines is 5ft 6in) also had a number of narrow gauge lines, but unlike Spain, where they are metre gauge, in Northern Ireland these were 3ft. The NCC's narrow gauge lines were the Ballymena & Larne Railway, and a share in the County Donegal Railway, owned jointly with the GNR (I), which when completed in 1906 was Ireland's longest narrow gauge railway with a main line from Londonderry to Strabane in Northern Ireland and on to Killybegs in the Irish Free State. In 1924, the LMS took over the Ballycastle Railway. The Ballymena & Larne Railway was the oldest, and ran express boat trains, and had been one of four companies that had formed the Belfast & Northern Counties.

The LMS shared ownership of the 3ft gauge County Donegal Railways Joint Committee with the Great Northern Railway of Ireland. This illustration of an early 41-seat railcar shows how basic was the conversion from a bus. *(The LMS Magazine)*

The County Donegal had 125 miles of narrow gauge line, making it the longest such system in the British Isles, with 99 per cent of it single track. The 14½ miles from Londonderry to Strabane was owned wholly by the LMS. There were branches from Strabane to Letterkenny, Stranorlar to Glenties and from Donegal City to Ballyshannon. Speeds were hardly sparkling, the journey from Londonderry to Strabane taking 50 minutes for example.

So it happened that Londonderry had no fewer than four railway termini, two on each side of the River Foyle. On the eastern side were the termini for the NCC line from Belfast and for the GNR (I) lines from Belfast (a meandering route along the border with the Free State), and from Dublin. On the western side was the County Donegal terminus, Victoria Road, with a line that ran south roughly parallel to that of the GNR (I) but on the other side of the Foyle, and that of the narrow gauge Londonderry & Lough Swilly Railway, which served the northern part of County Donegal. Three of the four termini could fairly be said to handle 'international' traffic, with only the NCC being a truly domestic railway.

The one problem that partition brought in addition to customs' checks and the cross-border railways, was that it cut Londonderry off from its hinterland in County Donegal to a great extent.

Developing the Irish lines

The Dundalk, Newry & Greenore Railway was an isolated oddity with little prospect of growth, and to tidy up its operations in Ireland the LMS handed over the working of the line to the GNR (I) in 1933. The Irish Great Northern put its own 2-4-2Ts on the passenger trains, and relegated the 0-6-0Ts to freight workings, but the six-wheel carriages were retained, albeit re-painted into GNR (I) green, until the line was finally closed in 1951.

The policy of 'scrap and build' was soon applied to the NCC. This was no isolated system but a network in its own right with more than 201 route miles of Irish 'standard' gauge and almost 64 route miles of 3ft gauge, and the LMS treated it as such. The first locomotives to be sent to Ireland by the LMS were five of the typical Midland Railway 4-4-0 tender locomotives, but these were later followed by a special build of four of the larger 2-6-0 tender locomotives and then, shortly before Nationalisation, by some fine 2-6-4Ts. The latter clearly showed their LMS heritage. Standard LMS carriages, regauged of course, were also sent across, with an initial batch of 30 built at Derby in 1924 which the *LMS Magazine* noted were 'the most up-to-date in Ireland'.

Locomotives and carriages were painted in standard LMS maroon, but while the locomotives simply bore the letters NCC, the carriages carried LMS NCC at waist level.

The County Donegal Joint Railway had locomotives painted geranium red while the passenger carriages were painted red to waist level with cream upper works. Under LMS involvement, between the two world wars, the CDJR established a stud of 17 tank engines, mainly used on freight trains, three Gardner-engined diesel railcars, a Drewry railcar, two Reo

The use of first petrol and then diesel railcars, or in fact rail buses, on the County Donegal resulted in a worthwhile increase in frequencies between 1922, upper, and 1938, lower. (*Bradshaw*)

petrol-engined railcars and four Ford petrol-engined railcars, and a shunting tractor. The railcars were an attempt at both modernisation and cost reduction and were largely the brainchild of the general manager, Henry Forbes. The first were petrol railcars bought second-hand from the Derwent Valley Light Railway in England in 1926. Being Ireland, nothing could be simple, and initially, the government of the Irish Free States insisted on duty being paid on these 'imports', arguing that they were buses. These vehicles were eventually replaced by diesel railcars, but they improved the passenger service and passenger numbers began to climb, despite the low population of County Donegal and the restrictions of having to cross the border.

The advent of the railcars meant that steam haulage accounted for just 30 per cent of the total annual mileage. Despite their small size, no fewer than 12 of the tank engines were superheated, and three of them were scheduled to haul trains of 450 tons, which seems implausible, but this was according to the *LMS Magazine*. The railcars generally had around 32–41 seats, but the Fords were small, with just 20 seats. In appearance, the railcars were angular and at one end looked like a normal control bus (that is with the engine in front of the driver). Later, the early railcars were augmented and in some case replaced by articulated diesel sets acquired from England, so that by the time the LMS was nationalised almost all passenger workings were by railcar or multiple unit.

Although the Irish standard gauge locomotives and carriages were built on the mainland, the rolling stock for the narrow gauge lines was built in Northern Ireland. The narrow gauge lines had rolling stock that for the most part looked as if it were scaled down main line rolling stock, in contrast to the variety of highly individual styles found in Wales, although the Welsh lines have a much narrower gauge. The LMS attempted to boost the appeal of the narrow gauge lines by introducing corridor rolling stock, built in its Belfast works, for the Ballymena & Larne line, but in 1933 it was decided to transfer the passenger service to the standard gauge line.

The County Donegal seemed to realise the importance of tourism, with its timetable having a poem entitled 'Longings' printed on its front page, which ended with the lines:

. . . And voices forever are calling me
From the wilds of Donegal

While passenger carriages and locomotives were sent to Northern Ireland from Derby, the appearance of this railcar suggests that it may have been built in the NCC's own workshops, as nothing like it ever ran on the LMS on the mainland. Care seems to have been taken to give the driver a good view ahead.

The CDR tried to minimise the disadvantages of its 3ft gauge by building carriages with considerable overhang.

The NCC itself, doubtless encouraged by the success of the County Donegal railcars, introduced its first example in 1933. Again it was petrol engined, although later converted to diesel, and No. 1 then survived until the early 1960s. A number of other railcars were also introduced by the NCC, but these were diesel-engined from the start.

The LMS also invested in the infrastructure. On the main line to Londonderry, a new viaduct was built over the River Bann at Coleraine, but this must have been planned by the Midland before Grouping as it opened in March 1924. Being built further down the river, the new viaduct eliminated some sharp curves and severe gradients. The viaduct's eleven spans included a lifting span for shipping to pass through. Later the LMS built the Greenisland loop and a new viaduct over Valentine's Glen in 1934 at a price of £200,000 (equivalent to £12.5 million today, which avoided the need for main-line trains to reverse at Greenisland, and a flying junction that carried the line to Larne clear of the mainline to Portrush and Londonderry.

Signalling was also improved, allowing trains on the main line to run at intervals of just three minutes on the busiest section between Belfast and Greenisland. Part of the line to Larne was doubled. An idea of the traffic being carried can be gained from the fact that trains from Larne Harbour to Londonderry could consist of as many as 17 bogie carriages. A train control centre was built at Belfast, and this was to be a considerable asset, especially after the outbreak of the Second World War, when the NCC lines became exceptionally busy with Londonderry becoming a major base not only for the escort vessels protecting the Atlantic convoys, but also with a Royal Naval Air Station at Eglinton, which was later joined by a second at Maydown. Bases were built for RAF Coastal Command, with some of them taken over by the United States Navy, while that at Ballykelly in County Londonderry had a runway built across the main line. The trains had priority!

There were some economies possible as a result of the Grouping. In addition to handing over operation, but not ownership, of the Dundalk, Newry & Greenore Railway to the GNR (I), the company rationalised the ferry services and ports, closing the former LNWR port and service from Fleetwood and concentrating the Belfast ferries on the Midland Railway's port at Heysham. This was not necessarily a case of the former Midland managers riding roughshod over their former LNWR colleagues as Fleetwood had a bar at the harbour mouth that restricted the draught of vessels crossing it.

An artist's impression of the new viaduct at Greenisland in Northern Ireland. Its construction, and that of a loop line, meant that trains between Belfast and Portrush or Londonderry, the NCC's main line, no longer had to reverse. (*Irish Steam Railway Preservation Society*)

Chapter 14

Shipping and Ports

With Great Britain not just an island, but one of a cluster of islands, it was not surprising that all of the grouped railway companies had extensive interests in shipping and docks. The railway companies soon saw the appeal of providing ferry services across the English Channel, the North Sea and the Irish Sea, as well as on lakes and rivers and across estuaries, but this was hard-won, and at first the railway companies were not allowed to operate ferries for fear that they might compete unfairly with the established operators. It was not until 1863 that the railway companies were finally allowed to operate shipping services.

The business was such an important part of the new LMS that the *LMS Magazine* wasted little time in reminding its readers that the company had the largest steamship operation of any railway in the world. This included no fewer than 29 cross-channel (meaning the Irish Sea) steamers with a total gross registered tonnage of 49,258; 21 Continental steamers with a total grt of 19,917; 11 steamers on the River Clyde with a total grt of 4,523; eight ferries with a total grt of 1,317; 17 lake steamers with a total grt of 1,782; nine tugs, 36 hoppers, dredgers and barges, and seven pontoons. All this amounted to a total gross registered tonnage of 92,614. This may seem little today when a single cross-channel ferry can be as much as 40,000 tons, but ships were much smaller at the time and a ferry with a tonnage of around 3,000grt was regarded as a substantial ship.

The company inherited the docks at Barrow from the Furness Railway, while the LNWR provided the docks at Deganwy Quay and Foryd Pier which were in Wales, as was Holyhead on the island of Anglesey, and Garston near Liverpool. Fleetwood had been built and operated by the LNWR and the LYR together, while the latter also had the Wyre Dock and on the Humber the port at Goole. This was, as usual, nothing compared with the Midland, which had two docks at Bristol, Avonside and Kings Wharf, plus the port of Heysham in Lancashire, and then on the River Thames, a landing stage at Tilbury, the Town and West Piers at Gravesend, and docks at Poplar, where the North London Railway also had a separate facility. The Severn & Wye Joint Railway had docks on the River Severn at Lydney in Gloucestershire, while the Somerset & Dorset Joint Railway had docks at Highbridge in Somerset.

The railways were major port operators while the LMS had the largest railway-owned shipping fleet in the world. Many of the vessels were engaged in humble duties, such as this Gravesend ferry, *Rose*.

A commonplace scene until the 1970s would have been railway wagons on a quayside, full of goods either to be loaded aboard, or just discharged from a ship. This is Grangemouth on the Firth of Forth with the steamer SS *Mall*, which had brought a large consignment of pit props. *(HMRS AEP101)*

In Scotland, the Caledonian passed on its docks at Bowling, Grangemouth and Alloa, as well as the Railway Pier at Oban and piers on the Clyde at Gourock and Wemyss Bay. The Glasgow & South Western also had Clyde piers at Fairlie, Largs and Renfrew, as well as docks at Ayr and Troon. The Highland Railway had a port at the Kyle of Lochalsh, while the Portpatrick & Wigtownshire Joint Railway had its important port at Stranraer.

The LMS also inherited several canals, with more than 540 miles altogether of which more than 490 miles were in England. Unlike the docks and ferry services, these lacked any real potential for growth and it was to be a case of managed decline, as we will see later.

The ferry routes that emanated from these various docks and piers did not simply reach across the Irish Sea, but there were also services across the North Sea, a legacy from the LYR.

The LNWR's port at Holyhead had services to Kingstown and Dublin North Wall, although at the time of Grouping the latter had its passenger services suspended, a throwback to economies made during the First World War, but it still carried cattle and cargo. Holyhead also had the service to Greenore, supported by the DNGR's services in Ireland. There were services from both Fleetwood and Heysham to Belfast, and from Liverpool to Drogheda. This network of routes was augmented by the service between Stranraer and Larne, the shortest crossing to Ireland, but one renowned for rough seas and also needing a lengthy journey for those from the North West of England, not to mention anywhere further south.

Thanks to the LYR, the LMS also had services from Goole on the River Humber to Dunkirk, Ghent, Antwerp, Rotterdam, Amsterdam, Hamburg and Copenhagen, but these were mainly general cargo services. Goole never ever reached the size of its neighbours at Hull and Grimsby, but a joint service existed with the LNER for passengers to Zeebrugge from Hull.

There were also the railway steamers on the Firth of Clyde, on Loch Lomond, Loch Tay and Loch Awe, as well as on Lake Windermere and Coniston Water. Ferries included those between Tilbury and Gravesend, Heysham and Fleetwood, and the Kyleakin ferry. The Clyde steamers were operated through a subsidiary which had been part of the Caledonian Railway's dowry for the LMS, the Caledonian Steam Packet Company, one of the predecessors of today's Caledonian McBrayne.

Rationalisation and expansion

The ferry services were an integral part of the railway business. The LMS not only served its own ships, but also the sailings of other companies, such as Burns & Laird on the services to Northern Ireland. At first this had a service from Glasgow to Londonderry as well as from Ardrossan to Belfast while others were the Belfast Steamship Company's service from Liverpool to Belfast, the Isle of Man Steam Packet Company operating from Fleetwood and Liverpool, and B&I from Liverpool to Dublin. The company rationalised its own services by pulling out of Fleetwood in 1928, and concentrated its passenger sailings to Belfast on Heysham, while it also passed its services to the Isle of Man to the Isle of Man Steam Packet Company that same year.

In the meantime, a new packet service had started between Tilbury and Dunkirk in May 1927. This was operated by the Angleterre-Lorraine-Alsace Company, and the LMS provided an express from Manchester to Euston with a free connection by bus to St Pancras, from which a boat train ran to Tilbury to connect with the sailings.

St Pancras was the major terminus for LMS boat trains, which from July to the end of September 1934 totalled 105 between St Pancras and Tilbury, while between Euston and Liverpool there were another 80. These were in addition to the boat trains for the company's own Irish Sea services. The boat trains in question were for the Cunard liners for the United States and Canada sailing from Liverpool, while those for Tilbury were for P&O and the Orient Line sailing to India, the Far East and Australia.

This traffic did not remain with the LMS for long as the new West Docks and the Ocean Terminal at Southampton soon saw the three shipping lines move there. Southampton was closer to the open sea, and also avoided the long haul around the North Foreland for ships using Tilbury. The Southern Railway gained this traffic at the expense of the LMS.

While the LMS commissioned new ships for its services, it also improved the ports, including introducing the first British roll-on/roll-off ferries which entailed building a ramp at Stranraer in Scotland that was deliberately over-specified so that it could handle heavy military vehicles and tanks.

Having concentrated its services from the North West of England on Heysham, the LMS introduced three new sister ships (which means ships of the same class) of 3,600grt: *Duke of Argyll, Duke of Lancaster* and *Duke of Rothesay*, ironically following the Fleetwood tradition of naming these ships after dukes. The service was so successful that in 1935 a fourth ship, *Duke of York*, was commissioned.

Further north, on the short crossing between Stranraer and Larne, the tradition, which the LMS upheld, was for the ships to be named after princesses. The most important ship that the LMS introduced on this route was *Princess Victoria*, Britain's first drive-on/drive-off, or in nautical terms, roll-on/roll-off, car ferry when she entered service in 1939. She was requisitioned

At the other end of the scale were the fast packet steamers, such as the *Duke of Lancaster*, involved in the Heysham–Belfast overnight ferry service which connected with the 'Ulster Express' to and from Euston.

LONDON MIDLAND AND SCOTTISH RAILWAY.
FIVE ROUTES TO IRELAND.

ROYAL MAIL ROUTE.
Via HEYSHAM and BELFAST.

New Cross Channel Steamers:
"DUKE OF ARGYLL," "DUKE OF LANCASTER," "DUKE OF ROTHESAY," & "DUKE OF YORK"
will sail as follows:—

ROYAL MAIL SERVICE.
Via HOLYHEAD and KINGSTOWN.
Through Bookings between all the Principal Stations in England and Ireland.
FASTEST AND BEST PASSENGER ROUTE.

[Detailed sailing and fare tables for the Heysham–Belfast, Holyhead–Kingstown, Liverpool–Dublin (British & Irish Steam Packet Co.), Liverpool–Belfast (Belfast Steamship Co.), and Stranraer–Larne routes follow.]

Via LIVERPOOL and DUBLIN.
(British & Irish Steam Packet Co.)

ROYAL MAIL ROUTE.
Via LIVERPOOL and BELFAST.
(Belfast Steamship Co.)

Direct connections at Belfast with trains to all parts of Antrim, Derry, and Donegal.

ROYAL MAIL AND SHORTEST SEA ROUTE.
Via STRANRAER and LARNE.
The Services between CARLISLE and BELFAST are given on Week-days only, and until further notice will be as follows:—

There was no shortage of choice for those travelling to Ireland, as the LMS not only had its own steamer services from Holyhead, Heysham and Stranraer, but also provided good connecting expresses for British & Irish Steam Packet Company ferry services between Liverpool and Dublin, and from the Belfast Steamship service between Liverpool and Belfast. (*Bradshaw*)

by the Admiralty in December and sunk by an enemy mine the following year. Her successor of the same name, built by British Railways, was equally ill-fated, as described later, in Chapter 17 Accidents.

At Holyhead, the LMS inherited no fewer than six ships: *Curraghmore, Anglia, Hibernia, Cambria, Scotia* and *Slieve Donard*, all commissioned by the LNWR between 1919 and 1921. These were largely to replace wartime losses, and while some older ships were scrapped, the LMS did not provide any new tonnage for this route. One reason for this was that in addition to the poor economic situation, the new Irish Free State was beset by civil war during its early years and traffic, especially tourist traffic, was badly affected.

The losses suffered on war service by the London & North Western Railway steamers, and the award of the mail contract between Great Britain and Ireland after the First World War, meant that the LMS inherited a fine fleet of modern steamers, the 'Anglia' class, for the Holyhead service.

Canals

History as taught in many schools implies that the railway age meant the end of the canals, but this was far from the truth, and the railways did not always close the canals. The London & North Western, for example, used the Birmingham Canal to feed traffic to exchange depots, and in return paid a guaranteed dividend to shareholders. Other railways found that canal ownership was a quick and non-Parliamentary means of penetrating the territory of a rival line. Eventually, almost a third of the canal network fell into railway ownership, and while it is true that many were closed, converted or neglected, this was not always the case, and some continued to trade profitably into the 20th century. Canals which had extensive development along their banks often did well.

The LMS became one of the biggest canal owners in the country, if not the biggest, but this was an asset that was past its best. There had been a revival of interest after the success of the Manchester Ship Canal, but this was a particular canal designed to solve a particular problem. The years between the two world wars were not ones in which massive new investment could be contemplated. The main canals in LMS ownership were the Montgomeryshire Canal, the Ellesmere Canal, and the Chester Canal.

The first of these, the Montgomeryshire Canal, was actually profitable until the end of the First World War, following which it began to make heavy losses. Owned by the Shropshire Union Railways & Canal Company, it passed to the LMS, but its decline continued. In 1936 a breach occurred near Frankton Junction, and despite having a statutory duty to maintain it, the LMS decided to abandon the canal, promoting an Act of Abandonment for this and other canals, that was passed by Parliament in 1944, stating that the waterway had not been used for some years.

The same legislation also permitted the LMS to close the Ellesmere Canal to navigation, apart from a short stretch between Ellesmere Port and Chester, while the section from Hurlesdon to Llangollen was retained to provide water for the Shropshire Union Canal. The oldest part of the Shropshire Union Canal network was the Chester Canal which remained profitable and was retained when the other sections were closed as a result of the 1944 legislation.

Although the LMS owned many canal barges in addition to those of independent operators who used its network, it has not been possible to ascertain exactly how many.

Chapter 15

Road Transport

The railways had been involved in road transport from an early stage in their history, but their involvement was limited. They could run buses from a town or village to their station, and they could collect goods for shipment and bring them to a goods depot or station, or deliver them to a customer from a station or goods depot, but they could not provide a door-to-door goods service without rail being involved, and could not run buses other than for railway passengers. As with shipping, the approach of Parliament was that for the railways everything was forbidden unless it was permitted, which traditionally has been the opposite of British legislation. As the railways were creatures of Parliament, needing an act to authorise their construction, they were relatively easy to control.

The reluctance to give the railways ever greater powers was born out of the belief that they could damage the existing operators, at sea and then on land. There was from the early days a distrust of the railways because the new mode of transport was so superior in terms of speed, reliability and cost to anything that had gone before. The impact of the railways on the canals was noticed, even though many canals survived in railway ownership. There was also the case that the railways became local monopolies competing with their neighbours at the edge of their operating area, and there was concern that this would extend to road transport as well.

On the other hand, the railways felt that they were at the mercy of road transport which boomed after the end of the First World War as many men were demobbed from the armed forces with the ability to drive and maintain road vehicles, while war surplus lorries were also sold off cheaply. The typical ex-army lorry in 1919 could easily be converted into a bus as they usually had the same design of chassis, and buses had still to receive the low centre drop axle that would allow floor heights to be lowered.

On its formation, the LMS had 9,100 horses for its cartage operations, and 1,350 road vehicles.

The powers to operate road vehicles in their own right were granted to the railways in 1929. Despite the jealous statements about the freedom of road hauliers to carry what they wanted, to pick and choose, and charge what they wanted, the first move by the LMS and other railway companies was into passenger road transport. In September, the LMS proudly announced that it had entered into agreements with 36 bus companies operating in England and Wales, and with the Scottish Motor Transport Company, SMTC, a group that owned many of the larger Scottish bus companies, mainly operating rural and inter-urban services, although the smaller towns were also served by companies, leaving just Aberdeen, Dundee, Edinburgh and Glasgow with municipal operations.

The catalysts for this move was that the LMS had promoted its own legislation a year earlier, and the LMS Road Transport Act 1928 in effect paved the way as Parliament could not allow one thrusting railway company to press ahead and invest in road transport while denying the other three the same rights.

Sir Josiah Stamp, the chairman, sent a circular to all staff advising them of the bus companies in which the LMS had acquired an interest as it would 'be useful to the staff when considering in what way they may assist further to improve the company's business.'

In Scotland, as well as SMTC the company was also involved in Ayrshire Pullman and Gourock Pullman Services. The list in England and Wales was far more extensive, and consisted of:

Birmingham & Midland Motor Omnibus Company
   (BMMO, more usually known as Midland Red)
Crosville Motor Services
Cumberland Motor Services
East Midland Motor Services
Eastern National Omnibus Company
Hebble Omnibus Services
Holyhead Motor Services, trading as Mona-Maroon
Lincolnshire Road Car Company
Llandudno Coaching and Carriage Company
North Western Road Car Company
Ortona Motor Company
Peterborough Electric Traction Company
Ribble Motor Services
Trent Motor Traction Company
Yorkshire Traction Company
Yorkshire (Woollen District) Electric Tramways Company

Sir Josiah also advised the company's employees that the company was interested in omnibus services operated by the local authorities in Sheffield, Leeds and Halifax, without actually explaining what the 'interest' was. 'Other arrangements with Municipalities and Omnibus Companies are pending,' he concluded.

The *quid pro quo* for this measure was that from 1930 the railways were no longer to run buses on their own account, so the extensive network of LMS and NCC bus services was merged into existing local companies, strengthening the company's 'interest' in them. The NCC was in fact replacing some of its less remunerative branch line passenger services with buses, in what would today is called 'bustitution'. The problem was, of course, that the new measures meant that the railways could be heavily involved in bus services, but they were to gain no advantage over other bus operators by doing so. It could have been this as much as any technical difficulties that inhibited further development of road-rail vehicles.

In many cases the company was involved with most transport operators who competed with its own services, especially the longer distance coach services that the larger bus operators provided.

Bus companies operating in and around London were affected by the creation of the London Passenger Transport Board in 1933. In the case of the LMS, Eastern National lost vehicles and routes to the new London Transport.

While the railway companies made their own, entirely regional, arrangements with bus companies, when it came to road haulage they operated in unison. The reasons for this were simple. First, the companies were increasingly being forced to collaborate in marketing freight services and in collection and delivery in order to contain costs. Secondly, although bus operators were usually local or at the most regional businesses, road haulage was even more fragmented than bus operation, in which many substantial groups had emerged, even by the late 1920s. There were just two haulage operators with a national presence, Carter Paterson, the parcels specialist, and Pickfords, the removals specialist.

In a few cases, two railway companies would invest in a bus company whose operational area crossed into both of their areas, but in no case did all four grouped companies combine to buy a bus or coach operation, but on 31 October 1933 the 'Big Four' combined to buy Carter Paterson and Pickfords.

Ireland

In Northern Ireland the LMS found the NCC with its own fleet of buses and lorries, which by 1935 totalled 131 buses and 56 lorries. This was an impressive fleet given the much lower population of Northern Ireland, especially away from the coast, while Belfast had its own municipal bus and tram system.

The struggle between the railways and road transport in Northern Ireland was much the same as on the mainland, with the railways losing business to the more competitive road transport operators. The reaction of the Irish railways was different, however, as they approached the government of Northern Ireland and proposed that it create a road transport monopoly, setting a dangerous precedent. Only the Irish standard gauge companies, the NCC and the GNR (I) as well as the Belfast & County Down, were involved.

The government sought the very best advice it could, from none other than the former general manager of the Great Western Railway, Sir Felix Pole, and asked him to investigate. He took evidence from both sides, and also from transport users and the trades unions. When his report was published in July 1934, he recommended setting up a road transport board to control all bus and lorry operations, and to encourage cooperation and coordination with the railways. His proposals were accepted and on 1 October 1935 the Northern Ireland Road Transport Board came into being, acquiring the railway bus and lorry fleets and the Smithfield bus station in Belfast. The NCC facilities at railway stations were made available to the NIRTB, and a joint passenger timetable was issued. Despite this, the coordination that was expected did not materialise and the NIRTB itself became a new competitor for the railways, but with a far better coordinated road transport service! As so often happens in road transport, the diseconomies of scale appeared and prices rose.

There were three exceptions to the sweeping control of road transport wielded by the NIRTB. Belfast Corporation continued to run its trams, trolleybuses and motor buses, as did the two narrow gauge cross-border bus companies, although later the County Donegal buses were taken over by the Irish transport operator, CIE.

One vehicle that offered the tempting possibility of involving the railways in doorstep-to-destination transport, by running on roads as well as rails, was the Leyland 'Ro-Railer', but like many such vehicles it was heavy and costly, while the earning potential was meagre. Acquiring bus companies was much more likely to be profitable. (*LMS*)

Chapter 16

Air Services

Given the long delay in authorising railway involvement in shipping and, much later, road transport, approval to become involved in air transport came relatively quickly. The first British commercial flights were in 1919, but the railways were involved with air transport from 1933. At first the more ambitious companies acted independently, but a combined operation, Railway Air Services, was formed in 1934 involving the LMS as well as the GWR and the Southern. The LNER was not involved, and while this may seem strange, it was the one company without many obvious services on which the aeroplane would be an asset, although the heavily indented coastline between Aberdeen and Edinburgh or Newcastle might have presented some opportunities. Air services within Scotland were operated by Scottish Airways, which collaborated with Railway Air Services, as did the airlines operating to the Isle of Wight and Channel Islands at the other end of the British Isles.

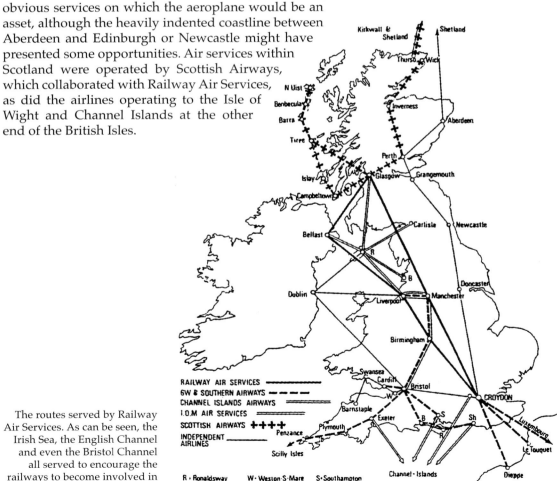

RAILWAY AIR SERVICES ————
GW & SOUTHERN AIRWAYS — — —
CHANNEL ISLANDS AIRWAYS ————
I.O.M AIR SERVICES ========
SCOTTISH AIRWAYS +++++
INDEPENDENT AIRLINES ————

R · Ronaldsway   W · Weston-S-Mare   S · Southampton
B · Blackpool   B · Bournemouth   R · Ryde   Sh · Shoreham

The routes served by Railway Air Services. As can be seen, the Irish Sea, the English Channel and even the Bristol Channel all served to encourage the railways to become involved in air transport.

This is typical of the de Havilland Dragon aircraft in the Railway Air Services fleet, seen here loading cargo. (*NRM 494/93*)

The vice-president in charge of scientific research at the LMS, Sir Harold Hartley, became the first chairman of Railway Air Services.

Given the competition posed by air travel and its threat to first-class revenues and sleeper services, railway involvement in air transport might seem strange. Nevertheless, the railways knew that if they didn't become involved, other operators would do so. There were also routes where the aeroplane showed a distinct advantage over surface transport, such as Plymouth to Liverpool, which opened on 7 May 1934. The aircraft flew via Haldon, the aerodrome serving Torquay, and continued via Cardiff and Birmingham. The service offered connections at Cardiff with Western Airways and with the Dutch airline, KLM Royal Dutch Airlines, at Liverpool, where passengers could change on to a flight to Amsterdam via Hull. There were further extensions to the route network in 1935.

The aircraft used were well suited to the service being provided, with elegant de Havilland Dragon Rapide twin-engined biplanes. These could only carry six passengers, and had a crew of two.

Nevertheless, not all seemed to be well with Railway Air Services, as the LMS seemed far less interested in aviation than the Great Western and the Southern, while these two companies did not like the heavy losses being incurred on routes outside their own areas of operation. This could have been a case of differences in route structures and opportunities for air transport to develop, or it could simply have been that the laggards were the companies with the poorest financial situation. In 1938, a new airline was formed from Great Western Air Services and Southern Air Services, Great Western and Southern Air Services.

In the meantime, during the summer of 1937, RAS, still with LMS involvement planned to fly a million miles during the season. Those with an LMS involvement included the Royal Mail service between London Croydon and Belfast, calling en route at Birmingham, Stoke and Liverpool, with two services daily in each direction that year for the first time, offering an out and back in one day opportunity for passengers. Readers of the *LMS Magazine* were reminded that there were connections at Croydon for onward travel to many European destinations. Railway passengers could complete part of their journey by air on payment of a supplement, and book through any railway booking office. There was also a Glasgow to Belfast service, with three flights in each direction daily, and services from the Isle of Man to Belfast, Blackpool, Carlisle, Glasgow, Leeds and Bradford, and Liverpool. At Glasgow, there were onward connections to Perth and Inverness, but, strangely, not to Aberdeen.

No supplement was charged for those wishing to send their luggage in advance, and it seems that this convenient arrangement was using the railway rather than the airways. On the other hand, fares were expensive, with Liverpool to Belfast costing around £3 10s; about the average weekly wage for a skilled man at the time.

While the outbreak of war saw the suspension of domestic air services, Railway Air Services did provide a number of domestic services for the use of members of the government and their officials. A limited service was also available across the Irish Sea to Dublin and the Isle of Man.

By 1944, many believed that the end of the war was in sight, at least in Europe, and started to plan post-war air services. On 13 November 1944, Railway Air Services was able to reintroduce scheduled air services between London and Liverpool and Liverpool and Belfast, while there was a connection from Liverpool's airport at Speke to the Isle of Man with Isle of Man Airways. New aircraft were planned for these services post-war, with ex-RAF Douglas C-47 Dakotas, as well as the 32-seat Bristol Wayfarer, a passenger development of the Bristol 170 Freighter.

Far less fruitful were the plans being laid for a new airline, British & Foreign Air Services, formed during the war years and owned jointly by the 'Big Four' railway companies. This was to be overtaken by events, for not only did the post-war Labour government nationalise the railways, it also nationalised most scheduled air transport.

Weight was extremely critical in the smaller, early airliners, so not only the luggage but also the passengers had to be weighed. (NRM LMS7143)

Chapter 17

Accidents

Railway accidents during the first half of the 20th century were far more prevalent than in recent years, and usually more serious when they did happen. By the time of Grouping, interlocking of signals and points was becoming more widespread, but even so, fog remained a persistent danger and far worse than today because of almost all domestic heating and much industrial production, as well as the railways themselves, being fuelled by coal. Most railway carriages were largely constructed of wood, many were still wooden framed, and offered no protection to their occupants in a collision or derailment. The 'scrap-and-build' policies of the LMS and its preference for all-steel construction contributed considerably to improving safety. On the other hand, the company still produced some rolling stock with gas lighting, and this was another weakness of the older rolling stock which meant that serious accidents could often be accompanied by fire.

There were a number of serious accidents during the life of the LMS, although some could be attributed to the unnatural pressures of the Second World War. Like any other railway, some accidents highlighted problems hitherto unnoticed or which railway management thought had been resolved. Interestingly, there were no accidents on the NCC during the period.

The new company was faced with a serious accident at its most important terminus, Euston, some 16 months after grouping.

Euston, 26 April 1924

Shortly after the inauguration of the electric services, at 7.53am on 26 April 1924, a six-car up electric train struck the rear of the 5.30am excursion from Coventry as it was standing at the up slow home signal carrying football fans to the FA Cup Final at Wembley. There were 14 carriages in the excursion train and all five passengers who were killed were aboard it, while another 68 passengers on both trains and both guards, as well as the motorman, were injured. The motorman of the electric train was trapped in his cab for five hours. The blame was laid on the signalman who had given 'train out of section' for an up Scottish express but used the up slow instrument instead of the up fast. The motorman of the electric train had not been able to see the tail light of the excursion train until he was within 16 yards of it because of the smoke and steam lingering under the Park Street railway bridge.

Lytham, 3 November 1924

Wheel failures had been a major contributor to railway accidents in the early days, but by the time of Grouping, the number of such failures had dropped considerably and was mainly confined to wagons. On 3 November 1924, the front steel tyre of a locomotive at the head of the 4.40pm Liverpool to Blackpool failed as the train was moving at around 50mph, derailing the train at a level crossing, after which it hit a bridge and the signalbox at Warton. The engine toppled, dragging the two leading carriages on to their sides, and coals from the fire grate set the carriages alight. Fourteen people were killed.

During the accident investigation, the inspector found part of the broken tyre 50 yards away in a field. On examination, it was found that a large cavity had been introduced to the tyre during casting. The wheel had run more than 100,000 miles since the new tyre had been fitted in 1920. All the remaining tyres from the same batch were removed from service and broken up, without finding any further cavities.

Parkgate & Rawmarsh, 19 November 1926

The 10.10am express passenger train from York to Bristol, on 19 November 1926, was approaching Rawmarsh, near Rotherham, at speed on the fast up line when the line was blocked by wreckage from the derailment of the 7.20am mineral train from Westhouses to Royston, which had been running on the adjoining down slow line. The locomotive of the express was not damaged and none of the carriages were derailed, but the debris from the derailment scraped the sides of the first three carriages and then ripped out the sides and interior of the last two carriages. It was in these that nine passengers were either killed outright or died later from their injuries; two others were seriously injured and another 25 suffered minor injuries or shock, while the guard was also injured. The carriages were of wooden construction and the outcome could have been less serious had all-metal rolling stock been in use, but this was still to come.

Penistone, 27 February 1927

Penistone, high in the Yorkshire Moors, and its immediate area have suffered a disproportionate number of railway accidents over the years. The line was a meeting point between the LMS and the LNER.

On 27 February 1927, an LMS locomotive was running around a train obeying a green signal, unaware that this was meant for an express. The LMS locomotive, a radial tank, had worked a train through on the Huddersfield line, and had arrived and its passengers had alighted. It needed to clear the line to allow an empty stock working from Bradford to enter the station and so shunted its rake of carriages on to the other LMS platform. Although not necessary, it was usual for the locomotive to run around to the other end of the train, which required a number of shunts backwards and forwards, ending with a move to the front of the train on the LMS up line.

Sending the fireman to brew tea in the porter's room, the driver was on his own, but was given a hand signal by the duty Huddersfield Junction signalman, who promptly forgot to set the points for the LMS line leaving the locomotive on the LNER line. The driver realised that he was on the wrong line and stopped, but when he saw a signal at the eastern end of the station go to 'off', he thought that this was meant for him and moved forward believing that he would run back on to the LMS line. The signal was meant for the express from Manchester to Marylebone, with five carriages, which had eased to 20mph because of speed restrictions at Penistone, and this prevented the accident from being more serious.

While the Huddersfield Junction signalman was blamed for the accident, the crew of the LMS locomotive was also blamed as the driver should have sent the fireman to the signalbox to remind the signalman of his locomotive rather than to brew tea.

Charfield, 13 October 1928

The Leeds to Bristol night mail failed to stop at the signals protecting the sidings at Charfield in Gloucester on 13 October 1928. It was a misty evening, but the mist was not thick enough for the signalman to call for fog signalmen. At the time, a freight train was being shunted from the main line into the sidings, and a train of empty goods wagons was running in the opposite direction to the night mail. The mail train collided with the freight train and was derailed, after which it was struck by the empty wagon working as it passed under the road bridge at Charfield station. Gas used for lighting on the mail train then ignited, with four of the five carriages completely burnt out. The fire was so intense that identification of the dead was difficult, and it was impossible even to be sure of the number of bodies. The official report lists 16 dead and 41 injured, but some believe that the numbers should be between 15 and as much as 23, although only eleven are known beyond all doubt to have died.

The driver of the night mail maintained that he had been given a clear distant signal and so had naturally assumed that the home signal protecting the points was also clear. He was charged with manslaughter, but acquitted.

Ashchurch, 8 January 1929

At Ashchurch, near Tewkesbury, in fog on 8 January 1929, the 7.20pm up express Bristol to Leeds mail train passed signals at danger and collided side-long with a shunt of goods wagons being propelled over the trailing crossover from the up to the down main line at the northern end of Ashchurch station. In the accident, the driver of the express and three passengers were killed, while eleven passengers and twelve postal workers were injured.

Leighton Buzzard, 22 March 1931

The 12.30am 'Midday Scot' from London Euston to Glasgow and Edinburgh was derailed at high speed on 22 March 1931, as it traversed the junction from the down fast to the down slow line just south of Leighton Buzzard station. It had been diverted because of engineering work on the line ahead, but the driver had not slowed to take the points, probably forgetting the instruction that would have been given to him as he started his shift, and there is no mention of warning detonators having been laid. The ten leading carriages were derailed, with the locomotive and the first three carriages being destroyed and the fourth carriage badly damaged. Three passengers were killed in the accident along with the driver, fireman and the dining car chef. Three passengers and two others of the train crew (probably working in the dining car or kitchen car) were badly injured, while another twelve passengers suffered from minor injuries.

The SS *Calder*, 17/18 April 1931

The LMS lost one ship, a new general cargo vessel, the SS *Calder*, on passage from Hamburg for Hull and Goole. She sailed from the German port on 17 April 1931 with 960 tons of general cargo, of which 200 tons was stowed on deck. The weather was stormy and the following morning two steamships, the *Hodder* and *Nottingham*, found wreckage that was identified as coming from the *Calder*. It seems that the ship foundered with all hands: her ship's company consisted of 18 men. It is difficult to be sure why she foundered, but either she could have been swamped by a large wave or her ability to cope with rough seas might have been compromised by the relatively large volume of deck cargo.

Great Bridgeford, 17 June 1932

Excessive speed was also the cause of this accident on 17 June 1932, less than 15 months after the accident at Leighton Buzzard. The train that had departed Crewe at 7.23pm for Stafford and Birmingham consisted of four carriages with an empty four-wheel wagon behind, and was completely derailed immediately after crossing through the cross-over from the up slow to the up fast line at the southern end of Great Bridgeford station. The engine and tender overturned, with the engine partly buried in the shallow cutting in which the line was located. The first carriage was completely wrecked, coming to rest at right angles across the four running lines. The remaining three carriages were derailed and partly overturned, with the body of the second carriage wrecked for about two-thirds of its length as it telescoped into the first carriage. Three of the 90 passengers aboard the train were killed outright, while a fourth died the following day. Nine passengers, the driver and fireman were seriously injured.

Port Eglinton, 6 September 1934

Head on collisions between trains are rare, but after passing signals set at danger on 6 September 1934, the 5.35pm passenger train from Glasgow St Enoch to Kilmarnock was crossing from the main line to the fast Canal line when it collided with the 5.12pm passenger train from Paisley to St Enoch. In the accident, the firemen of both trains and the driver of the Kilmarnock train were killed, as were six passengers, while the driver of the St Enoch train and ten passengers were seriously injured, and another 20, including the two guards, suffered minor injuries.

Winwick Junction, 28 September 1934

There is seldom a single cause in railway accidents, but most are the result of either a sequence of events or at least have several contributing factors, and one of these was at Winwick Junction, near Warrington, on 28 September 1934. This was a busy junction with a complicated layout, with four running lines for the main line between Warrington and Preston, and a junction for the Warrington–Earlestown branch line. Recognising the workload the LMS had given the signalman a booking lad, whose job it was to maintain the train register and remind the signalman of the position of any trains in the section.

Shortly after 9pm, a local train running from Warrington to Wigan entered the section to take the Earlestown branch, but the signalman was preoccupied with no fewer than seven other trains at the time, and is believed to have been on the telephone to control discussing a change to the running order for an express goods train carrying fish. The local train was stopped at the home signal and the fireman left the cab to walk to the signalbox so that he could remind the signalman that his train was stopped in the section. Before the fireman could reach the signalbox, the signalman at Winwick Quay, the next box to the south, rang 'call attention' for a Euston to Blackpool express, expecting to have to follow this with the call to shunt the local train out of the way. Instead, the Winwick Junction signalman forgot about the local and replied that the train was out of section, clearing his signals. The signal lad failed to warn him that the local was still standing at the home signal because he had been distracted by a telephone call about a timetable change and as he believed that he had missed the local train passing through on to the branch, he filled in the register to show that it had passed.

As the signals cleared, the driver of the local began moving forward slowly to pick up his fireman, but was almost immediately struck by the express. Despite the local train having modern steel coaches, three of them were badly telescoped, killing the guard and five passengers as well as another three passengers in the express. Two passengers later died in hospital, although it is not known which train they were on.

The signalman admitted responsibility, but the booking lad was considered to be the main culprit, although track circuiting or even a telephone at the home signal would have averted the accident. The inspecting officer recommended that track circuiting be installed at the junction.

King's Langley, 13 March 1935

Most accidents involve two trains, and occasionally three, but an accident involving four trains is, fortunately, rare, but such an event did occur at King's Langley on 13 March 1935. The 4.55pm up express freight, with 42 fitted vans and a brake van, carrying meat from Alexandra Dock to Broad Street stopped on the up fast line because a fracture in the vacuum pipe of the locomotive automatically applied the brakes. The driver managed to effect a temporary repair and in about six minutes the train was able to restart, but was almost immediately struck in the rear at around 25mph by the 5.50pm Stafford to Euston milk train. This had 22 fitted milk tanks and vans, which had entered the section under clear signals after being checked earlier by signals, accounting for its relatively low speed.

The accident fouled the down fast and down slow lines as well as the up fast by the rear four vans and brake van of the meat train, with the guard having a lucky escape, and the locomotive and eleven tanks and vans of the milk train. The driver of the milk train immediately sent his fireman forward to stop the 10.50pm down express passenger train from Euston to Edinburgh and Aberdeen, while he left the footplate to stop the 12.25pm coal train from Toton to Willesden, which was on the up slow and which he had just overtaken. Before he could do this, he was killed by the 10.30pm partially fitted Camden to Holyhead freight which was running under clear signals at around 40mph on the down slow line. The freight train's locomotive and 14 of its 42 wagons were wrecked as it struck the vehicles derailed earlier. This left the coal train, with 70 wagons and a brake van travelling at more than 20mph which then ran into the wreckage, derailing the engine and another 20 wagons were added to those off the rails.

This was the consequence of the signalman prematurely clearing his block instrument and allowing the first two trains into the section. It seems to have been a miracle that there was just one fatality, but the chaos was such that it took until 9.45pm the next day to find the body of the unfortunate driver who had done his duty attempting to prevent further collisions. His body was found between the up fast and down slow lines, buried beneath wreckage which in places reached a height of 30 feet.

Wartime

The problems created by wartime conditions, including the blackout, added to the dangers faced by railwaymen and passengers, so the accidents on the LMS during this difficult period are covered in Chapter 20.

Ecclefechan, 21 July 1945

As the wartime accident at Bletchley, covered in Chapter 20, showed, the railways were quite capable of adding to their problems without enemy help. Just after the end of the war in Europe, on 21 July 1945, the 1pm express from Glasgow to Euston was travelling at around 60–65mph as it approached Ecclefechan, south of Lockerbie, when it ran past a distant signal at caution and then overran the home signals, to collide with a goods train that was setting back into the down (the train ran down to the border and then up to London) siding to allow the express to pass. The express locomotive, No. 6231 *Duchess of Atholl*, a non-streamlined 4-6-2, finally stopped on its right side, 138 yards on from the point of collision, with the locomotive badly damaged and both its crew killed. The locomotive of the goods train was moved forward 100 yards. Aboard the express, 31 passengers were injured.

One result of this accident was that later, smoke deflecting plates were added to the 'Duchess' class locomotives, as in wet weather the smoke and steam from these locomotives tended to cling to the boiler top, obscuring the view for the driver. Cautious drivers would frequently cut off steam so that they could see the signals, but those anxious to make up time were less likely to do this.

Bourne End, 30 September 1945

Shortly after the end of the Second World War, a serious accident occurred at Bourne End, near Hemel Hempstead in Hertfordshire, and like the Harrow disaster some years later in 1952, it involved the

Perth to London sleeping car express, although in this case it only affected the one train.

On 30 September 1945, the sleeping car express with 15 carriages, was supposed to divert from the up fast to the up slow lines because of engineering work in Watford tunnel. The driver failed to react to signals before the turnout, which had a 15mph speed limit, and instead took the turnout at 60mph. The locomotive and the first six carriages were derailed and plunged down an embankment, and only the last three carriages remained on the rails. Casualties were heavy, with 43 killed and 64 injured.

The weather was fine and the visibility was good, and the driver was both experienced and had a reputation for being conscientious, but he had been working without a rest day for 26 consecutive days because of a shortage of drivers in the aftermath of the Second World War. It is believed that he had either been working automatically because of his exhaustion, or had dropped off to sleep. Had a GWR-style automatic warning system been present, he would have been alerted to the signals. One of the most unusual aspects of this accident was that the alarm was raised by a pilot who had just taken off from RAF Bovingdon and who alerted the control tower.

Lichfield, 1 January 1946

The 2.50pm express freight with seven fish vans and a guards van from Fleetwood to London was passing Lichfield Trent Valley station at 55mph on 1 January 1946, when a points failure diverted it off the through lines and it collided with the back of a four-carriage local train waiting in the station on the passing loop. The passenger train consisted of elderly wooden coaches built in 1912, and the last three of them were completely destroyed while the locomotive at the head of the train was propelled forwards by 90 yards. Twenty people were killed and another 21 injured.

Polesworth, 21 July 1947

The LMS had always taken a great pride in the quality of its track (signalling was another matter altogether). But wartime restrictions on materials and having many skilled employees away on war service (even though the railways were worked hard to support the military and industry), meant that peacetime standards could not be maintained. Even with the return of peace, the railways received only a fraction of their normal peacetime needs from the Ministry of Supply, and nothing at all to make up for the arrears of maintenance or war damage. This drop in standards was directly responsible for the derailment near Polesworth on 21 July 1947.

The 8.30am down express from Euston to Liverpool headed by a streamlined 'Coronation' class Pacific was travelling at more than 65mph with 16 carriages when it was derailed to the outside of a left-hand curve, blocking all four running lines; 14 of the carriages were also derailed. Fortunately, the Polesworth signalman was expecting the train and when it didn't arrive he took the precaution of stopping an up express. A freight train already on the down slow section was stopped by a fireman travelling as a passenger in the derailed express, while the driver and fireman went forward to stop any trains on the up lines.

The express locomotive was overturned and carried on for 400 yards past the point at which it had derailed, but damage was superficial. The two leading carriages were also overturned and wrecked, while the ends of the following six carriages were crushed together, but fortunately did not telescope. It was a credit to the LMS rolling stock that all of the couplings held and the inspector reported that all carriages retained a good line despite the derailment. A further reflection of the continued shortages and hardships affecting the railways even with the return of peace was that the train was packed with around 800 passengers with 130 of them standing, and naturally these were far more exposed to serious injury than those who were seated. Four passengers were killed in the accident and another died later, while 64 people were injured, including six members of the dining car staff.

Chapter 18

The Infrastructure

More than any other mode of transport, railways are heavily dependent upon their infrastructure for safe and efficient working. The LMS record in this area was mixed, far more so than for rolling stock. As the previous chapter has shown, accidents were not uncommon and many of them were extremely serious. It is even possible to discern a pattern in some of them. Just as the LMS inherited many elderly steam locomotives from the LNWR and too many locomotives that were too small from the Midland, even if they were much more modern and much better maintained, it also inherited an infrastructure that was in some respects dated and not as productive as it should have been. For example, of the 260 running shed and workshops that passed to the new LMS, far too many were out of date and inefficient, using methods that would not have been tolerated in a modern engineering plant. Just five depots, all part of the legacy handed down from the LNWR, had mechanical coaling plants. One of the LNWR depots, at Liverpool Edge Hill, was not so much mechanical as natural, as the site was on two levels and hopper wagons on the upper level could discharge directly into storage bunkers, from whence the coal could be loaded by gravity into locomotive tenders.

The LMS took particular pride in its permanent way, and to maintain this to a high standard was no easy matter. On much of the system, the men working on the line, the gangers, had to contend with a busy service and keep track possessions short, but in the North West of England, the Midlands and the London area, the job was helped by the extensive multiple lines that separated fast and slow trains, but which enabled trains to be switched from one to the other when necessary. At the other end of the system, there was much single track, especially in Scotland and Northern Ireland. In the Scottish Highlands, old rolling stock had to be converted to provide temporary accommodation for permanent way gangs working far from any other accommodation. This was the penalty of inheriting a substantial route mileage north of the border, and it is to be doubted if any of these lines ever paid their way. The travelling dormitories as they were called were far more basic and bleaker than the camping coaches introduced for holidaymakers during the 1930s.

Relaying track was no small business. It took 70,000 tons of rails in 1933 to relay 596 track miles out of the total route mileage of 6,954. This was a high rate of replacement which suggests that some areas had been neglected by the pre-Grouped companies, for they were, after all, a mixed lot with widely varying standards, but the following year the mileage to be relaid remained high, and still above 500 miles.

This must have been an expensive year for the company as it was the same year that it moved its offices from Euston to Euston House. The move was undoubtedly necessary as while the offices in the station may have sufficed for the LNWR, many of the former Midland people had to be moved down from Derby, and there were the other companies as well. There was a cost in the Midland having stubbornly or loyally, depending on one's point of view, kept its headquarters in Derby, but even if the Midland had build a London headquarters, it would still have meant that the head office departments would have had to be split between two locations as it would have been unlikely to have been adequate, and the LMS was also much more than simply the Midland added to the LNWR.

The permanent way

By the time Grouping started, railways were using rail that weighed 96lb per yard and came in 60ft sections, a dimension introduced by the LNWR and subsequently adopted by the other railways until continuously welded rail was adopted. Despite the increased weight of the rails, which should have ensured greater durability, there were still problems at the rail joints, which became dipped due to the bending of the rail ends as the wheels of a heavy train ran off one length and onto the next. This was made worse by fishplate wear and ballast settlement. Trials with different types of fishplate so that the joint sleepers would be moved closer together were not successful because of the difficulty in getting ballast under the sleepers.

More successful was the decision to switch to using flat-bottomed rail, an American concept, of 113lb per yard, with cast iron base plates and bolted fastenings.

The LMS also attempted to up-date layouts at junctions, with a new type of turnout which retained long crossing timbers but allowed cant or tilt to be provided for the diverging line and allow speed through the turnout to be increased. While the crossing timbers were also canted in the ballast, the rails rested on two level chairs. Wear on locomotive wheels was also reduced by the use of switch diamonds on flat-angle crossings.

Running at higher speeds was only possible on track that did not suffer from tight curves. The arrival of the 'Coronation Scot' called for some work at Trent Valley Junction to ease the alignment, although this was not done until 1938, a year after the service started. The progress of the crack express was inhibited by Queensville Curve, which slowed the train to 30mph for ¾ of a mile. The solution was to raise the speed limit to 55mph by relaying the junction with two level chairs and switch diamonds. The approach of the original Grand Junction route was realigned and its speed limit remained at 30mph, but the Queensville Curve was slewed by more than 11½ft and given additional cant, all for a cost of £8,000 for track work and another £2,000 for alterations to the signalling.

Cant on a railway line increased the speed at which trains could run through, but if they did have to stop, or ran very slowly, passengers could find themselves sliding along their seats into one another.

The permanent way or track was much more than simple track for trains running at any speed, it also included such features as water troughs, essential if fast, and thirsty, express locomotives were not to be delayed stopping for water. One problem with water troughs was that when the water scoop plunged into the trough, the water level at the sides rose, while that in the middle fell, leaving spillage over the sides of the trough and reducing the depth available for collection. One small, but important advance made by the company's engineers was to place two vertical blades 16 inches in front of the scoop, with the blades angled to push the water towards the centre of the trough, reducing wastage and also ensuring that the volume of water collected by the locomotive increased. The engineers maintained that this saved as much as 400 gallons when the scoop was left down for the entire run of the trough.

Two requirements were necessary for the successful use of a water trough. The first was the locomotive had to be running fast enough to generate sufficient pressure for the water to be forced up into the tender. The second was that the water tank in the tender had to be big enough and strong enough to cope with the pressure. Tank engines could not use a water trough as their small tanks tended to split under the pressure.

Servicing

The job that needed to be done most with the steam locomotive may have been filling it up with water, often at intervals of every 80 miles or so which was why only the Southern Railway did not bother with water troughs, but next on the list was coal. Coaling a locomotive could take time. The railway companies built special coaling stages so that wheel barrows could be used to carry coal to the locomotive tender, saving much hard work shovelling coal, and also much waste as not all of the coal shovelled into a tender actually went into it.

Coaling was still expensive in terms of manpower. The next step was the coaling plant, introduced after the First World War, which took a standard goods wagon with about eight tons of coal, and lifted it up the side of the coaling plant, until it reached the top, tipped over and its load then thundered down into the tender of the locomotive. This was known as the wagon hoist type of coaling plant.

During the 1930s, two other types were introduced, known to the LMS as the No. 1 Type Coaling Plant and the No. 2 Type Coaling Plant. Neither of these lifted the wagon. The No.1 had the wagon tipped so that its contents were fed into a jigger, a succession of buckets that lifted the coal to the top of the plant and into a storage bunker. The wagon could be one of the modern 20-ton type, which increased the productivity of freight trains. The No. 2 type did not tilt the wagon, but instead a hopper wagon was used, dropping the coal into the lower buckets of the jigger loader, and then into a bunker, from where another smaller jigger loader could pass the coal into the locomotive tender. Both methods cut down on manpower and enabled a locomotive crew to coal without assistance from the shed staff.

Signalling

The LMS inherited some fine rolling stock from the Midland Railway and while it had weaknesses in its locomotive fleet at first, it eventually set about remedying this and produced some of the finest steam locomotive of its day. There was much attention given to improving the permanent way so that it really was the 'best way', but the major weakness lay in its attitude to signalling. The train control system was a matter of pride, while technology was applied to marshalling yards and to such matters as coaling steam locomotives. Yet, for the most part, the signals inherited by the LMS on 1 January 1923 were those that it bequeathed to British Railways on 31 December 1947.

This would have been a problem with a railway that did not endeavour to run its trains faster, or even a railway which had all of its trains the same and following the same route and stopping pattern, as happens on the London Underground lines, for example. The LMS was neither of these, but handled the full variety of railway train, freight and passenger, stopping, fast, express, and even tours by train. It had electric and diesel as well as steam. Yet, it simply toyed with colour light signalling and did nothing towards creating an automatic warning system along the lines followed by the GWR.

The interior of the signalbox at the busy Settle Junction, with instruments on the shelves for indication of trains being passed from one section to another.
(HMRS ACW805)

Poverty alone is not a sufficient answer to this allegation. As the previous chapter shows, the LMS suffered many accidents that must have cost it dearly, and not just in the tangible costs, the disruption, the compensation, the cost of replacements and repairs, but in other ways such as reputation at a time when passengers on certain routes had a choice between the LMS and the LNER, or the LMS and the GWR. The trains might have run faster and smoother while the carriages were more comfortable and spacious, but . . .

In essence, the signalling systems that the LMS inherited from its predecessors had one thing in common, which was that they all depended on signalmen and drivers observing the rules completely, and did not take into account human weakness or frailty, or for the case mentioned earlier where a signalman was looking after no fewer than seven trains at one time with the help of a young lad.

As far as signalling went, the best that the LMS had from its predecessor companies came from the Midland, which had a rotary interlocking system, with track circuits and treadles that confirmed that a train had passed through a block section before the next train could be accepted. Track circuits were appearing at some locations, and from the turn of the century some stations had power operation. Yet, these features were not widespread. The attitude at Euston and later at Euston House, the new head offices built for the LMS, were that increasing automation was unnecessary, just so long as the signalmen and drivers followed the rules.

Euston should have been a showpiece, both for safety and efficient operation, but it wasn't, and even Belfast York Road, terminus for the NCC, was more up-to-date than Euston, which was far busier and which should have been a showpiece premier station for the LMS.

The absence of block instrument locking controls resulted in accidents where the wrong block instrument was cleared on multi-track sections, as indeed happened at Euston shortly after the LMS came into being. Despite some routes being heavily used, such as the electrified line between Liverpool and Southport, there were no block controls to help the signalmen. Between Euston and Watford, the electrified line had both track circuiting and colour light signals that

A general view of a motive power depot, that at Bangor, in steam days, but some years after nationalisation as can be seen by the locomotives with their BR 'lion and wheel' logo and, of course, the new style of tender. (*Colour-Rail 20605*)

followed US practice, with the added feature of automatic call-on. Although protected by a trip apparatus similar to that used on the London Underground, it was possible to get more than one train into a section and even to run nose to tail following a delay, which did result in a number of minor shunts when drivers underestimated the need to be careful. The lights provided speed indications rather than routes, with the top light referring to the main high-speed route and the lower light to the lower medium speed route. There was also a bottom marker light and if a four-aspect signal was installed, the second from the top provided an extra yellow. All very confusing as a driver could be faced with four lights, two of which could be red and one green!

The extent of modernisation of signalling on the LMS was the introduction of upper quadrant signals. A double yellow aspect was added to colour light signals, which were fairly extensive on the West Coast and Midland main lines, in addition to green and single yellow, in areas otherwise largely still working on semaphore signalling, to give advance warning that speed would have to be reduced at the next signal. The truth was, of course, that the LMS was simply too big to embark on wholesale conversion of its signalling to colour lights.

Running sheds

Well organised operation of a running shed was essential to the efficient operation of a railway. Of the 260 sheds that came to the LMS on Grouping, the best were almost certainly those of the Glasgow & South Western Railway, many of which had high roofs to allow smoke to clear quickly and improve the amount of light within the building. Despite the romantic picture shown in the famous LMS poster *The Day Begins*, locomotive sheds were filthy, dark, smoky, cold, draughty, leaky, and the workers had to mind where they put their feet on the uneven floors which also contained such traps as inspection pits, a turntable well if it was a roundhouse, and occasionally a length of exposed track. The railways were outside the scope of the various factory acts that had done so much to transform the Victorian workplace.

The pattern of sheds varied. The G&SWR favoured straight sheds, while the Midland had square 'roundhouses', so called because up to 24 stabling tracks would radiate from a central turntable. The reason for the different approach could well be that the Midland was so much larger and had so many more locomotives at any one location. At very important locations, such as the former Midland shed at Leeds Holbeck, there could be two roundhouses.

In fact, most of the work on servicing locomotives was done out of doors in the open. Here, engines had their ash pans and fire grates cleaned out at the end of the day, while soot was removed from smokeboxes, a filthy job given to the youngest newcomers to the industry, usually hoping to progress to fireman and eventually driver, and locomotives were even washed by hand. The impact on the health of those working there was hardly beneficial. At least one account relates how, when footplatemen – that is engine drivers and firemen – eventually succumbed to chronic bronchitis, they were relieved of their duties and put 'on the brush' sweeping up in loco sheds and helping to remove the constant stream of ash and soot that accumulated in the yard, which no doubt helped their condition considerably!

This was the 'below stairs' aspect of railway operation, kept out of sight.

The situation was clearly awful to an outsider, but railwaymen brought up in these conditions and often unaware of changes elsewhere took a less concerned view: in short, little changed at first. In 1925, a twin-bunker coaling plant with wagon hoist was ordered for Glasgow Polmadie. Not all of the inaction was that of an overlarge organisation struggling to come to grips with itself. To be fair, the new management team was taking time to decide on the best way forward and shed analysis committees were visiting every shed to evaluate the different methods of working and varying layouts. There was no doubt that much time was wasted in many sheds, with servicing and coaling taking much time and many locomotives having to queue before they could be attended to. It was estimated that the average locomotive was worked for just 11 hours 24 minutes a day, but to be fair, no matter how efficient a steam locomotive might be, the need for coal and for ash and soot to be removed ensured that it could never work 24 hours a day. The result of the analysis, which no doubt sometimes involved a fair amount of what has been called 'work study' or looking for 'best practice', was that a three-stage approach to improvement was set in hand and between 1929 and 1939, the number of sheds was reduced steadily to 200.

The first stage involved those depots not needing major layout changes, at which modernisation started in 1931, with orders for mechanical coal and ash handling plants. Some of the former were built of steel, as at Polmadie, but others were concrete, some used wagon hoists, others wagon tipplers, known to the LMS as the No. 1 Type Coaling Plant, while later hopper wagons were used with jiggers. For the others, the second stage was to establish and introduce an optimum yard layout, and this proceeded gradually until the outbreak of war. The third stage was organisational.

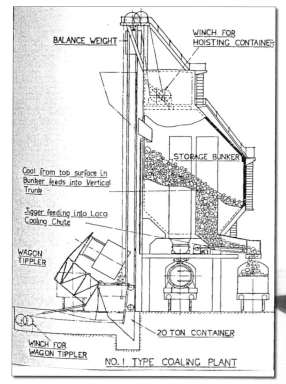

Two types of coaling plant were introduced by the LMS, respectively No. 1 on the left, and No. 2 on the right.

The LMS placed much emphasis on mechanised coaling to improve productivity. This is the coaling plant at Corkerhill in 1935, with 2P 4-4-0 No. 637 awaiting coal. (*HMRS AEP034*)

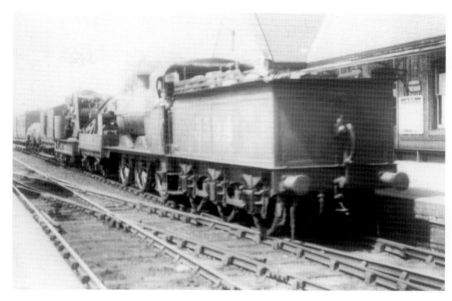

The date is 1926, so it is not too surprising that this ex-Midland locomotive still has its number on its tender. Johnson 3F 0-6-0 No. 3594 is seen with a breakdown train at Sutton Park. *(HMRS AEW214)*

In 1935, the LMS was divided into 29 motive power districts, later increased to 32 when it became obvious that some of the Scottish districts were overlarge. In each district, a shed was designated the 'concentration depot', for which it was given an 'A' suffix, and suitably equipped to handle every maintenance need, able to overhaul valves and pistons, overhaul axleboxes and repair boilers. A full list of sheds is given at Appendix I. This would have been a major step forward, but limited funds for the necessary investment meant that this was sometimes done at the cost of denuding many of the less important sheds of much of their equipment and skilled labour. Amongst these changes, water softeners were also introduced at those sheds in hard water areas so that limescale coating on boilers and boiler tubes was much reduced as was coal consumption. The only new shed to be built by the LMS was at Carnforth, completed in 1944, although two others were started, at Leicester and Carlisle Upperby, before Nationalisation, with both being concrete roundhouses. In the meantime, many sheds lost their roofing, either by courtesy of the Luftwaffe or because the structures were no longer sound.

Fruits of the changes were apparent by 1936, with locomotives working an average of 13 hours 42 minutes, an improvement of just over 20 per cent over the earlier working figure, and giving availability in excess of 84 per cent.

The works

Clearly, with the aim of 'scrap and build' to produce a highly standardised stud of locomotives and fleet of carriages, there was also the need to standardise production methods and concentrate on fewer works. Virtually every railway company of any size had its own workshops, and the main ones inherited by the LMS were the old LNWR works at Crewe, the former Midland works at Derby and the old LYR works at Horwich. The former London Tilbury & Southend Railway workshop at Bow was small, cramped and inefficient, as was that of the Furness Railway at Barrow, with a roof that until it was raised, was too low for an overhead crane, a necessity in any well-equipped and productive workshop. Wolverton was special, because it was home to the Royal Train.

Under the new regime, Wolverton and Derby produced most of the 700 or so new railway carriages needed each year at the outset, so that a smaller carriage works at Newton Heath, near Manchester, was closed in 1932.

The first of a triptych of aerial photographs showing Derby works in 1936. In the foreground is a locomotive on a turntable. *(HMRS AAE409)*

The main locomotive workshop was to be Crewe, but this needed extensive and costly rebuilding as it had expanded piecemeal since the London & Birmingham had opened it, and by 1923 it possessed no fewer than nine engine erecting shops with four of them very small. The reconstruction of Crewe, originally planned by the LNWR after the First World War but kept on ice due to the uncertainty over grouping, saw one large new erecting shop opened for all major overhauls and new locomotive construction. The older erecting shops, 1 to 4, were converted into a single new boiler building workshop to provide all of the boilers needed by the LMS. The remaining erecting shops, 5 to 9, were converted to other functions, such as stores. When the new central erecting shop opened in 1927, repair times were more than halved, down from 29 days to just 13 days. The number of locomotives awaiting repair dropped to five per cent of those allocated to Crewe.

The second view shows just how much space was needed for a major locomotive and carriage works. *(HMRS AAE410)*

The final photograph shows more of the works, with a concrete water tower in the foreground.
(HMRS AAE411)

When Stanier took over as CME, there came an emphasis on electric welding and on high surface finishes for machined surfaces to reduce fatigue cracking.

The other workshops at Derby, Horwich and the old Caledonian works at St Rollox, were confined to repairs.

With a new centralised system of building and repairing locomotives, the lesser works could be closed. Barrow was one of the first, and it was followed in 1930 by Highbridge on the Somerset & Dorset where the Southern and the LMS had decided to look after the railway themselves rather than allow it to continue to leech money. Stoke was another victim that year.

Two contrasting types of water tower are seen in this 1937 view of Derby, with a concrete structure to the left and a steel one on the right. Stanier 2-6-0, No. 2960, has been fitted with test equipment in front of the smokebox.
(HMRS AAN212)

A distant view of the Somerset & Dorset Joint Railway locomotive and carriage works at Highbridge, closed in 1929, with the LMS and SR taking over responsibility for locomotives and carriages respectively, to cut costs. *(HMRS AAC428)*

Distance saved Kilmarnock and Inverness, while Rugby was busy enough and good enough to survive. Bow survived because it was easier and less disruptive than moving rolling stock around from the Fenchurch Street lines.

As one can understand, there was much resentment amongst those whose workshops closed or were downgraded, and those whose workshops were not, mostly at Derby which had at the outset seemed due to set the standard for the new company. Derby also regarded itself as having far better craftsmen than Crewe, which Stanier himself often found unsatisfactory at first. It went a little way towards healing the wounds when, in 1935, Derby was commissioned to build ten 'Jubilee' class locomotives. Even after the war, on the eve of Nationalisation, Derby was building 2-6-4Ts for the NCC.

This preserved locomotive is the former London & North Western Railway 2-2-2 No. 3020 *Cornwall*, at Crewe Works in 1938. *(HMRS AAG429)*

Chapter 19

Railways at War

There were two aspects to the story of Britain's railways in wartime. On the one hand, there is the story of the railways struggling to meet their increased wartime commitments and the relationship between the railways and the state, which became both their biggest customer and also their controller, imposing restrictions and effectively taking their revenue and using them as subcontractors. On the other hand, there was the way in which the railways and railway personnel, both men and women, coped with enemy aerial attack.

Government interest in the potential of the railways dated from as early as 1871 and the Regulation of the Forces Act of that year, which allowed the government to take control of the railways in a national emergency. The real interest at the time seems to have been more a concern with internal unrest rather than an external threat. The first major use of the railways for military purposes came later, with the Boer War, but that did not require control of the railways, and indeed it really only affected one company, the London & South Western Railway, one of the Southern Railway's ancestors. In common with the other companies, the London Midland & Scottish Railway did not have the benefit of what amounted to a practice run during the Boer War, when the LSWR was the prime mover of men and horses from London and the military training grounds across the south of England to Southampton. The LSWR experience had been unique. When the First World War came, in common with every other railway in Great Britain, the 'predecessor' companies of the LMS found themselves under state control between 1914 and 1918, and in 1917 this was extended to the Northern Counties Committee, and the Dundalk, Newry & Greenore Railway, as well as the other railways in Ireland, then all under the control of London in the days before partition. The addition of the Irish railways reflected not only their importance in moving military personnel and horses, since Ireland was always a major source of both to the British Army, and food, but also because of the increasing civil unrest in the country.

The actual basis for state control had occurred in 1912, with the formation of the Railways Executive Committee consisting of the general managers of ten leading railway companies, including the London & North West and the Midland. The role of the REC would be to run the railways as a single entity in the case of war. When war came, the main pressure fell upon the companies in the south, especially those serving the Channel ports closest to France.

The railway companies not only had to adapt to centralised control, they also lost some 200,000 of their employees, who numbered around 600,000 in total, to the armed forces. Passenger services were cut back to allow paths for troop trains and to save fuel as well as wear and tear on track and rolling stock. Some minor branch lines were closed to save fuel and manpower, and a number of them never reopened. Nevertheless, it was not until 1917 that cheap fares were abolished and ordinary fares increased by 50 per cent, with even greater restrictions on the number of trains available for civilian passengers. On the other hand, in contrast to the practice during the Second World War, while the availability of restaurant cars was reduced considerably the facility did not disappear completely during the First World War.

Fortunately, the railways had, for the most part, enjoyed a period of considerable prosperity during the years leading up to the First World War, and so the problems encountered in assessing fair payment for the use of their facilities in the later conflict were not so serious. One or two companies encountered delay in receiving the grants due for abnormal maintenance costs, and there were some disputes that had to go to law. Overall, for the First World War, the government paid the railways £60 million to be shared between the companies.

The attitude of the government towards the railways during the First World War was still remembered by many of those running the railways. After all, the period between the two world wars had amounted to slightly less than 21 years. Directors and senior managers were also painfully aware that the years between the two world wars had not been good ones for the railways, which had not managed to achieve the revenues set out for them by the government on Grouping.

In the case of the companies that amalgamated to form the giant London Midland Scottish Railway, the London & North Western had paid a healthy 6.5 per cent in 1912, and even in Scotland there were dividends, with the Glasgow & South Western leading the way with 4.87 per cent, followed by the Caledonian at 3.75 per cent and the Highland at 2.25 per cent, while the Midland, famous for the comfort of its trains, was not too well rewarded for its care with just 2.5 per cent on its preference stock and 3.87 per cent on its deferred stock, possibly a side effect of running too many double-headed trains. The LMS was renowned for its adoption of modern American management practices, but despite this the LMS failed to pay a dividend in 1935 and could only manage 1.25 per cent in 1936, and although this rose to 1.5 per cent in 1937, it disappeared once again in 1938! The reason for this was simple, as 1937 had been a busier and brighter year for the railways as the Coronation of His Majesty King George VI had stimulated traffic, and possibly the wider economy as well. But even in that year, dividends were less than shareholders would have received had they invested their money in a Post Office savings account!

As any government compensation would be based on average turnover for the years immediately preceding the war, it was with considerable foreboding that the new conflict was anticipated. Added to which everyone realised that this time the growing potential of the bomber, a nuisance to the railways during the First World War rather than a serious threat, meant that they would be in the front line. The feeling was that the 'bomber would always get through', based on what had been seen of the Spanish Civil War and Japanese attacks in China. There were also problems of administration, with key personnel evacuated to areas where it was hoped that they could continue with their work uninterrupted by heavy bombing.

Preparing for war

Preparation for the wartime operation of the railways was put in hand as early as 1937. In September 1938, the Ministry of Transport warned that as soon as the danger of enemy aggression was imminent, a Defence of the Realm Act would be passed, and that one of its provisions would be for the government to take control of the railways and the railway operations of the London Passenger Transport Board. It was realised that bombing would be a threat, and in 1937 a technical committee laid plans for dealing with the effects. Meanwhile, Lord Stamp, the President, as chairman of the Railway Companies Association, was in charge of negotiations of the government over the state's use of the railways in wartime. As expected, in late September 1938, once again a Railway Executive Committee was formed, with the LMS represented by its general manager. Initially, the REC was chaired by Gilbert Szlumper of the Southern Railway, but he later became Director-General of Transportation (sic) at the War Office.

One of the early tasks for the Committee was to draw up a list of measures, including protection of employees and their administrative centres, as well as material for emergency repairs and any additional equipment needed. For the railway companies and London Transport, the total estimate came to £5,226,400, and a foretaste of things to come followed when the Government decided at the end of 1938 to provide a grant of just £4 million, of which £750,000 was to go to the LPTB, with the companies left to fund the balance themselves. The LMS share of this much-reduced sum was £1,359,700, the highest for any of the grouped companies. The total paid to the railway companies and the LPTB was £3,093,250, with the remainder being spent on equipment that would be pooled between the four railway companies.

The main line railway companies evacuated their head offices just before the outbreak of war, but even so, no risks were taken and air raid drills were conducted. This is LMS office staff entering the air raid shelter at the temporary offices at The Grove, Watford. *(IWM FLM1184)*

Part of the money was spent on relocating the headquarters as it was vital that the railway continued to function no matter what happened. Despite its size, the LMS achieved one of the more successful relocations of any of the 'Big Four' railway companies, taking The Grove, a large country mansion near Watford, which had no fewer than 300 acres of parkland on which many temporary buildings could be built.

Stores were created for materials that would be necessary to enable a railway to remain operational despite heavy aerial attack. The civil engineers received an additional three months' supply of materials to repair and maintain the permanent way, including baulks of timber and strut joists. A three-months' supply of locomotive and carriage spare parts was ordered over and above usual needs.

Meanwhile, many employees enrolled in the civil defence and air raid precautions services, while others were already in the Territorial Army, many of them in the Railway Supplementary Reserve of the Royal Engineers, or were planning to join. As early as late 1937, the LMS announced that it had converted two old carriages into an ARP lecture carriage and a decontamination unit at Wolverton. This was understandable as memories of the havoc and hardship created by the use of gas in the First World War were still fresh. Air raid precaution (ARP) exercises also began, and the *LMS Magazine* carried a photograph of a guard wearing a gas mask.

Believing that 'the bomber will always get through' meant that steps were taken to ensure that air raid shelters were constructed at all railway workshops and at other centres such as marshalling yards. Although there were deep level underground lines, the tube lines, at or close to the major London termini, other than Fenchurch Street, there was no intention at first of using these as additional air raid shelters and it was public pressure that eventually forced the authorities to relent and open the tube stations at night for the public to use as shelters. Unfortunately, official misgivings about their suitability as shelters were partly justified as there were a number of cases of tube stations being bombed and those sheltering in them killed.

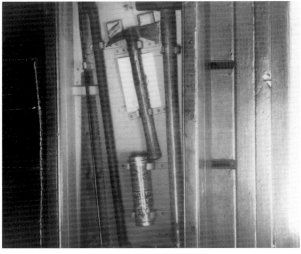

The interior of an ARP training unit, with a fire extinguisher and an axe as the most prominent features. (HMRS AAK320)

This appears to be a wartime view from the tender into the cab of a Bowen-Cooke 5XP 'Claughton' 4-6-0 showing the canvas tarpaulin used to stop enemy aircraft from spotting the locomotive fire at night. (HMRS AAG630)

A close-up showing
more detail of the
'Claughton' cab interior.
(HMRS AAG628)

State control

On the eve of war, as threatened, the Minister of War Transport, as the Minister of Transport
had become, moved quickly to seize control of the railways on 1 September 1939, using powers
granted to him under the Defence Regulations Act 1939. There was considerable delay in fixing
the basis on which the railways would be paid, with the state taking all of the receipts and
allocating what it regarded as a suitable sum to each of the four main-line railway companies
and London Transport on a predetermined basis. There was little real negotiation, with the
government hinting at acceptance or nationalisation. The inclusion of the London Passenger
Transport Board in the scheme was opposed by the 'Big Four' railway companies who believed
that passenger traffic would slump in wartime, and that as the only all-passenger operator,
London Transport would become a liability for the others. It certainly meant that the allocated
funds would have to be spread around more thinly.

The state also decided what resources could be made available in terms of raw materials and
manufacturing capacity to keep the railways running. This was not nationalisation in the true
sense of the word, but it was a bureaucratic straightjacket, although it must be borne in mind
that the control and direction of labour, raw materials and manufacturing capacity applied to
the entire economy and not just the railways.

Despite the haste to grab control of the railways, there was considerable delay in finalising
the means of working. The system of state control meant that the railways effectively became
contractors to the government, with all revenue passing to the government which then allocated
a share out of a pool, which was set at a guaranteed £40 million. The LMS share of the pool was
fixed at 34 per cent, while the LPTB received 11 per cent, the GWR received 16 per cent, the
same as for the Southern Railway, and the LNER 23 per cent. These percentages were based
on the average net revenues for the companies and LPTB in the three years 1935–37, which the
government regarded as the standard revenue for each company.

Once the guaranteed £40 million had been paid, any balance was allocated to the five train operators on the same percentage terms up to a maximum of £3.5 million. After this, the arrangements became complicated, since if there was a further balance, the revenue over a total of £43.5 million would be divided equally between the government and the pool until the pool total reached £56 million. At this stage, if the revenue share allocated to any of the companies then exceeded its standard revenue, the figure the companies had been expected to earn annually at the time of the Grouping, the excess would be shared out proportionately among the other companies.

Costs of maintenance and renewals had to be standardised, while the cost of restoring war damage would be met up to a total of £10 million in a full year. Privately owned wagons were also requisitioned by the Ministry of War Transport, and the individual companies had to meet the costs and revenue attributed to the wagon owners out of their share of the revenue pool.

This was a 'take it or leave it' type of agreement, with the government leaking threats of nationalisation if the companies failed to agree, although these were officially denied. The years in question had not been good ones for the British economy, although 1938 had been worse and the railways had had to work hard to get the government to recognise this. The difficult economic conditions that had prevailed for almost all of the inter-war period had meant that none of the railway companies had ever achieved the standard revenues anticipated by the Railways Act 1921, the measure that authorised the Grouping. The best that can be said for the deal was that the government was anxious to avoid inflationary pay claims from railway employees, and no doubt anxious to ensure that it did not play a part in war profiteering, since it was likely to be its own single biggest customer.

However, the inescapable fact was that the railways were having their revenues more or less fixed while costs were bound to rise as they struggled to meet the increased demands that wartime would place upon them. Placing an upper limit on the cost of making good war damage was another instance of either political expediency to keep the unions quiet, and the Labour Party within the wartime coalition government, or simple naivety since normal insurance measures were not available in wartime.

Nevertheless, within little more than a year, the Ministry of War Transport reneged on the original agreement and left the railway companies to pay for war damage out of revenue. The fixed annual payments were also changed, with the provision for extra payments dropped so that any surplus would be taken by the government, which generously also offered to meet any deficit, which was an unlikely event given the demands placed on the railways. The new deal provided for the following annual payments:

London Midland & Scottish	£14,749,698
Great Western Railway	£6,670,603
London & North Eastern Railway	£10,136,355
Southern Railway	£6,607,639
London Passenger Transport Board	£4,835,705

The railway companies were once again left with little option but to accept. The mood of the times was that any argument was unseemly as it seemed that invasion was a very real danger.

Bus services were not included in the scheme and neither was road haulage. The reasons for this were ones of practicality, as there were so many operators, including a number of owner-driver operations, especially in road haulage and coach private hire, that it would have been extremely difficult. In any case, the state had other means of regulating these modes of transport, by tight controls on the allocation of fuel and vehicles, with the armed forces free to requisition vehicles as necessary, and the Ministry of War Transport was able to allocate vehicles from one operator to another if it thought fit. The irony was that many bus operators in the provinces and especially in what would in peacetime have been resort areas, found wartime demand heavier as new bases for the armed forces were often established in these areas, especially along the southern and eastern coasts of England. Areas in which transport had been heavily affected by

Looking very much the worse for wear, this is a wartime view of the *Duke of Argyll*, one of the Heysham–Belfast ferries serving as a hospital ship. She is far from her normal route, being alongside a port in northern France.

the Blitz, such as London and Coventry, often had their vehicles replaced by vehicles from other operators before the limited production of utility vehicles was finally authorised.

Ferry services were badly disrupted as ships were taken over by the Ministry of War Transport, with many needed to help move the British Expeditionary Force (BEF), to France and then to keep it supplied. Other small ships were taken up by the Admiralty as they were needed for the many tasks around the main naval bases.

For all of the grouped railway companies, shipping was part and parcel of their operations. The LMS was no exception and its main shipping routes were those across the Irish Sea, although it also operated from the Humber to ports in Belgium, the Netherlands, Denmark and Germany until first Germany was dropped on the outbreak of war, and then the other countries after the German advance north in April 1940, and then west in May. Its own ships were used on the company's three shipping services to both parts of Ireland. The Irish Mail service from Holyhead used three 25-knot steamers *Cambria*, *Hibernia*, and *Scotia*, while the *Duke of Argyll*, *Duke of Lancaster*, *Duke of Rothesay* and *Duke of York* worked the Heysham–Belfast service. A further three ships, *Princess Margaret*, *Princess Maud* and *Princess Victoria*, worked the short route between Stranraer in Scotland and Larne. On the outbreak of war, the government immediately requisitioned six out of these ten ships, leaving *Cambria* and *Hibernia* at Holyhead, *Duke of Lancaster* at Heysham and the *Princess Margaret* at Stranraer.

Princess Victoria was fitted out as a minelayer, and ironically struck a German mine in the North Sea, sinking with heavy loss of life. The other ships were used as troopships, with the first priority being the movement of the BEF to France. This was accomplished without any loss, but a different story arose during the evacuation of the BEF from Dunkirk. The *Scotia* was so heavily bombed while at her moorings that she had to be abandoned before she sank. *Princess Maud* was also badly damaged but survived, and after Dunkirk was sent to Valery-en-Caux to evacuate further troops with the *Duke of York*, and between them brought back more than 2,000 men safely with little further damage. The *Duke of Argyll* is believed to have taken part in the evacuation of the civilian population from the Channel Islands, before becoming a hospital ship.

Princess Maud was soon returned to the Irish Sea so that she could move men and equipment between Stranraer and Larne, and this traffic proved so intense that she was soon joined by the SR English Channel train ferries *Shepperton Ferry* and *Twickenham Ferry*, being used as vehicle ferries. The short crossing between Stranraer and Larne became very popular as the war dragged on as it made the best use of shipping with a voyage of just two hours, as opposed to eight hours or more on the routes from England, and this also meant that the ship was exposed to the risk of U-boat attack for the shortest period.

Railways at war

There had been much rehearsal of wartime operating conditions on the railways over the previous year or so. Railwaymen had practised working in blackout conditions, which meant that no lights could be shown externally, with all windows screened, while station platforms could only be lit by blue lights or, as there were still many illuminated by gas, specially shaded gas lamps. Drivers and motormen had to pull up their trains beside oil lamps placed on the platform as markers. Steam locomotives had canvas draped between the engine cab and tender to hide the light of their fires, while the side windows that had appeared on the more modern locomotives were blanked out.

As war loomed, glass was removed from station canopies which were then covered in dark material, more to prevent any chink of light being seen from above than with wind or water-proofing in mind. This is Partick Central in Glasgow after an air raid in 1943 – had the glass still been in the roof, the damage would have been even more severe with the risk of death or serious injury to anyone in the vicinity. *(HMRS AAM309)*

None of this, of course, can truly give a real impression of what it must have been like operating a railway in the blackout, or of the problems of individual railwaymen, and women, having to report for work after a broken night's sleep in a crowded air raid shelter, or of coming off a night shift in the morning to find that their home no longer existed, and perhaps face the loss of family members and neighbours as well. The efficient working of a railway required skill and experience, but under wartime conditions most adults had to be available for either the armed forces or prepared to be directed to essential war work, and as skilled men volunteered or were conscripted into the armed forces, many of their places were taken by women. This may have been a factor in the eventual Allied victory as many historians believe that one factor in the defeat of Germany was that the Germans were reluctant to mobilise the civilian population and instead relied too heavily on slave labour and people conscripted from the occupied territories, or Vichy France. No country mobilised its population as thoroughly as the United Kingdom.

Wartime acted as a spur to extending loudspeaker announcements to stations, and while initially station name signs were no longer lit, those under station canopies were allowed to be illuminated later, provided that they were swung round at right angles to the platform. Those stations that had had their names painted on the canopies to help airmen with their navigation had them blanked out. A final safety measure at stations was the removal of glass from roofs and canopies, essential since even a small bomb could create so many shards of broken glass as to be an effective anti-personnel weapon.

As a fuller understanding of the implications of working a railway in wartime dawned on those involved, many regretted that the LMS had not followed the GWR in fitting speedometers, other than to some of its diesel shunters, as in the blackout picking up those points of reference that would give an experienced driver an idea of his speed was to become so difficult as to be almost impossible. Indeed, in a number of accidents the evidence suggests that the driver had either become completely disorientated or was exhausted and stressed for understandable personal reasons, and quite possibly both.

Unlike the Great Western and the Southern, the LMS abandoned its house publications at the outset of war, although admittedly there were no fewer than three of these, *LMS Magazine*, *On Time* and *Quota News*, and these were replaced by a monthly newsletter, *Carry On*, which was provided free whereas the *LMS Magazine* was paid for. Lord Stamp provided a message in the first issue with the headline: 'Railways Vital to Nation's Cause: Whatever Befalls, We Must Carry On.'

'It will ever be a source of pride to those connected with the railways that when war did come it found us prepared to the last man and the last vehicle to play our part speedily, safely, and efficiently in the sudden special movements of traffic....May we be able to say – as was said of the railways twenty years ago – that when the final victory is won, our share in it shall have been a worthy one.'

Nevertheless, communications with employees in wartime were also taken over to some extent by the state. The magazines or newsletters provided for employees were subjected to censorship and firm rules were laid down that editors had to follow. Over and above that, the Ministry of Information published hard-hitting posters that were intended to dispel rumours or careless talk. Railway workers were prime targets as the very nature of their work meant that they knew much about the war effort. Troop trains were an obvious example, but they also knew if trains were moving munitions or even large aircraft parts, new wartime traffic for the railways, or armoured vehicles.

Typical of these was a poster intended for railway premises:

If you've news of our munitions
KEEP IT DARK
Ships or 'planes or troop positions
KEEP IT DARK
Lives are lost through conversation
Here's a tip for the duration
When you've got private information
KEEP IT DARK

Another poster was more direct:

YOU
Know more than other people.
You are in a position of trust.
Don't let the fighting forces down.
A few careless words may give something away
that will help the enemy and cost us lives.
Above all, be careful what you say to strangers
and in public.

Evacuation and emergency measures

After the false hopes raised by resolution of the Munich Crisis of 1938, it soon became clear that war was more of a probability than a possibility. Preparations were made by the railway companies, although these were not helped by threatened industrial action by their employees which was only averted at the last moment. Anticipating a possible surprise attack, on virtually the eve of war, evacuation of children and many others, including their teachers and expectant

Another view of Partick Central from the footbridge – the severe damage to buildings close to the line can be seen, suggesting that for the railway, this was a near miss. *(HMRS AAM311)*

and nursing mothers, started to get them away from London and other major cities, especially those such as Birmingham, judged to be likely targets. The pressure on the LMS and other railways was such that during the four days of the operation, from 1 to 4 September 1939, only a skeleton service could be provided for the public outside the rush hours.

As anticipated, on 31 August, the order to begin the evacuation was given. Evacuation from London was shared by all four railway companies, while that from Birmingham was shared by the Great Western and the LMS. Children assembled at their schools and from there either walked or were taken by bus or underground train to the station allocated to them, with many having to use suburban stations either because of convenience or because the London termini could not handle all of them.

All four railway companies handled this traffic, although not every parent sent their child away, and some made their own arrangements. Meanwhile, the railways were running evacuation specials in and around the main industrial conurbations and other likely target areas, such as Glasgow, Merseyside, Manchester, Tyneside, Birmingham, Portsmouth and Southampton. The LMS carried most of the 46,934 people evacuated from Birmingham and provided most of the 170 trains needed. In Glasgow and Merseyside, the LMS was *the* evacuation railway, although some of that from Manchester was shared with the LNER.

Many of the evacuees must have made their own way to the departure stations or been taken on the London Underground as the total carried by the railways from London was 617,480, using 1,577 trains. While London was the biggest evacuation, many were being moved from other major industrial areas. After London, Merseyside was the next biggest evacuation, with 161,879 evacuees in 382 trains. Clydebank and Glasgow accounted for 123,639 evacuees with 322 trains, followed by Manchester with 115,779 evacuees and 302 trains. Nowhere else provided more than 100,000 evacuees, with a big drop between the Manchester total and that for Tyneside, where

73,916 evacuees were spread over 271 trains. Even Birmingham only provided the surprisingly low figure of 46,934 evacuees and 170 trains. Most of the evacuation trains seemed to have an average of around 400–500 passengers, but the two trains run from Rosyth must have been very crowded with a total of 2,187 evacuees between them.

The railways also had to arrange 34 ambulance trains for the partial evacuation of hospitals in these areas. These measures were not just to move patients to places of greater safety, but to free beds for the bombing when it came, and to empty hospitals near the coast in case of an invasion.

Meanwhile, in addition to handling the evacuation, between 1 and 3 September 22 special trains conveyed around 10,000 service personnel to the King George V Dock in Glasgow for passage to the Mediterranean, where they were to reinforce the garrisons in Gibraltar, Malta, Cyprus and Alexandria. Civilians were also reporting to labour exchanges as they received their call-up papers, meaning that there was yet more travel, albeit most of it over short distances. The achievement becomes still more incredible when it is also borne in mind that, during the evacuation and after it ended, 158,000 men were conveyed to the Channel ports and across the Channel to France, along with more than 25,000 vehicles, over a period of five weeks.

The problem was, of course, that at this early stage of the war, no one knew just how the situation would develop. The fall of France was not anticipated, nor was the invasion of Denmark and Norway or the Netherlands. This was because most members of the military believed that there would be a re-run of the First World War with major fighting for the duration of hostilities on French or Belgian soil. The additional feature was to be heavy bombing, but only of those cities within range of German airfields. Plymouth, which was to suffer badly from the attentions of the Luftwaffe, was seen as being 'safe'. In fact, a further evacuation was to be necessary, but that would overlap with the evacuation of British forces from Dunkirk, and in the meantime, as the period of the so-called 'Phoney War' drifted on through the winter of 1939–40, many evacuees drifted homewards.

After the initial evacuation of children from London in September 1939, and during the lull before the evacuation of the BEF from Dunkirk and enemy air operations, many children were brought home by their parents despite a 'STAY PUT' campaign. This is the scene at Euston with the prams and luggage of returning evacuees. *(IWM HU82779)*

Drastic cuts

On the outbreak of war, excursion and cheap day tickets were withdrawn, but day tickets were reintroduced on 9 October, although with tighter conditions which meant that they were not available before 10am and could not be used on trains departing from London between 4pm and 7pm, Monday to Friday.

After the evacuation was over, services had returned to normal but briefly, for on 11 September drastic cuts were imposed on the train services, meaning great hardship for passengers since, although the late holiday and day-tripper traffic had virtually disappeared, normal business travel was still virtually at pre-war levels, especially with large numbers of people commuting to their offices in the City. Like the railways, some large companies had dispersed, especially those with strategic importance such as the shipping lines, but it was not possible for everyone to do so, for apart from business considerations, the number of suitable venues outside London and other major cities was limited. The many smaller businesses and professional practices remained in London.

Not only did this lead to unacceptable levels of overcrowding, with many passengers left behind, it also meant that station dwell times were extended as passengers struggled to alight from trains or struggled to climb aboard. After the uproar that followed, normal services were reinstated on weekdays from 18 September.

Nevertheless, this was simply a temporary reinstatement and indicated nothing more than that the blanket reductions of 11 September had not been properly thought out in the short time available to the timetable planners. Wartime conditions meant that services had to be reduced, both to save personnel, fuel and wear and tear and to make trains and paths available for the military. New timetables imposing reductions in passenger services followed on 25 September, with the LMS being one of the first companies to introduce its new timetable, although on this occasion better allowances were made for peak-period travel. Off-peak, most main line services lost their usual trains with the service halved, often running to extended timings.

Some idea of the impact of the cuts on the travelling public can be gathered from the fact that the service from Euston and St Pancras to Glasgow was cut from twelve trains in 1938 to six in 1939. The average journey time was increased from 8 hours 6 minutes to 10 hours 4 minutes, but the fastest in October 1938 had been just 6 hours 30 minutes for the 401 miles. The service between London and Manchester was reduced from 22 trains daily to 14, while the 188 miles from Euston were covered in an average of 4 hours 52 minutes instead of the pre-war 3 hours 43 minutes, and a best of 3 hours 15 minutes. Inverness took 16 hours 26 minutes from London instead of 13 hours, while the number of trains was halved from four to two. There was considerable debate over whether sleeping car services could continue, but a number did, although for the ordinary traveller, the reprieve was short-lived.

Meanwhile, carriages were converted for use on ambulance trains for the military and others converted for the evacuation of civilian casualties in anticipation of widespread disruption by heavy bombing, although the latter were never needed. Locomotives were also modified, with a number fitted with condensing gear and pipes for obtaining water from streams, anticipating widespread disruption to water supplies following bombing. The major stations and depots formed their own volunteer fire-fighting forces, while there were also fire-fighting trains, able to rush to wherever they might be needed, not only because of the greater speed of the railway than road transport, but also because many fires might be more easily accessible from the railway than from the road.

The spread of rationing, introduced in early 1940, and the difficulty that many had in shopping with so many women working, and many of them working very long hours, led to a growth in the number of staff canteens on the LMS. Rolling stock was also modified and equipped as 'mobile canteen' trains, able to be sent to wherever such facilities were needed, either because the station canteen had been bombed or because large numbers were involved in dealing with the after-effects of an 'incident'.

Despite many railway jobs being classified as 'reserved occupations', the LMS saw a growing number of its personnel leaving to join the armed forces for the duration of the war. Their work on the railway and in the workshops was taken over by women, who even undertook some of the heavier jobs, including those of porters. At first, the new recruits did not have uniforms, but this was quickly remedied. Uniforms were important on a railway not only because much of the work was dirty, but also for security and so that passengers knew who to turn to for advice and help.

Although there was a cut in the number of trains, passenger traffic was 3 per cent higher in December 1939 than for the previous December. As industry got into its stride and was placed on a war footing, general goods traffic rose by 51 per cent while that for coal rose by 41 per cent. Goods train mileage increased by 18 per cent. In the docks, traffic was up by 31 per cent. All of this happened on a railway which had already lost many skilled personnel for service with the armed forces, as well as losing almost 40 locomotives which had been requisitioned and sent overseas. Employees were given the first of a series of wartime advances on their pay in recognition that the cost of living was increasing.

The New Year started badly, with many trains cancelled in what the company proclaimed as the 'Worst Winter Ever', as heavy falls of snow blocked lines and trapped trains.

Not only were the in-house publications abandoned, but bright posters extolling the virtues of the many resorts on the LMS, and on other railways were soon to be replaced by stern messages from the Ministry of War Transport, demanding to know 'Is your journey really necessary?' The Railways Executive Committee did its bit to discourage travel, raising fares in May 1940 by 10 per cent, both to discourage travel and to cover the mounting costs of the railways. There was to be a constant conflict between the authorities and the public at Christmas and the New Year, and in the summer months during the war years. A war-weary and bomb-battered population would do all it could to get away for a summer holiday, while the authorities made it as difficult for them as possible. At Christmas, people working away from home were anxious to get back for a day or two. To try to help, the armed forces eventually refused to issue forces leave passes at peak periods, which was harsh if the individuals concerned were about to be posted abroad, as so many were, as even before the invasion of Europe, Allied forces waged a long-running campaign against the Axis in North Africa.

Dunkirk

In 1940, the Whitsun holiday was cancelled by the government since the Germans were sweeping through the Low Countries and into France. This ultimately led to the evacuation of the British Expeditionary Force from Dunkirk, along with many French troops and some from Belgium as well.

While the Great Western and the Southern Railways provided most of the railway steamers used in the Dunkirk evacuation, several LMS ships were also present as they had been commandeered by the government on the outbreak of war.

Ashore in England, all four railway companies were already hard at work handling special trains, many of them sending trains south, to get the soldiers away from the Channel ports. At 5pm on 26 May, the code-word 'Dynamo' was sent to the railways, warning them that the evacuation was due to start. The railway companies provided a 'pool' of 186 trains, of which the LMS share was 44.

A problem arose with finding sufficient locomotives capable of running over Southern metals, especially since the route from Reading to the Channel ports was far from being a masterpiece of railway engineering! Many of the locomotives used were the highly capable Stanier 'Black Five' 4-6-0s. At the outset, the railways did not know how many journeys would need to be made by these trains and just where the troops would land. While the entire operation ran from 27 May to 4 June, the busiest days were 1 June and 4 June, when the entire operation was achieved by having holding points for empty trains at Faversham, Margate, Queenborough and Ramsgate. Possibly the railways managed so well because they were used to the demand for special trains caused by major sporting events.

Added to the difficulties of organising the railway end of the Dunkirk evacuation was the sudden realisation on the part of the authorities that a second evacuation was needed of many children moved from London to the south coast, but who were now too close for comfort to German airfields. Neither the railways nor the military knew how many men to expect from Dunkirk; in the end, more than 338,000 were carried. This of necessity meant massive disruption to ordinary services with even the slimmed-down wartime timetable suspended in many cases. The trains with the troops from Dunkirk joined the LMS at Willesden.

While in many ways, the whole exercise has been seen since as a masterpiece of organisation and improvisation, it took place in an atmosphere of chaos. No one knew how many troops would arrive or when, and certainly they had no idea of how many were fit and how many were wounded, and still less of where to send them when they did arrive. The chaos was such that trains were turned round at Dover and sent off before the authorities had any idea where they could send the rescued troops, so often drivers were instructed to 'Stop at Guildford and ask where you are going to.' This didn't apply to many LMS drivers, however, as most LMS trains were run through the West London Line, avoiding the bottleneck at Redhill, where trains had to reverse, and the busy junction at Guildford.

Volunteers tried to ensure that the arriving troops were given tea and something to eat, as well as a card so that they could write home to let their families know that they were safe. A collection at one station to provide food and drink for the troops, organised by the stationmaster's wife, raised more than £1,000 from passengers and from people who had been drawn to the station by the continuous flood of the heavily laden troop trains. Inevitably, everything was under unforeseen pressure. One example was that at some stations used as refreshment stops, there weren't enough cups: tins had to be used as improvised cups, and just before a train left from a refreshment stop, the order was given for these to be thrown out so that the volunteers could wash them ready for the next train.

Restrictions

Throughout the war years there was an almost constant trimming of services to reduce fuel consumption and eliminate underused train miles. The trains themselves were lengthened, often requiring a call at a station to involve two stops as passengers alighted from the front of the train, which then had to be moved forward to allow those in the back of the train to alight or for others to board. Although in peacetime the LMS had been used to running trains of 15 or 16 carriages, under wartime pressures this rose to 20 or more. These very long trains had the disadvantage that time had to be spent dividing the train on arrival, so that its carriages could be put into two platforms, and then the reverse would happen after it had left, with the front half being drawn clear of the station and then reversed onto the back half.

Often, journeys were delayed by the need for heavy trains to be given banking assistance, usually requiring a stop while the banker was coupled and then later uncoupled.

At first, the instruction was given on all railways that when an air raid warning was given, passenger trains were to stop and passengers allowed to alight and seek shelter if they wished, after which the train would continue at a maximum speed of just 15mph. As the full impact of the Blitz took effect and air raids became so frequent, this slowed traffic down to an unacceptable extent, and the instruction was revised with trains allowed to proceed at 25mph from early November 1940. The danger of a derailment to a train running on to bomb-damaged track at high speed during an air raid was obvious, but away from the most heavily blitzed towns, many drivers took a chance and often ignored the speed limit, guessing that the risk of bomb damage was relatively light.

Shipping services did not escape the cuts. The main service to continue throughout the war was that between Stranraer and Larne, although a reduced frequency remained between Holyhead and Dublin and from Heysham to Belfast. One other absence from the railways during the Second World War were the travelling post office trains, probably to both free the lines for other more essential traffic and also release manpower for the war effort.

In addition to trimming services, as the war progressed other restrictions were applied. On 6 October 1941, under the directions of the Minister of War Transport, all London suburban trains became third-class only, with the definition being that this applied to any train starting and ending its journey within the London Passenger Transport Board's area. The reasons for the move were practical, the idea being not only to make the best use of all accommodation on the reduced number of trains, but also to recognise the difficulty in finding the right class of accommodation in a hurry during the blackout. To drive the point home, carpets were removed from first-class compartments and the first-class indications on the compartment doors painted out, while timetables and departure indicators described trains as 'Third Class Only'.

After the withdrawal of first-class accommodation, blackout or not, regular travellers seemed to be able to find their way to the most comfortable part of the train and gravitated towards the superior legroom and elbow room, and plusher upholstery, of the former first-class compartments, so that these soon became shabby with intensive use.

There was constant debate over whether sleeping cars should or should not be withdrawn. Many felt that passengers needed this facility, which was once again restricted to first-class only, but others argued that extra day carriages provided better use of the limited number of trains being run. This was a major problem for the LMS and the LNER with their long Anglo-Scottish services, but from December 1942, these ceased to be available for civilian passengers, though a skeleton service was maintained for those travelling on government business.

While main-line trains retained first-class accommodation, after a period of reduced catering facilities with only a limited number of trains allowed to offer this facility, on 22 May 1942, all catering facilities were withdrawn from trains on the LMS. It then became important to discourage unnecessary travel. The lack of sporting events and the fact that the coastal resorts had their beaches wrapped in barbed wire, meant that the normal leisure pursuits were not available. Again on the instructions of the Minister of War Transport, on 5 October 1942 off-peak cheap returns were scrapped, leaving seasons as the only 'cheap', or discounted, tickets. This gives little idea of the impact of the service on the traveller, since the 'reduced' wartime service included a substantial number of troop trains.

In an attempt to economise, heating was another area in which fuel could be saved, so the pre-war system of switching on full heat on main-line trains between October and April when the temperature fell below 48°F at any one of a number of monitoring points, and half-heat when the temperature fell below 55°F, had been reduced to having full heat when the temperature fell below 45°F and half-heat when it fell below 50°F between November and March.

Shortages of skilled staff in the workshops and the conversion of many of these to war production, as well as shortages of materials, meant that the intervals between routine overhauls were extended. Economy measures on the LMS included a new simplified colour scheme for passenger carriages lacking the extensive lining-out of peacetime, while locomotives were painted plain black without any lining-out on being sent for overhaul or repair. The colour of the locomotives soon became immaterial as standards of cleanliness dropped.

Another aspect of railway operation in which standards dropped, aided by poor lighting and encouraged by wartime shortages of everything, was honesty. There was much concern about the rising level of what was described as 'pilferage' on all of the railways.

Nevertheless, some wartime pressures had to be accommodated by investment in improved facilities. With the Port of London crippled by enemy bombing and by the unacceptable risks from attack for shipping in the Straits of Dover and the Thames Estuary, other ports became more important, including those on the Bristol Channel. South Wales was also a major area for the production of coal, steel and iron. This put pressure on the railway system as new traffic flows had to be accommodated. So, in 1941, the Ministry of War Transport gave authority for the conversion of a six-mile length of line from Lansdown Junction at Cheltenham to Engine Shed Junction at Gloucester from double to quadruple track. This stretch of line was owned 50:50 by the GWR and the LMS, and it was agreed that the LMS would do the construction work and the GWR would lay the track and provide the signalling. Starting in September, the work required considerable land drainage because of the low-lying ground before the embankments could be built.

Another instance of expansion was a new branch opened to a Royal Ordnance factory at Swynnerton, near Stone, which carried 3 million passengers a year from 1941 on trains that never appeared in the public timetables.

From December 1941, anxious to ensure that large numbers of standard locomotives be built, the Ministry of War Transport had decreed that all locomotive production would be of the LMS Stanier 2-8-0 design. Even the GWR at Swindon built 80 of these. The choice of design was influenced by War Office requirements for locomotives capable of handling heavy goods trains, with passenger trains receiving a much lower priority. On the other hand, given the extended length of wartime longer-distance passenger trains, sometimes a freight locomotive was the best option even for them. The Ministry of War Transport was also reacting to the War Office's need for locomotives to be sent overseas, and at this stage of the war the North African campaign was in full swing.

Like all of the grouped railway companies, the LMS was a major manufacturer in its own right. In fact, the London Passenger Transport Board was the exception amongst railway operators, buying its rolling stock from manufacturers such as Metro-Cammell. The 'Big Four' were not above buying from outside, but they also maintained a steady flow of work through their own workshops. Even while the LMS was completing its work on the special 'Coronation Scot' London to Glasgow express, the War Office approached the company asking it to design a medium army tank. During the Second World War, the works at Crewe and Horwich became major centres for tank manufacture.

Nevertheless, while also playing their part in war work, Crewe and Derby, like the other railway company workshops, had to produce and repair locomotives. While tanks were produced for the British Army at Crewe, which turned out four Covenanter tanks a week, it still had a target of three new steam locomotives per fortnight, but under the pressures of production for the military this soon began to fall behind. At Derby and Wolverton, production lines were set up for the production and repair of wings for Handley Page Hampden and Avro Lancaster bombers. At Barassie, the old Glasgow & South Western Railway works in Scotland, a landing strip had to be built so that it could handle the repair of damaged aircraft, including Supermarine Spitfire fighters, on which at one time no fewer than 500 women were employed.

Despite all of this activity, it was to the LMS's credit that in 1941, its works repaired 54 Pacific locomotives, 119 'Royal Scots', 193 'Jubilees' and 'Patriots' ('Baby Scots'), and 38 of the massive Garratts. Even so, routine maintenance at the locomotive sheds was less thorough than it had been in peacetime, while wartime loads were much heavier, and the quality of coal provided could never be guaranteed. Such strenuous operating conditions soon began to expose inherent weaknesses and strengths in the different locomotive classes. The cracking of locomotive frames became a problem, and not just with the older locomotives, as this affected a substantial number of the famous 'Black Fives'. One oddity that could never be explained was, despite having almost identical frame designs, the 5X 4-6-0s gave little trouble, but the 'Baby Scots' proved troublesome. The 'Patriots' soon became very unpopular with the footplatemen. Fractured frames meant that a major overhaul took around 14 days, compared with the six to eight days that under wartime conditions was the standard for more robust locomotives.

Once the United States entered the war, convoys bringing American troops across the Atlantic placed an extra burden on the railways and the LMS in particular. It was often not known until the last minute whether convoys would head for Liverpool or for the Clyde, with the landing spot being changed at short notice.

Chapter 20

Under Attack

Not simply Britain's largest railway, but the biggest business in the British Empire, the London Midland & Scottish Railway was almost as dependent on goods traffic as its rival on the Anglo-Scottish services, the LNER. Like the LNER, it was preoccupied with its express traffic, and its poverty between the two world wars was only slightly less than the LNER. Having inherited a wide variety of locomotives from an equally varied number of predecessor companies, from Grouping until the outbreak of war, the LMS had pursued a policy of 'scrap and build' for both its locomotive stock and its carriages, and this was to stand it in good stead in the difficult years that followed. Not only did the LMS have some very good freight and mixed traffic locomotives, which it built in large volumes, of which the famous Stanier 'Black Five' 4-6-0 mixed traffic locomotive was the best known and most numerous, with no fewer than 471 built between 1935 and 1938, and was to be well-suited to the demands of wartime. Nevertheless, when it was something heavier that was needed for the heavy freight demands of the war years, it was Stanier's 2-8-0 freight locomotive that was to become the austerity standard, being built by the LMS and by the other companies.

In fact, despite its poor financial status between the two wars, the LMS had done well to update its rolling stock. In other ways too, the LMS had prepared for war. In 1938, a new ramp had been built at Stranraer so that motor vehicles could be driven straight on to the vehicle decks of the steamers, and this was over-designed so that it was wide enough and strong enough to take heavy tanks.

Nevertheless, the LMS suffered from serious internal problems and it could also be said that it had been simply too big to manage efficiently, given its huge size and geographical spread. This was something admitted on one occasion by Sir William Wood, who took over from Lord Stamp as president when the latter was killed with his family during an air raid, there being a shortage of money and an uncertain industrial and economic situation. It did have a reputation for building fine locomotives and its long distance carriages were regarded as being the very best on any of the grouped railways, even better than the 'Centenary Riviera' wide-bodied stock on the GWR's 'Cornish Riviera' express.

This was a company with 20,000 passenger carriages, 10,000 steam locomotives, 30,000 road vehicles and, before the outbreak of war, more than 70 steamers either in its own fleet or in fleets, such as the Caledonian, in which it was a partner.

Probably the first major British company to import modern management techniques from the United States, the LMS believed in mechanisation and in science. It worked to mechanise the coaling of locomotives, with large coaling hoists lifting up coal wagons and tipping their contents into the tenders of its large express and goods locomotives, dispensing with the use of smaller wagons or hand barrows which were labour intensive. It also led the way with control centres, which had authority over the signalmen and controlled a larger area, although it did not assume the role of the signalman in the modern sense.

On a war footing

As with the other railways, the war started quietly for the LMS, although the restrictions were as substantial for its passengers as for the other companies, and arguably even more so than for those travelling on the Southern and the Great Western. As so many of the LMS's passengers were travelling very long distances, so the speed limits and additional stops made an even greater impact. Despite adding many extra carriages so that trains with more than twenty became commonplace, a substantial number of passengers were forced to stand, all day or all night as journey times extended.

Fighting the weather and the censor

In common with the other railway companies, the LMS had to introduce severe cuts to its services and restrict the facilities on offer after the evacuation. As elsewhere, this resulted in much adverse comment in the press. More importantly, this was not all ignorant criticism by people knowing little about railway operation in the general press, for much of it came from the railway press.

In one important respect, the criticism was well deserved, for many of the October 1939 schedules were worse than those of October 1918, when the First World War was still raging. For example, on the busy London to Birmingham service, which on LMS metals was 112.9 miles, the best train in 1918 completed the journey in 2hr 40 min, and this had been reduced to 1hr 55min by 1938, but in 1939 it was stretched to 2hr 41min. Average times were much worse, at 2hr 53min between Euston and Birmingham in 1918, 2hr 5min in 1938, and 3hr 10min in 1939. Faring a little better was Manchester, 188.5 miles, which had taken 4hrs 35 min by the best train in 1918, 3 hrs 15 min by 1938, but in 1939 took 4hr 32min, while again the average times to and from Manchester were 5hr 10min, 3hr 43min, and 4hr 52min in 1918, 1938 and 1939 respectively. Glasgow, on the other hand, was another instance of a worse schedule than 1918 when the best train had taken 9hr 30min for the 401.4 miles, compared with 6hr 30min in 1938, but 9hr 35min in 1939.

The average was slightly better than in 1918, at 10hr 4min against 10hr 20min, but this was still worse than the 1938 average of 8hrs 6min. Nevertheless, those travelling between London and Birmingham had only lost a quarter of their daily trains, down from 20 to 15 and this was better than the 1918 figure of eleven trains, while Manchester suffered rather more with a cut from 22 trains to 14 between 1938 and 1939, while in 1918, there had been 16 trains, as well as losing some of its trains from Marylebone. The number of through trains between London and Glasgow was halved, down from 12 to six, the same as in 1918.

While this reflected badly on the LMS, as did similar cuts on the other railway companies, it is important to remember that the decisions were not taken by the LMS, or indeed any of the other companies, but by the government-controlled Railway Executive Committee (REC), which had taken over the railways on the eve of war.

Wartime provides its own problems but without any corresponding let-up on those that a railway might normally expect. The most serious of these was to prove to be the weather, with some exceptionally harsh winters during the war years. The bad weather that hit the railways after Christmas 1939 was the worst since 1916. The weather was most severe in the north of England and in Scotland. One day, the train due at Euston at 4.17pm from Manchester, Stockport and Rugby arrived 7hrs 20min late, while the train from Liverpool due at 6.08pm was 3hr 20min late, and the 'Irish Mail' from Holyhead was 4½ hours late. Emergency buffets were placed at the larger stations for passengers stranded in trains that had been disabled by the weather, or whose trains had been cancelled. Food rationing did not start until early 1940, so adequate supplies seem to have been provided easily, although there must have been some serious disruption to the movement of fresh food.

All in, the LMS alone suffered 238 separate cases of lines being blocked by snow, affecting 1,056 route miles. No fewer than 71 trains were blocked by snow drifts and out of these, just

15 locomotives managed to break free to get help. Especially distressing was the plight of the passengers aboard three expresses that had left Glasgow Central on the morning of 28 January, 1940, which were blocked near Beattock summit and then almost buried. They were stuck for five days. Further south, the cutting between Brock and Garstang was blocked for four days because water troughs meant that snow ploughs could not be used. This was another problem for the running of reasonably fast trains over anything more than a relatively short distance – water. With water troughs frozen, extra stops had to be made, and water could even freeze in the water towers. No Anglo-Scottish expresses could run either by the main line or the Settle & Carlisle route between the nights of 27/28 January and 2/3 February 1940.

The Railway Executive Committee was unable to issue the normal apologies or warnings to intending passengers due to wartime censorship, but got its own back some months later when it issued the following poster:

CENSORED
In peace-time railways could explain
When fog or ice held up your train

But now the country's waging war
To tell you why's against the law

The censor says you must not know
When there's been a fall of snow

That's because it would be news
The Germans could not fail to use

So think of this, if it's your fate
To have to meet a train that's late

Railways aren't allowed to say
What delayed the trains today

This might sound melodramatic, but a massive German aerial attack, difficult to mount though it would have been given that airfields in France and the Low Countries were not then available, would have been an intolerable burden on top of the other difficulties. As it was, much of northern Europe was equally badly affected and the Luftwaffe seems to have been snowed in at its airfields, but while weather reconnaissance was to assume considerable importance later in the war, at this early stage the belligerents were edging cautiously around each other, even though there was some hard war-making going on in the air and at sea, 'Phoney War' or not.

Doubtless lured by the peace of the 'Phoney War', the LMS was looking forward to a further season's holiday business, and this despite the fact that, on 11 March 1940, anticipating the German invasion of Norway, a substantial part of the north of Scotland was declared a protected area by the War Office. The area included everywhere north of Inverness and Inverness-shire and Argyll west of the Great Glen, although not the town of Inverness itself. This meant that travel to the area was restricted to residents and members of the armed forces, while anyone else had to apply for a special pass.

Nevertheless, the LMS, like the other railways, continued to approach the coming summer with considerable optimism. In the spring, it published its annual guide, *Holidays by LMS*, with no fewer than 684 pages, including 100 with photographs. It could have been a godsend to the Germans if they had intended to invade. The publication appeared at the beginning of May, and on 10 May the invasion of the Netherlands and Belgium, and then France, started. The special programme of extra trains for holidaymakers and for the Whitsun holiday in particular, was cancelled, along with the bank holiday itself.

Also shortly to be curtailed was a programme to build 240 2-8-0 Stanier 8F freight locomotives for the Ministry of Supply to augment the ex-Great Central 2-8-0 locomotives taken up from the LNER and which had gone to France with the British Expeditionary Force in 1939. The first of these locomotives was ready by late May 1940, but by this time the situation in France was so bad that they were all retained at home until later, when they were sent to Egypt and the Middle East. Nevertheless, these locomotives were to provide the basis of the Second World War 'standard' freight locomotive and be built not only by the LMS, but also by the other main-line companies for their own use.

Accidents

As with the other companies, the wartime blackout imposed considerable difficulties in train operation. Nevertheless, the LMS was unfortunate enough to suffer one of the first serious accidents in which the blackout was a contributing factor. On the night of 13 October 1939, the 7.50pm Euston to Stranraer boat train was running double-headed, but despite four drivers and firemen on the two locomotives they managed to pass no fewer than six adverse signals. While the train was due to stop at Bletchley, it approached the station at such speed that it could not stop before it hit a shunting engine that was attaching carriages to another train. In the resulting collision, four people were killed and manslaughter charges brought against the driver of the pilot locomotive, although he was found not guilty.

The fireman of the pilot engine admitted that he had become disorientated and did not realise where he was until the engine exploded detonators at Bletchley, while the experienced driver of the train engine had simply left the duty of watching for signals to the driver of the pilot locomotive. As in an accident on the GWR at Norton Fitzwarren, the situation was confused by parallel tracks. The Chief Inspecting Officer of Railways, Lt-Col Mount, was convinced that the conditions of working in the blackout were substantially to blame for the accident.

'It is for consideration whether, and to what extent, blackout conditions on very dark nights affect the normal efficiency of enginemen,' he reported. 'It has been stated that such conditions actually make the driver's task easier, and it is true that the 'pattern' of lights today as compared with the maze of different light which may be observed in peacetime on the approach to a big station or town, is generally confined to a few signals relating only to the line on which the train is running, and perhaps to a parallel line, as at Bletchley.

'On the other hand,' he continued, 'experience shows… the clarifying of the resulting signal "pattern" has not the safety value it otherwise would have, as the landmarks, by which the driver instinctively locates himself, are also eliminated under blackout conditions. If locating objects even signalboxes are no longer visible, a driver… may well lose his whereabouts temporarily, and for sufficient time to permit of speed in excess of that corresponding to signal indications…. On moonless or cloudy nights a driver in the blackout speeds through almost impenetrable darkness, relieved only by the lights of signals. The assessment of distances between signals is uncertain… drivers may be at considerable disadvantage in assessing their speed and location, particularly after years of operation at 70–80mph, and it is not inconceivable that, without a speedometer, speed may be allowed to rise…'

His main conclusion was that the extension of automatic train control was to be pressed ahead with as far as wartime shortages of labour and materials allowed. He also lamented the fact that only on the Great Western were speedometers fitted to locomotives. Amidst the conflicting demands and pressures of wartime, his recommendations were ignored.

On 5 March 1940, a more easily understood accident occurred on the Highland main line between Aviemore and Slochd summit, a difficult section at the best of times. Two 'Black Five' locomotives were double-heading an unfitted mineral train of thirty wagons and a brake van, giving a total of 460 tons, from Aviemore to Slochd. It was stopped as it approached Slochd home signal and then diverted into the down loop line. It was at this point that it was realised that there were only nine wagons, and that the guard's van and 21 wagons were rolling back down a 1-in-70 gradient towards Aviemore. The theory was that the guard's van should have been able to hold the wagons if a coupling broke, but this was impossible against such a gradient and realising this, the guard jumped from his van, suffering injuries as he did so. The signalman at Slochd was slow to realise that there was not a complete train, but then telephoned the box at Carr Bridge 5½ miles away, where the gradient was 1 in 60. The signalman at Carr Bridge saw the train race past his box and could do nothing more than send the 'obstruction danger' signal to Aviemore, where another northbound double-headed goods train had just departed. As this train was 2½ miles north of Aviemore, the crew of the leading locomotive saw red lights approaching, but before they could do anything, the runway wagons crashed into them, overturning the pilot locomotive and killing the crew, while no fewer than 14 of the wagons and the brake van were destroyed.

There was a yet another wartime accident on the LMS, in late autumn 1940, at Wembley station.

At 7.10pm in the darkness of the blackout, a four-wheeled luggage barrow with around half-a-ton of goods and luggage for a down slow train was being manhandled by three porters up the ramp at the end of the platforms for the up fast and down slow lines. The barrow was overloaded because the porters were trying to move the contents in one move, and as a result it was heavier than they could manage. As they went up the ramp, they slipped, and despite their best efforts, it ran back and stopped, fouling the up fast line just as the 11.50am express from Liverpool to London approached, travelling at about 55mph.

The locomotive struck the barrow and it is believed that possibly only the bogies' wheels of the 4-6-0 'Patriot' class No 5529 were derailed initially. The driver acted quickly to close the regulator and apply the brake, but beyond the platform lay a double cross-over leading from the fast to the slow lines. On reaching the cross-over, the locomotive derailed completely, overturning while the weight of the carriages behind jack-knifed the tender, killing the driver and fireman. Fortunately, the train consisted of modern carriages, confining serious damage to the leading three coaches, in which four passengers were injured, but on the platform another nine people were killed.

Only a limited amount of clearance work could be carried out in the blackout, and with wreckage scattered over all four tracks, Euston was closed to steam services, although the electric trains to London could continue. It took a week before full services could be restored.

Although this accident has been attributed by some to the blackout, even in normal circumstances the locomotive driver would have had little chance to react. The accident to the barrow occurred just before his locomotive reached it, and in any case, a bend and a road bridge obscured the view of the station for trains on the up line. Some accidents seem beyond the power of any imaginable safety device, other than, in this case, the common sense of the porters.

Within a year, on 14 September 1941, another wartime accident occurred on the LMS at Holmes Chapel, between Crewe and Manchester, again when a signalman cleared his block instrument prematurely and allowed another train into a section.

At 1.23am, the 12.35am Crewe to Leeds passenger train was pulling away from the station when it was struck in the rear by the 12.50am Crewe to Manchester passenger train travelling at around 35mph. Six passengers aboard the Leeds train were killed immediately and another three died later, while 45 people were injured. The rescue efforts were helped by ARP personnel and by the local Home Guard. The Leeds train comprised a goods wagon and six bogie carriages, while the Manchester train consisted of nine bogie carriages. The accident might have been worse had not the Manchester train been slowing down for an engineering speed restriction.

As the year drew to a close, there was another accident, this time in fog. Wartime increased the dangers on the railways, especially at night with the blackout, which was also much more dangerous in fog. At Eccles, near Manchester, on 30 December 1941, a westbound train passed danger signals in fog and collided with an eastbound train traversing a crossover, and although travelling at just 30mph, 30 people were killed. The main cause was found to be that the signalman had suspended fog working, which would have extended the distance between trains, because he did not know if fogmen were on duty. The site of the accident was close to the Manchester Ship Canal, where visibility was as low as 10 yards.

There was a further accident while the war continued, at Ecclefachan near Lockerbie, but as this occurred after the war in Europe had ended it is dealt with in Chapter 17 Accidents.

Wartime operations

The LMS share of the evacuation trains for Dunkirk was 44, and while this was far from the highest contribution, some of these trains had to convey troops as far north as Aberdeen.

No fewer than 50,000 LMS workers joined the Local Defence Volunteers, and when the title was changed to Home Guard in July 1940, the LMS organised a ceremonial naming of a 'Patriot' class 4-6-0 locomotive No. 5543 at Euston by Lt Gen Sir Henry Pownall, Inspector General of the Home Guard.

To save fuel and wear and tear on track as well as locomotives, during the war, the railways initially had maximum speed permitted reduced to 60mph, although on the main long-distance routes of the LMS this was later increased to 75mph. The increase in speed was accompanied by drivers being told to use their locomotives to the limits of their ability to make up for lost time. Some drivers used this instruction in the true spirit that it was intended, and even with trains of 15 carriages or more, managed to make up lost time, but others were content to maintain the scheduled timings.

For almost ten months, the widely anticipated bombing did not come, with only a few small-scale raids. While this soon changed with the Battle of Britain as the Luftwaffe tried to put the Royal Air Force out of action prior to an invasion of England, the LMS was sufficiently well away from the main fighter bases in the south of England to have been little troubled at this stage of the war. All this was set to change with the Blitz however, the heavy air raids that started in late 1940 and continued through the winter to early summer 1941. At first, the tactics consisted of largely area bombing, against a particular town rather than specific targets. Even so, much serious damage was done, and at Coventry in November 1940, and Liverpool in May 1941, every possible route in the area was damaged, but hard work by repair crews meant that line closures could generally be measured in hours rather than days.

The first LMS casualties of the war were, as mentioned in the previous chapter, some of the company's ships which had been requisitioned, or in nautical terms 'taken up from trade', to fulfil a variety of wartime roles.

The air raid on Coventry on the night of 14/15 November 1940, saw the LMS suffer no fewer than 122 incidents on its lines around the city. Traffic between Euston and Birmingham had to be diverted at Rugby and sent via Leamington and Kenilworth, returning to the main line at Berkswell. Nevertheless, within two days one platform was available at Coventry station and the London to Birmingham trains returned to their usual route, using the Coventry avoiding line, a week after the raid. The fact that the Great Western also served Birmingham ensured that there was some flexibility in the arrangements.

From the point of view of maintaining the LMS's operations, the worst raid was that of 10/11 May 1941, when a 1,000lb bomb fell through the roof of St Pancras, continued through the floor of the station, itself basically a deck of wrought iron plates on wrought iron main and cross-girders, resting on cast iron columns, and buried itself in the London clay below, exploding when some 25 feet down. The explosion created a large crater at the concourse end of Platforms 3 and 4, but even more serious it destroyed the tunnel carrying the Metropolitan Line and the Midland trains to the City for about 20 feet. Clearing up the mess and starting repairs was made difficult by the presence of an unexploded bomb halfway along No. 2 platform. Nevertheless, undamaged platforms were used and within seven days, with the exception of two platforms, all lines were working again.

Euston was missed by the Luftwaffe, but even before the heavy raid that so battered St Pancras, Broad Street had suffered badly. On the night of 3/4 October 1940, the lines into the terminus were wrecked by bombing and the station had to be closed for several days. It was hit yet again on 13 October and on 11 November. The station had also served the LNER with services reaching it over the lines of the former Great Northern Railway. These had been suspended from mid-September to early December 1939 to make space for essential war traffic, but were ended completely on 4 October as a result of the damage done by the previous night's bombs.

Services to East London were cut back after the heavy bombing resulted in many residents being evacuated from what was, in many places, a wasteland. After 14 May 1944, services were not worked east of Dalston Junction.

Fenchurch Street, on the eastern side of the City of London, was relatively unscathed, but services to North Woolwich were abandoned after the bombing of October 1940.

Apart from the occasional closure of London termini due to enemy action, the inner suburban stations at Shoreditch and Haggerston had to be closed for the duration in 1940.

One town that was an obvious target for the Luftwaffe was Barrow-in-Furness, in what is now Cumbria but was then part of Lancashire. Barrow had a major naval shipyard, Vickers, specialising in building aircraft carriers and submarines, although the commercial port itself was owned by the LMS having been part of the dowry on Grouping from the Furness Railway. This was also the site at which later many of the pontoons for the Mulberry Harbour, needed for the Normandy invasion, were built. During the Blitz of 1941, the hydraulic power system in the docks was badly damaged and sheds along the dockside destroyed. The main casualty was the old Central station with its all-over roof, and this was completely demolished, the only British railway station to suffer such extensive damage.

To cripple a railway, it is not always necessary to damage buildings, track or trains, as control centres play a vital role, especially when the system is under pressure or crippled, when their essential overview can help to maintain services. Each division of the LMS had its own control centre. That in Manchester looked after the Central Division, consisting mainly of the former Lancashire & Yorkshire Railway lines, and was the most sophisticated of any on the LMS. The emergency room had been built 30 feet below ground level with heavy bombing in mind. Just before Christmas 1940, a heavy air raid was under way when a reservoir in the vicinity was breached by a bomb and water began to flood into the control centre. Fortunately, those present were able to escape without serious loss, but operations were hampered as instructions for anything out of the ordinary had to be sent by car or by motorcycle dispatch riders until the control centre could be recovered and made operational again.

The LMS was the only 'mainland' railway company to operate in Northern Ireland through the Northern Counties Committee, with its lines from Belfast to Londonderry, Portrush and Larne. Many in Northern Ireland believed that they would be safe from aerial attack because of the distance from the nearest German bases, but before the war, in 1938, the senior manager in Northern Ireland, Major M.S. Speir, insisted on building air raid shelters in Belfast as well as strengthening the signalbox. The Luftwaffe did not mount a major air raid on Belfast until April 1941, but this destroyed the company's general stores and parcels office, as well as the audit office and the engineers' drawing office, but the signalbox survived. The following month, on 4 May, there was a further raid, which cost the Northern Counties Committee 20 carriages and 270 goods wagons, but control and communications remained intact.

On the other side of the Irish Sea, Liverpool was raided for seven consecutive nights in May 1941. During this period, on two occasions the railway network serving the city lost every route in and out of the area, and at one time the lines were cut in no fewer than 500 places.

Such raids obviously resulted in many members of the LMS workforce being killed or injured, but seniority was no guarantee of survival. On the night of 16/17 April 1941, Lord Stamp, the company's chairman, was killed in an air raid. This was a loss for the railway companies as a whole since he was involved in negotiations with the government which at the time was cutting back on its earlier deal to compensate the railways. The loss of Lord Stamp, and the fear of being viewed as unpatriotic as invasion threatened, combined to stifle railway opposition to the government's revised proposals.

The locomotive sheds, by this time known as motive power depots, were also obvious targets for the Luftwaffe, and either direct hits or near misses saw many lose their roofing, including Kentish Town. Others were, however, simply removed for safety reasons after years of neglect and the impact of acid rain from the country's then smoke-laden atmosphere.

Chapter 21

Peace and Nationalisation

When referring to the wartime record of the railways in 1944, Sir Alan Mount, the Chief Inspecting Officer of Railways, was able to say that it represented 'an eloquent tribute, to their efficiency, standard of maintenance, and on the high factor of safety attained, all of which reflects the greatest credit on every railwayman and woman for the part they played in this historic year.' Yet, these comments late in the war by an impartial public servant were ignored by the politicians.

It is hard to judge just how much railway passenger traffic was affected by the war since the available statistics do not show the average length of journey, which was likely to have increased considerably. The number of originating passenger journeys on the LMS was from 421 million in 1938 to 456 million in 1944, itself down 2 million on 1943. For all of the railway companies, the number of coaching train miles fell between 1938 and 1944, including empty stock workings. These figures tell little of the reality of wartime railway travel, as the number of passengers per train mile increased substantially between 1939 and 1943, without taking any account of the length of journey made, which seems to have increased substantially, still less the amount of time spent aboard the train. On the LMS, passengers per train mile rose from 4.1 to 6.5.

Freight ton-miles increased overall by 46 per cent between 1938 and 1943, with the biggest increase, 86 per cent, in merchandise, which doubtless included manufactured items such as munitions. While coal and coke traffic only rose by 13 per cent, the length of haul increased by no less than 30 per cent. In peacetime, there must have been a great deal of one-way traffic, no doubt due to the private-owner wagons, since loaded goods wagon miles rose by almost a third between 1938 and 1943, empty miles fell by around 8 per cent. The average load per wagon also went from just three tons pre-war to just over four tons.

The statistics are inadequate since they consist of totals provided by each company, not by the Railway Executive Committee, so that, for example, a train from, say, Portsmouth to Rosyth could count as four trains, running over the Southern, GWR, LMS and finally the LNER. Nevertheless, passenger specials for the government rose from 24,241 in 1940, doubtless boosted by the Dunkirk evacuation, and after a drop in 1941, to 47,381 in 1943. Freight specials showed a steady increase, from 20,888 in 1940 to 45,583 in 1943.

Naturally enough, throughout the war the hostilities took their toll on railway staff, many of whom continued to work under conditions that many would regard as incredible today. Not only was serious damage repaired as quickly as possible, sometimes with military help, to maintain services, but locomotives and trains were moved to safety during the height of air raids, and many continued to work amidst burning buildings.

The view of the Chief Inspecting Officer of Railways was not shared by the new Labour government elected in early summer 1945.

'This railway system of ours is a very poor bag of assets,' Hugh Dalton, Chancellor of the Exchequer, had told the House of Commons during the second reading of the Transport Bill on 17 December 1946. 'The permanent way is badly worn. The rolling stock is in a state of

The post-war period found the railways struggling to get back to normality. This was exacerbated by a shortage of skilled workers and money, but this Fairburn 4MT 2-6-4T No. 2270, taking a suburban train out of Glasgow Central in 1946, seems have been very well looked after. *(HMRS AAL409)*

great dilapidation. The railways are a disgrace to the country. The railway stations and their equipment are a disgrace to the country.'

At the time, MPs were discussing the terms of compensation to be paid to the shareholders, and the Chancellor had been pressed to justify the appalling compensation that was proposed. He managed to avoid mentioning the strains of war, but by the time the measure became law, the *Financial Times* was moved to point out that the claim that the railways were a 'poor bag of assets' had been disproved. Indeed, amongst those with an open mind, the railways were truly war battered, and exhausted. Not only had the system been worked to the limit, not only had it endured heavy enemy aerial attack, it had seen its locomotives and rolling stock taken as far away as Persia, present day Iran, and at home hastily trained labour had taken the place of the skilled men who had either volunteered to join the armed forces or had been conscripted. In addition to the shortage of materials and manpower, the workshops had in many cases been given over to war production, and faced with the need to repair bomb damage the priority was repairing and rebuilding while routine track and rolling stock maintenance had to be neglected.

If Britain's railways were such a poor bag of assets indeed in 1947, one might wonder why it was that the lines on the Isle of Wight continued to operate Victorian locomotives and rolling stock right up to 1966, and when these were replaced it was by elderly rolling stock dating from the 1930s that had been withdrawn from the London Underground?

Grey days

Despite the end of the blackout, preceded in any case by 'dim out' with reduced lighting permitted in the closing days of the war in Europe, these were grey days for the country as a whole. Much has been made of the return of the bright lights with the end of the restrictions enforcing the blackout by VE Day, but the population had to continue with rationing of almost everything, except that one or two items such as fresh fish and bread, which had not been rationed during the war years, were now rationed post-war!

The railways post-war nevertheless were in the position of trying to do more with considerably less resources than they had employed pre-war. The mass of the public were anxious to make up for the holidays lost during the war years, they wanted to travel. If 1938 had been a poor year for the railways, 1946 and 1947 brought an embarrassment of traffic. On the LMS, the average train was carrying 140 per cent of its pre-war loading, with passenger miles up 70 per cent while train miles were down by 30 per cent. Engines, carriages, stations, track, signals and bridges were all worn out, crying out for attention while the workshops that had given them regular overhauls had been committed to building tanks, guns, invasion barges and aircraft. All of this was aggravated by poor quality coal and frequent cuts in the volume of coal allowed to even such a vital industry as the railways, on whose performance other industries depended.

At the time, even the better off had to use public transport, and even if one could get hold of a car, which would be old since with the exception of a few models for military use, car production had stopped for the duration of the war, petrol was still difficult to obtain. Buses, including those of London Transport which had come to pride itself on the condition of its fleet and its overhaul arrangements, now included many with holes in their bodywork; others had chassis that sagged alarmingly in the middle. In just under six years of total war, the country had been so battered and its circumstances so reduced that it resembled what would today be described as a third world state, with little that worked. Large areas of many towns and cities had been razed to the ground, or had the skeletal remains of gutted buildings standing bleakly against the sky.

Just how much of the public enthusiasm for nationalisation resulted from onerous wartime travel restrictions and the controls that left the timetable often halved or worse, when additional traffic had to be handled, or extended journey times by a third or more, is hard to say in retrospect. On the other hand, the vote for Labour may not have been a vote for nationalisation but a vote against what many had come to see as the unfairness and inequality of some aspects of British life. It would be tempting to think that the denial of electrification by the LMS was in part to blame for nationalisation finally reaching the Statute Book, but the railways, with the possible exception of the Great Western, had little public sympathy. The railway companies were blamed for the restrictions on services during the war years, even though they were no longer in control as all decisions were taken by the Railway Executive Committee.

There were other factors at work here. The full evil of the Soviet system had still to be revealed, and in the post-war period Communism was even considered respectable. Few people were shareholders, and few understood, or even cared, how the system worked.

Apart from enthusiasts, the railways never enjoyed great popularity. The errors and shortcomings of the worst obscured the achievements of the best. This still happens today. Part of the problem is, of course, that public expectations of the railways are often unattainable and unrealistic. One Ministry of Transport civil servant once told the author that the by then nationalised railways were making vast profits out of suburban commuters because the trains were so over-crowded, and refused to believe that if the train then spent the whole day idle in a siding, it was losing money. Most of its peak hour passengers were enjoying heavily discounted fares anyway, with savings on annual season tickets amounting to 40 per cent on suburban journeys and up to 60 per cent on longer-distance services.

The real problem over the nationalisation debate was simply that the public, the electorate and taxpayers, didn't care.

Who did care then? The railway shareholders were outnumbered by the railway workers. Nationalisation in the UK was driven by the workers in particular industries. Labour was committed virtually to the nationalisation of almost everything, although in later years some prominent ministers would deny that they would nationalise 'down to the last corner shop'. Railwaymen and coal miners all wanted to control their own industries in a series of 'soviets'. Labour also decided that air transport should be run by the state. How shipping managed to remain off limits is a mystery, although even this was in the sights of later Labour administrations. The docks belonging to the railways were nationalised, but the remainder left untouched simply because so many of them were in local authority control, or run by public bodies.

Nationalisation of the railways overnight gave the state control of the main ports, plus the railway hotels, haulage firms such as Carter Peterson and Pickfords, and the travel agency Thomas Cook. It provided a substantial ferry and coastal shipping fleet, and a large number of bus companies, especially when the state also managed to absorb the bus interests of Thomas Tilling, Scottish Motor Traction and the British Automobile Traction Group. The government's priority was nationalisation, greater state control and a cradle to the grave welfare state, rather than reconstruction and improvement of the manufacturing base and infrastructure. These assets were all acquired cheaply, but they had been neglected out of dire necessity during the war, and in the immediate post-war period the railway companies could not even obtain their usual peacetime allocation of materials for routine maintenance and renewals, let alone make significant inroads into the massive backlog.

Probably what counted more was the experience of those on some of the London, Midland & Scottish Railway's branch lines, where intending passengers had to open compartment doors and look inside to see whether there was room for them as the windows were so filthy. An acute shortage of labour had meant that even such basics as cleaning carriages and locomotives were neglected, and in any case, many carriages needed what is sometimes described as a 'deep clean'. Many recall the LMS locomotives in particular being so dirty that often engine numbers had to be chalked on to aid identification. Not for nothing did one wit scribble the graffito: 'LMS – a hell of a mess'. Schoolboys used to take a delight in swinging their satchels through the air and against seats to send a cloud of soot and dust into the air of an already murky compartment.

On the other hand, this was not simply a wartime or early post-war phenomenon as the same problems had been reported with the old LNWR, which also had to chalk locomotive numbers on cab sides.

The weather takes a hand

It almost seemed as if the fates were ganging up on the railways in the two years after the end of the war. One of the worst winters on record came in early 1947. It was inevitable that services were affected both by the bad weather and by the looming shortage of coal. Bad weather kept miners away from work, and the coal that was brought to the surface was often frozen at the pit head and difficult to load. The colliers bringing the coal that could be loaded were kept in port or delayed by the strong gales. For those railways operating steam locomotives, water was also a problem, as the water troughs were rendered useless by the low temperatures forcing longer-distance trains to make additional calls to take on water, itself a hazardous task requiring locomotive firemen to climb on top of tenders in freezing conditions and in strong winds.

The bad weather had started in January. Heavy snowfalls were accompanied by strong gales, and in between the periods of calm were marked by freezing fog. By early February, most railway motive power depots had enough coal for just one week, including coal for the LMS's own power station, and the government was forced to act, introducing curbs on the use of electricity by industry.

This extended to the railways, so that starting on 5 February cuts were enforced on many electric suburban services, followed within a week, on 11 February, by yet a further round of cuts, while still more followed on 15 February. The shortage of coal also affected steam-hauled services. The massive freeze continued until 8 March, when a thaw started, augmented by heavy rain on 10 March, that resulted in flooding of many low-lying stretches of line.

Worse was to follow. In Scotland, a severe snowstorm came with little warning on Wednesday, 12 March 1947. It started gently enough at around 5pm, but within two hours there was a heavy blizzard accompanied by gale force winds, and snow drifts had begun to emerge. The 5.10pm express from Glasgow to Stranraer reached Glenwhilly station at 7.53pm with the 'Black Five' having had difficulty surmounting Chirmorie summit despite the train having just four corridor carriages. Further progress was impossible as a northbound freight train was occupying the single-track line, eventually backing to New Luce which it had left earlier as operation in the direction of Glasgow was impossible. The only solution was to send for a snow plough, but in the severe winter snow ploughs were few and far between, and many of those in Scotland had been sent south to the north of England where the bad weather had arrived earlier.

At 11pm, a snow plough arrived at Glenwhilly and continued towards New Luce, which it reached at 11.58pm. After a wait of just over four hours at Glenwhilly, the Stranraer express was able to continue its journey. The section to New Luce was 4½ miles long and normally could be worked in eight minutes, but there was no signal from New Luce to tell the signalman at Glenwhilly that the train was out of section. At 1am, the guard of the Stranraer train struggled out of the snow and into the station to alert those present that the train was stuck in a fresh snow drift half a mile south.

Fortunately, those aboard the train had heat and light at this stage, while the guard explained that he had a consignment of food for a NAAFI (Navy, Army & Air Force Institute) canteen, which he was authorised to issue to the passengers. On returning to his train, the guard ensured that the 57 passengers were fed. At 7am, the stationmaster and his staff at the station carried a supply of hot tea to the train, by this time half-buried; the first of three such trips that day. The driver and fireman remained on the footplate keeping the fire burning, supplying heat to the carriages, but at noon the water in the tender dropped so low that the fire had to be put out to avoid the firebox crown collapsing and exploding. With the end of the heat, the carriages became colder, and with the return of darkness the cold and the weight of snow pressing on the windows caused them to crack, with one caving in and seriously injuring two passengers. The batteries that had provided light once the train stopped failed one by one. Snow ploughs had been sent, but one was stuck some ten miles to the north and the other more than five miles to the south.

The storm abated on Friday morning and fires were set in the booking office and the stationmaster's house before the passengers were escorted from the train to the station. The local people, mainly LMS employees, fed the passengers and looked after them, but supplies were scant as the previous day had been ration day and nothing had arrived and no one had been able to get to the nearest shops. As the coal ran short, teams with makeshift sledges began a shuttle between the station and the train to transfer its coal to the station.

At 5pm on the Friday, a Stranraer-based guard got through from New Luce to report that the southern snow plough had reached the station with a gang of workers, and a relief train was available for those fit enough to walk the 4½ miles through thick snow. The crew of the train and 32 passengers managed to struggle through to New Luce, and eventually reached Stranraer before midnight.

On Saturday, 15 March, the remaining passengers made their way to a relief train, which had got to within two miles of Glenwhilly, with the help of a large body of police and German prisoners-of-war, who carried the older and less fit passengers on stretchers. By late afternoon, all were in Stranraer. The crew of the train from Glasgow had to return home by steamer!

It was not until the following day that the train itself could be rescued, but by this time the line was only open from the south as the snowplough to the north had been badly damaged and a locomotive derailed, blocking the line further. The line was not fully open until Thursday, 20 March.

Chapter 22

What Might Have Been

Midnight on 31 December 1947 was marked by the sound of steam locomotive whistles being blown in celebration of Nationalisation. The 'Big Four' grouped companies were no more, but instead replaced by an even larger single nationalised railway that was itself a part of an even larger British Transport Commission. If the LMS had been too big to manage effectively, the BTC was still larger.

Speculating on what might have happened had railway nationalisation not happened is somewhat difficult. For a start, even had the railways escaped nationalisation in Great Britain, there was more than a fair risk that it would still have happened in Northern Ireland. While the railways in what is now the Irish Republic were nationalised even before those in Great Britain, the cross-border companies escaped because of their 'international' status. So, the County Donegal, the Londonderry & Lough Swilly and, of course, the Great Northern Railway of Ireland continued in private hands for a few years more. Yet, nationalisation of road transport meant that the days of private enterprise railways were numbered. While the Ulster Unionist Party, for long the governing party in Northern Ireland, is often seen as a partner to the Conservative Party in Great Britain, in many ways it is far to the left of the Conservatives, especially in economic policy.

The catalyst for nationalisation throughout the whole of Ireland could have been the collapse into bankruptcy in 1953 of the GNR (I), although the government of Northern Ireland might well have taken over the NCC and the Belfast & County Down earlier. This means that 1953 was the year when state ownership of all railways on both sides of the border would finally have come about.

In short, apart from the ferry services, we can now forget about railways in Northern Ireland. Indeed, nationalisation proved one thing, that they didn't have a future. The County Donegal soon became a bus operator owned by Coras Iompair Eirean, the Southern Irish transport operator, while the L&LSR also became a bus operator, albeit remaining in private ownership for a while longer. The former GNR (I) saw its lines to Londonderry closed, leaving it with just the Belfast–Dublin line, while the former NCC lost most of its lines other than those from Belfast to Larne and to Londonderry, with the branch to Portrush. The small Belfast & County Down retained only its short line to the coastal resort and dormitory town of Bangor.

The one thing that we can be sure about is that the LMS would have continued its diesel experiments. Dieselisation of shunting operations would have continued apace and would have been completed quickly. The main line diesels would have entered service with Nos 10000 and 10001 showing their paces on the main lines, but would this have led to a wholesale switch to diesel production? This is difficult to answer. The LMS, like the GWR, started to convert steam locomotives to oil-burning, but was ordered by the Ministry of Supply to stop when the country ran short of foreign currency, and before Marshall Plan loans could be gained from the United States the country could not afford to import crude oil. One can only imagine that little more would have been done before the early 1950s, when the economy began to improve and the return of a Conservative government would have removed the threat of nationalisation.

This is to suppose that the diesel experiments on the main lines would have worked well. Would two locomotives have been enough to prove the concept? Both Nos 10000 and 10001 were just 1,600hp, which experience has shown to be too little to handle an express passenger train of twelve or more carriages. Some pre-service artists' impressions show them operating in tandem. Perhaps the first generation of LMS diesels would have suffered from the same problem as the first-generation LMS steam locomotives, post-Grouping, too little and not powerful enough. On the other hand, at least one man could handle two, or even more, diesels, and the LMS might have copied American railways in having several locomotives at the head of its trains, even to the extent of adopting the US practice of cabless power cars.

The design of the main-line diesel-electric locomotive was much easier to establish, although the two prototypes ordered by the LMS were underpowered at just 1,600hp. This is the first, numbered No. 10000 by the LMS, the only one to be delivered before Nationalisation, but shown here in British Railways ownership. *(Colour-Rail 210373)*

This brings us to the next stage of railway development, electrification. Could electrification of the Fenchurch Street services have been delayed any longer? The pressure to get on with it would have been immense, but so would the cost. Would the LMS have had enough money, or would the Treasury have stepped in again? Treasury help might not have been needed as the heavy post-war traffic experienced by the railways would also have ensured that there was a good cash flow and reserves could have been accumulated ready for renewed investment once materials became available. In addition, as after the First World War, some deal would have been done with the government over the wartime use of the railways, and this money, if invested in modernisation, could have started to transform the railway. On the other hand, and with railways there so often appears to be an 'other hand', the priority would have been to repair wartime damage and maintenance arrears.

It is tempting to digress slightly and wonder what would have happened if, in 1912 at the age of 43 years, the then Herbert Ashcombe Walker had not been wooed away to become the last general manger of the London & South Western Railway, but had instead stayed with the London & North Western. Walker was the strongest British proponent of electrification. It is tempting to suppose that had he become the first general manager of the LMS, he might have steered the company in a completely different direction. The point is, of course, whether or not he would have emerged from the struggle for power on Grouping as general manager, or would he have been shunted into the sidings? It is most likely that he left the LNWR because he saw little chance of taking control there, and so it is most unlikely that he could have played the role with the LMS that awaited him on the Southern Railway where he became its first general manager.

Certainly, by the mid-1950s, the pressure to look at culling uneconomic branch lines would have arisen, and while some would no doubt have been converted to diesel railcar operation, copying not only the GWR but also the NCC, this in so many cases seems to have simply delayed the hard decision to opt for closure. From the same period onwards, the decline in consumption of coal would also have affected the viability of many branch lines in mining areas, and even those in areas with heavy industry at the other end of the coal trains' journeys. In fact, many believe that had the Second World War not happened, the LMS would have decided to cut many more of its uneconomic branch lines and also close a number of stations.

Perhaps finally the LMS would have been forced to consider the long-dismissed and derided option of operating trainload freight services between railheads, making even greater use of containers and, with the other railway companies, making the best use of their shared freight road transport interests.

It is also likely that the government would have been faced with hard choices, especially in areas with marginal parliamentary seats, of having to choose between closure and subsidy for uneconomic branch lines that the railways, and in fact their shareholders, had been carrying for some years.

If in some ways this looks so very much like what did happen under the nationalised railway, it is worth suggesting that two other factors would have come into play.

First, dieselisation would have taken longer and been steadier than actually happened under British Railways. The LMS would not have built steam locomotives right up to 1960, only to have them withdrawn within a decade. Steam locomotive production would have stopped by 1955, and steam operation would probably have lasted into the late 1970s. That said, the LMS would have been much slower to electrify its long-distance services, and any electrification would have concentrated on suburban services and, later, outer-suburban services as the commuter area grew. Later, the lines from Euston to Birmingham, Liverpool and Manchester would have been electrified, but probably later than in fact did happen under BR.

Secondly, competition between the LMS and LNER, and the LMS and the GWR, would have continued. Paddington would have kept its services to Birmingham, while Edinburgh and Glasgow would still have enjoyed competition with services from both King's Cross and Euston, and possibly from St Pancras as well since the LMS found that this duplication with its Euston services relieved pressure on the network, as well as providing a diversionary route, and also ensured good links between the East Midlands and Scotland. One feels that freed from Treasury constraints and interference, the LMS would have been more generous in maintaining competition and in ensuring the survival of duplicate routes.

At sea, the pressing need was to replace the ships on the services from Dublin, and no doubt this would have been done by introducing roll-on/roll-off, or if you prefer, drive-on/drive-off ferries, while replacing wartime losses elsewhere would also have included ships of this kind. Heysham–Belfast would have seen newer ships sooner than under British Railways. The LMS would have been much more reluctant to close the 'Port Road', so traffic between Stranraer and Larne would have been busier, and, of course, this route was the first to have roll-on/roll-off ferries.

The loss of a later *Princess Victoria** during an especially severe storm in 1953, would have been shaken off, as other ferry operators have done. On the other hand, anyone who has been involved with shipping to Northern Ireland will know that whenever a new ferry of this design is introduced, someone will raise the *Princess Victoria* tragedy. This doesn't happen elsewhere.

---

*On 31 January 1953, the *Princess Victoria*, carrying the name of Britain's first roll-on/roll-off car ferry which had been lost due to enemy action during the Second World War, left Stranraer for Larne in a bad storm. As she made her crossing, water started to enter the vehicle deck and as she rolled in the storm, it surged across the deck. Her engines failed and she radioed that she was 'not under command'. Despite a Royal Navy destroyer being sent to her aid, she sank, with the loss of 133 out of the 177 persons aboard, including her master and three prominent Ulster politicians. Only ten crew members and 34 passengers survived.

The combined effect of the troubles in Northern Ireland and the growth of private car ownership, which led many more people to use the shorter crossings, would probably have ensured the development of the Stranraer–Larne sailings while those from Heysham might have suffered the same fate as the former Belfast Steamship service from Liverpool, although the better ship-train connection at Heysham might have helped.

Whether or not someone would have bitten the bullet and started to split up the LMS, selling-off its 'non-core' interests, is an interesting thought. Many other groups, including Unilever, have sold off subsidiaries or even whole divisions and others have restructured completely. The statutory nature of the railway business would have meant that would have stayed, but no doubt the Railway Rates Tribunal would have had its powers cut or even been disbanded altogether as road haulage became more significant and the motorway network grew. The LMS might have sold its hotels, or even some of its docks and shipping interests. The remaining canals might have been closed completely. On the other hand, as a company that looked across the Atlantic, perhaps, the LMS would for once have looked not at US practice but at Canada instead, and remodelled itself along the lines of Canadian Pacific, becoming a multi-modal transport group with trains, ships, aircraft and hotels, as well as road haulage and buses. There's a thought!

Perhaps the real pressure to restructure would have come after 1979 when a new British government began to dismantle the restrictions on first long-distance coach operations, then road haulage, and finally buses. This created a much freer market, even if not quite the pre-1930–33 free-for-all. That would certainly have forced the LMS to look at its uneconomic activities.

The later *LMS* carriages influenced the British Railways Mk1 rolling stock, as can be seen here with this former *LMS* corridor composite carriage, clearly in British Railways ownership and operating on the London Midland region. *(Colour-Rail 20922)*

Appendix 1

Motive Power Depots

The steady reduction in the number of sheds meant that codes were changed from time to time and below is the last allocation of codes before the outbreak of the Second World War. By this time, these were officially motive power depots, with the parent depot for each district given a figure between 1 and 29, with the subordinate depots, in the company's own words, given the code of a the parent depot with an identifying letter. For the sake of clarity, the parent depots are in upper case letters.

Prior to this, each division had a separate series, except the Northern Division which used no special system, or perhaps none at all. Below the subordinate divisions came simple running sheds without a letter suffix, as at Market Harborough and Seaton.

The list below gives a good idea of the geographical spread of the LMS, especially in the way it penetrated South Wales, as at 31 December 1947.

Depot	No.		
		Clee Hill	
		Craven Arms	
WILLESDEN	1A	Knighton	
Camden	1B	Builth Road	
Watford	1C	Swansea	4B
		Carmarthen	
RUGBY	2A	Llandovery	
Market Harborough		Upper Bank	4C
Seaton		Gurnos	
Bletchley	2B	Brecon	
Leighton		Abergavenny	4D
Cambridge		Hereford	
Oxford		Blaenavon	
Newport Pagnell		Tredegar	4E
Aylesbury			
Northampton	2C	CREWE NORTH	5A
Nuneaton	2D	Whitchurch	
Warwick	2E	Crewe South	5B
Coventry	2F	Stafford	5C
		Stoke	5D
BESCOT	3A	Alsager	5E
Bushbury	3B	Uttoxeter	5F
Walsall	3C		
Dudley		CHESTER	6A
Aston	3D	Mold Junction	6B
Monument Lane	3E	Birkenhead	6C
Albion		Birkenhead North	6D
Tipton			
		LLANDUDNO JUNCTION	7A
SHREWSBURY	4A	Bangor	7B
Trench		Holyhead	7C
Coalport		Rhyl	7D
Ludlow		Denbigh	

EDGE HILL	8A	Coalville	17C
Warrington	8B	Rowsley	17D
Arpley			
Over & Wharton		TOTON	18A
Speke Junction	8C	Westhouses	18B
Widnes	8D	Hasland	18C
		Staveley	18D
LONGSIGHT	9A		
Stockport	9B	SHEFFIELD	19A
Macclesfield	9C	Millhouses	19B
Buxton	9D	Canklow	19C
		Heaton Mersey	19D
SPRINGS BRANCH	10A	(supervised from Longsight)	
Preston	10B	Brunswick	
Patricroft	10C	(supervised from Edge Hill)	
Plodder Lane	10D	Widnes (M)	
Sutton Oak	10E	Belle Vue	19E
		(supervised from Longsight)	
CARNFORTH	11A	York	19F
Barrow	11B	Trafford Park	19G
Lakeside		(supervised from Longsight)	
Coniston			
Lancaster	11C	LEEDS	20A
Oxenholme	11D	Stourton	20B
Tebay	11E	Carlton	20C
		Normanton	20D
CARLISLE KINGMOOR	12A	Manningham	20E
Upperby	12B	Ilkley	
Penrith		Skipton	20F
Durran Hill	12C	Keighley	
Workington	12D	Hellifield	20G
Moor Row	12E		
Beattock	12F	SALTLEY	21A
Leadhills		Bournville	21B
Dumfries	12G	Redditch	
Kirkcudbright		Bromsgrove	21C
Stranraer	12H	Stratford-on-Avon	21D
Millisle		Blisworth	
Newton Stewart			
		BRISTOL	22A
PLAISTOW	13A	Thornbury	
Devons Road	13B	Gloucester	22B
Tilbury	13C	Tewkesbury	
Shoeburyness	13D	Dursley	
Upminster	13E	Bath	22C
		Radstock	
CRICKLEWOOD	14A	Templecombe	22D
Kentish Town	14B	Highbridge	22E
St Albans	14C	Wells	
WELLINGBOROUGH	15A	BANK HALL	23A
Kettering	15B	Aintree	23B
Leicester	15C	Southport	23C
Bedford	15D	Wigan (C)	23D
		Lostock Hall	23E
NOTTINGHAM	16A	Walton-on-the-Hill	23F
Southwell		Ormskirk	23G
Lincoln			
Peterborough	16B	ACCRINGTON	24A
Kirkby	16C	Rose Grove	24B
Mansfield	16D	Colne	24C
		Lower Darwen	24D
DERBY	17A	Blackpool	24E
Burton	17B	Fleetwood	24F
Overseal			

WAKEFIELD	25A	PERTH	29A
Huddersfield	25B	Crieff	
Goole	25C	Balquhidder	
Mirfield	25D	Aberfeldy	
Sowerby Bridge	25E	Blair Atholl	
Low Moor	25F	Methven	
Farnley Junction	25G	Stirling	29B
		Loch Tay	
NEWTON HEATH	26A	Dundee	29C
Agecroft	26B	Blairgowrie	
Bolton	26C	Forfar	29D
Bury	26D	Arbroath	
Bacup	26E	Montrose	
Lees	26F	Brechin	
		Alyth	
POLMADIE	27A	Oban	29E
Hurlford	27B	Ballachulish	
Muirkirk		Aberdeen	29F
Beith		St Rollox	29G
Edinburgh	27C	Inverness	29H
Carstairs	27D	Dingwall	
Girvan	27E	Fortrose	
Ayr	27F	Fort George	
Dalmellington		Kyle of Lochalsh	
Greenock	27G	Tain	
Ardrossan	27H	Dornoch	
Corkerhill	27J	Helmsdale	
Dawsholm	27K	Lybster	
Dumbarton		Wick	
Airdrie		Thurso	
Yoker		Aviemore	29J
St Enoch	27L	Forres	29K
		Keith	
MOTHERWELL	28A	Burghhead	
Hamilton	28B		
Grangemouth	28C		

Backed on to the tender of another locomotive is Class 5XP 'Jubilee-class' No.5560 *Prince Edward Island* at Crewe North in 1937. *(Colour-Rail 2135)*

Appendix 2

Locomotive Numbering

A priority for the new London Midland & Scottish was to develop an integrated numbering system for the vast fleet of locomotives inherited from its constituent companies and subsidiaries. This was necessary as there was considerable duplication, especially with the lower numbers as every company had started from number 1. In many cases, the predecessor companies had also allocated numbers randomly and the LMS was keen to introduce some order, with all locomotives in the same class given consecutive numbers and classes of locomotive to be numbered in blocks. The former Midland Railway locomotives were for the most part an exception as they had undergone a similar renumbering in 1907, but there was the important difference that the LMS moved the numbers from the tender to the locomotive, breaking with Midland practice for practical reasons.

Until a further renumbering in 1932, the LMS used four groups of numbers into which locomotives from a set of companies were numbered, and within each group, locomotives were numbered in blocks which ran (low to high numbers) as set out below. Within each block, the least powerful locomotives took the lowest numbers.

This meant that:

Numbers 1–4999 were allocated to former Midland, LTS, North Staffordshire, and Stratford-upon-Avon & Midland Junction Railway locomotives, with passenger tender locomotives numbered 1–1199; passenger tank locomotives numbered 1200–1499 and 2000–2219; freight tank locomotives numbered 1500–1999 and 2220–2289, and freight tender locomotives were numbered 2290–4999. When the Somerset & Dorset Joint Railway's locomotives were absorbed in 1930, they were renumbered in the Midland series.

5000–9999 were allocated to former LNWR locomotives, including those of the NLR and the Wirral Railway, with passenger tender locomotives numbered 5000–6399; passenger tank locomotives numbered 6400–6999; freight tank locomotives numbered 7XXX, and freight tender locomotives were numbered 8XXX and 9XXX.

10000–12999 were allocated to former LYR, Furness Railway, Maryport & Carlisle Railway, Cleator & Workington Junction Railway, and Knott End Railway. Passenger tender locomotives were numbered 10000–10599; passenger tank locomotives were 10600–11199; freight tank locomotives 11200–11999, and freight tender locomotives were numbered 12000–12999.

14000–17999 were allocated to former Caledonian Railway, Glasgow & South Western Railway, and Glasgow & Paisley Joint Railway locomotives, with passenger tender locomotives numbered 14XXX; passenger tank locomotives were numbered 15XXX; freight tank locomotives numbered 16XXX, and freight tender locomotives were numbered 17XXX.

By 1932, with so many older locomotives withdrawn and replaced by significant numbers of new, standard LMS engines, the numbering system was modified, so that all post-Grouping locomotives were numbered in the 1–9999 series, with pre-Grouping locomotives being renumbered out of that series as required to accommodate them. In the years before the outbreak of the Second World War numbers were cleared for new locomotives by simply adding 20000 to the numbers of old locomotives.

Although a fresh series starting at 7400 was intended for diesel shunters, this was soon seen to be insufficient and a new series started at 7050. The prototype mainline diesel locomotives, the first of which was introduced at the end of 1947, just prior to Nationalisation, were numbered 10000 and 10001.

The LMS policy of numbering locomotives rather than tenders allowed fewer tenders to be built than locomotives, which is why this 4P Compound 4-4-0 No. 936 has a Stanier tender which is much younger than the locomotive. This is a Devon-bound express descending the Lickey incline in 1938. *(HMRS AEU307)*

Appendix 3

Locomotives as at 31 December 1947

This is the locomotive fleet of the LMS on the eve of Nationalisation. In addition, a small number of locomotives were on loan from the London & North Eastern Railway and also from the Ministry of Supply. NCC, CDRJC and DN&GR locomotives are at the end of this appendix, SDJR locomotives are included in the main LMS series as from 1930 the company supplied the motive power for the railway.

Although names such as 'Patriot' or 'Dunalastair' refer to classes of locomotives, the power classification given as such relate to the role for which the locomotive was designed, with 'F' for freight, 'MT' for mixed traffic, 'P' for passenger and 'XP' for express passenger, with the higher the number that follows, the greater the power. This system was another inheritance from the Midland Railway, but it was refined further by the LMS. 'U' referred to unclassified locomotives.

STANDARD L M S LOCOMOTIVES

Wheel arrangement.	Description.	Motive Power Classification.
	2 - 6 - 2 Passenger Tank Engine.	No. 3
	2 - 6 - 4 Passenger Tank Engine.	No. 4
	2 - 6 - 0 Freight Tender Engine.	No. 4
	4 - 4 - 0 Passenger Tender Engine.	Nos. 2 & 4
	4 - 6 - 0 Passenger Tender Engine.	No. 6
	0 - 6 - 0 Freight Tender Engine.	No. 4
	0 - 6 - 0 Freight Tank Engine.	Nos. 2 & 3
	0 - 8 - 0 Freight Tender Engine.	No. 7
	2 - 6 - 0 - 0 - 6 - 2 Beyer Garratt.	

The standard wheel and power classifications used by the LMS.

Battery electric shunters were used by several companies on an experimental basis. They must have earned their keep as they all seem to have enjoyed long working lives, but their use never became widespread with main line railway companies. This is the former Lancashire & Yorkshire Railway No. 2, designated as an 0-2-2-0, in the yard at Derby Works in 1946. *(HMRS AEL115)*

Battery electric
1550 ex-MR 0-4-0
1 Ex-NSR

Diesel-electric locomotives
7058 300hp 0-6-0 shunting
7074/6/9–99, 7110–29 350hp 0-6-0 shunting
10000 1,600hp Co-Co

Diesel railcars
29950–29953 Leyland

Electric multiple units
London area: 106 vehicles
Liverpool-Southport: 70 vehicles plus two baggage cars
Wirral: 19 vehicles
Manchester–Bury: 38 vehicles
Manchester South Junction & Altrincham Railway: 24 vehicles
Lancaster–Morecambe–Heysham: three vehicles

Seen in 1923, shortly after Grouping, are these two former LNWR three-car electric sets on a service near Hatch End, and still in pre-Grouping livery. These were known as 'Oerlikon' sets after the name of the Swiss manufacturer of the motors. *(HMRS AAQ633)*

The somewhat Spartan interior of the passenger compartment in one of the 'Oerlikon' driving cars. *(HMRS AAD007)*

Steam rail motors

10617 ex-LYR
29988 ex-LNWR

Steam locomotives

(Built by LMS unless specified as ex-predecessor or by commercial builder)

0-4-0T

1516/8/23 ex-MR saddle tanks, no power classification 0F
1528–1537 ex-MR Deeley, power classification 0F
7000–7004 Kitson, power classification 0F
7180–7184/90*/1* (* ex-SDJR locos) Sentinel, no power classification.
11202/4/6/7/12/16–18/21/2/7/29–32/4/5/7/40/1/4/6/53 ex-LYR 'Pug' saddle tanks, power classification 0F
16010/1/20/25–32/5/8/9 ex-CR 'Pug' saddle tanks, power classification 0F

The less busy branch lines were served by 'railmotors', although steam rather than the internal combustion engine provided the motive power. This is the Banbury branch railmotor at Bletchley and appears to be drawing a parcels van. *(HMRS AEU309)*

One advantage of the tank engine was that it could work equally well in either direction, although normally, it would still be at the head of the train. This is Johnson 1P 0-4-4 No. 1261 propelling, or pushing, a Romford–Upminster train in 1947. *(HMRS AEQ603)*

4-wheel Sentinel chain-driven
7190/7191, ex-SDJR 101/102

0-4-2T
7862/7865 ex-NLR Bissel truck,
power classification 1F
27217 ex-NLR Crane tank,
power classification 0F

0-4-4T
1239/46/7/9/51/2/5/60/1 ex MR,
power classification 1P
72/3/5/8/87/90/5/8/1303/7/15/22/
4/30/7/40–42/4/8/50/3/7/8/60/1/
65–68/70/1/3/5/7/9/82/5/9/90/6/
7,1402/6/11/3/6/20–26/9/30, ex-MR,
power classification 1P
1900–1909 power classification 2P
15051/15053 ex-HR, power classification 0P
15116/7/9/21–27/9/30/32–36/38–46/
59–62/64–99, 15200–4/06–40/60*–9*, ex-CR,
power classification 2P (* built by LMS)

0-6-0T
1660/1/4/6/8/71/2/4/6/82/6/90/5/9,
1702/6/8/10–14/8/20/24–27/

34/9/45/47–49/52–54/6/9/62/
3/67–70/3/7/79-81/8/93–95/7,
1803/1805/11/3/4/8/20/4/6/
9/33/5/8/9/42/4/6/7/52–57/
9/60/5/9/70/73–75/8/9/85/9/
90/3/5 ex-MR, power classification 1F
7160–7169 Standard Dock power
classification 2F
7200–7259 ex-MR, power classification 3F
7260–7455/7457–7552/54–88/7590–
7608/9/7608–7610/2/4–6/7618–
7658/61/2/64–81 Standard,
power classification 3F.
11307/13/6/18–21/3/5/36/
6/42/3/5/5/53/8/61
/71/5/6/9/81/90/6/
7, 11400/4/5/8/10/2/
3/5/9/23–35/7/9/32/
6/8/9/41/43-47/53/
7/8/60/2/4/67–72/4/5/7/9/81/2/4/
86–92/95–99, 11500/3/4/6/
11510–14/6/9/21/4/6/30 ex-LYR Barton
Wright, power classification 2F
11535–11537/44/5 ex-LYR Dock,
power classification 1F
16151–16173 ex-CR, power classification 2F
24780 ex-LNWR, power classification 2F
27505/9/10/12–15/7/20/2/5/7/8/30/2 ex-
NLR, power classification 2F

0-6-0ST
1500–1507 ex-SDJR, power classification 2F

0-6-2T
1980–1993 ex-LTS, power classification 3F
6876/8/81/3/99/6900/6/9/12/17/20/2/4/6
/31 ex-LNWR, power classification 2P
27553/61/2/80/5/6/91/6, 27602/3/19/
21/5/7/35/48/54/69/74/81, 7692/9/77
00/3/10/1/5/20/1/30/3/7/40/1/6/51/
2/6/7/9/65/9/73/80/2/7/9/91/4/6/9
, 7833/6/40/1, 27830 ex-LNWR Coal Tank,
power classification 2F
16905 ex-G&SWR, power classification 3F

0-8-2T
7875/7/8/81/4/5/7/8/92/6 ex-LNWR,
power classification 6F

0-8-4T
7930–3/6-9/48/51/4/6/8/9 ex-LNWR (but
delivered after Grouping),
power classification 6F

2-4-0T
6428 ex-LNWR, power classification 1P

2-4-2T
6601/3–5, 6616, 6620/8/32/5/7/9/43/54/
6/8/61/3/6/9/73/6/69–83/86–88/91/2,
6701/10–12/18/27/38/40/2/7/9/57 ex-
LNWR, power classification 1P
6762 ex-LNWR, power classification 1P
10621–3/5/30/1/3/4/6/9/40/2–4/6-8/50–
6/60/5/7/70/1/5/6/8/81/6/7/9/92/5–
7,10703/5/11/2/4/5/20/1/5/
8/31/2/5/6/8/43/6/48-50/2/5/7/62/4–
6/77/8/81/8/93/5/8/9/, 10800–
2/4/6/7/12/3/5/8/23/9/31/40
/2/4/9/50/2/5/9/65/9/72/3/5/80/6/7/9/
92/6/8/9 ex-LYR, power classification 2P
10835/91/93, 10901/3/9/25/34/43/5/50–3
ex-LYR, power classification 3P

2-6-2T
1–70 Fowler power classification 3P
71–99, 100–147/149–162/164–168/170–
202/204-209 Stanier, power classification 3P
148, 163,169, 203 Stanier rebuilt, power
classification 3P
1200–1209, Standard,
power classification 2MT

2-6-4T
2300–2424 Fowler, power classification 4P
2425–2494, 2537–2672 Stanier two-cylinder,
power classification 4P
2500–2536, Stanier three-cylinder,
power classification 4P
2187–2299 Fairburn, power classification 4P

4-4-2T
2092–2104/6–9 ex-LTS,
power classification 2P
2110–2160 ex-LTS, power classification 2P

4-6-2T
15350–15356/9–61 ex-CR,
power classification 4P

0-6-0
22630, 22846/53/64 ex-MR, double-framed,
power classification 2F
22900–02/4/7/11–13/5/8/20/21/6/9/
31–35/40/44–47/50/1/53–55//8/9/63/5/
67–71/74–78/82–84, 2987–90/92–99,
23000–03/5–14/6/8 ex-MR 4ft 11in,
power classification 2F.
3021/3/7/31/5/37–39/42/5/
47–52/4/8/61/2/4/6/71/3/4/8/84/90/
94–96/8/9, 3101/3/8/9/13/8/9/23/7
ex-MR 5ft 3in, power classification 2F
3130/4/8/40/4/49–51/3/4/6/7/61/
4/6/8/71/3/75–77 ex-MR 4ft 11in,
power classification 2F
3137/74/8/80/1/3/85–89 ex-MR 4ft 11in,
power classification 3F
3194, 3201/4/11/6/8/28/48/60 ex-SDJR 5ft
3in, power classification 3F
3190//5/6, 3229/62/4/70, 3311/60/72/7/85,
3420/23–25/37/45/51/66/73/7/9/85/
9/93/3, 3503/8/11/2/6/7/25–27/

Fowler 4MT 2-6-4T No. 2354 takes a suburban passenger train up Camden Bank in 1946. *(HMRS AAL525)*

33/6/7/9/43/5/51/9/61/4/6/71/9
2, 3602/3/17/32/48/55/88/9/91/6,
3703/7/25/6/38/9/64 ex-MR 5ft 3in,
power classification 2F
3191–3, 3200/3/5/7/8/10/12–14/9/
22–26/31–35/7/39–54/56–59/61/3/
65–69/71/73–75/7/8/81–84/6/7/90/
92–99, 3300/1/5–10/12–15/17–19/21/
23–27/29–42/4/51/55–57/9/61/4/
67–71/3/4/8/9/81/86–89/92/
94–96/8/9, 3400–02/5/6/8/10/11/9/
27–29/31/3/5/6/8/39–41/3/
4/6/8/9/53/4/56–59/62–64/
8/9/74/6/82/4/90/1/4/6/7/9,
3502/6/7/9/10/4/5/20–24/
9/31/8/40/4/6/8/50/3/8
/62/5/8/70/72–75/78–87/93–96/8/9,
3600/4/5/7/8/12/5/18–24/7/
29–31/3/4/36–39/44/5/50–53/56–58/
60–62/4/5/67–69/73–76/78–84/6/7/
90/3/8, 3705/9–12/4/5/7/21/3/4/
27–29/31/4/5/7/42/5/47–49/51/
53–57/9/60/2/3/65–67/9/73/75-79/
81–87/89–93/95–99, 3800–15/17–33 ex-MR
5ft 3in, power classification 3F
3835–4026 ex-MR, power classification 4F
4027–4606 Standard, power classification 4F;
4557-61 ex-SDJR, and 4466,
4552/85/98 oil-burning
12016/9/21–24/30–32/4/6/7/41/

43–47/9/51/3/6/9/63/4 ex-LYR Class 25,
power classification 2F
12088/9/91–95/8/9, 12100/
02–05/8/10–12/18–21/23–27/9/32/33/
35–41/3/50/2/4/6/7/59–67/
69–72/74-77/81–84/6/9/91/2/4/6/7,
12201/3/7/8/12/15–20/5/29–33/
35–40/43–46/8/50/2/3/5/6/8/60/2/
68–73/5/78–80/5/5/88–90/3/4/6/9,
12300/4/5/9/11/2/7/9/21/2/6
/8/30/1/3/4/36–38/41/3/5/48–51/3/
55–58/60/2/3/5/6/8/9/74/6/8/9/81/2/
86–90/3/7/9, 12400/01/03–5/7/8/
10–18/22/27–33/5/37–50/52–61/64–67,
12515, 7/8/21–27/9 ex-LYR Class 27,
power classification 3F
12494/9, 12501/08–10 ex-FR,
power classification 3F
12528/41/2/5/9/51/4/57-
59//61/8/9/72/74–76/78–83/90/2/8,
12602/07–09/15/6/8/9 ex-LYR Class 28,
power classification 3F
17230–47/49–80/82-92/94–96/8/9,
17300–75/77–99, 17400–27/29–73 ex-CR,
power classification 2F
17550–66/68–97/9, 17600–09/11–28 ex-CR
812, power classification 3F
17629–45 ex-CR 652, power classification 3F
17650–55/8/9/61/3/65–74/9/81/2/4/6/
88–91 ex-CR Pickersgill, power classification 3F

A former LTS 0-6-2T, Classification 3F, No.1988, is seen in 1939 over an ash pit at Plaistow. *(Colour-Rail 11)*

17693–5/97–99/17702 ex-HR,
power classification 3F
28088/91/3/5/7, 28100/04-07/
15/16/28/33/41/5/52/3/8/66/72/91/9,
28202/5/16/21/7/30/3/4/9/
45-47/51/3/6/62/3/71/95/6,
28308/9/12/13 ex-LNWR 17in Coal, power
classification 2F
28318/33/5/37–39/45/50/70/2/85/92,
28403/4/8/15/7/28/30/41–43/
50/1/7/8/60/45/84/7/92/4/9,
28505/7/9/11–13/5/21/25–27/9/31/2/
42–44/47–49/51/3/5/6/9/61/75/80/
3/5/6/9/92/4/7/8, 28608/11/6/9/22
ex-LNWR 18in Goods, power classification 2F

0-8-0

8892/4, 8902/4/6/8/10–13/24/9/31/5/9/62,
9011–13/5/7/30/2/8/40/3/52–54/6/58–
60/7/71/5/6/83/5/9/91/2/5/8,
9100/2/3/7/24/8/31/3/5/6/40/
51/2/6/9/62/5/6/71/5/9/83/4/7/90/93–
97, 9201/4/8/13/21/2/5/31–
33/6/41/8/50/1/5/9/61/3/9/72–

74/9/83/5/6/95/7 ex-LNWR G1, power
classification 6F
8893/95–97, 8901/3/7/9/14/5/7/20–22/
25–27/30/32–34/6/40–45/8/50–54/64/6,
9002–10/14/6/18–29/31/33–37/41/42/
44–51/5/7/61–66/68–70/72–74/
77–82/4/86–88/90/3/4/6/7/9, 9101/
04–06/08–17/19–23/25–29/9/30/2/4/
37–39/41–50/53–55/7/8/60/1/3/4/
67–70/72–74/76–78/80/1/5/6/8/9/91/2/
6/8/9, 9200/2/3/5/7/9–12/4/15–20/3/4/
26–30/4/5/37–40/42–47/9/52–54/
56–58/60/2/64–68/70/1/75–78/80–82/
4/87–94/6/8/9, 9302/04/06–08/10–19/
21–23/5/27–31/3/5/39–45/7/8/50–52/
54–58/60/1/3/65–69/81/2/85–99, 9400–54
ex-LNWR G2 and G2A,
power classification 7F
9500–9674, Standard power classification 7F;
9511/33/9613/42/70 oil-burning
12727/82, 12806/21/2/5/7/8/31/4/7/
9 ex-LYR, power classification 6F
12841/56/7/70/3/7/86,
12906/10/3/6/35/45/52/6/62/71 ex-LYR,
power classification 7F

Ex-Midland 4F No.3888 handles a passenger train near Skipton in 1938, with the heavy hauling capacity of a goods locomotive probably very welcome handling the steep gradients in this area. *(Colour-Rail 12148)*

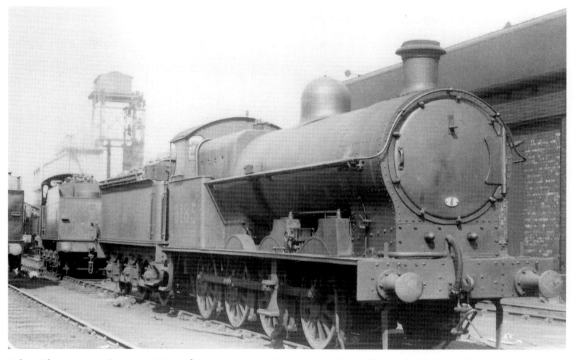

Behind the scenes at Crewe in 1936 with Bowen-Cooke 6F 0-8-0 No. 9185, with a coaling tower in the distant background. *(HMRS AAK930)*

The Lickey incline demanded a banker, or booster, locomotive or locomotives for most trains, and the Midland Railway ignored its tradition of small locomotives when it built this Fowler 0-10-0 'Decapod' just for that purpose. The only one of its type, it was numbered 2290 and is seen at Bromsgrove. *(HMRS AEU614)*

0-10-0
22290 ex-MR Lickey Banker

2-4-0
20155/85, 20216 ex-MR Johnson, power classification 1P

2-6-0
2700–2944 Hughes, power classification 5P4F
2945–2984 Stanier tapered-boiler, power classification 5P4F
3000–3002 Standard, power classification 4F
6400–6419 Standard, power classification s 2F

2-8-0
8000–8011/7/24/6/7/9/33/35–37/50/
53–57/60/62–65/7/9/70/73–76/78–85/
88-90/2/3/95–99, 8100–99, 8200–25/
64–85/93, 8301–99, 8400–79/90–95, 8500–59,
8600–8704 Standard, power classification
8F; 8064/79/191/8269/73/8370/85/86/86
06/53/96 converted to oil-burning, power
classification 7F
9670–80 Class 7F (inherited from SDJR, with
some rebuilt by LMS)

The Midland was far from having a monopoly of 4-4-0 locomotives as this Class 3P No.25350, seen in 1936 at Bangor in North Wales was inherited from the London & North Western Railway, a company known for working its locomotives hard. *(Colour-Rail 12474)*

One of the most satisfactory locomotives for mixed traffic was the Stanier 5MT 4-6-0, such as No. 4869, seen here with a train of goods vans in 1947. Unlike many photographs taken at this time, the locomotive is reasonably clean and the number is clear to see. Post-war, a number of these locomotives were converted to burn oil, until a balance of payments crisis led to the programme being abandoned. *(Colour-Rail 12079)*

Sitting idly at Derby in 1936 is standard locomotive 4F 0-6-0, one of a type also supplied to the Somerset & Dorset while others in the class were converted to oil-firing, but clearly this wasn't one of them. *(Colour-Rail 12203)*

Ex-Midland Railway No. 1000, a Deeley 4P Compound 4-4-0, pulls away with a passenger train at Derby in 1935. Today, it is preserved in the National Collection. *(HMRS AAK902)*

4-4-0

322–326 ex-SDJR, power classification 2P
383/85/91 ex-MR 6ft 6in saturated, power classification 2P
332/7/51/3/6/9/62/4/70 /7/94/7, 400–27/30/32–34/ 36–39/43/4/46–48/50/52–56/ 8/9/61–64/6/8/70–72/77-80/ 82–99, 500-62 ex-MR 7ft rebuild superheated, power classification 2P
563–590/92–99, 600–38/40–99, 700 Standard, power classification 2P
711/5/20/26–29/31/34–36/ 39–41/3/5/7/8/56–58/62 ex-MR, power classification 3P
900–939, 1045–1199 Standard Compound, power classification 4P
1000–1044 ex-MR Compound, power classification 4P

14363 ex-CR 'Dunalastair IV', power classification 2P
14379/85 ex-HR Loch, power classification 2P
14397–14399, 14401/3/4/9/10/15/6 ex-HR, 'Ben', power classification 2P
14434 ex-CR 'Dunalastair III' superheated, power classification 2P
14438–14441/43–60 ex-CR 'Dunalastair IV' superheated, power classification 2P
14461–14508 ex-CR Pickersgill, power classification 3P
25297 ex-LNWR 'Precursor' superheated, power classification 3P
25231/50/73 ex-LNWR 'King George V', power classification 3P

2-6-0+0-6-2

7967–7999, Garratt articulated

The need to handle heavy goods trains led to the LMS Beyer Garratt articulated locomotive, but Midland influence still prevailed and the locomotive failed to achieve its full potential and was soundly beaten by Stanier's 2-8-0s when they arrived. *(Colour-Rail LM111)*

It almost seems an oddity to see a former Midland Railway 4-4-0 handling a passenger train on its own without double heading. This is Class 4P No.932 at Hellifield in 1933. *(Colour-Rail 2955)*

4-6-0

4758–5499 Standard, power classification 5MT; 4826/7/9/30/44 oil-burning
5500–5513/15–20/22–25/7/32–39/41–51 'Patriot', power classification 5XP
5514/21/6/26–31/40 'Patriot' rebuilt, power classification 6P
5552–5734/37–42 'Jubilee', power classification 5XP
5735/6 'Jubilee' rebuilt, power classification 6P
6100/2/05–07/10/3/23/30/4/6/7/ 40–43/8/51/3/56/8/62-65/7, 'Royal Scot', power classification 6P
6101/3/4/8/9/11/2/14–22/24–29/ 31–33/5/8/9/44–47/9/50/2/7/59–61/6/ 68–70 'Royal Scot' rebuilt, power classification 6P
6004 ex-LNWR 'Claughton', rebuilt power classification 5XP
8801/24/34 ex-LNWR 19in Goods,

power classification 4F
10412/23/9/32/42*/8*/55* ex-LYR Hughes, power classification 5P (* built by LMS).
14630/1/34–54 ex-CR 60, power classification 4P (many built by LMS)
14764/7 ex-HR 'Clan', power classification 4P
17950/1/3–6 ex-HR Cumming Goods, power classification 4P
25648/73, 25722/52/87, 25827 ex-LNWR 'Prince of Wales', power classification 4P

4-6-2

6200/1/3–12 'Princess Royal', power classification 7P
6202 Turbomotive, power classification 7P
6220–6256 'Princess Coronation'/'Duchess', power classification 7P;
6220-6229 streamlined

Jubilee-class classification 5XP 4-6-0 No. 5579 *Punjab* heads a passenger train at Llandudno Junction in 1936. Judging by the age of the rolling stock, this was not an Irish boat train, but more probably a semi-fast service. *(Colour-Rail 12076)*

Northern Counties Committee
5ft 3in gauge unless stated otherwise

Diesel locomotive
17 Class X

Diesel railcars
1–3 Leyland
4
0-4-0T
16 Class N

0-6-0T
18/19 Class Y

0-6-0
13–15 Class V

2-6-4T
1–10 Class WT (built by LMS)

2-6-0
90–104 Class W (built by LMS)

4-4-0
33/4/58/62/4–6/9 Class A1
4A Class U1
70–87 Class U2

3ft gauge 2-4-2T
43/111 Class S
41/42 Class S1

County Donegal Railways Joint Committee
3ft gauge

Diesel locomotive
11 0-4-0 Gardner-engined diesel mechanical converted from a steam locomotive

Rail motors
7/8, 12/14/15 Gardner 75hp diesel.
9 Ford 36hp petrol
10 Gardner 75hp diesel, ex-Derwent Valley Railway
16/17/18 Gardner 103hp diesel

2-6-4T
1–3 Class 5
4–6/8 Class 5A

4-6-4T
9–12 Class 4

Dundalk, Newry & Greenore Railway
5ft 3in gauge, operated by GNR (I), but in LMS ownership

0-6-0T
1–4/6 ex-LNWR

Designed for goods services, here 3F 0-6-0 No.12441 is on a double-headed passenger train at Sowerby Bridge in 1934. The locomotive was inherited from the LYR and so it is still in its native territory. *(Colour-Rail 2255)*

Sitting not in steam in the siding at Polmadie in 1938, but with a tender full of coal, is classification 2F 0-6-0 No.17459, an ex-Caledonian Railway locomotive. *(Colour-Rail 2924)*

Named LMS Standard Locomotives

The LMS almost seemed to name its locomotives as an afterthought with none of the logic or consistency that one could see with the Great Western and the Southern, with nothing as straightforward as 'Castles', 'Kings' or 'Halls', 'Schools', 'Merchant Navy' or 'West Country' classes. Even the 'Jubilee' class, with its echoes of empire, added some of the great names of the First World War, whom one might have expected to be members of the 'Patriot' class. From time to time, the *LMS Magazine* would list names to be bestowed on classes of locomotives. Many of the inherited locomotives came complete with names. There are some oddities to be found, but it was an act of generosity to name a 'Patriot' after Sir Herbert Ashcombe Walker, general manager of the Southern Railway, who had led the Railway Executive Committee when he was general manager of the London & South Western Railway during the First World War.

'Patriot' class 4-6-0s
(also known as 'Baby Scots'; very extensively rebuilt from LNWR 'Claughtons') Some members of this class were given names or re-named after Nationalisation.

5500 *Patriot* (*Croxteth* until 1937)
5501 *St Dunstan's* (*Sir Frank Ree* until 1937)
5502 *Royal Naval Division*
5503 *The Leicestershire Regiment*
5504 *Royal Signals*
5505 *The Royal Army Ordnance Corps*
5507 *Royal Tank Corps*
5511 *Isle of Man*
5512 *Bunsen*
5514 *Holyhead*
5515 *Caernarvon*
5516 *The Bedfordshire and Hertfordshire Regiment*
5518 *Bradshaw*
5519 *Lady Godiva*
5520 *Llandudno*
5521 *Rhyl*
5522 *Prestatyn*
5523 *Bangor*
5524 *Blackpool*
5525 *Colwyn Bay* (*E. Tootal Broadhurst* until 1937)

5526 *Morecambe and Heysham*
5527 *Southport*
5528 *R.E.M.E.*
5529 *Sir Herbert Walker K.C.B.* (until 1937)
5530 *Sir Frank Ree*
5531 *Sir Frederick Harrison*
5532 *Illustrious*
5533 *Lord Rathmore*
5534 *E. Tootal Broadhurst*
5535 *Sir Herbert Walker K.C.B.* (from 1937)
5536 *Private W. Wood V.C.*
5537 *Private E. Sykes V.C.*
5538 *Giggleswick*
5539 *E.C. Trench*
5540 *Sir Robert Turnbull*
5541 *Duke of Sutherland*
5543 *Home Guard*
5546 *Fleetwood*
5548 *Lytham St. Annes*

'Jubilee' class 4-6-0s

5552 *Silver Jubilee*
5553 *Canada*
5554 *Ontario*
5555 *Quebec*
5556 *Nova Scotia*
5557 *New Brunswick*
5558 *Manitoba*
5559 *British Columbia*
5560 *Prince Edward Island*
5561 *Saskatchewan*
5562 *Alberta*
5563 *Australia*
5564 *New South Wales*
5565 *Victoria*
5566 *Queensland*
5567 *South Australia*
5568 *Western Australia*
5569 *Tasmania*
5570 *New Zealand*
5571 *South Africa*
5572 *Eire* (*Irish Free State* until 1938)
5573 *Newfoundland*
5574 *India*
5575 *Madras*
5576 *Bombay*
5577 *Bengal*
5578 *United Provinces*
5579 *Punjab*
5580 *Burma*
5581 *Bihar and Orissa*
5582 *Central Provinces*
5583 *Assam*
5584 *North West Frontier*
5585 *Hyderabad*
5586 *Mysore*
5587 *Baroda*
5588 *Kashmir*
5589 *Gwalior*
5590 *Travancore*
5591 *Udaipur*
5592 *Indore*
5593 *Kolhapur*
5594 *Bhopal*
5595 *Southern Rhodesia*
5596 *Bahamas*
5597 *Barbados*
5598 *Basutoland*
5599 *Bechuanaland*
5600 *Bermuda*
5601 *British Guiana*

5602 *British Honduras*
5603 *Solomon Islands*
5604 *Ceylon*
5605 *Cyprus*
5606 *Falkland Islands*
5607 *Fiji*
5608 *Gibraltar*
5609 *Gilbert and Ellice Islands*
5610 *Gold Coast*
5611 *Hong Kong*
5612 *Jamaica*
5613 *Kenya*
5614 *Leeward Islands*
5615 *Malay States*
5616 *Malta G.C.* (*Malta* until 1943)
5617 *Mauritius*
5618 *New Hebrides*
5619 *Nigeria*
5620 *North Borneo*
5621 *North Rhodesia*
5622 *Nyasaland*
5623 *Palestine*
5624 *St. Helena*
5625 *Sarawak*
5626 *Seychelles*
5627 *Sierra Leone*
5628 *Somaliland*
5629 *Straits Settlements*
5630 *Swaziland*
5631 *Tanganyika*
5632 *Tonga*
5633 *Aden* (*Trans-Jordan* until 1946)
5634 *Trinidad*
5635 *Tobago*
5636 *Uganda*
5637 *Windward Islands*
5638 *Zanzibar*
5639 *Raleigh*
5640 *Frobisher*
5641 *Sandwich*
5642 *Boscawen*
5643 *Rodney*
5644 *Howe*
5645 *Collingwood*
5646 *Napier*
5647 *Sturdee*
5648 *Wemyss*
5649 *Hawkins*
5650 *Blake*
5651 *Shovell*
5652 *Hawke*
5653 *Barham*

5654 *Hood*
5655 *Keith*
5656 *Cochrane*
5657 *Tyrwhitt*
5658 *Keyes*
5659 *Drake*
5660 *Rooke*
5661 *Vernon*
5662 *Kempenfelt*
5663 *Jervis*
5664 *Nelson*
5665 *Lord Rutherford of Nelson*
5666 *Cornwallis*
5667 *Jellicoe*
5668 *Madden*
5669 *Fisher*
5670 *Howard of Effingham*
5671 *Prince Rupert*
5672 *Anson*
5673 *Keppel*
5674 *Duncan*
5675 *Hardy*
5676 *Codrington*
5677 *Beatty*
5678 *De Robeck*
5679 *Armada*
5680 *Camperdown*
5681 *Aboukir*
5682 *Trafalgar*
5683 *Hogue*
5684 *Jutland*
5685 *Barfleur*
5686 *St. Vincent*
5687 *Neptune*
5688 *Polyphemus*
5689 *Ajax*
5690 *Leander*
5691 *Orion*
5692 *Cyclops*
5693 *Agamemnon*
5694 *Bellerophon*
5695 *Minotaur*
5696 *Arethusa*
5697 *Achilles*
5698 *Mars*
5699 *Galatea*
5700 *Britannia*
5701 *Conqueror*
5702 *Colossus*
5703 *Thunderer*
5704 *Leviathan*
5705 *Seahorse*

5706 *Express*
5707 *Valiant*
5708 *Resolution*
5709 *Implacable*
5710 *Irresistible*
5711 *Courageous*
5712 *Victory*
5713 *Renown*
5714 *Revenge*
5715 *Invincible*
5716 *Swiftsure*
5717 *Dauntless*
5718 *Dreadnought*
5719 *Glorious*
5720 *Indomitable*
5721 *Impregnable*
5722 *Defence*
5723 *Fearless*
5724 *Warspite*
5725 *Repulse*
5726 *Vindictive*
5727 *Inflexible*
5728 *Defiance*
5729 *Furious*
5730 *Ocean*
5731 *Perseverance*
5732 *Sanspareil*
5733 *Novelty*
5734 *Meteor*
5735 *Comet*
5736 *Phoenix*
5737 *Atlas*
5738 *Samson*
5739 *Ulster*
5740 *Munster*
5741 *Leinster*
5742 *Connaught*

'Royal Scot' 4-6-0s

(Several locos were renamed at various times, and Nos 6100 and 6152 exchanged identities in 1933.)

6100 *Royal Scot*
6101 *Royal Scots Grey*
6102 *Black Watch*
6103 *Royal Scots Fusilier*
6104 *Scottish Borderer*
6105 *Cameron Highlander*
6106 *Gordon Highlander*
6107 *Argyll & Sutherland Highlander*

6108 *Seaforth Highlander*
6109 *Royal Engineer*
6110 *Grenadier Guardsman*
6111 *Royal Fusilier*
6112 *Sherwood Forester*
6113 *Cameronian*
6114 *Coldstream Guardsman*
6115 *Scots Guardsman*
6116 *Irish Guardsman*
6117 *Welsh Guardsman*
6118 *Royal Welch Fusilier*
6119 *Lancashire Fusilier*
6120 *Royal Inniskilling Fusilier*
6121 *Highland Light Infantry*
6122 *Royal Ulster Rifleman*
6123 *Royal Irish Fusilier*
6124 *London Scottish*
6125 *3rd Caribinier*
6126 *Royal Army Service Corps*
6127 *Novelty*
6128 *Meteor*
6129 *Comet*
6130 *The West Yorkshire Regiment*
6131 *Planet*
6132 *Phoenix*
6133 *Vulcan*
6134 *Atlas*
6135 *Samson*
6136 *Goliath*
6137 *Vesta*
6138 *The London Irish Rifleman*
6139 *Ajax*

6140 *Hector*
6141 *Caledonian*
6142 *Lion*
6143 *The South Staffordshire Regiment*
6144 *Honourable Artillery Company*
6145 *The Duke of Wellington's Regiment (West Riding)*
6146 *Jenny Lind*
6147 *The Northamptonshire Regiment*
6148 *The Manchester Regiment*
6149 *Lady of the Lake*
6150 *The Life Guardsman*
6151 *The Royal Horse Guardsman*
6152 *The King's Dragoon Guardsman*
6153 *The Royal Dragoon*
6154 *The Hussar*
6155 *The Lancer*
6156 *The South Wales Borderer*
6157 *The Royal Artilleryman*
6158 *The Loyal Regiment*
6159 *The Royal Air Force*
6160 *Queen Victoria's Rifleman*
6161 *The King's Own*
6162 *Queen's Westminster Rifleman*
6163 *Civil Service Rifleman*
6164 *The Artists' Rifleman*
6165 *The Ranger (12th London Regt.)*
6166 *London Rifle Brigade*
6167 *The Hertfordshire Regiment*
6168 *The Girl Guide*
6169 *The Boy Scout*
6170 *British Legion*

Another ex-LYR locomotive was this 2F 0-6-0ST, rebuilt from a Class 2 tender locomotives, No. 11439, seen at Bolton in 1937. *(Colour-Rail 2253)*

A 'Princess Royal' 4-6-2, No. 6224 Princess Alexandria, imbibes. The blue livery with white stripes was replaced in 1938 by red with gold stripes. *(Colour-Rail LM20)*

'Princess Royal' 4-6-2s

6200 *Princess Royal*
6201 *Princess Elizabeth*
6202 'Turbomotive' (An unofficial, but
    widely used name for this locomotive.)
6203 *Princess Margaret Rose*
6204 *Princess Louise*
6205 *Princess Victoria*
6206 *Princess Marie Louise*
6207 *Princess Arthur of Connaught*
6208 *Princess Helena Victoria*
6209 *Princess Beatrice*
6210 *Lady Patricia*
6211 *Queen Maud*
6212 *Duchess of Kent*

'Princess Coronation'/'Duchess'

4-6-2s

*Streamlined locomotive originally painted blue with white stripes.
+ Streamlined locomotive painted red with gold stripes.

6220 *Coronation**
6221 *Queen Elizabeth**
6222 *Queen Mary**

6223 *Princess Alice**
6224 *Princess Alexandra**
6225 *Duchess of Gloucester*+
6226 *Duchess of Norfolk* +
6227 *Duchess of Devonshire* +
6228 *Duchess of Rutland* +
6229 *Duchess of Hamilton* +
6230 *Duchess of Buccleuch*
6231 *Duchess of Atholl*
6232 *Duchess of Montrose*
6233 *Duchess of Sutherland*
6234 *Duchess of Abercorn*
6235 *City of Birmingham*
6236 *City of Bradford*
6237 *City of Bristol*
6238 *City of Carlisle*
6239 *City of Chester*
6240 *City of Coventry*
6241 *City of Edinburgh*
6242 *City of Glasgow*
6243 *City of Lancaster*
6244 *King George VI* (*City of Leeds* until April 1941)
6245 *City of London*
6246 *City of Manchester*
6247 *City of Liverpool*
6248 *City of Leeds*
6249 *City of Sheffield*
6250 *City of Lichfield*

6251 *City of Nottingham*
6252 *City of Leicester*
6253 *City of St Albans*
6254 *City of Stoke-on-Trent*
6255 *City of Hereford*

6256 *Sir William A. Stanier, F.R.S.*
One further locomotive was built after Nationalisation: No. 46257 *City of Salford*.

The dark appearance of this 'Coronation' class 4-6-2, No. 6236 *City of Bradford*, suggests it is painted in red with gold stripes, seen here descending Shap in 1939 with an up express. *(HMRS ACW506)*

Appendix 5

Locomotives absorbed at Grouping

Overnight, the LMS found itself with a very mixed fleet of steam locomotives passed on to it by the constituent and subsidiary companies that Parliament decreed should be its lot. The whole of 1922 had been devoted to finalising the arrangements for the Grouping, but the creation of a new management team and some outlines of a structure were all that could sensibly be achieved.

Records are not always entirely accurate, but below are the locomotives that are recorded as being absorbed on 1 January 1923, and which were renumbered into LMS stock. In addition, the LMS acquired the former LYR electrification on Merseyside, that of the Midland around Heysham, and that of the LNWR and NLR in the London area, and in each case this meant that electric vehicles were also included.

As with the LMS locomotives in Appendix 2, although names such as 'Claughton' or 'Renown' refer to classes of locomotives, where possible, the power classification is given as such relates to the role for which the locomotive was designed, with 'F' for freight, 'MT' for mixed traffic, 'P' for passenger and 'XP' for express passenger, and so should really have been described by the LMS as 'power classification', with the higher the number that follows, the greater the power. 'U' means unclassified.

The Derby-based breakdown train being pulled by Fowler 4F 0-6-0 No. 4157 in 1946. *(HMRS ABH601)*

Caledonian Railway

0-4-0ST
16000 CR Class 781, acquired second-hand;
LMS power classification U
16008–16025 CR Class 264;
LMS power classification U
16026–16039 CR Class 611, but similar to
Class 264 above; LMS power classification U

0-4-2ST
15000/15001 CR Class 262;
LMS power classification U

0-4-2
17000–17020 CR Class 670;
LMS power classification U

0-4-4T
15100–15114 CR Class 171;
LMS power classification 1P
15115–15124 CR Class 19;
LMS power classification 2P
15125–15136 CR Class 92;
LMS power classification 2P
15137–15146 CR Class 879;
LMS power classification 2P
15147–15158 CR Class 104;
LMS power classification 1P
15159–15226 CR Class 439;
LMS power classification 2P

0-6-0ST
16150 CR Class 486; LMS power classification 1F
16100–16102 CR Class 272;
LMS power classification U
16202–16224 CR Class 323;
LMS power classification 3F
16225–16229 CR Class 211;
LMS power classification 3F

0-6-0T
16151–16173 CR Class 498;
LMS power classification 2F
16231–16239 CR Class 29,
fitted with condensers;

LMS power classification 3F
16240–16376 CR Class 782;
LMS power classification 3F

0-6-0
17230–17392 CR Class 294;
LMS power classification 2F
17393–17473 CR Class 711, but similar to
Class 294 above; LMS power classification 2F
17550–17628 CR Class 812;
LMS power classification 3F
17629–17645 CR Class 652, similar to Class
812 above; LMS power classification 3F
17646–17649 CR Class 30, a superheated
development of Class 652 above;
LMS power classification 3F
17650–17692 CR Class 300;
LMS power classification 3F

0-8-0T
16500–16505 CR Class 492;
LMS power classification 4F

0-8-0
17990–17997 CR Class 600;
LMS power classification 4F

4-2-2
14010 CR Class 123;
LMS power classification 1P

4-4-0T
15020–15031 CR Class 1;
LMS power classification 1P

4-4-0
14100–14107 CR Class 179;
LMS power classification 1P
(known as 'Oban bogies')
14108–14115 CR Class 80;
LMS power classification 1P
(known as 'Coast bogies')
14290–14295/14297-14309 CR Class 66;
LMS power classification 1P
14296 CR Class 124, an exhibition engine
derived from Class 66;

LMS power classification 1P
14308–14310 CR Class 13;
LMS power classification 1P
14311–14325 CR Class 721 'Dunalastair I';
LMS power classification 2P
14311–14325 CR Class 766 'Dunalastair II';
LMS power classification 2P
14430–14433 CR Class 766 'Dunalastair II'
rebuilt 1914 with superheaters;
LMS power classification 3P
14434–14436 CR Class 900 'Dunalastair III'
rebuilt 1914–18 with superheaters;
LMS power classification 3P
14337–14348 CR Class 900 'Dunalastair III',
LMS power classification 2P.
14438–14439 CR Class 140 'Dunalastair IV'
rebuilt 1915–22 with superheaters;
LMS power classification 3P
14349–14365 CR Class 140 'Dunalastair IV';
LMS power classification 2P
14440–14449 CR Class 139, superheated,
LMS power classification 3P
14450–14460 CR Class 43, superheated;
LMS power classification 3P
14461–14476 CR Class 113,
LMS power classification 3P
14477–14508 CR Class 72;
LMS power classification 3P

2-6-0
17800–17804 CR Class 34, a variant of Class 30
0-6-0; LMS power classification 3F

4-6-0
14600–14608 CR Class 55;
LMS power classification 4P
14609–14618 CR Class 908;
LMS power classification 4P
14619–14626 CR Class 60;
LMS power classification 3P (another 20,
Nos 14630–14649, built after Grouping)
14750–14751 CR Class 49 rebuilt 1911 with
superheaters; LMS power classification 4P
14752–14755 CR Class 903 rebuilt 1911 with
superheaters; LMS power classification 4P
14756–14761 CR Class 938 'River' originally
built for Highland Railway;
LMS power classification 4P
14800–14803 CR Class 956;
LMS power classification 5P
15227–15236 CR Class 159;
LMS power classification 2P
15237–15240 CR Class 431; LMS power
classification 2P (another ten,
Nos 15260–15269 built after Grouping)
17900–17904 CR Class 918;
LMS power classification 3F
17905–17909 CR Class 179;
LMS power classification 3F
17910–17915 CR Class 184;
LMS power classification 3F

4-6-2T
15350–15361 CR Class 944;
LMS power classification 4P

Although stated to have been taken in 1938, this photograph of Fowler 4F 0-6-0 No. 3875 shows it still in pre-Grouping livery, with the old Midland number just visible on the tender! It is working a train of banana vans from Avonmouth to St Pancras. *(HMRS AEV112)*

Preservation may have gained momentum in the latter half of the 20th century, but even in the 1930s, the LMS was aware of its history, even if Stanier was not, and several historic locomotives were retained for museum display. This included Caledonian 'Single' 4-2-0 No. 123 seen inside St Rollox Works in Glasgow, stored in works grey finish. *(HMRS AEN931)*

Furness Railway

0-4-0T
11258 no LMS power classification

0-6-0T
11547–11562 LMS power classification varied, 1F or 2F

0-6-0
12000–12014 no LMS power classification
12065–12076 LMS power classification 1F
12468–12483 LMS power classification 2F.
12494–12512 LMS power classification 3F

0-6-2T
11622–11622 LMS power classification varied, 2F or 3F

2-4-0
12100 no LMS power classification

2-4-2T
10619–10620 no LMS power classification

4-4-0
10131–10146 LMS power classification 1P
10185–10188 LMS power classification 2P

4-4-2T
11080–11085 LMS power classification 1P

4-6-4T
11100–11104 LMS power classification 4P

Glasgow & South Western Railway

The locomotive stock of the G&SWR suffered greatly under LMS ownership with no less than 80 per cent being withdrawn very quickly after Grouping and with just one surviving to see Nationalisation in 1948. This may have been a question of the age and suitability of the locomotive stock, or it could be that in Scotland, the Caledonian view prevailed.

0-4-0T
16040–16049 no LMS power classification

0-4-2
17021–17075 LMS power classification 1F

0-4-4T
15241–15254 LMS power classification 1P
16080–16085 no LMS power classification

0-6-0T
16103–16117 no LMS power classification
16377–16379 LMS power classification 2F

0-6-0
17100 LMS power classification 1F
17103–17212 LMS power classification 2F
17474–17524 LMS power classification varied,
2F or 3F
17750–17764 LMS power classification 4F

2-4-0
14000–14002 LMS power classification 1P

2-6-0
17820–17830 LMS power classification 4F

4-4-0
14116–14270 LMS power classification varied, 1P or 2P
14366–14378 LMS power classification 2P
14509–14521 LMS power classification 3P

4-6-0
14656–14674 LMS power classification 3P

4-6-4T
15400–15405 LMS power classification 5P

Highland Railway

0-4-4T
15050–15054 no LMS power classification

0-6-0T
16118/16119 no LMS power classification
16380–16383 LMS power classification 2F

0-6-0
17693–17704 LMS power classification 3F

0-6-4T
15300–15307 LMS power classification 4P

4-4-0T
15010–15017 no LMS power classification

4-4-0
14721–14285 LMS power classification 1P
14379–14422 LMS power classification 2P
14522/14523 LMS power classification 3P

4-6-0
14675–14693 LMS power classification 3P
14762–14769 LMS power classification 4P
17916–17930 LMS power classification 4P
17950–17957 LMS power classification 5P

Lancashire & Yorkshire Railway

Electric locomotives
2-2-2-2 not numbered but retained for shunting
0-4-0 battery electric shunter

0-4-0ST
11200 built by Vulcan Foundry, LYR Class 3;
no LMS power classification
11201–11257 LYR Class 21;
no LMS power classification

0-4-0 Railmotor locomotives
10600–10617 LYR Class 5;
no LMS power classification

0-4-2T
12015–12064 LYR Class 25;
LMS power classification 2F
(most were converted to saddle tanks)

0-6-0T
11533–11546 LYR Class 24;
LMS power classification 2F

0-6-0ST
11303–11532 LYR Class 23;
LMS power classification 2F
(rebuilt from Class 2 tender locomotives)

0-6-0
12083–12467 LYR Class 27;
LMS power classification 2F
(with superheater, to become Class 28 below)
12515–12536 LYR Class 28;
LMS power classification 3F, superheated
12537–12556 LYR Class 28;
LMS power classification 3F
12557–12619 LYR Class 28; LMS power
classification 4F (rebuilds of Class 27 above)

0-6-2T
11600/11601 built by Kitson, LYR Class 22;
LMS power classification 1F
11602–11621 14 built by Kitson and 20 by
Dubs, LYR Class 22; LMS power classification 1F

0-8-0
12700–12759 LYR Class 30;
LMS power classification 5F
(one rebuilt as below)
12760–12770 one rebuilt from above,
the rest built as new
12771–12839 LYR Class 30;
LMS power classification 6F
(33 rebuilds with larger boiler, 40 new)
12840–12994 LYR Class 31;
LMS power classification 7F
(40 rebuilds of Class 30 above, 115 new)

0-8-2T
11800–11804 LYR Class 32;
LMS power classification 6F

2-4-2ST
10621–10869 LYR Class 5;
LMS power classification 2P
(26 rebuilt with superheater as LYR Class 6)

2-4-2T
10870–10899 LYR Class 5;
LMS power classification 2P
(44 rebuilt with superheater as LYR Class 6)
10900–10954 LYR Class 6;
LMS power classification 3P
(44 rebuilt from LYR Class 5)

2-6-2T
11700–11716 LYR Class 26;
LMS power classification 3F

4-4-0
10100/10101 LYR Class 2;
LMS power classification 1P
10102–10130 built by Beyer-Peacock, LYR
Class 2; LMS power classification 1P
10150–10183 LYR Class 3;
LMS power classification 2P
(six rebuilt with superheaters to become
power classification 3P, as below)
10190–10195 LYR Class 4; LMS power
classification 3P (rebuilt from above)

4-4-2
10300–10339 LYR Class 7; LMS power
classification 2P

4-6-0
10384–10404 LYR Class 8; LMS power
classification 3P (4-cylinder with 15 rebuilt
with superheaters)
10405–10474 LYR Class 8;

LMS power classification 5P (15 superheated
rebuilt from above, remainder new)

4-6-4T
11110–11119 LMS power classification 5P
(superheated and delivered after Grouping)

London & North Western Railway
(including North London Railway)

0-4-0ST
7206–7210 LNWR Class 835;
no LMS power classification
7211/7212, 7217–7219 LNWR Class 1201;
no LMS power classification
7213–7216 LNWR Class 1201;
no LMS power classification
(rebuilt as 0-4-2 crane tanks)

0-4-0WT
7200–7205 LNWR Class 2360;
no LMS power classification
(used as service locomotives)

0-4-2PT
6400–6419 LNWR classed as 'dock tank';
LMS power classification 1P

0-6-0PT
7458–7502 LNWR unclassed;
LMS power classification 1F

0-6-0ST
7220–7457 LNWR classed as 'special tank';
LMS power classification 1F

0-6-0
8088–8314 LNWR classed as '17in coal
engine'; LMS power classification 2F
(45 rebuilt as pannier tanks as shown below)

8315–8624 LNWR classed as '18in goods';
LMS power classification 2F
8000–8087 LNWR classed as 'special DX';
no LMS power classification

0-6-2T
7550–7841 LNWR classed as 'coal tank';
LMS power classification 1F
6860–6936 LNWR classed as '18in tank';
LMS power classification 1P

0-8-0
8900–8952 LNWR Class B;
LMS power classification 3F (many rebuilt)
8953–8967 LNWR Class C
(most rebuilt from Class A);
LMS power classification 4F
9002–9064 LNWR Class D (rebuilt from Class
A with many rebuilt as Class G0;
LMS power classification 4F
8968–9001 LNWR Class C1 (rebuilt from
Class A); LMS power classification 3F
9065–9153 LNWR Class G (many rebuilt from
Class B); LMS power classification 4F
9154–9394 LNWR Class G1;
LMS power classification 6F
9395–9494 LNWR Class G1;
LMS power classification 7F

0-8-2T
7870–7899 LNWR Class 1185;
LMS power classification 4F

0-8-4T
7930–7959 LMS Class 280;
LMS power classification 5F

2-4-0T
6420–6434 LNWR Class 2233;
LMS power classification 1P

2-4-0
5000–5079 LNWR classed as 'renewed
Precedent'; LMS power classification 1P
5080–5109 LNWR classed as 'Waterloo/
Whitworth'; LMS power classification 1P

2-4-2T
6515–6600 LNWR classed as '4ft 6in tank';
LMS power classification 1P
6601–6757 LNWR classed as '5ft 6in tank';
LMS power classification 1P

2-8-0
9600–9609, LNWR Class E
(mainly rebuilt from Class B);
LMS power classification 3F
9610–9615 LNWR Class F
(mainly rebuilt from Class E);
LMS power classification 3F
9616–9645 LNWR Class MM (supplied by
government as Robinson ROD type);
LMS power classification 7F

4-4-0
5156* LNWR classed as 'Iron Duke'
(converted from simple 4-4-0 to compound);
LMS power classification 2P
5157* LNWR classed as 'Black Prince'

compound; LMS power classification 2P
5110–5117* LNWR classed as 'Jubilee'
4-cylinder compound:
LMS power classification 2P
5118–5130* LNWR classed as 'Alfred the
Great', 4-cylinder compound;
LMS power classification 2P
5187–5319 LNWR classed as 'Precursor'; LMS
power classification 2P/3P
(most later provided with superheating)
5131–5186 LNWR classed as 'Renown'
(rebuilds of 'Jubilee' and 'Alfred the Great'
classes); LMS power classification 2P
5320–5409 LNWR classed as 'George the
Fifth' (ten rebuilt from 'Queen Mary' class);
LMS power classification 2P

*Most rebuilt as 'Renown class'.

4-4-2T
6780–6829 LNWR classed as 'Precursor Tank';
LMS power classification 2P

4-6-0
5450–5554 LNWR classed as 'Experiment';
LMS power classification 3P
8700–8869 LNWR classed as '18in goods';
LMS power classification 4F
5600–5845 LNWR classed as 'Prince of Wales';
LMS power classification 3P
5900–6029 LNWR classed as 'Claughton';
LMS power classification 5P (later rebuilt as
'Patriot' class)

4-6-2T
6950–6996 LNWR Class 2665;
LMS power classification 3P

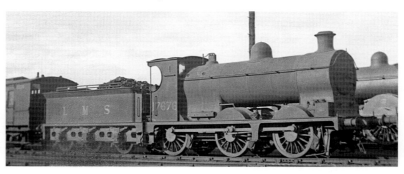

Ex-Caledonian Railway
Classification 3F 0-6-0 No.
17676 sits idly, out of service
and out of steam, at Stirling in
1935. (*Colour-Rail 1003*)

Midland Railway
(including London Tilbury & Southend Railway)

*Indicates groups of numbers with some locomotives withdrawn prior to Grouping.

0-4-0T
1500–1537* no LMS power classification

0-4-4T
1200–1430* LMS power classification 1P

0-6-0T
1605–1899* LMS power classification 1F
1900–1959 LMS power classification 3F

0-6-0
2369–2867* LMS power classification varied, 1 or 2
2900–3834 LMS power classification varied, 2 or 3
3835–4026 LMS power classification 4

0-6-2T
2220–2233 LMS power classification 3F

0-6-4T
2000–2039 LMS power classification 3P

0-10-0
2290 'Lickey Banker';
no LMS power classification

2-4-0
1–281* LMS power classification 1

4-2-2
600–683* LMS power classification 1

4-4-0
300–327* LMS power classification 1
328–562 LMS power classification 2
700–779 LMS power classification 3
1000–1044 LMS power classification 4

4-4-2T
2120–2179 LMS power classification varied, 1P or 2P
2200–2209 LMS power classification 1P

4-6-4T
2100–2107 LMS power classification 3P

North Staffordshire Railway

0-4-4T
1431–1435 NSR Class M;
LMS power classification 3P
1436–1439 NSR new Class M;
LMS power classification 3P

0-6-0ST
1600–1601 NSR unclassed (built by Hudswell Clarke); LMS power classification 1F

0-6-0T
1550–1598 NSR Class D;
LMS power classification 2F
1602–1603 NSR unclassed (built by Kerr Stuart);
LMS power classification 1F

0-6-0
2367 NSR unclassed (experimental engine and not numbered until rebuilt from tank to tender locomotive in 1924);
LMS power classification 2F

2320–2342 NSR Class E;
LMS power classification 1F
2343–2350, 2357–2358 NSR Class 100,
LMS power classification 2F
2351–2356 NSR Class 159;
LMS power classification 2F
2359–2366 NSR Class H;
LMS power classification 3F

0-6-2T
2234–2239 NSR Class DX;
LMS power classification 2F
2240–2273 NSR Class L; LMS power
classification 3F (many built after Grouping,
before Stoke Works closed)

0-6-4T
2040–2047 NSR Class C; LMS power classification
5F (but often used for passenger work)
2048–2055 NSR Class F;
LMS power classification 4P

2-4-0T
1440–1451 NSR Longbottom Class B;
LMS power classification 1P

2-4-2T
1454–1459, NSR Longbottom rebuild Class B;
LMS power classification 1P

4-4-0
595–598 NSR Class G;
LMS power classification 3P
599 NSR Class KT; LMS power classification 3P

4-4-2T
2180–2186 NSR Class K;
LMS power classification 3P

Somerset & Dorset Joint Railway

The S&DJR was operated jointly with the Southern Railway, but to economise, the joint owners divided the responsibility of maintaining the line and the rolling stock between themselves in 1930 when the LMS absorbed all the locomotives.

Stratford upon Avon & Midland Junction Railway

0-6-0
2300–2311 LMS power classification varied,
2F or 3F

2-4-0
290 LMS power classification 1P

Wirral Railway

0-4-4T
6770–6776 LMS power classification varied,
1F or 2F

0-6-4T
6948, 6949 LMS power classification 3F

2-4-2T
6758–6762 LMS power classification varied, 1F or 2F

4-4-2T
6830 LMS power classification 1F

4-4-4T
6850, 6851 LMS power classification 1F

Bibliography

Given the wide scope of Britain's railway history, it is not possible to provide a complete list of books on the subject. A look at the library lists for the LMS alone shows around 200 titles, with many others for its predecessor companies. These detail subjects such as locomotives, carriages, goods wagons, stations, motive power depots, signalboxes and signals, all covered exhaustively, while there are also books of reminiscences by those who worked for the LMS. Old copies of *Bradshaw's Railway Guides* and *Timetables*, originally published monthly, are illuminating when they can be found, but the reprints by David & Charles are better value than the originals, which are now collectors' items. A good sample of books would include some at least of the following:

Allen, Cecil J., *Titled Trains of Great Britain*, Ian Allan, London, 1946–67. Shepperton, 1951 & 1974

Beaumont, Robert, *The Railway King: A biography of George Hudson railway pioneer and fraudster*; Review, London, 2002

Bishop, D., & Davies, W. J. K., *Railways and War since 1917*, Blandford, London, 1974

Christiansen, Rex, *A Regional History of the Railways of Great Britain: Volume 7 – The West Midlands*, David & Charles, Newton Abbot, 1973

Gourvish, Terry, *British Railways 1948–73*, Cambridge University Press, 1987
   – *British Rail 1974–1997*, Oxford University Press, Oxford, 2002

Hamilton Ellis, C., *The Trains We Loved*, Allen & Unwin, London, 1947

Jackson, Alan A., *London's Termini*, David & Charles, Newton Abbot, 1969

Jenkinson, David, & Essery, Bob, *The Illustrated History of LMS Standard Coaching Stock Volumes 1, 2 & 3*, Oxford Publishing Co, 1991–2000

John, E., *Timetable for Victory: A brief and popular account of the railways and railway-owned dockyards of Great Britain and Ireland during the six years' war, 1939–1945*, The British Railways, London, 1946

Joy, David, *A Regional History of the Railways of Great Britain: Volume 8 – South and West Yorkshire*, David & Charles, Newton Abbot, 1975

Morrison, Gavin, *London Midland, Then and Now*, Ian Allan, Shepperton, 1995

Nash, G.G., *The LMS at War*, London Midland & Scottish Railway, London, 1946

Neele, George Potter, *Railway Reminiscences*, 1904

Nock, O.S., *A History of the LMS*, 3 vols, George Allen & Unwin, London, 1982–83
    – *Britain's Railways at War, 1939–1945*, Ian Allan, Shepperton, 1971

Peacock, A.J, *The Rise and Fall of The Railway King*, Sutton, Stroud, 1995

Rowledge, J.W.P., *Diesel Locomotives of the LMS*, Oakwood Press, 1975

Smullen, Ivor, *Taken For A Ride,* Herbert Jenkins, London, 1968

Simmons, Jack, & Biddle, Gordon, *The Oxford Companion to British Railway History*, Oxford University Press, Oxford, 2000

Thomas, John, *A Regional History of the Railways of Great Britain: Volume 6 – Scotland*, David & Charles, Newton Abbot, 1971

White, H.P., *A Regional History of the Railways of Great Britain: Volume 3 – Greater London*, David & Charles, Newton Abbot, 1963

Whitehouse, Patrick, & St John Thomas, David, *LMS 150: The London Midland & Scottish Railway – A Century and a Half of Progress*, David & Charles, Newton Abbot, 1987

Wragg, David, *Wartime on the Railways 1939–1945*, Sutton, 2006
    – *Signal Failure – Politics and Britain's Railways*, Sutton, 2004

Index

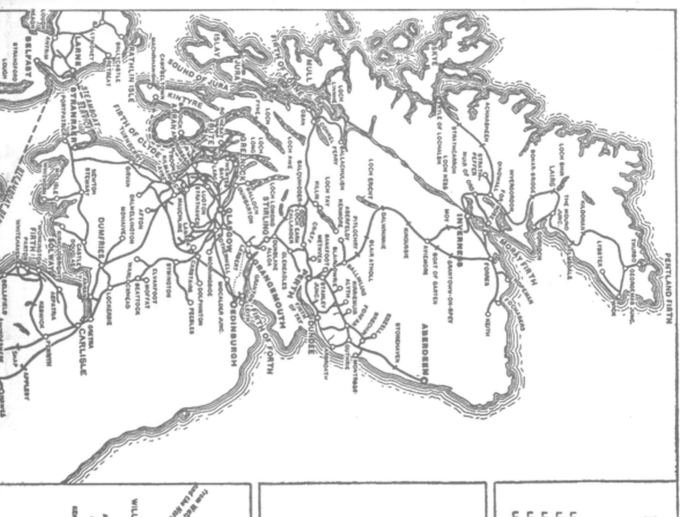

LONDON MIDLAND AND SCOTTISH RAILWAY
Map of the System

Scale
10 5 0 5 10 15 20 25 30 35 40 Miles

LINES OWNED BY THE COMPANY ... ... _____

LINES PARTLY OWNED ... ... _____

LINES LEASED OR WORKED JOINTLY ... ... _____

LINES OVER WHICH THE COMPANY EXERCISES RUNNING POWERS CONTINUOUSLY .... – – – –

LINES OVER WHICH JOINT COMMITTEES EXERCISE RUNNING POWERS CONTINUOUSLY ....

STEAMBOAT SERVICE ⌐⌐⌐⌐⌐⌐

MAP OF RAILWAYS IN THE NORTH OF IRELAND

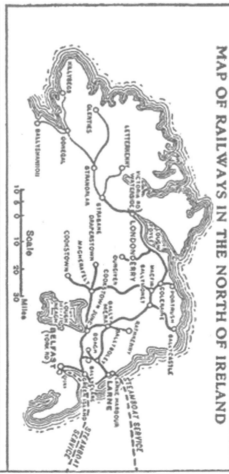

Scale
10 5 0 10 20 30 Miles

ENLARGED MAP OF LONDON AREA

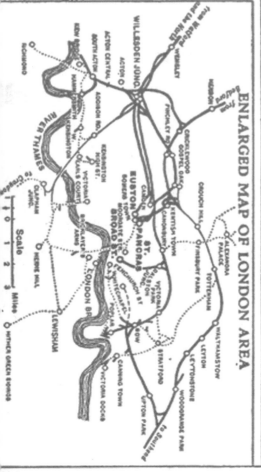

Scale
2 1 0 1 2 3 Miles